Air Transport Networks

Theory and Policy Implications

Kenneth Button

Professor of Public Policy, School of Public Policy,
George Mason University, USA

and

Roger Stough

NOVA Endowed Professor of Public Policy, School of Public Policy,
George Mason University, USA

TRANSPORT ECONOMICS, MANAGEMENT AND POLICY

Edward Elgar
Cheltenham, UK • Northampton, MA, USA

Published by
Edward Elgar Publishing Limited
Glensanda House
Montpellier Parade
Cheltenham
Glos GL50 1UA
UK

Edward Elgar Publishing, Inc.
136 West Street
Suite 202
Northampton
Massachusetts 01060
USA

A catalogue record for this book
is available from the British Library

Library of Congress Cataloguing in Publication Data

Air transport networks: theory and policy implications / edited by Kenneth Button and Roger Stough.
    (Transport economics, management and policy)
    Includes bibliographical references and index.
    1. Airlines—United States. 2. Airlines—Europe. 3. Airlines–United States–Management. 4. Airlines–Europe–Management. 5. Airlines–Rates–United States. 6. Airlines–Rates–Europe. I. Button, Kenneth John. II. Stough, Roger. III. Series

HE9780.A395 2000
387.7—dc21
                                   00–034827

ISBN 1 84064 429 X
Printed and bound in Great Britain by MPG Books Ltd, Bodmin, Cornwall

Contents

List of Figures   vi
List of Tables   viii
Preface   xi

1.   Introduction   1
2.   Airline Economics   15
3.   Airline Networks   46
4. ○ Regulation of International Airline Networks   59
5.   Early Impacts of US, Canadian and EU Airline Deregulation   83
6.   Filling Incomplete Networks: International Air Transport   148
7.   Issues of Market Stability   169
8.   Airports: Pricing and Access   190
9.   European Airports Policy   204
10.   The Economics of Being a Hub City   231
11.   Air Freight Transport   265
12.   Interaction with Other Networks   290
13.   Safety and Environmental Issues   310

References   345
Index   371

List of Figures

2.1   Losses due to non-cost minimization   26
2.2   Price discrimination according to service quality   30
2.3   Stages in arriving at yield-maximizing revenue   33
2.4   Fares and passenger miles associated with an airline
      prior to making an alliance and after making an alliance   36
2.5   Network implications of airline alliances   38
3.1   Optimal networks   49
3.2   Congestion costs   50
3.3   Pre-US deregulation linear route structure   52
3.4   Post-US deregulation hub-and-spoke route structure   53
3.5   Typical hub-and-spoke route structure   54
3.6   Multiple hub system   55
3.7   Multiple hub system with directional hubs   56
3.8   Competition between alliance hub-and-spoke networks   57
7.1   The Viner case   178
7.2   Non-identical firms   179
7.3   Low elasticity of demand case   180
7.4   The situation with market slumps   180
7.5   Demand fluctuations   181
8.1   The long- and short-run costs of airport provision   192
8.2   Marginal cost pricing with shifting capacity and increasing
      demand   197
9.1   Nature of airport services   207
9.2   European departure delays, 1993–7   211
9.3   Costs to overfly Europe, 1997   212
10.1 The series of stages in the assessment of the impacts of
      relaxing the perimeter rule at Dulles airport   243
10.2 Growth in income in case study areas   259
10.3 Passenger traffic at case study airports   260
10.4 Trends in high-technology employment   261
11.1 Growth in the air cargo market, billions of FTKs,
      1985–2015   267
11.2 US air freight by weight imported into and exported
      from the US in 1995 (ranked by combined total weight
      of air exports and imports)   268

11.3	Comparison of actual air freight rates with the N rate for 1993	273
11.4	US cargo ton miles by scheduled carriers	278
11.5	Average US cargo freight revenue per ton-mile	280
11.6	Role of air cargo transport in US/Canadian and US/Mexican trade	283
12.1	Air trucking in the freight logistics chain	295
12.2	Shift in the cost function	298
12.3	Airfreight forwarders' systems architecture	299
12.4	Communications network	302
12.5	Forwarder benefits	306
13.1	Swissair and the Global Quality alliance, 1994	319
13.2	The stages of the environmental chain	339

List of Tables

1.1   European airlines (AEA members only)   4
1.2   European airline profits in 1996   5
2.1   Demand elasticities of air passenger travel   17
2.2   Demand elasticities for air travel on the North Atlantic,
       1964–74, by country (expressed as absolute values)   18
2.3   How often US business travelers choose flights to build
       up frequent flyer miles   20
2.4   Global airline alliances, 1999   34
4.1   ICAO seven year forecast and actual flights on the
       North Atlantic (thousands)   69
4.2   A general indication of the adequacy of international air
       transport data   75
5.1   Economic features of perfect competition, perfect
       contestability and pure monopoly   92
5.2   Service changes in selected markets   96
5.3   Changes in aircraft and seat departures, 1978–84   96
5.4   Fare discounts pre and post deregulation   97
5.5   Airline fares as a percentage of the CAB formula
       (2nd quarter of 1983)   98
5.6   Real costs of air travel between various forms of hub   101
5.7   Entrants to and leavers from the scheduled aviation
       market, 1978–87   102
5.8   Concentration ratios (% of domestic revenue passenger
       miles)   104
5.9   Number of scheduled carriers serving each market   105
5.10   Labor costs of the major US airlines, 1978–85   106
5.11   Rate of return on annual total invested capital in US airlines   108
5.12   Foreign gateways served by selected US carriers   115
5.13   Average annual percentage decline in unit costs and sources
       of unit costs for US and non-US carriers, pre- and
       post-deregulation   116
5.14   Share of the domestic Canadian aviation market, 1987   126
5.15   Major airline affiliations, 1988   127
5.16   Changes in competition on selected EU scheduled routes   143
5.17   Scheduled airfares from Brussels (Belgian Francs)   144

5.18	Capacity of air system (total number of seats available in thousands) on scheduled return flights within the EU	145
5.19	Average size of aircraft used by AEA members on European and domestic air services	146
7.1	Differing conditions for rent seeking and stability collusion	175
8.1	Approaches to runway congestion management	196
8.2	Movement in flight departure times following changes in the pax peak period at Heathrow	202
8.3	Airport and handling charges (1993 ECU) for a scheduled A320-100 service	203
9.1	Summary statistics for the ten worst departure and the ten worst destination airports	214
9.2a	Traffic statistics for the busiest city in each European state	215
9.2b	Recent traffic statistics for the busiest city in each European state	216
9.3a	Passenger traffic for the busiest city in each European state	217
9.3b	Traffic growth for the busiest city in each European state	218
9.4a	Traffic statistics for the top 40 European airports, 1997	219
9.4b	Cargo and international passenger traffic at the top 40 European airports	221
9.5a	Passengers at the top 40 European airports	223
9.5b	Changes in traffic at the top the top 40 European airports	224
9.6	Simple correlations using combined ACI and CODA air traffic statistics	225
9.7	Air passenger traffic between EU countries (million passengers, 1994)	226
10.1	Use of Washington Dulles International Airport, 1977–97	245
10.2	Implications for airport use	247
10.3	Impact on employment at Dulles Airport	248
10.4	SICs constituting high technology industry	249
10.5	The employment implications by high-technology classifications of scenario one	250
10.6	The employment implications by high-technology classifications of scenario two	251
10.7	Services from the case study airports	261
11.1	Air cargo volumes by market segment, millions, RTKs	269
11.2	Air freight traffic in Europe by market segment, 1993	270
11.3	Top 10 air freight carriers, 1993	270
11.4	Concentration in the international express sector, daily shipments volume, 1997	271
11.5	US all-cargo air operators	280
11.6	Canadian air cargo carriers providing feed to US hubs, 1996	284

11.7	Air freight traffic in Europe by geographical market segment, 1993	287
12.1	Rail links at selected European airports	292
13.1.	Estimates of the implications of noise nuisance effects on property values (percentage change per decibel increase)	327
13.2	Relative fuel consumption of air transport	328
13.3	Comparison of long-run average social costs of passenger transport	329
13.4	Meta-regression parameters	337
13.5	Taxonomy of policy instruments	341

Preface

In the late 1990s, the then Institute of Public Policy at George Mason University made a decision to devote resources to the study of air transport policy. One obvious reason for this is the importance of the sector, it is the fastest growing mode of transport. Another is that efficient air transport networks contribute to economic growth and are highly influential in determining the spatial distribution of the economic growth process. Both passenger and cargo aviation are key elements in the development of modern logistics and supply chain management.

The result of this initiative has been a number of studies that have explored various aspects of air transport networks both domestically in the US and more generally at the international level. It has also produced work that has focused specifically on the links between the quality of local air transport access and regional economic prosperity.

This book brings together some of the findings generated by these studies and sets them in a wider context of developments in our broader understanding of how network industries function in the modern world. Much of the work in the book, therefore, has practical policy implications.

In one sense this book represents an on-going trend. It is increasingly appreciated that networks are important in the current age where information and mobility are key components in furthering the advantages generated by the global economy. Our understanding of the nature of networks, is however, comparatively sparse. Networks are often complex, overlapping and frequently changing. This book, although it has a substantial economics content, makes use of a number of disciplines to explore the nature of some of these networks.

The book also can be seen as a coming together of a number of earlier studies. In this sense it has inevitably benefit from collaboration with others and a major indebtedness is owed to Aisling Reynolds-Feighan, Peter Arena, Kirk Johnson, Piet Rietveld, and Somik Lall.

Kenneth Button
Roger Stough

1 INTRODUCTION

1.1 INTRODUCTION

Air transport is a network industry. It is only comparatively recently that economists have taken an explicit interest in networks. In the past the issue of networks has somehow fallen between the strands of industrial economics and the theory of the firm. The extensive regulation and public ownership of many network industries, most notably transport, energy and communications has meant that many of the features of networks have been obscured. The regulatory regimes in the past, however, have essentially treated them in a similar fashion to other forms of economic activity. The approach of the US domestic air transport regulators until the late 1970s, for instance, was to effectively ignore network effects when determining fares and license allocations.

Air transport is also the fastest growing transport industry. It is a major consumer of high-technology output, involves an extensive and sophisticated infrastructure, is a substantive contributor to the national income and trade accounts of many countries and is an important lubricator of trade more generally. It is also an industry that has grown within a heavily regulated institutional environment although there have recently been important changes with moves towards greater liberalization.

To understand some of the implications of the sector it is important to initially provide some background information. If for no other reason this is important just to illustrate that air transport is a significant sector and one that is worthy of serious study. The following section paints a broad picture of the scale and nature of air transport.

1.2 THE AIR TRANSPORT INDUSTRY

1.2.1 Passenger air transport

Globalization and internationalization are two major industrial trends of the late twentieth century (Thurow, 1996). Part of this is reflected in the significant trade growth that has taken place in the 1990s, with real export growth in the industrialized countries that make up the Organisation for Economic Cooperation and Development (OECD) at over 7% per annum. Comparatively, from 1964 to 1992, first world production was up by 9% per annum, exports by 12%, and cross-border lending by 23%. Equally, there has been a significant rise in foreign ownership of assets that are now estimated to total about $1.7 trillion.

Whether these trends are passing fads or genuine long term adjustments to the way production and trade is conducted is premature to judge. Preliminary indications are, however, that they are more than transient.

All this has been taking place when the institutional structure of the provision of air transport services has seen significant developments. The US's deregulation of its domestic markets for air freight since 1977 and for passengers in 1978, combined with subsequent commitments to an 'Open Skies' approach to international aviation in 1979, has changed the way US policy is conducted but also, through both demonstration effects and direct knock-on effects, the ways in which other air transport markets are now regulated (Button, 1990; Organisation for Economic Cooperation and Development, 1998).

The intra-European market is moving rapidly towards a situation found within the United States. Many European countries unilaterally liberalized their domestic markets while the EU, since 1988 through a succession of 'Packages', has moved to a position that will leave air transport largely free from economic regulation since the middle of 1997.

These measures, partly stimulated by a number of legal judgments in the European Court, initially opened up regulated fare and capacity bands but then limited fares and entry controls to instances where governments at both ends of a route agreed to them. The creation of a Single European Market from 1993 also means that international air transport within Europe is essentially deregulated, with full cabotage within member states being allowed from 1997.

The majority of national markets in South America have been liberalized with various types of privatization programs. Australia and New Zealand markets have also been deregulated. Additionally, the World Trade Organization (WTO) brought into play (albeit in an extremely small role) a new and geographically wider policy making institution to supplement the roles already played by bodies such as the International Civil Aviation Organization (ICAO) and the International Air Transport Association (IATA) (Katz, 1995). Aviation issues are also on the agenda of new regional groupings such as the Asian-Pacific Economic Council (APEC).

This combination of market trends and institutional reforms, together with rising incomes and increased leisure time, have contributed to the steady growth of demand taking place in aviation markets. Additionally, technology advances have allowed aircraft efficiency to rise and air traffic control systems to handle greater volumes of traffic, thus exerting positive effects on the cost side of the international air transport equation.

As a result, air passenger traffic since 1960 has grown world wide at an average yearly rate of 9% and freight and mail traffic by 11% and 7% respectively. In 1995, for example, some 1.3 billion passengers were carried by the world's airlines. Civil aviation has become a major service industry contributing to both domestic and international transport systems. It facilitates wider business communications and is a key component in the growth of tourism, now one of the world's major employment sectors. In addition to carryingpassengers, aviation is an important form of freight transport, with some estimates suggesting it carries up to 60% of world trade by value and forecast to rise 80% by 2014.

The Association of European Airlines (AEA) members have seen a steady growth in their traffic in geographical Europe since 1992. Overall traffic increased by 8.1% in 1994, the biggest rise for 15 years leaving aside the 9.1% in 1992 following the drop in traffic recorded in 1991. This trend continued in 1995, with growth reaching 6.1% and a new record of 8.3% in terms of passenger kilometers for all the AEA airlines taken together (Table1.1). This fairly sustained growth in traffic, coupled with a more moderate increase in output, was reflected in an improved load factor for all the national carriers which, like the productivity improvements, brought many of them back into profitability.

After running a deficit for several years, most airlines managed to get back into the black in 1995. Net profits for the 12 main EU airlines are in the region of US$800 million against a net overall loss on the same scale in 1994. However, financial performances have varied with only British Airways, Finnair and KLM achieving universally favorable results over the entire period from 1990 to 1994. Among the medium-sized and regional airlines which have been particularly active since the introduction of the Third Package,[1] good results were achieved in 1995 by Regional Airlines and Air Littoral with net profits of Ffr9 million and Ffr8.5 million respectively, by EBA (net profit of Bfr200 million) and by Tyroletan Airways (net profit of US$3 million). Airlines continued to perform significantly differently in the latter part of the 1990s (Table 1.2).

As a sector, aviation will continue expanding into the foreseeable future, albeit at differential rates, in various geographical sub-markets. A number of international agencies, aircraft manufacturers and airlines regularly produce forecasts of aviation traffic (e.g. Airbus Industrie, 1993; Boeing Commercial Airplane Group, 1996; and International Civil Aviation Organization, 1994). While forecasting remains an art rather than a science, it seems likely that passenger traffic will grow at a rate between 5% and 7% into the foreseeable future, much of it in the Asian–Pacific region (up to 9% a year). Forecasts have also foreseen slower growth in the more mature US and European markets.

In line with other sectors, aviation has experienced significant moves towards globalization and internationalization. Indeed, it is the stated objective of the UK carrier, British Airways to become a 'global carrier'. In pursuit of wider market coverage and in an effort to enhance their own internal efficiency, other airlines have followed a similar number of strategies. The most recent development is the creation of various forms of airline alliances.

---

[1]   For details of the various 'Packages' of reforms, see Button *et al* (1998).

Table 1.1 European airlines (AEA members only)

		Short/medium Haul		
		ASKs (billions)	RSKs (billions)	FTKs all services (millions)
1990		129.47	77.34	1 189.9
1991		124.68	72.03	1 047.6
1992		144.09	83.79	1 182.6
1994		167.25	101.89	1 652.1
1995		178.50	110.33	1 791.1
1996	Jan	14.71	7.78	148.1
	Feb	13.69	7.49	146.1
	Mar	15.17	9.69	168.3
	Apr	15.71	9.70	156.5
	May	16.25	9.95	150.0
	Jun	16.42	10.64	154.1
	Jul	17.60	11.44	159.7
	Aug	17.87	11.99	150.7
	Sep	16.50	11.20	167.0
	Oct	16.69	10.72	182.5
	Nov	15.48	8.71	181.6
	Dec	15.39	8.61	180.4
1997	Jan	15.78	8.31	154.1
	Feb	14.49	8.20	159.7

		Long Haul		
		ASKs (billions)	RSKs (billions)	FTKs all services (millions)
1990		273.88	192.61	15 688.6
1991		269.44	183.31	15 688.6
1992		297.43	207.06	15 860.0
1993		318.51	223.47	16 789.9
1994		333.53	243.47	17 481.3
1995		319.21	261.90	20 707.0
1996	Jan	29.41	20.48	1 514.4
	Feb	27.09	18.41	1 648.6
	Mar	29.63	23.07	1 926.6
	Apr	30.84	21.93	1 743.2
	May	32.38	22.73	1 756.6
	Jun	32.40	25.09	1 822.9
	Jul	34.39	27.49	1 792.8
	Aug	34.79	28.24	1 720.5
	Sep	33.99	26.98	1 839.6
	Oct	33.88	26.23	1 959.0
	Nov	31.65	22.83	1 907.2
	Dec	32.69	23.14	1 841.3
1997	Jan	32.69	21.30	1 538.4
	Feb	29,27	21.30	1 673.9

Table 1.2 European airline profits in 1996

Airline	Revenues ($billion)	Pre-tax profits (#billion)
British Airways*	13.26	1.02
Lufthansa	13.88	0.46
SAS	5.25	0.26
KLM*	5.96	0.77
Air France*†	8.13	0.04
Iberia	3.77	0.02
Swissair	6.63	−0.36
Alitalia	5.06	−0.78

* Year end March 1997.
† Excluding Air Inter.

Later, this book will focus on alliances involving scheduled airline services. These have also been formed involving charter carriers but are less common.[2] There is also one airport alliance (between Schiphol Airport in the Netherlands and Vienna Airport in Austria) which embraces a number of cooperative features and a 1% cross-share holding. Scheduled airline services and airport alliances, however, are outside the scope of this study.

In the past, airlines in Europe have formed alliances to economize on aircraft maintenance. This generally requires fleets of twenty or so large commercial aircraft that few carriers could operate in isolation. In 1968, UTA, SAS, KLM and Swissair formed KSSU – an organization which subsequently underwent a number of metamorphoses as airlines joined and left. Economies of scale and standardization in maintenance were exploited through different carriers specializing in maintaining particular aircraft types. Subsequent groupings, such as Atlas, were of a similar nature. Equally, the cooperation of scheduled airlines to develop computer reservation systems represents another form of an aviation sector alliance. The development of Amadeus in Europe is an example of this (Humphreys, 1994a). The scope and nature of modern strategic airline alliances transcends in importance these early efforts at cooperation.

1.2.2 Air cargo

The modern air cargo providers are a heterogeneous group of operators, offering different types of services and different levels of logistical expertise. This is a

[2] For an account of charter alliances, particularly between UK and German companies, see *Avmark Aviation Economist* (1994).

somewhat different picture to that found twenty or so years ago and represents both the consequences of changed institutional structures and the advent and adoption of new technologies. To simplify, one can consider three main categories of air freight operators: line haul operators, integrated (express) carriers (such as TNT, Federal Express and DHL) and niche operators.

Line haul operators move cargo from airport to airport and rely on freight forwarders or consolidators to deal directly with customers. Line haul operators embody scheduled and non-scheduled all-cargo undertakings moving only freight in dedicated freighter/cargo aircraft (for example Cargolux in Europe and Nippon Cargo Airlines in Japan); combination passenger and cargo operators that use both dedicated freighter aircraft and the belly-holds in passenger aircraft to move freight (for example Lufthansa and Air France); and passenger operators that use belly-hold capacity in passenger aircraft (such as British Airways). The size of these undertakings varies considerably.

All-cargo operators offer relatively high reliability and have the capability to move large volumes over long distances. For the combination carriers, the cargo operations are mainly long haul, with a large amount of freight being interlined onto shorter haul feeder services. The high utilization of long haul aircraft often justifies the purchase of new aircraft for these services. Passenger carriers in many countries have tended to view cargo as a by-product of passenger operations[3]. They move cargo in the belly-holds of passenger aircraft where it has traditionally taken second place to passenger services.[4] If, for example, an aircraft has a full passenger and baggage load, the cargo/freight would be delayed until the next available flight. Unlike passenger services, shippers do not normally have access to price information analogous to passenger Computer Reservation Systems (CRSs).[5] Freight forwarders play an important role in consolidating shipments for line haulers.[6]

Integrated/courier/express operators offer a variety of products to shippers and supplement air services with extensive ground transport to provide time-definite

---

[3]   They are also generally seen to offer the lowest prices and the least reliable service (GECAS, 1994). The former is because of the traditional tendency to pass most of the avoidable costs onto passengers and to price cargo at or near short run marginal cost.

[4]   In some instances they use aircraft that can rapidly be converted from a passenger carrier to a freight carrier.

[5]   Although now highly sophisticated tracking technologies exist and are gradually being adopted (Newton, 1994).

[6]   Many freight forwarders, however, must depend upon cartage companies and airlines to invest in the more sophisticated technologies and this has hindered the development of some of these types of operation. This is not only because of freight handling procedures themselves but also because forwarders have tended to work on small margins, with a narrow asset base (Malkin, 1992; Button and Owens, 1999).

delivery with continuous shipment tracking and, if necessary, logistical expertise to support just-in-time (JIT) inventory control strategies. In order for courier operators to be able to offer door-to-door next day deliveries, they require night-time operations. In terms of aircraft requirements, they need to operate quiet, reliable aircraft with low utilization levels (as few as two hours flying time per day in some cases). Courier operators seek to purchase a combination of new aircraft, with high capital costs and better utilization on long haul segments, with less expensive renovated second-hand aircraft for the medium haul operations with lower utilization.

The integrated carriers, because of network economies on the cost side and the need for market presence on the demand side, are large operations. For example, Federal Express employs 110 000 people and has a fleet of over 200 jet aircraft of Boeing 727 size and above, plus some 250 small feeder planes. United Parcels Service (UPS) specializes in world-wide package deliveries and operates around 160 large jet aircraft and employs 300 000 people (Ligon, 1992). They also operate hub-and-spoke networks from major airports, often specifically catering for their particular needs; e.g. Federal Express has a major hub at Memphis.[7]

Niche operators operate or leverage specialized equipment or indeed expertise in order to fill extraordinary requirements: for example, Heavylift (Netherlands). These carriers attract business through their capabilities for handling outside freight or special consignments, including line haul to locations with poor infrastructure facilities. They are often small companies. For chartered freight and niche operators, the discontinuous use of aircraft makes it financially preferable to acquire freighter aircraft on a second-hand basis.

Air freight services are sold and marketed in a number of different ways. The line haul operators sell a relatively small proportion of their cargo space directly to their customers. The greater proportion of their space is sold through general sales agents (GSAs) or freight forwarders, who negotiate with the airlines for fixed amounts of space. The agents or forwarders then sell on the freight space to customers. The line haul airlines publish their cargo tariffs as agreed at IATA tariff conferences. In practice, only a small percentage of customers pay these published tariffs, which can be considered as an upper-bound on air cargo rates. This makes it difficult to monitor variations in real tariff rates.

As with air passenger fares, discounting is widely applied in the case of cargo, with rates being determined on the basis of a number of characteristics and

---

[7]   Since cargo is not sensitive to routings and scheduling in the same way that passengers are, the criterion for freight hubs differs from that for passenger hubs. Much cargo is moved at night and use can be made of passenger hub capacity that is free at that time (e.g., as DHL does at Cincinnati). Equally, as with Federal Express, a cargo hub may be located at a city generating relatively little passenger traffic. The hub networks of integrated carriers also differ from most US passenger airlines in that they have a single large hub rather than a multi-hub interactive network.

circumstances, including: commodity type; volume, density and weight; routing; season; regularity of shipments; imports or exports; and priority or speed of delivery.[8] Consolidated shipments aggregated by forwarders and carried by the line haul operators typically travel under a single air waybill. Integrated operators offer a variety of products or services depending on the weight of the consignment and the speed of delivery required by the customer. Discounting is applied to these services on the basis of the volume and regularity of custom. Because each consignment is treated as a separate piece of freight, with an individual air waybill and customs declaration, the integrated carriers provide and practice electronic tracking of individual shipments.

The demand for air cargo services is derived from the demands of producers and consumers.[9] Air freight has contributed to and benefited from the recent rapid growth of the world economy and to the globalization and internationalization of production. The process of physical distribution of freight has, in particular, become a highly sophisticated operation with increasingly greater reliance being placed on the use of new technology to assist in the movement, storage and tracking of consignments. Inventory control and integrated logistics management is now widespread (Brown, 1997).

Air cargo is important in this context because it offers a fast and relatively safe mode of transport for low volume, low weight but high value products. It also provides an important back-up service in terms of meeting demands for spare parts and emergency repair equipment. Additionally, it often offers the only viable means of freight transport to remoter, peripheral regions of countries such as Canada, Australia and Russia where the high costs of fixed, tracked transport infrastructure and climatic conditions put other modes at a major disadvantage.

Consistent, reliable, and complete data on all air freight markets are, however, not available.[10] Data do exist for many countries on physical volumes of goods

---

[8]   This follows the pattern of dynamic price discrimination or 'yield management', found in passenger air transport and poses similar problems for analysts interested in tracking price trends.

[9]   Chapter 2 provides more details of the technical nature of the market for air transport services.

[10]   The use of air trucking is, for example, not fully recorded. One problem is that air freight is increasingly a private sector activity and there are thus inevitable questions of commercial confidentiality. In terms of economic data, much of the traffic is not charged by segment but rather by entire movement cost making the isolation of the air freight component difficult. Equally, many of the combined carriers still treat cargo as a marginal cost in their financial calculations. For country-specific information, the International Civil Aviation Organization (ICAO), the US Department of Transportation (USDOT) and the Association of European Airlines (AEA) provide data, although these are increasingly less reliable as scheduled national flag carrier's shares of national air freight traffic decline. Recently, significant numbers of carriers

transported by air but these are often deficient or incomplete. Economic data relating to international movements are often more comprehensive because of the need for reporting to meet customs requirements. Data relating to the transition economies are, however, sparse and those from many Third World nations are very unreliable. There are, however, a number of commercial and governmental sources where efforts have been made to bring the available information together in a systematic way.

For the past decade air freight has grown faster than air passenger volumes[11] and this trend is expected to continue.[12] The growth, however, has not been evenly spread. The Organisation for Economic Cooperation and Development (OECD) countries accounted for nearly 70% of the total world revenue ton kilometers in 1993 and for 67.4% of the international revenue ton kilometers (RTKs). The US, Japan, Germany and France accounted for over 75% of the total RTKs and over 72% of the international RTKs. The dominant flows of cargo are on the North Atlantic, between Europe and the Far East and in the Pacific Rim. The US share of the global market stood at 43% in 1975 but fell to 32% of RTKs in 1995 as new markets have emerged.

The European share of air cargo traffic has remained relatively unchanged over the same period (24.2% in 1975; 22.9% in 1995). The main growth region has been Asia and the Pacific. This region's share of world air freight RTKs rose from 12.4% in 1975 to 28.5% in 1995. In 1995, non-US charter freight RTKs accounted for 6.6% of world air freight.

In global terms, the dominant air cargo flows are in three main markets – the North Atlantic; Europe-Far East and the Pacific Rim. These markets accounted for 60% of world scheduled traffic in 1993. The Europe–Asia market is expected to have one of the highest growth rates over the period 1996–2015, with Boeing (1996) estimating that air freight will grow by 7.4% per annum.[13] Intra-Europe

---

have also failed to report or delayed reporting statistics to ICAO. Where national data are made available they are typically published some time after the comparable passenger statistics.

[11]   Air cargo revenues have also become an important component of overall airlines revenue amounting to 16% of the total in 1996.

[12]   This follows the forecasts of such bodies as the International Civil Aviation Organization, Boeing and Airbus

[13]   Air freight markets are shifting as the economic growth pattern of developing countries accelerates with the main drivers being the following:

- primary influence of world economic activity (world GDP is the best single measure of global economic activity with a high correlation between changes in world GDP and changes in world air cargo RTKs);
- impact of the range of services in the express and small package market;
- inventory management techniques;
- deregulation and liberalization;

freight has the lowest forecast growth rate of 4.3%. The international air express market is expected to grow rapidly over this period.[14] and Boeing forecasts an annual growth rate of 18% which it claims will result in such services accounting for about 40% of total international cargo business by 2015. They currently account for 5% of the market.[15]

The European air freight market is dominated by the flag carriers of the member states, as are the passenger markets. In 1993 some 94% of total revenue ton kilometers (RTKs) were performed by the flag carrier. The main exception was the UK, where British Airways performed about 51% of total RTKs. Europe's air freight is essentially carried by passenger carriers and by combination passenger–cargo carriers (such as Lufthansa and Air France). The integrated carriers have increased the size of their European operations in recent years and it has been suggested that they now perform most of the total Intra-European RTKs (Triangle Management Services, 1990).

All European Union (EU) flag carriers offer freight services on passenger aircraft with Lufthansa, Air France and Iberia also offering substantial all-freight services. British Airways and KLM handle just under 10% of their air freight using all-freighter aircraft. Air freight within Europe carried by the Association of European Airlines carriers tends to account for a small proportion of carrier's total RTKs and tons carried. For Association of European Airline (AEA) carriers covered by the Third Package, intra-European traffic accounts for 17% of RTKs on average, and for 36% of freight tons. For many of the carriers, the North Atlantic is the most important market sector which reflects the significantly larger stage length on these long haul routes compared with intra-European routes.

To give some indication of the importance of air freight in Europe and the types of issue that it raises,[16] the growth rates in Irish air freight traffic have been similar to the growth rates in Irish trade during the 1990s. Between 1990 and 1995, exports grew by 90%, while air freight traffic increased by 70%. The shares of exports going to UK and other European Union markets have been declining

- national development programmes;
- stream of new air-eligible commodities.

[14]   In commercial terms, Boeing also anticipates a long term yield decline of 1% per annum, while in terms of air freight capacity charges, large freighters (with more than 50 tonnes) will show the greatest proportional increase. The small and medium capacity fleets will be increasingly dominated by freighters of express carriers.

[15]   This mirrors the US where express services accounted for 4% of the US market in 1977, with an average annual growth rate of about 25%. Express operators now claim close to 60% of the US domestic market in 1996 (Air Cargo World, 1996). It is believed that the US experience raised customer expectations for air freight services world-wide.

[16]   For more details of the Irish situation, see Reynolds-Feighan and Durkin (1997).

(both declined by 9% between 1990 and 1995) with the trade share destined for beyond the EU growing. The value of Irish export trade per ton tends to increase with distance to markets and it is in the longer haul markets that air freight has significant advantages over surface modes. For all but one of the top 21 of Ireland's trading partners located outside the EU, the volume of imports significantly exceeds the volume of exports. This trade imbalance, along with differences in the average value per ton of imports compared with exports, gives rise to complicated logistical and schedule planning problems for the carriers operating into and out of Ireland. The significant growth in non-EU trade has stimulated the development of a small number of new long haul air freight services.

Unlike the passenger air transport market, the US carriers do not exercise such a dominant role in the cargo market. One reason for this is that in many markets, such as those in the Asian Pacific region, use has been made of non-scheduled specialist charter cargo operators to circumvent restrictions placed on scheduled carriers. Another factor is that with the advent of wide-bodied jets significant belly-hold capacity became available[17]. While the passenger demands of the US domestic market, with banks of flights requiring rapid turn-arounds at hubs to offer high service quality, gave little time to load and unload freight, European and Asian carriers operating largely in regulated international markets could exploit these technical economies. The result was that, with the exception of Northwest, which has a large long haul international presence, US passenger carriers have not become large freight carriers.

Recent years have seen considerable structural changes occurring in the industry. This is in part due to regulatory changes (see below) but also reflects technical developments. The share of air freight handled by the line haul carriers has, following global trends, been declining steadily in Europe. The express operators are expected to account for 40% of total international cargo business by 2015, according to Boeing. Express operators currently account for about 60% of the US domestic market and the US experience remains an important indicator of key trends. The different types of operators also face a variety of cost, revenue and operating conditions.

1.3 NETWORK INDUSTRIES

The exact definition of a network is not unambiguous. According to Capineri and Kamann (1998), '...a *network* [is] a collection of nodes (actors, cities) connected

---

[17]   A Boeing 747 with a full complement of passenger can carry 20 tonnes of cargo: less than the 60–70 tons of a dedicated 747 freighter, but offering a high marginal return.

by facilities (links, arcs, ties, relationships, waves) through which entities (such as goods, cars, passengers, services, power) pass' (italics in original;). Networks may be physical, as with roads, or non-physical, as with relationships. Economic analysis tends to focus mainly, but not exclusively, on physical relationships.[18] Indeed here much of the attention is on airline networks.

Delineating a firm in more traditional areas of economic study is becoming increasingly difficult but so is he task of drawing the boundaries around networks. There are often geographical boundaries to consider which can become opaque when there is multinational ownership involved. The size and scope of the market poses particular problems in the application of antitrust and similar regulatory policies as has been seen with respect to both telecommunication laws and with regard to investigations into international airline alliances. In this book we adopt a fairly practical approach to networks and do not attempt to refine a formal definition. This seems sensible in a situation where there are many overlapping and often interacting physical and informational structures.

1.4 THE BOOK

The main body of the book is designed to examine both the theoretical and the empirical side of air transport networks. It includes looking at both the direct suppliers of air transport services, the airlines, and the infrastructure that they use, the airports and the air traffic navigation and air traffic control systems. It is essentially an economics book. It does not concern itself with engineering issues and only pays limited attention to many of the managerial and operational issues that are of importance to air transport. The aim is not to produce an encyclopaedia of air transport networks. Rather it is to offer some insights into the economic factors that have influenced their development and that play a continuing role in the way the sector is treated, both by those within it and by those responsible for the wider public policy that regulates it.

All books require a structure and in all cases there are a number of possibilities available. The approach here is essentially very conservative. The remainder of the book initially sets out some basic economic principles as they apply to the air transport industry. This entails looking at some of the evidence that we have regarding the basic economics of the airline industry (e.g. regarding costs and efficiency). It contains only limited information about networks *per se* but does provide important information about the particular features of the sector that influence the way air transport networks have emerged. While there are some economic features common to all networks, and these are discussed to an extent in

---

[18]   In particular the work of the Nobel Prize winning economist, Gary Becker has broadened the scope of economics.

Chapter 3, equally there are distinguishing features that pertain to each particular network industry or sector. These features are partly determined by institutional arrangements, in the widest meaning of the term, but are also partly determined by the intrinsic economics of the sector.

Chapters 4, 5 and 6 are more institutional in their orientation and consider public policies, both domestic and international, that regulate the way air transport networks have developed and currently operate. They pay particular attention to the trend towards liberalization of markets that has characterized transport policy over the past twenty years. In Chapter 5 a detailed examination is conducted of the implications of moving to a liberalized air transport market in the US and Canada. The attention is mainly on the first decade after the reforms to avoid the problems of defining a longer-term counter factual. Chapter 6 looks more specifically at the implications of international airline regulation that, through its structure of bilateral agreements, has produced partial network structures. To some extent, Chapter 7 takes up the theme of regulation from a somewhat different perspective and focuses on potential instability issues in air transport networks and the possible policy responses that are available to counter the problem.

With Chapters 8, 9 and 10 there is a move away from the airlines and towards the economics of the air transport network infrastructure. Particular attention is paid in these three chapters to the economics of airports and to their wider role in economic development. A major problem with these nodes in the air transport network is that they are not normally supplied or operated according to market principles and this leads to problems of sub-optimal investment and utilization. From a wider policy perspective, the air transport infrastructure issues that have confronted European policy makers, and the policy approaches that have been adopted, are taken as a sort of case study in Chapter 9. The impacts of hub airports on economic development in the US have been taken as another case in Chapter 10.

While air freight transport networks are examined in a number of places in the preceding chapters, Chapter 11 gives them a more explicit treatment. They are important economic networks in their own right and this in itself may be said to justify this coverage. They bare also increasing in importance as globalization in production takes place and as the demand for movement of high value/low weight manufacturers grows. In addition, they raise a number of interesting questions that are somewhat different to those covered in the body of the book where passenger transport is often the primary focus.

Chapter 12 extends this theme somewhat by considering the interaction between airports and other modes of transport. In particular, issues of airport access and inter-modal transport are looked at. Access to an increasingly heavily used airport system throughout the world is having serious and detrimental knock-on effects on the surface transport that moves people and goods to and from airports and on the ability of the large number of people who now work at airports to reach their employment. The chapter is also concerned with the competitive interactions between air transport networks and other networks (including telecommunications networks); transferring some types of traffic to other modes has important implications for issues of access to airports.

The final chapter takes a somewhat wider look at the economics of air transport networks and considers issues of safety and environmental damage. While air transport is a very safe mode of transport, the nature of the incidents that do occur tends to attract considerable public attention and this inevitably affects public policy and the way airlines prioritize their own internal decisions. Air transport also has a number of major environmental implications that are increasingly being considered as public policies are developed.

2   AIRLINE ECONOMICS

2.1   INTRODUCTION

The title 'Airline Economics' for a chapter is slightly misleading although it does
largely convey what is covered here. It is misleading because it implies that
somehow there is a special branch of economics that applies particularly to
airlines. This is not so. Economic principles are universal. What we are interested
in here are the particular economic features of airline markets and institutions that
are important in a network context. The depth of coverage should enable a basic
appreciation of the issues to be gleaned, although there are far more technical
accounts available.

The material largely, but not exclusively, focuses on the scheduled
airlines industry. Many of the main arguments are also germane for non-scheduled
carriers although since charter and other markets often involve somewhat simpler
networks there are inevitable differences. The arguments are also broadly
applicable to passenger carriers and freight carriers although again there will be
differences.

Airline operations have a number of peculiar economic features that need to
be viewed as an entity. They provide network services that are non-durable (in the
sense that once a flight leaves, it has been 'consumed'). For any flight there is a
finite capacity involving the carriage of a variety of different clients, not only
passengers and freight but also various classes of passenger. These different
classes extend beyond explicit divisions into such categories as 'business class'
and 'coach' and embody differences in time preferences, fares, and ticket flexibility
that characterize the vast diversity of users of air transportation. Airlines provide
an intermediate product (few people travel for the pure pleasure of it,[1] but rather
because of what they will find at the destination) and air transportation imposes
externalities on third parties (such as environmental effects).

There are also various forms of economy associated with scale of the services
provided, the length of time an operator has served a market and the structure of

---

[1]   Having said this, airline operations do seem to retain a sort of romantic
appeal to many and sometimes it would appear that investors and owners become
involved simply to be close to aircraft. This aspect of the sector is not treated in any
great detail here, although the motivations for individuals to become involved in an
industry that has historically earned a low long-term rate of return would seem to
justify more research.

the network adopted. To support airline operations a large and technologically sophisticated infrastructure is required.

While none of these features are unique in themselves, their combination does pose specific problems when trying to understand the economics of the industry. This means that while conventional economic concepts are valid, they must be applied to allow for these particular characteristics.

2.2 THE DEMAND FOR AIR TRANSPORT

The demand for air transport services, as is the demand for all transport services, is derived from the demand to enjoy some final activity. There is a tendency to discuss air travel in simple terms of business and leisure travel but this misses many important attributes of demand.

Transport services, although not unique in this respect, are characterized by their non-durable nature.[2] once a plane takes off the trips that it had for offer have either been taken up or have been lost for ever. Passenger air travel, like other forms of transport, is also a participation activity. Its consumption requires a considerable amount of the user's (i.e. the traveler's) inputs of time and energy in addition to the fare that must be paid. This means that demand patterns are normally influenced by 'generalized cost' considerations that embrace these personal inputs as well as the fares involved.

Third, air travel is seldom taken in isolation from other travel. In the context of passenger trips these at the very least involve travel to and from airports and may involve using several aircraft; they are almost inevitably multi-modal activities. Similarly, for freight transport, consignments must be transported to and from the airport as well as flow between terminals.

A fourth feature of demand is that the price that a consumer is willing to pay can be influenced by the availability of complementary products. In particular, loyalty to one airline can allow a traveler to accumulate frequent flyer miles that may be used for additional flights. The miles are in that sense a complement to the main purchase.[3] From an airline point of view they are designed as loyalty payments aimed at retaining customers.

[2]   Other goods that fall into this category include theatre performances and some types of energy.
[3]   Frequent flyer programs were initiated in the US in1981. By 1986 all major US carriers operated a program, and by 1993 membership of frequent flyer programs had reached 30 million people with 1.7 trillion accumulated miles to their accounts. Programs have emerged less rapidly outside of the US, in part because some airlines felt that involvement was essentially a zero-sum game, while within the EU it was unclear where such programs stood with respect to competition policy. They have now, however, become widespread across all international markets. Often linked to

Analysis of demand has been handicapped in recent years because the airlines have increasingly engaged in dynamic price discrimination (yield management) as computerization, and in particular the development of computer reservation systems, has given more information on the way seats are selling and the ability to adjust fares very rapidly. This means that there is effectively no such thing as a fare for a flight and often an aircraft will carry passengers paying a wide range of fares. Airlines, for commercial reasons, are reluctant to release detailed breakdowns of fares paid and consequently demand analysis tends to be based on yield (i.e., the total revenue from flight divided by the number of passengers).

Fare demand elasticity for air travel depends on the nature of the final demand of passengers (e.g., leisure or business activities) and whether one is looking at the long term or short term elasticities (i.e., using a cross-section or time series approach). An analysis of demand elasticity estimations by Oum *at al.* (1992) summarized in Table 2.1 indicates a range of estimates from –0.4 to 4.51.[4] There is some evidence that the estimated elasticities vary by fare class (first class, standard economy and discount) and by distance. This corresponds to the intuitive notion that price-sensitive leisure travelers form the majority of long distance passengers while less price sensitive business travelers make shorter journeys.

Table 2.1 Demand elasticities of air passenger travel

	Time series	Cross-section	Others*
Leisure travel	0.40-1.98, 192	1.52	1.40-3.30,2.20-4.6
Business travel	0.65	1.15	0.90
Mixed or unknown	0.82,0.91,0.36-1.81 1.12-1.28,1.48	0.76-0.84, 1.39, 1.63, 1.85, 2.83-4.51	0.53-1.00,1.80- 1.90

* Included here are studies with unknown data sources.
Source: Oum *et al.* (1992).

frequent flyer programs is membership of an airline club. Some of these stem directly from miles traveled (e.g., British Midland's, Diamond Club) while others require payment of a membership fee (e.g., Qantas's, Australian's Flight Deck) but all offer members private lounges, refreshments and, often, business facilities. They represent sunk costs to airline travelers and hence, at the margin, are an incentive to stay with an airline once a club is joined.

[4]   These are estimates of the Marshallian demand elasticities. Compensated demand functions are difficult to estimate because utility is not directly measurable.

The data in the table confirms that the demand for business travel is less sensitive to fare changes than is the demand for leisure travel. How exact these estimates are is, though, open to some question since many of the studies used full fare as a proxy for business travel but some of these studies used data prior to full deregulation of markets when leisure travelers were forced to pay the full fare.

There has also been analysis of the differences in fare elasticities that seem to exist in different markets. Table 2.2, for instance, presents the results of an investigation of air travel across the North Atlantic conducted by Mutti and Mural (1977). The general impression is of price inelasticity but there is obvious variability between routes. Examinations of internal air traffic within the US, however, produce much more varied results. Brown and Watkins (1968) and Gronau (1970) show a remarkable degree of consistency in their findings by producing price elasticities of −0.85 and −0.75, respectively. Jung and Fujii (1976) came to a somewhat different conclusion, namely, 'The empirical evidence suggests that demand for air travel for distances under 500 miles in the south east and south central portions of the US is price elastic.' Devany (1974) also found variations in elasticities with respect to distance very much in accord with this.

Table 2.2 Demand elasticities for air travel on the North Atlantic, 1964–74, by country (expressed as absolute values)

Market	Income elasticity	Fare elasticity
United States	2.15	−0.99
United Kingdom	4.38	−0.40
Netherlands	1.77	−0.28
Italy	2.00	−0.72
Germany	2.71	−0.19
France	2.03	−0.14
Total	1.89	−0.89

Source: Mutti and Mural (1977).

It is not only fare that can be important in determining demand, as suggested above, factors such as 'bonuses' associated with frequent flyer programs may also be important.[5] Frequent flyer programs may, as incumbents are prone to argue, be a form of quantity discount rewarding good customers. The alternative view, in the context of business travel, is that they represent attempts to exploit the principal–agent problem by encouraging traveling employees to make decisions that are not necessarily in the interests of their employers (Humphreys, 1991).

In terms of demand for the services of specific carriers, frequent flyer programs provide incumbent airlines, and especially large carriers, with significant advantages. Large incumbents with their extensive route networks give travelers a greater opportunity to earn miles and also have a more diverse set of destinations to offer when the traveler accumulates enough miles to earn an award. Large carriers can, therefore, benefit significantly from the non-linear nature of the award structure. By concentrating flying on one or two large airlines a traveler becomes eligible for more attractive awards as mileage accumulates. Placing expiration dates on earned miles makes it even more important for a traveler to remain with one carrier.

US business travelers seem sensitive to frequent flyer incentives (e.g., Proussaloglu and Koppelman, 1995). A US General Accounting Office (1990) study revealed that 81% of business travelers choose flights to build up their frequent flyer mileage more than half the time (Table 2.3). Further, the US Department of Transportation (1990) concluded that frequent flyer programs influence choice and give an advantage to large carriers. This was also a view expressed in Canada when its Competition Tribunal in 1993 reviewed the failure of Wardair. Quantification of this effect, however, is difficult. Tentative evidence sheds some light on the extent that programs may give an artificial advantage to large incumbent carriers in the US. It asks what would happen to the market shares of airlines if frequent flyer programs were abandoned. The results suggest that while, in general, larger carriers would seem to lose most and the smallest to gain most, there are numerous instances where this does not hold.

One can also consider what would happen if any airline takes unilateral action and, without changing any other attributes of the services offered, withdraws its frequent flyer program. The evidence is that the largest carriers in the US, American Airlines and United Air Lines, would lose market share (Morrison and Winston, 1995). Smaller carriers would lose less but still enough to explain why they continue their frequent flyer programs. It would see from this work that, once accustomed to frequent flyer programs, many travelers expect all airlines to offer one. The study does not explain, though, the success of low cost carriers that do not have frequent flyer programs.

---

[5]   Other studies have explored the importance of wealth effects (Alperovich and Machnes, 1994) and service quality effects (Ippolito, 1981) on demand.

Table 2.3 How often US business travelers choose flights to build up frequent flyer miles

Percentage of travel agents reporting	
Always or almost always	57
More than half the time	24
About half the time	9
Less than half the time	4
Rarely, if ever	2
Other	3

Source: US General Accounting Office (1990).

Demand is also influenced by the information the customer has available. Computer reservation system (CRS) services provide computerized systems that contain up-to-date information about air carriers' schedules, availability, fares and fare rules, and through which reservations can be made or tickets may be issued. They have for about 25 years formed an integral part of airlines' marketing strategies.

The power of CRSs to benefit owning airlines has long been appreciated. It has been argued that, without regulation, airlines could suffer considerable discrimination by carriers owning such systems. On this basis CRSs have been the subject of regulation in the US (since 1984), in Canada (1989) and in the EU, and a Code of Conduct was initially established in 1991 by the ICAO setting standards of information display and access. The aim has largely been to limit potential exploitation of customers by CRS-controlling airlines.

One major problem has been display bias in favor of the owner and this has been tackled by the legislation. Although historically important, halo effects (booking practices by agents that favoring CRS-owner airlines[6]) are diminishing. Advances in computer technology, the development of the Internet and the ability for passengers to book directly through personal computer systems have reduced the importance of travel agents.

[6]   In the US, 51% of travel agents choose the airline for their clients at least half the time, and at least two-thirds of agents choose the airline on at least one-quarter of the flights they book. Further, a Louis Harris survey found that travel agents choose carriers 41% of the time for business travelers and 55% for leisure travelers – the former being more frequent travelers and thus better informed. The survey also found that 51% of the agents selected a carrier because of commission incentives at least some of the time.

2.3 THE NATURE OF THE COST FUNCTION

The cost structures of airlines are complicated by the multi product nature of the services offered. There is also the question of defining the appropriate unit of input. Is it the plane, the seat or the segment of the service that is being costed? Technically, significant advances have been in the ways in which airline cost functions are estimated. An improved understanding of cost structures, coupled with more sophisticated models and estimation procedures, has been important in this process.[7]

Much of the traditional work on costing had a basis in accounting and was mainly concerned with separating and attributing cost items. This has now progressed, at least in terms of economic analysis, to the use of flexible cost functions and the deployment of programming techniques.

The conventional accountancy procedures and basic econometric models (e.g. Leontief or Cobb-Douglas-based functions) deployed until the late 1980s have been supplemented by more rigorous techniques as the understanding of the subtleties of cost functions has advanced, as methods of estimation have developed, and as relevant computer software has become available (e.g. Caves *et al.*, 1987).

On the theoretical side, traditional neo-classical ideas of economies of scale have been supplemented by notions of economies of scope, networks, density and of experience.[8] Also on the demand side, ideas of economies of market presence have come to the fore in terms of influencing the optimal scale of activities and largely underlie the development of frequent flyer programs and code-sharing alliances. Econometric models have been able to accommodate these features and to allow parameter estimation through the use of flexible form models. The transcendental-logarithmic (translog) function is, for instance, now widely deployed because of its flexibility although putting input prices on items such as capital still poses serious problems.[9]

---

[7]   Additionally the move away from rate-of-return regulation that was practiced in many air transport markets has removed the ability to pass on cost increases to consumers and stimulated a more careful approach to cost analysis.

[8]   Economies of scale reflect declining costs of production as an airline's output increases; economies of scope are present when one airline can produce two or more services more cheaply than if these services were produced by separate airlines; economies of traffic density occur when the average unit cost of production declines as the amount of traffic increases between any given set of points served; and economies of network size exist when the average cost of production declines as the number of city points served by an airline's network increases. Economies of experience reflect falling costs with total sales in a market over time.

[9]   The standard approach is to estimate the-log cost (or production) function in combination with share equations using Zellner's seemingly unrelated least squares

The traditional linear economic cost model was based on the premise of a production where factors were always combined in fixed proportions (i.e. a Leontief technology). The Cobb-Douglas model (involving a log-linear specification) improved on this and provided a degree of transferability but only with a constant elasticity of substitutability. The translog and other flexible forms remove this constraint. The general form of the translog cost model is:

$$LnC = A + \alpha lnQ + \Sigma\beta_i lnP_i + 0.5\delta(lnQ)^2 + 0.5\Sigma\Sigma\gamma_{ij}lnP_i lnP_j + \Sigma\rho_i lnP_i Q \qquad (2.1)$$

where: C is the total cost, Q is output and ρ_i is the price of the ith factor.

The function is assumed to be an exact representation of the minimum cost function. For it to be well-behaved a minimum requirement is that it be positive and homogeneous of degree one in prices. This implies the following restrictions:

$$\Sigma\beta_1 = 1; \quad \Sigma\rho_i = 0; \quad \Sigma\gamma_{ij} = \Sigma\gamma_{ji} = 0 \qquad (2.2)$$

It is assumed that the market for factors is competitive.

The results of cost analysis using these techniques do not yield a consensus. Early work (White, 1979) looking at traditional scale economies found these did exist for the smallest operators but were rapidly exhausted. At least one study of the US domestic air transport sytem indicates that there are possible diseconomies at the largest firm size (Spraggins, 1989). Economies may, however, exist in specific areas such as marketing and advertising.

Given the complex nature of the air transport industry product, it is not surprising that empirical studies using aggregate measures of airlines' output can give inconclusive results. If measured as revenue passenger miles, the scale of operations of a carrier can be extended by increasing *ceteris paribus*, the flight frequencies or the number of passenger per flight. Frequency changes could lead to economies of network size, where density effects might occur in connection with the amount of use made of the networks involved.

In more detail, evidence suggests that airlines' unit costs do not fall greatly as they expand (e.g., Caves *et al.,* 1983). Strictly the evidence indicates that within any city pair markets there are rapidly declining costs of service but that there are approximately constant returns to scale for airline systems that have reached the size of the US trunk carriers. Savings come from attracting more traffic rather than expanding the network to cover additional origin/destinations; any additional routes increase the operator's quasi-fixed costs which may negate the benefits derived from more traffic. Further, good regional connections may be a more effective marketing tool than large, less coherent networks.

procedures. This increases degrees of freedom, means the estimates are invariate to the share equation omitted and converge to yield maximum likelihood estimates.

Standard economic analysis focuses on firms producing a single output. This does not adequately reflect the complexity of relationships in the aviation industry. Airlines supply a range of outputs by operating more than one service on any given city-pair route and providing a number of interconnected ones. Economies of scope occur when it is less costly for one airline to provide a range across a fixed network than for a number of airlines to provide them separately. In terms of market entry, economies of scope imply that entry needs to be across a range of markets if costs of the entrant are to match the incumbents. Conversely, successful entry of low-cost point-to-point airlines in the 1990s US domestic market demonstrates that costs can in some cases be lower for such services than for larger networks.

US regulatory reforms have airlines seeking this diversity of service, primarily via hub-and-spoke operations. In the international market, flag carriers tend to focus their operations on national hub airports. The empirical evidence is not conclusive that this generates significant economies of scope. One of the main difficulties has been isolating potential effect from other aspects of airlines' cost functions. Further, a major rationale for these structures comes as much from marketing advances (i.e., on the demand side) as cost savings. Providing a diverse range of services leads to market visibility and makes frequent flyer programs more attractive, thus enhancing customer loyalty. These attributes are features of network value or value of presence and utility to customer.

Reaping economies from traffic density is often as important as exploiting economies of scope, although their effects are entwined.[10] As more passengers travel, it becomes possible to use larger aircraft that are cheaper to operate per seat kilometer and offer more frequent services. This lowers the cost per available seat kilometer. As we have said, economies of density occur when unit costs fall as the size of the market increases. Hub operation adoption, by increasing city-pairs served, allows a carrier to utilize better its unsold seats inventory. Early empirical evidence from the US domestic market points to significant economies of density, with a 1% rise in passengers an airline carries over a given network, increasing

---

[10]   Strictly, economies of scope relate to falling costs of providing services as the range of services offered by a carrier increases while economies of traffic density refer to falling costs as the amount carried increases between any given set of points served (Brueckner and Spiller, 1994).

The technical distinction between economies of scale and scope can be seen by reference to the following equation where C denotes cost and Q is output. Economies of scope are assessed as:

$$S = \{[C(Q^1) + C(Q^2)] - C(Q^1 + Q^2)\} / \{C(Q^1 + Q^2)\}$$

$C(Q^1)$ is the cost of producing Q^1 units of output one alone, $C(Q^2)$ is the cost of producing Q^2 of output two alone, and $C(Q^1 + Q^2)$ is the cost of producing Q^1 plus Q^2. Economies of scope exist if $S > 0$. There are economies of scale if C/Q falls as Q expands.

total costs by only 0.8% (Caves *et al.,* 1983). Later studies have pointed to a possibly of even greater economies than this (Brueckner and Spiller, 1994). Competitive market entry on any route in these conditions again requires entry on a large scale. Recent low-cost carriers entering US and EU routes, however, suggest that some markets are amenable to a smaller-scale entry.

Economies in operating a standard fleet of aircraft also seem to exist. In particular, communality of spare parts, maintenance procedures and flight crews can reduce unit-operating costs. This is exemplified in the US domestic market by the savings Southwest Airlines has achieved, partly through its total reliance on variants of the Boeing 737 aircraft. These economies are being exploited in short-haul markets, with few impediments to market entry. In some instances, airlines make use of the large used aircraft market to equip themselves from the outset with a standard fleet of aircraft.

An outcome of airline liberalization is the ability of many incumbents to remain in the market and strengthen their position. There may exist economies of experience. Part of this effect can be due to residual endowments of market power after reforms (those, for example, associated with the grand-fathering of landing slots) and part to initial diversity and scope of an incumbent's operations. On top of this, an additional effect stems from airlines simply having been in existence for a time and from being in the market with the experiences that this provides them.

Experience provides incumbents with buffers against new market entrants in a number of ways:

- Goodwill. When confronted with a number of carriers, potential users of aviation have varying levels of information and quality of services. Risk aversion encourages a 'better the devil I know' mentality that favors incumbent suppliers. The need to circumvent this with advertising and promotions pushes up costs for new entrants.
- Knowledge. Incumbent supplies have more information on the market being served and can tailor service to specific customer needs. New entrants must sink resources into acquiring such information.
- Organization. New entrants must assimilate needs of the new service over their other routes, and this entails learning costs throughout the remainder of their organization.

Empirical evidence on economies of experience in air transport is scant and exact causal links are often difficult to define. One early study of the US domestic experience (Baker and Pratt, 1989) looking at the nature of entrants to domestic routes after federal deregulation found that established intra-state airlines had a much larger impact on the inter-state market than did newly established carriers. This is supported by data on entry to new routes in the US after deregulation. In the first three quarters of 1980 from a sample of 281 market entries, the newcomers already served both endpoints in 245 cases and at least one endpoint in 277 cases (Berry, 1990). Analysis of the efforts of Compass Airline to enter the Australian domestic market after liberalization also points to the difficulties of establishing goodwill and brand identity (Nyathi *et al.*, 1993). More recent experience in the US suggests that new entry can be successful in serving markets of less than 750 miles if their costs are low – Morris Air was an example (Bennett and Craun, 1993).

All this analysis assumes that the airline is on its minimum cost curve and may or may not be able to reduce unit costs by moving along it. Leibenstein (1966) and others have argued that this may not be the case and as a result there may be significant resources losses; there may be X-inefficiency. The differences in this approach compared to more conventional concerns about economic inefficiency can be explained by reference to Figure 2.1. An X-inefficient airline that is not attempting to keep costs to a minimum when confronted by a marginal cost curve MC* sets price at P1. This results in a deadweight loss of **A** due to allocative inefficiency, when monopolists, whilst managing their undertaking efficiently, keep prices above the competitive level or output below it (Harberger, 1954). And also a Posner (1975)/Tullock (1967)/Bhagwati (1982) rent-seeking loss of up to **B** results from monopolists using their rents to protect their positions, for example by lobbying or holding under-used slots. If cost-minimizing behavior were pursued, then the X-efficient marginal cost curve would be lower at MC. The resultant welfare differences, when contrasted with marginal cost pricing based upon the X-efficient MC curve, are:

- **C**, the X-inefficiency loss at the price P1;
- **D**, the additional allocative loss because marginal cost pricing is not being practiced at the X-inefficient MC* cost level; and
- **E**, the additional allocative loss because marginal cost pricing is not being practiced on the lowest possible MC curve.

The three most popular techniques for teasing out these latter losses are parametric programming (Aigner and Chu, 1968), non-parametric programming (Charnes *et al.*, 1977) and parametric stochastic, or composed error, frontiers (Aigner *et al.*, 1977).

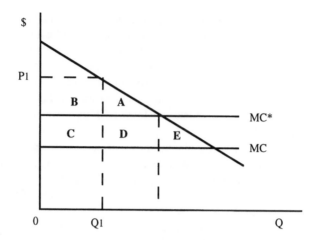

Figure 2.1 Losses due to non-cost minimization

Amongst these techniques there are many possible categorizations and taxonomies, but a fundamental difference between the second technique and the other two relates to their respective assumptions regarding maximizing behavior. In the first and third sets of techniques, a parametric frontier is postulated based on a behavioral maximization hypothesis. This is usually a production frontier, a cost frontier or a profit frontier. The production frontier assumes the existence of a functional relationship: f(x) describing the maximum output obtainable from a vector of inputs, x. The observed output of the typical carrier falls short of this maximum output by an amount, ε equal to its technical inefficiency:

$$\ln y = \ln f(x) + \varepsilon; \quad \varepsilon \leq 0. \tag{2.3}$$

Duality relationships may be used to construct a parametric cost function for given input prices, w, or the parametric profit function for given input and output prices, w and p. In either case, there is an implicit assumption that maximizing behavior is present, and that it is exhibited by the most efficient firms in the sample. Inefficiency is measured by the size of the error between observed cost, or profit, performance, and the parameterized maximum given by the functional relationship;

$$w'x = C(y,w) + \varepsilon; \quad \varepsilon \geq 0 \tag{2.4}$$
$$\text{or}$$
$$py - w'x = \pi(w,p) + \varepsilon; \quad \varepsilon \leq 0. \tag{2.5}$$

In the case of parametric stochastic frontier measurement, not all of the deviation of observed from maximal performance is attributed to inefficiency. Instead a composed error assumption is made that partitions ε between an asymmetrically distributed inefficiency term, u, and a symmetrically distributed noise term, v.[11]

What many of the empirical studies using these techniques fail to do is ask what *a priori* grounds exist for assuming that the best practice firms in the sample - whose observations trace out the frontier – actually adopt optimizing behavior. Most analysts, including those looking at airlines, choose industry-wide data sets and investigating the degree of measured inefficiency against an optimized frontier without setting any controls on the nature of the constraint pressures that will determine the degree of inefficient behavior. For example, in the composed error cost frontier, measured inefficiency is:

$$u = \varepsilon - v = [\text{observed cost - parameterized frontier minimum cost}] - \text{noise} \qquad (2.6)$$

In different parts of the industry, however, and at different times, the parameterized frontier minimum cost may contain considerable unmeasured X-inefficiency depending on the degree to which constraint concern pressures of various types are operating.

In this respect the non-parametric programming approach may have an attraction. The non-parametric programming approach (also known as DEA - data envelopment analysis) proceeds by constructing, under different assumptions about free disposability and returns to scale, the convex hull of the observed input-output observations for a given set of firms or organizations. For example, if X and Y are all the observations on inputs and outputs in an airline wide sample of n carriers, and x and y are the corresponding observations of a typical carrier, then that airline's efficiency index, θ, assuming free disposability and variable returns to scale, is the solution to the linear program:

choose $\{\theta, \lambda\}$ to : min θ such that: $\qquad \theta x \geq \lambda' X \qquad\qquad\qquad (2.7)$
$$y \leq \lambda' Y$$
$$\lambda_i \geq 0, \ \Sigma \lambda_i = 1, \ i = 1, ..., n$$

As such this technique constructs a frontier based simply on the distance of the best practice firms from the rest. There is no implicit assumption of maximizing behavior on the part of any of the firms, including the best practice firms on the frontier. It is still the case, though, that many DEA or non-

---

[11]   Different estimation methods for such models are suggested by Greene (1980) and Stevenson (1980).

parametric efficiency studies ignore the nature of the efficiency pressures likely to be operating on any given sample.

Work applying these approaches on the airline sector has indicated quite marked differences in levels of productivity, and *ipso facto* costs. Much of this work has been related to the US market. Caves *et al.* (1981) examined levels and growth rates of output, inputs and total factor productivity of 11 US trunk airlines over the period 1972 to 1977. The relative international efficiency of US carriers was subsequently examined by Caves *et al.* (1987) for the period 1970 to 1983. Changes in the returns to scale and total factor productivity were studied by Bauer (1990) using data on 12 US carriers for the period 1971 to 1981. The stochastic frontier method was deployed by Good *et al.* (1993) to compare the efficiency and productivity of four large European airlines with eight US carriers in 1976--1986. The same period was used in Good *et al* (1995) to conduct both DEA and stochastic frontier analysis on eight European and eight airlines, and found that the former would save about $4billion a year (1986 dollars) if they became as effective as US airlines.

Outside the US, Gillen (1990) used a total cost function to look at the performance of seven Canadian airlines between 1964 and 1981, while Encaoua (1991) examined European airline costs and found some convergence between 1981 and 1986. Distexhe and Perelman (1994) used DEA methods to find reduced X-inefficiency amongst 33 airlines over the years 1973 to 1983. The Australian Bureau of Industry Economics applied DEA techniques to a cross section of 309 airlines to examine efficiency variations.[12]

Oum and Yu (1995), in an international comparison of 23 airlines for the period 1986 to 1993 and using a total factor productivity framework found significant differences in the performance of carriers from different regions. With the exception of the Japanese airlines, Asian carriers were found to have lower unit costs than European or American airlines. The period also saw important productivity improvements in the European and Asian carriers compared to their US counterparts; a probably catching up effects as these markets began to be dergulated.

2.4   PRICING

As we see in later chapters, air transport fares and cargo rates have a long history of regulation. This led to price structures that were often far from those that would emerge in commercial markets. Things have been changing and rate

---

[12]   DEA analysis has also been used to examine airport productivity. Gillen and Lall (1997) looked at 21 US airports over a five year period and found significant X-inefficiency at government owned airports. ˙

controls have gradually been removed. Freed from rate regulations in many markets, the pricing of air transport services has developed considerably over recent years as airlines have developed sophisticated forms of yield management, a dynamic form of price discrimination.

Airline services are non-durable in the sense that, if a seat is not sold when an aircraft takes off, that service is lost forever. Those demanding air transport services are not a uniform group but represent a wide range of individuals – business travelers of differing seniority, holiday-makers etc. – with various priorities. This combination of non-durability of service and heterogeneous demand has led many airlines to adopt yield management techniques to maximize their revenue flow.

Price discrimination does not only permit suppliers to recover their costs, it also helps travelers and consignors in that services can be retained without subsidies even if, as in some cases, it is necessary to differentiate the quality of service provided as well as the fare charged. International air travel offers some initial examples of this type of situation where differential prices are charged over a route according to the specifications of the types of service the travelers are willing to pay for.

The gradual breakdown of the International Air Transport Association's (IATA) system of regulating air fares across the Atlantic in the 1970s, for example, was accompanied by the introduction of cut-price services such as 'Skytrain', operated by Laker Airways (Abe, 1979). No-frill flights were introduced at low fares with seat allocation dependent upon the willingness of potential passengers to queue – tickets could not be purchased until six hours prior to take-off. Subsequently, this type of service was modified and regular scheduled airlines now offer a variety of ticketing arrangements on their flights. A clear segmentation of the market had been recognized based upon elasticities of different groups.

Figure 2.2 provides an illustration of the sort of situation that has emerged in many air transportation markets. If there are three different groups of potential travelers each characterized by the separate demand curves D_1, D_2 and D_3, then three separate fares should be charged (P_1, P_2, P_3) to maximize the consumers' surplus enjoyed. P_1 is charged for the highest quality flight, equaling the marginal cost of that service, with lower fares for poorer quality flights.

On the surface it appears that ON_1 passengers will travel first class reaping a consumer surplus of ABP_1, and N_1N_2 passengers will pay P_2 for the slightly lower quality of service and enjoy consumers' surplus of HIG. This ignores the possibility that first-class travelers may switch to the poorer quality but cheaper services (that is, there may be some 'revenue dilution'). In fact, travelers N'_1N_1 could switch and increase their welfare. Similarly, N'_2N_2 passengers appear to be the probable number of customers for the poor quality service but again a further N'_2N_2 may be induced to join them by the lower fare.

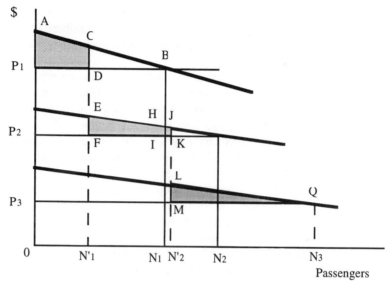

Figure 2.2 Price discrimination according to service quality

Whether people take advantage of the possibility of switching to cheaper, but less convenient, forms of service is uncertain. It depends on information flows, the way the airlines market their seats and the sensitivity of travelers to service quality. The availability of the range of services, however, means the total potential consumer surplus (the shaded areas) will exceed that generated if only a single price and service package were available.[13]

[13]   With perfect price discrimination the airline will extract all consumer surplus from users although the resources devoted to the sector will (with Pareto conditions met elsewhere) be optimal. This can be seen in the diagram below.

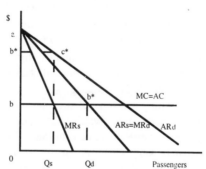

If a monopoly airline with constant costs were to charge a single maximizing price it would be b* and consumer surplus would be ab*c*. With perfect price discrimination

This type of practice is an integral part of what has become known as yield management. Essentially it is the ability of management to maximize the revenue from a pre-defined activity (e.g., a scheduled flight) by a combination of price discrimination and product differentiation.[14] Yield management is essentially a dynamic form of price discrimination whereby, rather than an identical fare being charged to each passenger, users are charged different fares reflecting their elasticities of demand.

The use of CRSs by airlines enables them to track how sales are going on each services, to adjust the fares offered on a given flight, the seats available at each fare and the preconditions for booking at any fare. The preconditions (combined with some relatively minor quality differentials inherent in first class, business and coach class areas of an aircraft) introduce product differentiation into the management equation while the various fares charged for what are, in many ways, very similar services represent the price discrimination element. As with any form of price discrimination this allows the airline to convert consumers surplus (the difference between the price the user pays and that he is willing to pay) into producers surplus. In the case of yield management, the airlines adjust their prices of seats over time as sales proceed, slow sales precipitating a fall in price in the next period (Kraft *et al.*, 1986; Oum *et al.*, 1986.

The combinations offered and the adjustments made by an airline as the time of any flight departure approaches are designed to maximize the yield from the predetermined decision to offer that particular service. The technique is somewhat different to that of the classic economic model of price discrimination where management increases revenue by charging different groups of customers (differentiated by their price elasticities) different prices for the same product. The cost of serving each customer is, in the classic model, identical.

There is, however, normally some qualitative or other form of product differentiation involved in yield management that implies cost differentials in the provision of services to customers. First-class air travel does cost an airline more than discount travel. Equally, however, the existence of economies of scope may mean that the supplier of a range of different services can keep unit costs lower than a number of suppliers each specializing. In overall resource terms, therefore,

down the demand curve (ARs), the monopolist has the incentive to push output out to Qd that will yield profits of abc but no consumer surplus. It is, however, the marginal cost level of output. The fact that many of the empirical studies cited in later chapters find significant levels of consumer surplus in deregulated markets indicates that price discrimination as practiced by the airlines is not perfect.

[14]   It has become a key element in, for example, the scheduled airline industry where the chief executive of one major operator, R.L. Crandall of American Airlines, stated, 'I believe that yield management is the single most important technical development in transportation management since we entered the era of airline deregulation in 1979' (cited in Smith *et al.*, 1992).

yield management may provide for the development of a more efficient market structure.

The set of decisions confronting industries practicing successful yield management is often complex. The interactions and options available are too numerous for fare levels, fare structures, constraints and capacity distribution to be determined simultaneously. This leads to a further common feature of yield management, namely sequential decision making. The form this takes varies between both sectors and firms within sectors but a broad indication of the decision sequence adopted by many airlines when considering a particular scheduled service is set out in Figure 2.3. In this case the nature of the technology does permit a degree of interaction between some of the stages (e.g. discount levels and allocation of seats to different fare classes) as the time of the flight approaches.[15]

The financial benefits to airlines from yield management can be considerable. American Airlines estimated the incremental revenue attributable to its yield management system amounted to $1.4 billion for the three years to 1992 and thereafter contributed at least $500 million a year annually (Smith *et al.*, 1992). The system employed by American Airlines then involved three functions, the optimization of overbooking, the allocation of discount fares and traffic management (and specifically meeting demands for connecting flights).

Airline alliances are now a major feature of airline networks and in many ways are logical extensions of yield management as well as being important in stimulating demand. There is no accepted definition of an airline alliance. In a strict legal sense, in some countries it can mean some degree of equity ownership of one carrier by another, but more often it is interpreted, in looser terms, to embrace such things as code-sharing agreements, interchangeable frequent flyer programs and coordinated scheduling of services.[16] They can also extend beyond this to embrace aircraft maintenance and servicing. There are also a limited number of alliances between airports (e.g., Vienna and Amsterdam).[17]

---

[15]   Interestingly, it is only recently that some yield management systems have had demand elasticities explicitly introduced into their algorithms.

[16]   There were some 513 airlines alliances covering these categories in 1999 involving 204 airlines.

[17]   Airport alliances involving coordination of pricing strategies can theoretically generate social benefits in certain conditions where there is strong complementarity between airports (Oum *et al.*, 1996). The limited alliances that currently exist are more to do with the exchange of information and ideas.

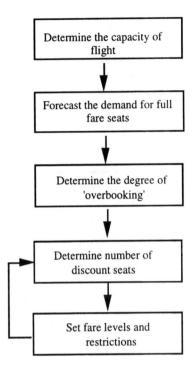

Figure 2.3 Stages in arriving at yield-maximizing revenue

Airlines are often involved in a large number of different alliances embracing a single partner, but they may involve several others carriers. Increasingly, a more relevant feature is several major carriers linking activities in so-called 'galaxies'. Table 2.4 shows the major global alliances at the end of 1999. These alliances are coming to dominate air transport. Members of the Star Alliance in 1999, for instance, do 21.4% of world revenue passenger kilometers and account for 20.7% of world airline revenue. The oneworld alliance accounts for 18.2% of RPK and 16.3% of revenue.[18]

---

[18] At the time of writing (June, 2000) there are discussions taking place between United Air Lines and US Airways, and less formal ones between American Airlines and Northwest Airlines, with the intention of possible merger or take-over. Outside of the US British Airways and KLM are also discussing merger. If these negotiations produce actual mergers or take-overs then this will represent a move to even stronger alliances. Especially given the international interconnections involved.

While not unique to the aviation sector,[19] from an historical perspective, alliances have emerged in a number of distinct conceptual forms. Horizontal alliances embrace undertakings that serve the same market, vertical alliances link specific activities, and external (or diversification) alliances involve agreements with suppliers in other industries.

Table 2.4 Global airline alliances, 1999

Alliance	Air France/Delta	oneworld	Qualifyer	Star Alliance	Wings
Core members	Delta Air Lines Air France Aeromexico	American Airlines British Airways Quantas Cathay Pacific Canadian Int'l Iberia Finnair	Swissair Sabena THY Turkish TAP AIR AOM Lauda Air Crossair Air Europe	United Air Lines Lufthansa Air Canada Thai International SAS Varig Air New Zealand Ansett Australia	Northwest KLM Continental Alitalia
Future members	LanChile		All Nippon	Austrian Singapore Airlines Mexicana	

Traditionally, the international aviation system of agreements within the IATA framework involved revenue pooling, fare controls and service frequency coordination fit within the framework of horizontal alliances. The development of more liberalized international aviation markets, however, has reduced this form of alliance in air transport.

More common instead are vertical forms of alliances. Within the confines of international aviation itself, agreements exist between carriers providing complementary services (e.g., feeders to hubs served by major trunk carriers). Abutting these strict aviation activities is a group of alliances between airlines and complementary services. Over time, British Airways has been partnered with hotels such as Marriott and the Ritz-Carlton Group and Son, car rental agencies such as Hertz, and charge card companies such as Diners Club. Airlines in the US and Australia have become involved in terminal ownership, although public ownership of airports precludes this in most EU countries.

External alliances have generally involved hiving off specialized activities to outside companies such as catering. Neither management science nor economic theory can provide an uncontroversial specific reason why airlines unite. In basic terms, an airline alliance can impact the demand for a carrier's services and its cost structure. The ultimate effect on customers will depend on characteristics of the

---

[19]   For instance within transport there has been a trend towards alliances in the maritime sector and between railway companies in North America.

market where the airline alliance operates; if an alliance forms but is only a small part of a large competitive market, the incentive for carriers to maximize efficiency and keep prices low is likely to produce considerably different results to when the carriers dominate a market and erect barriers to new entry.

Because of the diversity of forms that alliances take and the ways potential elements can be combined, it is dangerous to generalize but some broad points can be made using a simple diagram.[20] In Figure 2.4, D_1 and C_1 represent the demand and cost curves confronting a carrier on a particular route. They are linear, and the cost curve horizontal is simply for presentational clarity. If the airline joins with one or more competitors, then, by virtue of joint marketing, code-sharing, common frequent flyer programs, coordinated scheduling and so on, the demand for an airline's services will move out (e.g., to D_2) and because of the potential for rationalizing services, the scope for reducing ground costs and so on, costs will fall (e.g., to C_2).

In this framework, it is assumed the market is stable and viable prior to any alliance being formed. In practice, an alliance may keep loss-making carriers in a market, but this is not dealt with here.

The extent and nature of these shifts in demand and cost schedules would depend not only on the details but on the response of carriers outside the alliance. If the alliance results in other, non-partner carriers becoming more cost conscious, cutting fares or improving services, then the demand curve in Figure 2.4 will not shift or only slightly move out. Equally, pure code-sharing alliances may have

---

[20]   Most frequent flyer programs are somewhat more complex than indicated in the text. They are targeted at particular groups of travelers and, as such, do not impact equally along the demand curve. In the diagram, α is the level at which fares move from economy (coach) to business or first class. By offering extra 'miles', airport lounge facilities, easier check in facilities and so on an airline will attempt to push this part of its demand curve out most vigorously with less concern about attracting lower fare-paying customers. This can kink the overall demand curve as shown or at least cause its curvature to become steadily steeper.

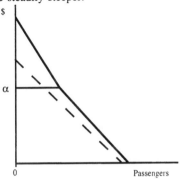

minimal effects on costs. For purposes of exposition, very simple cases are
shown in the diagram.

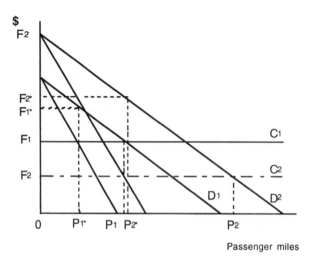

Figure 2.4 Fares and passenger miles associated with an airline prior to
making an alliance and after making an alliance

Making matters more realistic only strengthens the case that predicting full
economic implications of any alliance is extremely difficult. A number of
possible outcomes emerge from this simple framework.

- If the market is initially competitive and the alliance has no significant effect
  on conditions (e.g. two small players enter a large market), full benefits of
  any cost reductions and service improvements (reflected diagrammatically in
  enhanced demands) will be passed to consumers. In other words, fares will
  fall from the old cost related level of F_1 to the new cost level of F_2, and
  passenger seat miles will rise from P_1 to P_2.
- If the market is initially monopolized and the alliance, through a blocked
  space arrangement, brings new players into the game, then both fares may
  fall and passenger miles increase. Initially, the fare level would be F_1^* if
  there was no price discrimination, but it would fall to F_2.
- If the alliance gives partners monopoly power on a route previously
  competitive (associated with all capacity in an international bilateral
  agreement over landing slots, dominant frequent flyer program, etc.) and they
  seek to maximize profits, then the outcome will depend on the strategy both
  adopt. If a single fare approach is used, conventional monopoly theory

indicates that fares charged by the airline under review will change to F_2^* and passenger numbers to P_2^*. The ultimate fare level may be higher or lower than the original competitive level, depending on the extent to which the alliance results in cost savings. Equally, the number of passengers may be higher or lower than P_1, depending on the elasticities of demand involved.

- Widespread practice of 'yield management' enables carriers 'to price down demand curves' rather than charge a single uniform fare. If there is perfect price discrimination, then the airlines will price differentially to the point where demand meets cost, to a level where it carries P_2 passengers. (This gives the same number of passenger miles as the competitive final outcome but all the surplus that users enjoy with competition is translated into airline profits.) In this case, fares would vary between F_2^+ and F_2. The airline would also benefit by generating additional revenues equal to the area under the demand curve above C_2 and to the left of P_2.
- The alliance carriers may decide not to maximize monopoly profits from the arrangement as managerial slack emerges (so-called X-inefficiency). In this case, the carrier's cost function may not fall entirely to C_2, and the pricing decision not exploit the full potential of price discrimination. The result would be fewer passenger miles than in previous scenarios with reduced revenues going to the carrier.
- While enjoying short term monopoly power, the airline alliance may be concerned that excessive profits could encourage new entry that is difficult to combat. Alternatively, these profits may bring policy responses from the government that might influence their actions. In this case, fares may be set below those associated with the single price monopoly or of yield management.[21] The extent to which this deviation would occur depends on the degree of risk aversion felt by carriers in the alliance.

This all is a gross simplification of reality, but it illustrates some of the problems associated with assessing the implications of alliances. The situation in practice is actually more complicated particularly because aviation is a network industry and any effect on one link impacts elsewhere on the network[22]. Shifts in demand and costs should also be treated in this matter.

Linked to this are problems in defining the relevant market for analyzing alliances. This issue was not explored in the diagram, but from an anti-trust policy perspective, this is a matter of crucial importance. In many cases, individual routes may have alliance carriers providing services but not enjoying

---

[21]   This is known as 'limit pricing'.

[22]   The theories relating to economics of networks are often complex. A brief overview in the air transport context is offered in Chapter 3; for a more general technical survey see Economides (1996).

any significant monopoly advantage. There may be competition from a variety of indirect alternatives, or the service itself may act only as one element in a wider complex network where many different routings exist.

Figure 2.5 is a simple illustration of the types of issues in assessing the economic effects. If an alliance involves carriers operating between A and B which results in a monopoly position along this route, then the actual degree to which they can exercise power depends on a variety of factors. For example, if there are indirect services between A and B via C or D or even F, then airline demand services will be conditional on what happens along these alternatives.

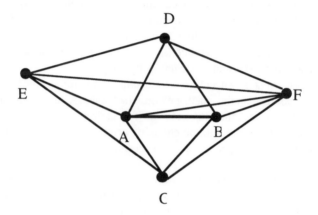

Figure 2.5 Network implications of airline alliances

If the link between A and B forms only part of many longer trips involving travel between A and F for example, then the number of options to travelers becomes even larger. They may avoid the link by a direct flight from A to F or on other, alternative indirect routes via C or D. If the services between A and B are used frequently in more complex travel patterns involving several inter-changes as one link in a trip from E to F, the number of possible, competitive options is increased.

The situation in Figure 2.5 relates, therefore, only to a point-specific route alliance (namely between A and B). A strategic alliance poses more complex problems in defining relevant markets for public policy purposes. By co-ordinating activities across a network, airlines forming in a strategic alliance may be in a position to influence fares and service quality on the indirect routes that potentially compete for traffic in A to B services. This could occur, for example, if partners were dominant hub carriers at these two airports.

Whether such an alliance is against the public interest would depend on whether efficiency gains outweigh efforts by the airlines to extract supernormal profits (i.e. those beyond a normal rate of return on an investment). In turn, this is often determined by the exact details of an alliance. If it is the blocked space variety where each carrier buys space on the other planes then, even if the alliance were a monopolist in a market, competition between members within the aircraft themselves could keep fares to a level of workable competition.[23]

Strategic alliance arrangements involving a degree of market segmentation where, despite prior hub dominance, competition existed before are less likely to provide consumer benefits. These will not occur unless the activities coordinated by the airlines significantly reduce costs or there is significant countervailing power exercised by potential new market entries or the threat of government regulations tempers the strategic alliance's fare setting strategies.

Even if a threat of entry remains, cooperative undertakings may contain competitive implications when actions reduce their costs. By adopting limited price strategies below what small, independent suppliers can offer, such cooperatives may still be pricing in excess of their own costs. In other cases, undertakings may set prices to attain a reasonable return for shareholders, but, at the same time, not maximize them; essentially, management aims to create conditions subject to less competitive stress.

There is also a theory suggesting that airline alliance cooperation introduces stability into markets where excessive competition would discourage adequate supply. The commitment to provide scheduled services encourages carriers to price down short-run marginal costs, although this does not allow them sufficient income to cover fixed costs. Knowing this, many otherwise efficient carriers will not enter the market.

2.5 REGULATORY ISSUES

The practical issue of economic regulation is looked at in some detail in Chapters 4 and 5 and that of social regulation in Chapter 13 and so only a few passing remarks are offered here. These are primarily designed to summarize the main economic reasons why regulation has been so prevalent in air transport. Little is said about some of the wider, non-economic reasons for intervention.

Economists have long recognized that markets may, in practice, suffer from serious imperfections. Most obviously, these imperfections, or market failures, could adversely affect the users of transport services, perhaps because fares would be sub-optimally high or the service offered dangerous. But equally, they may harm third parties through, for example, generating excessive environmental pollution or the predatory pricing behavior of incumbent operators may reduce the

---

[23] Workable competition involves an imperfectly competitive situation but one that cannot be improved upon by government intervention for reasons such as high transactions costs or inadequate knowledge on the part of the authorities.

potential viability of other firms wishing to supply transport services and thus deter them from entering the market.

A wide range of arguments, some of doubtful economic logic, have been drawn into debates over air transport regulation, and indeed transport regulation more generally. Broadly the types of market failure which have attracted most attention embrace the following (Button, 1993):

- *Containment of monopoly power.* This has particularly been the case on thin routes where there were fears that traffic could only sustain one carrier. It has also been a major reason for the national or local ownership and control over major pieces of air transport infrastructure such as airports and air traffic control systems. More common today perhaps is the fear that the alliances formed by suppliers of air transport services may result in cartels to limit output and prevent new entrants coming into the market.
- *Control of excessive competition.* Unregulated competition may limit the quality of service offered to customers and result in instability in the industry – in technical terms there may be no 'sustainable' equilibrium or an 'empty core'. The actual problem is not competition *per se* but rather the possibility that certain market features such as declining costs or fluctuations in demand may result in certain sections of the community not being provided with adequate services. Chapter 7 offers more details.
- *Regulation of externalities.* Imperfections in the market mechanism may result in air transportation activities imposing costs which are not directly included in the private sector's decision making – noise, atmospheric pollution and danger being the main causes for concern. This subject is explored more fully in Chapter 13.
- *Provision of public goods.* Because certain items of infrastructure, such as air navigation systems, are thought to exhibit public goods characteristics (that is, non-excludability and non-rivalness) their provision, it is argued, would be at best inadequate without government intervention. The degree to which such infrastructure should be seen as conforming to a public good, however, often depends upon the initial policy in place – for example, it is relatively easy to exclude planes from a navigational system if wished.
- *Provision of high-cost infrastructure.* The sheer cost and long pay-back period, combined with possible high levels of risk, makes it unlikely that all major pieces of infrastructure such as international airports would be built or expensive transport engineering research undertaken without some form of government involvement.
- *Assistance of groups in 'need' of adequate transport.* Some groups in society may be geographically isolated and as such require basic air transportation. In a marketplace this would not be forthcoming unless these communities paid but, for social or other reasons, such as fostering national cohesion, the

government may elect to subsidise the services. In effect, it is felt that for a variety of reasons, including faults in the existing pattern of income distribution, effective demand is not an adequate guide to transport resource allocation and wider, social criteria should, therefore, be sought.

- *The existence of high transactions costs.* An efficient market is dependent on the complete allocation of property rights and the ability to trade these rights. In practice such an allocation may not be possible and trading may prove expensive. In this case governments lay down laws and priorities that govern behavior. Rules on the use of flight paths are an example.
- *The integration of transport into wider economic policies.* Land-use and transportation are clearly interconnected and some degree of coordination may be felt desirable if imperfections exist in either the transport or the land-use markets. Additionally, intervention in the transport sector may form part of a wider government macroeconomic strategy (for example, price controls or investment programs), industrial policy or development policy. Chapter 10 looks at some of these issues in more detail.
- *The need to reflect the genuine resource costs of transport.* In the case of certain finite, non-renewable resources (for example, mineral fuels) the market mechanism may fail to reflect the full social time preference of society. The government may, therefore, intervene to ensure that the decision maker is aware of the true shadow price.
- *The improvement of transport coordination.* Because there are numerous suppliers of air transport services, inefficient provision may result if their decisions are made independently. There is also the prospect of duplication of transport facilities, and consequential wastage of resources, without some degree of central guidance. For these reasons the planning of airports has been a governmental concern, as has the nature of air traffic control.

In general, most official policies claim to cover a range of different problems although conflicts may, and do, emerge. For example, policies designed primarily to contain externalities may have adverse effects on income distribution or could run counter to a national economic policy that is pursuing a course of maximizing gross national product. Similarly, measures to ensure that adequate high-cost research is conducted may mean conferring monopoly powers on private suppliers (for example, through the patent system or in terms of government contracts to purchase the fruits of a new technology). Consequently, there is an inevitable blurring across these justifications for government involvement when various policy measures are discussed or introduced. Even more uncertain than the exact justification or objectives underlying some policies is the exact effect the different policy tools employed by policy makers is likely to exert.

Air transport has traditionally been one of the most regulated sectors of the economy. While the situation is now changing somewhat, regulations still remain. Many of these regulations governing airlines are categorized in the US as social regulation and in many other countries as quality controls. They cover such matters as safety and environmental regulation. By and large they have been put in place to compensate for the negative externalities that can be associated with air transportation. Other regulations are of a more traditional economic nature and relate to such things as fares and service characteristics. They are aimed at meeting what are seen as economic failures in the working of the airline market due to the existence of monopoly power or predatory behavior.

Traditionally, the concern of antitrust authorities is that alliances concentrate market power and exploit monopoly advantages that partner airlines forge. The result may be a reduction in supply and higher prices for users. This judgment, however, may not be automatically justified because merger or cooperative behavior can often increase economic efficiency. Where there are potential economies of scale, density, or scope, the public policy challenge is to ensure these advantages are maximized without suppliers extracting all the economic rents. Equally, alliances may circumvent the economic problems of market instability that can exist in network industries as well as offering a mechanism of avoiding the worst excesses of any other intervention failures.

A particular concern in recent years, both with the growth of alliances and with the emergence of large carriers, has been that of the possibility of predatory behavior by airlines (Hanlon, 1994). There has been a difficulty in defining predation and distinguishing it in practice from competitive behavior. A reputation for predatory conduct may, however, be an impediment to efficient market entry.

Potential entrants that consider entering a portion of an existing network may be deterred if they fear that incumbents are likely to cut fares significantly or initiate a large capacity increase on the contested route. The predatory threat here is latent in the sense that potential entrants base their decisions on expectation rather than actions. In the sense that the power of incumbency *per se* can limit the actions of potentially more efficient newcomers, it can distort the market.

There is general agreement that the predatory practices, where clearly shown to exist, should be regulated but that action on latent predatory behavior is particularly difficult to handle. It is difficult in most cases for regulators to distinguish at the time of new entry between pricing to maximize profits (or minimize losses) when moving to changed competitive conditions, pricing to fill empty seats, pricing to reflect falling costs due to enhanced efficiency and pricing to drive new entrants out of the market.[24] Latent predatory power is even more

---

[24]   This has been reflected in debates in the US during the late 1990s where the Department of Transportation has sought to impose new guidelines for tackling predatory behavior in air transport. A discussion of their arguments and the response

elusive. New potential entrants fear that incumbents with fighting funds will, in the short term, reduce prices below costs or introduce large amounts of additional capacity. Where regulation has been attempted, one approach to containing the problem is the Bright Lines approach. This indicates specific rules as to what constitutes predatory behavior (e.g., looking for prices set below a reasonable estimate of the relevant cost). An alternative favored by the EU is the Rule of Reason approach that looks at each case in its context (Dodgson *et al.*, 1991).

However, the application of these concepts to aviation is limited. There have not been detailed investigations of predation in the international airline industry. These facts, combined with the natural pressures for efficiency that exist in a strongly competitive market, have led some commentators to question whether it is worth trying to contain predation in liberalized aviation markets where other entry barriers are low. With the existence of subsidies and other imperfections, however, the potential for predation remains. Monitoring of a possible occurrence of predatory practices needs, therefore, to be maintained using conventional national competition policy instruments.

2.6 SOCIAL AIR SERVICES

While the majority of economic analysis contained in this book is of a positive nature, air transport has traditionally been an instrument in normative policy formulation. Early subsidies in the US were aimed at developing a nation-wide postal service and much of the early emphasis of UK international aviation policy concerned tying together a geographically disparate empire. The protection of domestic airlines or of specific airports is also common as part of wider industrial and development policies. A few brief comments on some of these wider aspect of air transport policy is offered.

Air transport has traditionally played an important role in providing transport services to remote areas and as a unifying force across large, sparsely populated regions. Governments have sought to provide air services within their territories for social, political and regional economic development purposes. A diverse set of regimes exists to finance such services. Until recently in the majority of the OECD countries, because the state owned the main airlines, social air services were provided as part of the carrier's mandate. In many instances regulatory structures have implicitly embraced this role of air transport by fostering cross-subsidization of services.

More recently, as domestic systems have been the subject of regulatory reform, direct subsidies (such as the US Essential Air Services Program and the

of an expert committee established to look into competition policy in the sector is contained in Transportation Research Board (1999).

national regimes permitted under the EU's Public Service Obligations - e.g. the Spanish services in the Canary Islands, Balearic Islands and Melilla) have become more common. Social service obligations have been less common at the international level other than in the context of linking specific regions or areas to the wider, international economy. They function much less as a social service than as instruments in economic development policy. This, for example, is the rationale of the Greek and Irish social service obligations. This is also explicitly recognized in EU policy where they do exist, and are deemed to have a valid long-term role to play in providing a social function. There are questions of how to fund them during structural change and what level of funding to provide.

In providing social air services, governments increasingly rely, as far as possible, on market forces to minimize the extent of subsidy payments. The strategies favored aim to allow for flexibility in service levels to small communities which are more vulnerable to cyclical downturns in traffic and to encourage the development and growth of all classes of airlines so that scope and density economics may generate efficiencies at all levels.

The social air services programs now in operation by the US, Australia and Canada, for example, all require a competitive bidding process for carrier selection in cases where subsidies are required. There is still, however, diversity in the ways in which civil, non-financially viable air services are funded. Even where policies of regulatory cross-subsidization have given way to direct subsidies, there remain problems with the comparability of financing structures. The evidence from other sectors is that financial assistance can take a variety of forms, but that it is possible to develop general guidelines that offer a measure of comparability.

As discussed later, air transport has been the subject of considerable structure change over the past twenty years and there has been the tendency in some cases for governments to protect carriers. In particular, in the international market assistance with the transaction costs of restructuring is often sought by airlines who have developed their capital base under different market conditions or under a previous regulatory regime. Airlines as a whole, for instance, may have invested in fleets more suited to the old market or institutional structure than to the new.

In some instances, because of restrictions on flight numbers, there has been a tendency for regulatory regimes to result in the use of large aircraft, while more liberalized short-haul markets are often best served by smaller aircraft. Change, therefore, can leave carriers with fleets ill matched to new market conditions. The natural reaction of those adversely affected is to seek some form of transitional protection so that at least some of the sunk costs may be recovered. The extent of market rigidity should not, though, be exaggerated, since there is an active world-wide market for used aircraft of all sizes.

The issue, at one level, concerns distribution matters (Gordon, 1981).[25] Structural change in most types of industry leaves an overhang of sunk costs which must be borne either by those that carried out the initial investment or by limiting the speed of the reform process, by consumers and new investors who are deprived of the benefits of the new regime. In adopting a particular approach to this issue, however, there may be implications for the longer-term outcome of the reform process. Indeed, if inappropriately designed, government intervention may inadvertently frustrate the ultimate economic or political goal of change. It may, for instance, reduce the scope for new technologies being introduced or lead to inappropriate signals being sent to related sectors (e.g. to those providing aviation infrastructure).

The desirability of allowing time for appropriate restructuring, while at the same time ensuring that efficient use is made of sunk assets, underlies many of the arguments for subsidies to airline operators and for protective arrangements under bankruptcy law. The arguments contain elements of positive economics but also embrace notions of equity and burden sharing. There is an inevitable danger that subsidy and bankruptcy regimes may result in inefficiencies due to the direct misallocation of resources into inappropriate restructuring programs. They may also have serious secondary effects if, by diverting traffic, they lead to lower revenues among other operators that could restructure more efficiently.

[25] A more detailed discussion of the routes to deregulation is found in Chapters 5 and 6.

3 AIRLINE NETWORKS

3.1 INTRODUCTION

Airlines provide networks of services. They are not unique in this sense but networks industries do have a number of peculiarities that require specialized treatment in economics. In addition to the pure network aspects of supply, the air transport industry, as with most network industries, offers services that are non-durable and cannot be stored. This, as seen in the previous chapter, influences the way in which prices are set within the network of operations.

The network features of the sector are important both to those who supply and use the services and to those with wider responsibilities for policy making. From the airlines' perspective there are a number of possibilities for providing network services that are considered below. Which airline is chosen may, in reality, be a function of external factors (e.g. controls over flight paths, availability of airport capacity and entry regulation) as well the economic considerations that would exist in a free market, unregulated world. But even if institutional constraints were a minor consideration, airlines are confronted by a series of overlapping networks of consumer demand patterns and are tied in with a series of complementary markets.[1]

At its simplest, over any network the demands of business travelers differ from those of leisure travelers. Not only do the demand elasticities over different links vary but also the attributes of the services that are being are sought inevitably differ. Business travelers, as was seen in Chapter 2, are more sensitive to frequency and reliability features of service and to the facilities available at airports. This is also why in many geographical markets charter services can coexist with scheduled services.

In the past much of government policy has been founded on the notion that air transport can, with some modifications, be treated very much in line with other types of economic activity that have been the subject of regulation. More recently, and particularly since the late 1970s, it has become appreciated that the interaction between services poses specific issues that require more care in the ways policies are developed and implemented. This has led to modifications in the regulatory structure with policies being liberalized to permit air transport networks develop in ways more akin to those found in the marketplace.

---

[1]   In particular, airlines are highly dependent on information networks to ensure efficient provision of their services and to link demand for their services with the supply.

The aim of this chapter is to provide some basic discussion of network economics and to set this within the context of the broad ways in which airline networks have evolved through the long period of regulation to the contemporary situation of near free markets in many countries. Much of the discussion involves the US domestic market because this is large enough to have a geography akin to a natural market area for air transport. It is also the market that has most completely gone through the cycle to reach a free market situation. The different situation regarding this market and the market for US international services is also discussed.

3.2 NETWORK EXTERNALITIES[2]

For it to be worthwhile to develop a network of any configuration rather than simply provide single link services there must exist some form of network economy.[3] These economies may be on the cost side but they may also reflect the possibility of earning higher revenues on the demand side. On the cost side there may simply be traditional economies of scale linked to having larger operations and the ability to fixed costs over a larger number of customers. As discussed below there may also be additional network benefits associated with particular network configurations.

In terms of user benefits, larger networks can offer the advantage of access to a much larger range of destinations and generally greater service frequency. Additionally, any individual user helps ensure that this range of options is available to others. What this means in terms of an individual user of an air transport network is that, by paying the full attributable cost of using the service, the user helps ensure that the service is also available for other potential users as well as benefiting from their support of the network.

The main reason for this is that the costs borne by air travelers extend beyond those of simply the fares being paid to the opportunities that larger networks may

---

[2]   Strictly since these external benefits are enjoyed only by those using the airline network, they involve 'club good' issues.

[3]   The discussion here is largely about a network involving interconnectivity. Connectivity exists, as seen in the left diagram below, when there exists a connection between two points. Interconnectivity involves at least three nodes, as in the right portion of the diagram.

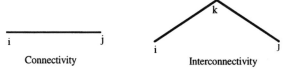

Connectivity   Interconnectivity

offer. In Figure 3.1, for example, it is assumed that the costs, C, to airlines of providing networks rise with the size of the network, proxied by passenger numbers, but at a decreasing rate (i.e., some scale benefits are implied but these diminish with the size of the network). For the user there are increased benefits associated with larger networks (U) but the rate of increase declines with the size of the network. To obtain any passengers there is a minimum size of network (X_{min}) but after X_{max} the additional traffic the airline will gain from adding links is less than the additional costs and further expansion will not be justified.

From the perspective of passengers, however, the optimum network is at X_m where there is a maximum deviation between the financial costs they must pay to cover airline costs and the network benefits to be enjoyed. Passengers, however, will continue to seek flights up to X_{max} since their marginal benefit exceeds the costs they will be charged.[4]

[4]   Another way of looking at this is to take the simple case of a positive externality, as seen in the diagram. Here an individual's demand (marginal benefit) for an airline service is shown as MB with the marginal costs involved of MC. For simplicity, it is assumed that there are no negative externalities arising due to congestion. The flights made by the individual help sustain the network for other potential users so that the marginal social benefit curve, where society is deemed in this club good context to embrace other air travelers, is to the right of the MB curve at MB*. It is assumed for simplicity that, in drawing this, the larger the number of flights taken by the individual, the greater the social benefit. If no allowance is made for this external effect then the fare is set at F and the volume of service used is V*. Allowing for the externality pushes the optimum volume of service out to V** and the fare up to F*. There is no incentive for the traveler to move out to V*, however, because he does not recognize these benefits. One policy solution is to subsidize fares down to F** which would achieve the optimal volume of traffic. Another approach would be to adopt a form of price differentiation that allows costs to be recovered by airlines at an output of V* by extracting consumers surplus from intra marginal users of the network.

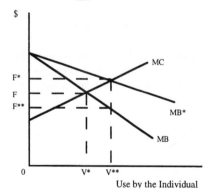

Use by the Individual

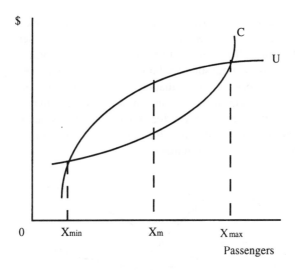

Figure 3.1 Optimal networks

In addition to the positive externalities that may be associated with larger networks, there are also issues of possible congestion that can arise both on links and at hubs.[5] There is an optimum level of congestion that that arises simply because there is interaction between those using elements of the network and without out this the facility would be underused in an economic sense. The bigger concern is that of excess congestion when a facility is overused and the benefits that are being derived from it are not maximized. This normally stems from inappropriate pricing of the facilities involved.

Figure 3.2 provides the standard explanation of how this problem can arise and indicates how it may be handled. The marginal cost of a flight as seen by the air traveler is represented as the MC curve – this embodies the cost to the airline of providing the seat, which is passed on in the fare, and the time costs of the trip to the traveler. Given a demand curve of D for the service, the volume of traffic will be T. This, however, ignores the congestion that each traveler imposes on other travelers, both in terms of aircraft using runways and the congestion on planes. If this congestion effect is allowed for then the marginal cost of a trip goes up to MC* and the optimal level of traffic falls to T*. A degree of congestion remains, the difference between the MC* and D curve at traffic flow T*, but this reflects the optimal level of interaction. This optimal outcome can be achieved by a pricing policy that pushes up the costs to travelers to F* or the same result could come by limiting travel through other means (e.g., slot controls) to T*.

---

[5]   Additionally, a range of environmental externalities often associated with concentrations of air traffic are considered in more detail in Chapter 13.

The extent to which congestion is an issue depends to some degree on how much of it is already internalized within the fares paid by passengers and cargo shippers. Unlike externalities such as those associated with noise or air pollution, the inefficiency costs of congestion are borne by the users of air services and those that provide those services. In situations where there is only one carrier monopolizing an airport, there is thus an incentive for that carrier to make efficient use of facilities and to allow for congestion costs when setting fares and establishing services. This is also true for scheduling committees at airports with a number of carriers operating from them.

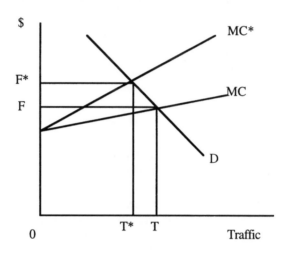

Figure 3.2 Congestion costs

3.3 FORMS OF AIRLINE ROUTE NETWORKS

Airline route networks can take a diversity of forms. In recent years, with the flexibility that freer market conditions have allowed, networks can also be very dynamic with links being continually added and removed. To some extent the networks that are observed are the result of the market structure in which air transport services are supplied. While this is partly determined by the nature of demand and cost considerations it is also often strongly influenced by the institutional structure in which airlines operate. The fact that air transport has been the subject of a wide range of economic and social regulations almost since its inception means that the notion of an unfettered network is a comparatively new one to the sector.

Further, given the lack of experience of how the sector functions, both in a static sense of being able to define an optimal network with given operators and knowledge and in the sense of innovation being held back by regulatory constraints, it is difficult to say exactly what optimality means in this context. There is no effective counterfactual to use as a basis for assessment. What has been observed is that the nature of airline networks has changed as regulatory liberalization has progressed but also the current situation does not seem entirely stable. There has been quite dramatic restructuring, for instance, in the US domestic market as low cost carriers have competed with larger hub-based airlines and the latter have themselves moved through various phases of dispersion and concentration across their hubs.

Many air transport markets have been subjected to major regulatory changes since 1978 but the US domestic market provides the benchmark for what has happened regarding the structure of airline service networks.

At the outset it should be said that the patterns that have emerged have been somewhat different according to the nature of the carriers involved. In particular, there have been important differences between the air cargo operators and the predominantly passenger carriers. One reason for this is that passengers are sensitive to routings while packages, being inanimate, have no such feelings and consignors generally have little preference regarding routes provided time windows are met. Cargo carriers find it easier, therefore, to focus on mega hubs and to channel considerable volumes of traffic through them at times passengers would see as antisocial. The growth of package services also means that good road accesses allowing intermodal operations with trucking play a role in the hubbing decision.

Focusing on passenger airline networks, the heavily regulated US domestic market from the 1930s through to the end of the 1970s really left network debates only for marginal consideration by the authorities. Routes were awarded to carriers with little regard to the network economies of supply. A carrier was effectively confronted with a constrained supply function when requesting new service licenses and only took network features into account in terms of instances where fleet and equipment could be used on small, inter linked sub-sections of the carrier's overall operations.

The result was that a carrier would have a pattern of operations of the type seen in Figure 3.3. There would be no focal point and interlining with its own services to provide an integrated network would be very limited. If someone wanted to travel from C to G, for example, the carrier could well offer a service that went C to B to I to G with the plane stopping at each point *en route*. Often the core routes were established prior to regulation with the carrier gaining additional ones piecemeal over time.

There were, from the passengers' perspective, some advantages to this structure in that numerically many direct services existed. Although, set against this, frequency was often low and fares were high, because of the inability of airlines to reap the synergy of cost savings from a more market-oriented route structure.[6] From a technical perspective, monopoly control over routes combined with the scale benefits of operating large aircraft led to a tendency to move to the use of wide-bodied aircraft as they became available and this further reduced service frequency.

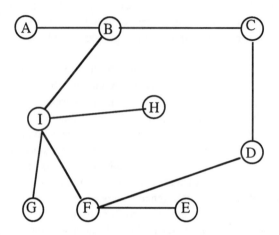

Figure 3.3 Pre-US deregulation linear route structure

This system did not mean that there were no hub airports where consolidation of traffic could take place. There were major interchange nodes but the passengers often had to change between carriers as well as between aircraft. Schedules were not fully coordinated and through ticketing could pose problems. In smaller countries hub and spoke operations were also the norm because governments often focused flights through a single major airport.

The deregulation of the US domestic air transport market from 1977 led to a very rapid adoption of hub-and-spoke operations by the larger airlines (Figure 3.4). These airlines (with one or two notable exceptions such as Pan American) were quick to exploit the potential economies of scale, scope and density that a freer market situation permitted. On the demand side there also came the gradual appreciation that network services provided economies of network presence that can add to the revenue flow.[7]

---

6   The regulatory authority's ability to regulate fares based on a cost determined formula added to the high levels of fares.

7   The ability of the main pre-deregulation carriers to survive the impact of reforms also suggests that there would seem to be some economies of experience in the industry (see Chapter 2). Essentially, the argument for such economies is that factors

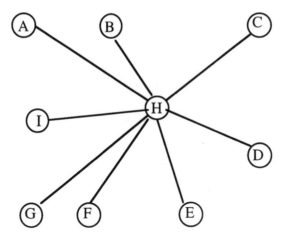

Figure 3.4 Post-US deregulation hub-and-spoke route structure

With this form of hubbing structure, flights are funneled in banks into a number of large hubs where substantial numbers of passengers changed aircraft to complete their journeys.[8] These banks involve the coordinated arrival of a large number of flights in a short space of time and then an equally coordinated departure of flights within a narrow time window. Larger hubs may well have up to seven or mare such banks a day. Travel time would be longer for many people but fares

such as learning by doing pulls the average cost of supply down as more units are produced.

[8]   There have been a number of other attempts to delineate different forms of airline hub system. Doganis and Dennis (1989), for example, separate the single hub model into 'hourglass' and 'hinterland' hubs. The former is represented in the left diagram where the hub is operated with flights from one region to points broadly in the opposite direction. The hinterland hub on the right feeds short haul connecting traffic to long haul flights. The hourglass hub operation tends to use aircraft all of a similar size, whereas the hinterland hub has aircraft of mixed sizes.

fell and the range of potential flight combinations available to any particular destination expanded considerably.[9]

In Figure 3.4, city H that previously (Figure 3.3) enjoyed only one air link becomes the hub for an entire range of airline services. Why H? In most cases with passenger transport a hub is located in a major city that generates significant 'local' traffic as well as being the point of interchange for transferring, 'flow' traffic. The airport must also have the physical capacity (runways, terminals, etc.) to handle the high volume of transit traffic. Its selection is also determined by location – a central position normally allowing for linkages to a larger number of spoke airports.

Initially, the large scale entry of carriers, often involving carriers originally supplying local services, into the national market led to some instability in terms of the hub-and-spoke structures that existed. Also the idealized form set down in Figure 3.4 could seldom be completely established. Structures more akin to those that seen in Figure 3.5 are more common. This may be because of thin traffic on some routes making linear structures of services more efficient (e.g., between A, B, J and H) or in other cases large volumes of traffic between adjacent cities such as K and C may make a shuttle service commercially viable.

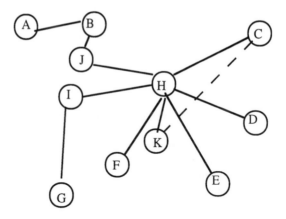

Figure 3.5 Typical hub-and-spoke route structure

As airlines have consolidated through mergers,[10] and have grown with the market, so the form of hub-and-spoke structure has evolved. The growth in

---

[9]   In the US initially, but recently much more generally, the banks of flights by major carriers at their hub airports have often been interspersed with flights by low cost carriers that make use of idle gate capacity.

international services, coupled with the move towards strategic alliances, has also influenced the pattern that has emerged in the late 1990s. There has been a growth in multiple hub operations along the lines seen in Figure 3.6. Here there are two large hubs (H1 and H2) that are linked by a direct service and themselves also serve a number of satellite cities. This type of structure can occur when an airline seeks to serve a very large market such as the entire US. It may then locate its central transit points at two or more locations to maximize market penetration – Northwest, for example has hubs at Detroit and Minneapolis while American Airlines has hubs at Chicago and Dallas-Fort Worth.

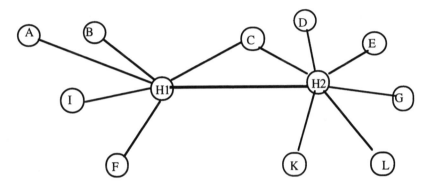

Figure 3.6 Multiple hub system

[10]   Market concentration through mergers is only likely, however, if there is adequate incentive for suppliers to combine. Take the simple network case discussed in Varian (1999). If it is assumed that the benefit of a network is proportional to the number of users on that network (n) and for simplicity the constant of proportionality is taken as unity, then following Metcalfe's Law the value of the network is n^2. A simple calculation shows that combining two networks of size n_1 and n_2 yields:

$$\Delta v_1 = n_1(n_1 + n_2) - n_1^2 = n_1 n_2$$
$$\Delta v_2 = n_2(n_1 + n_2) - n_2^2 = n_1 n_2$$

Each network gets equal value (v) from the interconnection. Those on the small network (2) each get considerable value from linking with the large number on the other network. The large number of people on the other network (1) each get smaller additional utility but there are a lot of them. This offers scope for reciprocation with the networks having settlement free access to the other network. The problem is that the large supplier may need to keep its market power to allow adequate price discrimination to recover costs and make an acceptable long term return. In this case the larger concern may merge with the smaller and attain twice the value of interconnecting:

$$\Delta v_1 = n_1(n_1 + n_2)^2 - n_1^2 - n_2^2 = 2n_1 n_2$$

International alliances have led to *de facto* multi-hub services with a carrier in, say, Europe basing its operations around a hub but linking its services with those of a US airline that has its own domestic hub-and-spoke network.[11] The service between H1 and H2 in Figure 3.6 would in this case be a code shared operation involving both carriers. This is the case of airlines in the Star Alliance with United Airlines having services based around its US hubs (Chicago, Denver, Dulles, etc) and Lufthansa having its services based around its Frankfurt hub. Similarly, KLM has integrated operations based at its Amsterdam hub with those of Northwest Airlines based at Detroit and Minneapolis.

In the international case the actual configuration of services may, therefore, be more akin to those in Figure 3.7. They are essentially unidirectional within the countries or markets involved. A passenger wishing to travel from Pittsburgh to Bonn can do so on the Star Alliance using a single ticket by travelling to Washington on United Air Lines, across the Atlantic to Frankfurt on either United Air Lines or Lufthansa and then to Bonn on Lufthansa. Figure 3.7 offers a variant on this where airlines in an alliance may also offer not only services between their main hubs but also some additional international services from other airports in their network (e.g., United Airlines offers a range of transatlantic services from its secondary hub at Dulles, Washington).

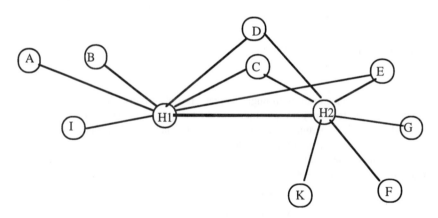

Figure 3.7 Multiple hub system with directional hubs

[11]   Such structures grew in importance in the 1980s and 1990s as airlines sought to offer through services from origins within their base country to airports within the destination country that were not designated as 'gateways' under prevailing bilateral air service agreements. It should be noted that the restrictive bilateral air service agreements that typified international aviation until recently effectively institutionalized hubs in many countries by giving monopoly rights to the flag airline.

With hub-and-spoke systems the main focus on competition is generally between the alternative networks rather than over individual links. There are some exceptions where two carriers may each have a significant share of a large hub – Chicago is an example. To illustrate this, we can consider Figure 3.8 where there are no direct services between the various 'behind-gateway cities with competition' but potential travelers have a choice of two alternative carriers (perhaps each being in an alliance of more than one airline) to fly between these points. The 'behind-gateway cities without competition have no network competition and as drawn each is a monopoly of one carrier or the other.

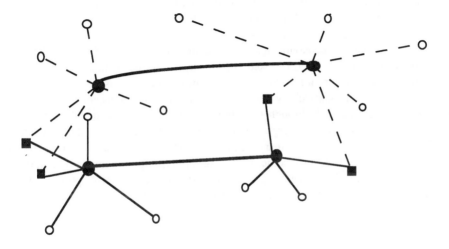

■   Behind-gateway city with competition

O   Behind-gateway city without competition

Figure 3.8 Competition between alliance hub-and-spoke networks

3.4   THE NON-HUB CARRIERS

Not all airlines operate hub-and-spoke systems, or possibly more correctly do not operate them quite as intensely as most of the US major carriers. One reason for this is that there are very dense routes where 'shuttle' styles of service meet demand considerations most effectively. These are very frequent services with the aircraft simply shuttering back-and-forth between two points. In the US major carriers, such as United, separate such services as individual operating units.

Southwest is often held up as an example of a non-hub operator in the US domestic market although it does in practice have coordinated services through a number of secondary hubs in addition to its non-hub-and-spoke operations. In the Southwest case the structure of services can be viewed as linear and somewhat akin to that illustrated in Figure 3.3. It keeps its costs down by offering minimal on-plane amenities and by selecting routes where it can turn its aircraft around quickly and thus maximize the time its fleet can be in the air generating revenue.

In other cases, services may be free-standing and not be part of a linked or hubbed structure. This is often a function of the geography of the market that is being served. The charter services traditionally providing flights to holiday destinations in Europe or between Canada and the southern states of the US may be seen as falling into this category.

The amount of economic analysis relating non-hub networks is relatively limited. Fujii *et al.* (1992) looked specifically at the economics of such direct flights, in this case from mainland USA to Hawaii's neighbor islands of Kauai and Maui. They were particularly concerned with the demand-generating effects of flights that did not hub through Honolulu. Using an attribual model, they found that such flights served to marginally increase the traffic to these islands (by about 2% in 1988) but their primary impact was to accommodate existing travel demands. There was also some switching of passengers between the various islands as a result of these options. The direct services also proved to be uneconomical and were, in one case, suspended after a short period of operation.

4 REGULATION OF INTERNATIONAL AIRLINE NETWORKS

4.1 INTRODUCTION

As pointed out in Chapters 1 and 2, airlines, and air transport generally, have traditionally been heavily regulated for economic and social reasons. As we see in subsequent chapters, the details of the nature of regulations that can be applied to air transport networks can vary considerably. However, although regulatory intensity and form have varied between countries, over the past two decades there has been a global move towards more liberal regimes of control. This parallels trends in other transport sectors and industrial policy more generally.

This chapter and the one that follows are concerned with the nature of network regulation and the ways in which it has evolved over time. It is also concerned with some of the problems that are encountered in trying to assess the implications of regulations and in reviewing changes in regulatory regimes. The issue is not a simple one because regulations are not changed in a vacuum but are part of broader policy movements that are in turn reflective of other shifts in economic, social and technological parameters.

Here the attention is on some of the issues concerning international air transport, and in particular problems in examining the implications of recent policy changes. Chapter 5 looks at domestic regulation, although the sections on the European Union (EU) really cross the domestic/international borderline. While there are many very large domestic markets, such as the US and Canada, and rapidly expanding ones, such as China, most countries are geographically relatively small and their domestic networks correspondingly limited. In these cases air transportation is almost exclusively an international activity.

The aim is not to go into depth about the nature of international regulation, this has been done elsewhere.[1] Rather we are concerned with the problems that can arise in assessing the implications of these regulatory structures. In particular, attention is paid to the problems of obtaining useful data to assess the effectiveness and efficiency of policy. To consider the impact of any policy it is important not only to have useful conceptual models but also to have a fairly good idea of the scale and qualitative implications of change. There have been marked advances on the modeling front and estimation procedures are now highly sophisticated, but there are major limitations regarding data availability.

---

[1] For example see, Organisation for Economic Cooperation and Development (1997), Williams (1993) and Hanlon (1996).

4.2   REGULATORY TRENDS

There is no single tool of economic regulation. There are many regulatory instruments that have been applied to air transportation. These are sometimes broken down into those which, adopting US jargon, are aimed at economic regulation and those at social regulation – quantitative and qualitative regulation in the English vocabulary. The former are concerned with controlling the amount supplied in transport markets, who supplies it and the price which consumers pay. Social regulation specifies the nature of the transport services provided relating; for instance, to vehicle design, maximum emissions levels, driving hours, training of personnel, etc. In practice there is an inevitable overlap between the two sets of instruments. Limiting market entry, for example, can contain many adverse environmental effects of transport while strict quality controls can act to contain competition.

It is perhaps more useful, therefore, simply to provide a listing of the various policy instruments under the following general headings.

- *Taxes and subsidies.* The government may use its fiscal powers either to increase or to decrease the costs of various forms of air transportation over different routes. It may also influence the factor costs of transport inputs and subsidies, both direct and indirect, for the development of new aircraft and air traffic control technology have been common place. Subsidies for air mail services were standard practice from the 1920s and in the post Second World War period many state-owned flag carriers received substantial sums from government to cover capital and operating costs.
- *Direct provisions.* Local and central government are direct suppliers, via municipal and nationalized undertakings, of a wide range of air transport services. Many airlines outside of the US are or have been under state ownership. In some cases ownership may be complete whilst in others it may entail a share-holding poisiton. Local and central government are also responsible for supplying a substantial amount of air transportation infrastructure, notably airports and air traffic control, supplementary services, and rapid transit systems to airports.
- *Laws and regulations.* Government may legally regulate the air transport sector and there has grown up an extensive body of law that, in effect, controls and directs the activities of air transport service suppliers and users in every country. At the international level there are air service agreements between states that control many of the characteristics, such as the levels of service and fares, of air transportation between them. A small number of regulatory powers have been given over to international agencies such as the United Nations and World Trade Organization (WTO).

- *Competition policy and consumer protection legislation.* It is useful to distinguish general industrial legislation, governing such things as restrictive practices and mergers, and consumer protection legislation, covering such things as advertising, which embrace all forms of activity in the economy and not just air transport. The general regulations and controls normally apply to air transportation but in some case there are explicit exemptions either for carriers in general or for particular airlines.
- *Licensing.* Government may regulate either the quality or quantity of air transport provision by its ability to grant various forms of licenses to operators, workers, aircraft or services. This approach is often tied in with more explicit regulations and controls.
- *Purchase of transport services.* Various non-transport activities of government require the use of air transport services. Hence, by means of its position as a large consumer, government may exert a degree of countervailing power over air transport suppliers. In the US, for example, as a *quid pro quo* for having a monopoly for the carriage of government personnel, US airlines agree to provide airlift and crew during times of national emergency (e.g., during the Gulf conflict).
- *Moral suasion.* In many instances moral suasion takes a weak form, usually being educational or the offering of advice on matters such as safety but it may be stronger when the alternative to accepting advice is the exercise, by government, of others of its powers (e.g., the withholding of a license or the introduction of legal restraints).
- *Research and development .* Government can affect the long-term development of air transport through its own research activities and the ways in which it funds research more generally. There are, for instance, strong links between military and civil aviation technologies.
- *Provision of information.* The government through various agencies offers certain technical advice to air transport users and provides general information to improve the decision making within the sector. Many of these services are specific to air transport (e.g., meteorological services) while others assist the air transport sector less directly (e.g., information on trading arrangements overseas). It can also ensure that users have adequate information to make rational decisions (e.g., regarding the way computerized information on flights is displayed or, as in the US, the flight time reliability of services).
- *Policies relating to inputs.* Air transport is a major user of energy, especially oil, and also its hardware utilizes a wide range of other raw materials and intermediate products. Government policy relating to the energy and others of these sectors can therefore have an important indirect bearing on the costs of air transport provision.

It seems logical that if market imperfections can be identified it is in the public interest to intervene to reduce their distorting effects. This is not a particularly contentious view. Difficulties arise, however, not from the notion of public interest as such but from the degree to which intervention can, in practice, produce public benefit. In the 1970s a body of opinion emerged that regulation in general had become excessive and no longer served the public interest.

In particular, the ideas of the Chicago School of economists questioned the motivation underlying the actions of regulators – most notably that they tend to act as rational economic entities and pursue policies aimed at furthering their position rather than necessarily that of the public interest. Others considered the power of the regulated and argued that because of their control of information flows (for example, regarding cost data which are needed to regulate fares) and their power to lobby, there was a tendency for them to capture the regulatory process.

Even if regulation is initiated in the public interest it is not free from problems. Ideally policy makers like to match one policy instrument with one objective, but this is seldom possible in air transport. The problem of interdependence in objectives arises but, in addition, the instruments themselves frequently have diverse effects. Taxation policies to reduce the use of air transport for environmental reasons may prove regressive, while licensing may result in quasi-monopoly powers being given to certain carriers.

Forecasting, monitoring and appraising the effects of alternative policy instruments can also prove difficult. Air transport policy is pursued through a package of instruments and policy changes usually result in several being varied in their intensity at once. The effects of such changes are likely to be fully felt only after a lag as agents in the air transport market respond and adjust to the new situation. Even if one could isolate occasions when a change is made to a single policy instrument it is unlikely that the full effect could be recorded before further changes take place.

Finally, there is the problem of determining the counterfactual – the course of events that would have ensued with no policy change. Government is frequently reactive in its approach, suggesting that changing circumstances are already observable by the time policy is enacted, but on other occasions policy changes are initiatives and actually anticipate change. One can never simply assume that events would have continued on the course set prior to a major policy change.

4.3 THE REGULATION OF INTERNATIONAL AIR TRANSPORT NETWORKS

Prior to the Second World War, there was little by way of a standardized system of regulation governing international aviation. Pairs of countries simply made *ad hoc* arrangements. The development of longer range aircraft during the war and the recognition that there would be ample capacity to rapidly develop commercial aviation after it led to efforts to coordinate international aviation policy, the primary event being the Chicago Convention of 1944.

This made some important steps forward. Articles 1, 6 and 17–20 of the Chicago Convention were particularly important. They recognized each contracting state's complete and exclusive sovereignty over the airspace above its territory, the requirement that aircraft should have a nationality by being registered in one particular state and the consequent need for aircraft registered in any state to obtain the permission of a state in order to operate air services to or from its territory.

Despite this there were conflicting views on how the international market should be regulated. Discussion at the Convention was dominated by governments claiming absolute sovereignty over the airspace above their territories. Opinions ranged from having a single, global carrier under a single authority to a completely free, competitive market. The hope lay that those signing would grant to all other signatories freedom of access to this airspace and to their airports. To this end certain freedoms of the skies were identified. [2]

In practice the Convention did not make very much progress because the commercially important third, fourth and fifth freedoms were not, with some minor exceptions, settled on the hoped for multilateral basis. Instead bilateral deals were brokered. This gave rise to a network of bilateral air services agreements – e.g., the UK and US concluded the first Bermuda Agreement in 1946. Under these

---

[2]   The 'Freedoms of the Skies' are:
- 1st freedom. The right of an airline of one country to fly over the territory of another country without landing.
- 2nd freedom. The right of an airline of one country to land in another country for non-traffic reasons, such as maintenance or refueling, while en route to another country.
- 3rd freedom. The right of an airline of one country to carry traffic from its country of registry to another country
- 4th freedom. The right of an airline of one country to carry traffic from another country to its own country of registry.
- 5th freedom. The right of an airline of one country to carry traffic between two countries outside its own country of registry as long as the flight originates or terminates in its own country of registry.
- 6th freedom. The right of an airline of one country to carry traffic between two foreign countries via its own country of registry. This is a combination of the third and fourth freedoms.
- 7th freedom. The right of an airline to operate stand-alone services entirely outside the territory of its home state, to carry traffic between two foreign states.
- 8th freedom. The right of an airline to carry traffic between two points within the territory of a foreign state (cabotage).

agreements two countries agreed upon the gateway airports through which each could enter the other's territory, restricted the entry of airlines to routes and shared out the traffic. They were generally restrictive and often allowed only one airline from each country to operate a route. This also meant that fifth freedom operators could only fly on the routes involved if the authorities at both ends agreed.

The matter of airfares was in the first instance determined within the ambit of another body – IATA. It operated a series of conferences where airlines discussed and coordinated fares, the agreements being subsequently ratified by governments. At a later stage membership of IATA did not require airlines to be bound by conference fare decisions and in some sectors (e.g., North Atlantic routes) fixed rates were replaced by zones of reasonableness. The Convention also gave rise to a United Nations agency (the ICAO) that was largely concerned with technical standards, the collection of statistical data, etc., rather than detailed economic regulation although it has become more involved in this in recent years.

This broad structure still remains in place although there have been important changes. The nature of the bilateral system has altered considerably over the years. As seen in the next chapter, a multilateral system has been initiated within the boundaries of the European Union. The US has, since 1979, and in particular since 1994, pursued a policy of adopting extremely liberal 'Open Skies' bilateral air service agreements whenever other countries will accept it. In some instances, this policy has been more than a passive waiting for co-signatures and US strategy has on occasions been to proactively pursue this approach through such tactics as liberalizing agreements with other states competing with the reticent partner.[3]

By 1982, the US had signed 23 liberal bilateral air service agreements, mainly with smaller nations, in pursuit of its Open Skies agenda. This was followed in the 1990s by a burst of agreements with European states including those with Switzerland, Luxembourg, Iceland, Sweden, Norway, Belgium, Denmark, Finland and the Czech Republic in 1995, Jordan in 1998 and Singapore, Brunei, Taipei, Panama, Guatemala, El Salvador, Honduras, Costa Rica, Nicaragua, New Zealand, Malaysia, Aruba, Chile, Romania and the Netherlands Antilles in 1997. More major agreements with the Netherlands and Germany came as a result of agreements on airline alliances between KLM and Northwest Airlines and Lufthansa and United Air Lines, respectively.

The 1995 agreement with Canada was not strictly an Open Skies arrangement but has, in a staged manner, opened up trade in air services between the US and Canada. The agreement led to a significant increase in transborder traffic, which was up by 10% to 14.3 million passengers in its first year as seat capacity rose by

---

[3]   In a few instances the agreements have, at least for periods, become more restrictive. Bermuda II in 1977 with the UK is a case in point and for a period in the 1990s the bilateral with France was reduced to a reciprocity agreement.

30%. Consumers benefited from 102 new transborder routes that offered residents of many cities their first nonstop transborder services. The agreement also enabled UZS airlines to develop integrated networks across the border, such as those established by American Airlines and Canadian International.

One area that poses particular problems concerns the interface between international and domestic air transport networks. While there has been considerable deregulation within many countries and often between countries, the ability of non-national airlines to operate in other countries' markets (cabotage) remains severely constrained. The same holds for owning foreign airlines; most countries have a limit on the amount of foreign investment and also on the control that foreign investors can exercise over an airline. This is a particular issue in large domestic markets such as the US where non-US carriers cannot operate and there are foreign ownership restrictions. These pose questions regarding the degree to which this lack of internal competition affects the efficiency of the US domestic market. They also have been an issue in negotiating more liberal bilateral air service agreements with countries such as the UK which would like complete freedom of trade including that within the US (Button, 1998c).

Where tight economic regulation continues, information is needed in the international horse-trading that is an integral part of the bilateral system of air traffic agreements. Where there are efforts to liberalize the regulatory structure, statistics are needed for private and government sector uses. Airlines, airport authorities, and suppliers of aircraft and other material inputs require quantitative information to make for effective management decision making and to permit longer-term planning. Labor unions require data to negotiate effectively with employers. Government needs to monitor the state of the industry, to enforce general regulations over such things as anti-trust behavior. Increasingly, data are being demanded on the wider, social implications of air transport as matters of safety and environmental damage attract public attention. Finally, academics and consultants require reliable and consistent data to perform basic analytical as well as policy-relevant research.

4.4 THE DATA PROBLEM[4]

4.4.1 Data requirements

Trade in international air transport services is extensive, growing and becoming more complex. International air transport statistics are, therefore, collected and analyzed for a variety of purposes. Such statistics are important to various public and the private sector groups in their decision-making processes. The needs of each group often differ. The use made of data and less solid information can also vary

---

[4]   A more complete account of these problems is contained in Button (1999a).

within a group according to the issues at hand. Over time these issues can also take on new dimensions. In consequence, compromise is inevitable in the way data are collected and summarized.

The aim here is to look at the needs of the various potential uses to which statistics are currently put and are likely to be needed in the foreseeable future. These needs are, therefore, in the context of overall medium term developments in air transport markets, public policy priorities, and commercial requirements. The needs of the public and private sector inevitably overlap in many instances and similar data are required to meet these needs.[5]

In recent years market liberalization has produced significant changes in the institutions governing international air transport. Within the post 1944 framework, the IATA acted as a clearing-house for information with fares, capacity and other features of the market being very closely monitored. Data were relatively simple to collect because many key parameters were effectively determined by fiat within the framework of an international cartel.

Initially, much of the debate over international liberalization was conducted in the abstract with logical argument used to support regulatory reform.[6] Statistical information supplemented these theoretical and political arguments with evidence drawn from a range of studies showing the benefits of freer aviation markets *per se*. The post-1978 developments in the US domestic market formed the bedrock for much of this work but early lessons were also learned from analyzing some of the liberal bilateral arrangements.[7] The number of studies of this kind looking strictly at international air transport was, however, relatively small.

---

[5]   One area of public concern that is not touched upon here is in that of security. Almost by definition there is limited knowledge of exactly what data are available to the security agencies and to what extent they are exchanged at an international level.

[6]   The new attitude towards economic regulation has been reflected in the criteria by which regulated markets are assessed. Regulation, aside from purely protective measures, has traditionally been viewed in terms of containing monopoly power whilst permitting economies of scale to be enjoyed. The focuses is now on minimizing X-inefficiency and maximizing dynamic efficiency (see table below). The result is that one is looking for different featuress in the institutional structure with more focus on cost minimization and innovation. Inevitably, this requires different models and data.

Allocative efficiency	- requires first or second best pricing of the final products.
Scale efficiency	- requires possible limitation on sub-optimal entry to the Industry.
Technical efficiency or X-efficiency	- requires cost minimization by the incumbent firms.
Product choice and dynamic efficiency	- requires innovation by incumbents.

[7]   For example, Barrett (1990) and the UK Civil Aviation Authority's (1993) work on the European markets.

The increased internationalization and globalization of airline services has produced a need for more current analysis and a longer-term need for different types of information and statistics. But as a prerequisite there are important issues of definition. First, there is considerable commercial interest, together with accompanying public and legal debate, about the desirability of airline alliance.[8] These debates require good data to be constructive but there is no accepted definition of what exactly constitutes an alliance. This has led to different sets of statistics emerging.[9]

Reforms are also resulting in the restructuring of airline networks leading to problems for poloicy makers in defining what constitutes an air service; simple point-to-point data provide only a partial picture when most trips involve transit through a hub airport.[10] This problem also brings to the fore the interface that exists between domestic and international air transport. Travelers and shippers are concerned about origin to destination characteristics but the public data are generally divided between the local and the trunk elements of a passenger or cargo movement.

Specifically, traditional data on the physical features of airline activities, such as route miles served and passengers carried, are important for some aspects of the new policy environment but they are often inadequate for the negotiations that take place leading to reform. These negotiations are basically concerned with matters of the comparative advantage of each nation's airlines rather than with physical parameters. Yet it is this type of commercial data that are generally lacking and the adoption of yield management practices makes it difficult to collect.

Freer, more commercially oriented markets inevitably bring with them concerns about their overall performance and the conduct of individual airlines within them. At one extreme there is concern that network industries are inherently unstable and, in economic terms, lack a core (see Chapter 7). Under supply is the result. At the other extreme is the fear that, given the existence of

[8]   Until recently, the majority of the strtegic airline alliances that have historically attracted most public interest have involved one or more European carriers joining with a large US airline. The situation has become more complex in 2000 as major US carriers seek merger possibilities among themselves (e.g., United Airlines and US Airways, the largest and tenth largest carriers in the world) while overseas alliance partners are also involved in discussions to merger (e.g., KLM and British Airways both of which have US alliance partners). Alliances are not unique to air transport nor indeed to transport in general, but are one of the most rapidly growing forms of business practice.

[9]   As an illustration, one can compare the number of airline alliances recorded in recent reports in the *Economist*, *Airline Business* and *Avmark Aviation Economist*.

[10]   This definitional question is important when assessing competition between carriers when there is a need to delineate the markets that are being served, e.g., regarding antitrust immunity matters surrounding alliance approvals.

economies of scale, scope, density and market presence there will be a long-term oligopolization or even monopolization; again under-supply results although accompanied by excessively high quality of service. Linked to this is a concern that opportunities for new market entry will be restricted by incumbent airlines pursuing predatory practices. Tackling these problems may involve individual case studies but background statistics are important as benchmarks against which to assess behavior.

The need for better data is also likely to be stimulated further in the long term by broader trends in trade policy. The gradual development of international liberalization of trade in services under the administration of the WTO has yet to have any major effects on air transport. The annex to the General Agreement on Trade in Services (GATS) dealing with aviation has very limited coverage. It does not cover hard rights but is limited to three doing business issues: aircraft repair and maintenance services, the selling and marketing of air transport services and CRSs.

There has been strong resistance to date by countries such as the US to giving international agencies extensive power to regulate their industries in international markets. In part this stems from concerns about losing control over what is considered a domestic matter. But if the role of WTO expands, the likelihood is that more reliable quantitative information will be sought by those developing policy.[11]

Often linked to public policy analysis and formation but extending beyond it is the role of statistical information in predicting demand for international air transport. There seems little doubt that iternational aviation will continue expanding into the foreseeable future, although at differential rates in various geographical sub-markets and for different types of travel. Whilst forecasting remains more of an art than a science, it is likely from the overview of recent forecasts outlined in Chapter 1, that passenger traffic will grow at a rate between 5% and 7% into the foreseeable future, rising as high as 9% in markets such as those in the Asia-Pacific region.

For decision making the nature of the long-term growth trend is less important than are details about individual markets and fluctuations in medium term traffic levels. It is this sort of detail that the airlines need for strategic planning and the aircraft manufactures and government authorities for hardware development. The evidence is that many forecasts are not particularly accurate in this latter respect. Table 4.1, for example, gives an indication of the performance of the earlier forecasting models used by Boeing on the important North Atlantic route.

---

[11]   It will also become increasingly germane as multilateral policing and monitoring if the regime demands standardization of information.

Table 4.1 ICAO seven year forecast and actual flights on the North Atlantic (thousands)

Base Year / Forecasts	1984	1985	1986	1987	1988	1989	1990	1991	1992	1993	1994	1995	1996	1997	1998	1999
1980	127.6	130.2	132.7													
1981	125.7	128.0	130.4	133.0												
1982	125.8	128.1	131.4	131.6	132.0											
1983	127.8	129.1	131.7	131.7	133.6	135.3										
1984	*132.7*	138.3	139.8	142.8	147.9	152.0	153.6									
1985		*140.8*	143.5	144.2	148.5	151.5	156.0	159.5								
1986			*141.4*	149.8	151.9	154.8	159.0	164.0	168.9							
1987				*158.5*	177.2	187.3	195.3	203.4	209.8	215.4						
1988					*175.7*	187.6	197.3	204.5	212.9	221.6	229.1					
1989						*192.0*	205.4	216.4	225.6	235.6	244.4	253.6				
1990							*206.1*	205.0	213.9	224.4	236.7	249.3	263.6			
1991								*213.0*	220.3	233.5	247.0	258.1	268.1	277.6		
1992									228.2	238.0	252.2	263.3	278.9	294.3	312.5	
1993										242.8	252.8	264.5	277.2	291.2	305.2	320.1

Note: Actual figures in italics.

These medium term forecasts are, however, important in many managerial decisions such as the ordering of new aircraft. One problem with demand forecasting is that traditionally it has relied on extrapolations of patterns discerned in time series of past events and relationships. Establishing the nature of past and existing relationships between a range of variables and air travel demand is not easy even with reliable data, but forecasting the future path of independent variables is generally more problematic. Assuming current and past relations will remain constant over the forecast period is also fraught with difficulties. Efforts at supplementing these procedures using Delphi and similar techniques do not resolve the problems and can in some instances worsen them.

More recently airlines such as British Airways (1995) and aircraft manufacturers such as Boeing have been using various scenario analyses in an attempt to develop strategies to confront uncertain futures. This approach is also often iterative with the various scenarios being continually modified as feedback from those involved in the company and industry allow refinements to be made. These, therefore, involve less traditional statistical inputs but use more qualitative material. They also employ a range of forecasts of possible trends in the factors that influence the demand for air services and the costs of providing them.

Costs of airline services are also relevant for policy makers and airlines. Airlines have a commercial interest in having a finger on the pulse of their costs. Governments require cost data to assess not only legal matters regarding general industrial policy but also for such things as the way taxation policy is applied. As seen in Chapter 2, conventional accountancy procedures and basic econometric cost models (e.g., Leontief or Cobb-Douglas functions) have been supplemented by more rigorous techniques. This has allowed analysis of economies of scope, networks, density and of experience. The recognition that inappropriate regulated market structures can lead to sub-optimal shifts in the cost function associated high levels of X-inefficiency has led to the adoption both of refined econometric procedures and of programming techniques.

Overall these developments have implications for the type of data needed to carry out detailed cost and productivity analysis and pose particular problems in policy assessment because much of the data requirement - e.g. regarding yields - often has commercial value associated with it. While this is an issue for analysis of any domestic system, it is even more of a problem when international comparisons are being attempted.

International air transportation relies on an extensive infrastructure that not only includes airports and the navigation and air traffic control systems but extends to the infrastructure required to get passengers and cargoes to and from air terminals. There is also the communications infrastructure needed to coordinate the activities of airline customers and the suppliers of services to airlines.[12] Infrastructure data requirements relate to on-going activities for immediate management and operational planning (e.g., slot, gate and parking space allocations) and to longer term capacity planning and investment decisions. The latter, given the time it takes to gain acceptance for capacity expansion, can require forecasts for thirty to forty years forward.[13] In many instances the banking pattern of flight arrivals and departures, involving flights converging and then leaving within narrow time frames, coupled with the need to integrate domestic and international connections, involves considerable interchange of information between airlines and airport authorities on the local scheduling committee.

It has been feared for some time that in many markets the available infrastructure is increasingly reaching its technical capacity.[14] While some of the problems lay in the poor management of much of the infrastructure there remain very real capacity issues. Expansion of capacity is difficult because of concern over adverse environmental impacts.[15] In most industrialized countries investment in more physical capacity requires extensive public inquiry procedures to be conducted. These inquiries are costly and take considerable time to complete.[16]

Air transport is the safest way to travel but there are accidents. Between 1987 and 1996 there were 205 commercial jet aircraft lost in the world. Over the same period there were 142 fatal accidents involving jet aircraft of which 108 involved passenger airlines and killed 6 156 people. Data on smaller commercial aircraft accidents are less complete. There are national differences in safety levels, although the number of incidents varies considerably on a year by year basis because of the lumpiness of incidents. The rate of accidents involving all US carriers has remained fairly constant since the mid-1970s at about 0.05 fatalities per 100 000

---

[12]   The work dealing with the role of CRS systems and passenger air transport is fairly extensive, but that on the cargo side is more limited (Button and Owens, 1999).

[13]   These need to be relatively accurate for engineering design purposes but since costs and benefits are discounted in cost-benefit assessments can be less accurate over the longer period. Good short-term data are also required for slot allocation purposes. At present allocations are usually done in an administrative fashion (Castles, 1997).

[14]   IATA in 1990, for instance, concluded that, without further enhancements, capacity of 16 European airports would be severely limited by the turn of the century, with Madrid, Frankfurt, Heathrow, Gatwick, Barcelona and Milan (Linate) worst affected. Even if potential measures helped to increase capacity, other than new runways put into place, 13 airports would still remain constrained by 2010.

[15]   It is no accident that perhaps one of the most expensive cost-benefit studies conducted was into the location of a new 'Third London Airport'. The recommendations of the enquiry team were rejected (Commission on the Third London Airport, 1971).

[16]   The process is not speeded up by the need in virtually all cases for the decision to be based on entirely new sets of studies. There seems to be little scope for deploying value transfer procedures in this area (Johnson and Button, 1997).

departures or 0.0008 per million aircraft miles. Non-US carriers as a group have slightly worse statistics. Individual aircraft accidents, however, attract considerable media attention and public concern because of the large numbers of individuals that can be involved in any incident.[17]

Improving safety, or indeed even convincing the public of the generally good safety record of international air transport, requires solid statistics. Aviation safety data are often incomplete, inconsistent or have serious gaps. This is in part because countries have developed different ways of collecting data and use different definitions and measures. The US National Transportation Safety Board, for instance, uses a very broad definition of an accident (any accident that involves a broken bone is classified as an accident). Other countries use tighter definitions. Equally, there are differences in the way air misses are defined and reported.

Efforts have begun to improve the ways in which these safety data are collected across countries. The 33 European Civil Aviation Conference states have followed the FAA in establishing a system called 'Safety of Foreign Aircraft' (SAFA) to collect data on incidents with foreign aircraft. It is intended that the incident data will provide enough evidence to approach the responsible state authority on the operational and technical qualities of its carriers' operations. The practical problem is how to collect these data.[18]

Safety policy involves making trade-offs. Accidents involve a variety of immediate costs in terms of aircraft loses and damage and there are also quantifiable financial costs of preventive policies although statistics on these are less easily obtained. The costs of lost life and injuries pose more of a challenge. There are, however, techniques available to put money values on these using revealed and stated preference methodologies, but they are not free of criticism.

Aviation activities impinge on the environment. There has been a long standing concern about aircraft noise nuisance and the local implications of accessing airports by land, but recently the focus has changed to the atmospheric pollution around airports and from the global environmental effects of flights themselves. Exact calculations of such cost are difficult because there are gaps in the scientific understanding of the issues and because data on the physical emissions themselves are limited. At the global level, British Airways (1994) has estimated that commercial aviation produces some 500 tonnes of carbon dioxide

---

[17]   This would imply the need for Bayesian statistical analysis but Guassian modeling still demonstrates the technical literature. There is some evidence, though, that safety considerations can affect the viability of air carriers (Button, 1999b).

[18]   The US has not traditionally made extensive use of standard recording devices on aircraft except when a major incident has occurred. This is in contrast to many other countries (e.g., the UK). In 1998 the FAA begun seeking ways of making better use of these data to gain insights on situations where incidents have been averted and on the general way crews perform their duties. This would allow a more proactive approach to safety. A concern is an unwillingness of labor to have incidents highlighted.

emissions per annum and thus contributes 1.25% to 1.5% of greenhouse gas emissions.[19] The ozone layer may also be affected by nitrogen oxide emissions in the middle atmosphere and at lower levels may at the margin contribute to acid rain. Concern has also been expressed about the implications of ice crystals from engine exhausts in the stratosphere.

Good data are required to monitor the use of aviation fuel by various types of aircraft in differing operating conditions to provide a more exact estimate of the environmental implications of air transport. Large aircraft are noisy and noise complaints are common around international airports. There are various methods of presenting the noise problem in a quantitative form using indices, but in themselves they are seldom useful for policy debates other than to show changes in the scale of the problem. For policy debates efforts have been made to provide monetary valuations of the noise measure based upon either hedonic price methods or contingent valuation techniques (Feitelson *et al.*, 1996). As yet, however, no consensus has emerged as to a universally applicable figure.

4.4.2 What data do we have?

There are a number of sources of international air transport statistics. In addition to published statistics there are numerous academic and consultancy studies that have collected primary data and that may be usefully for meta-analysis.[20] The competitive nature of the international air passenger and cargo sectors, however, means that much consultancy material is often confined to the 'gray literature'.

For many national agencies, global international air transport statistics are a secondary concern; most tend to focus their attention on the markets served by their own carriers. Data sets from international organizations are selective and limited. They tend to reflect those areas of activity over which the agency has responsibility. Organizations such as the ICAO and the IATA, mainly because of resource constraints and a lack of legal authority, usually have to rely upon airlines and national governments to feed data to them. These data come in at varying speeds, often making full sets of statistics dated upon their publication, and are reduced to the lowest common denominator for comparative analysis. Methods of collection vary between countries and reliability are sometimes suspect.

Those responsible for providing air transport also offer a range of data sources. Aircraft manufacturers provide technical details of fleets and, in some instances, develop particular data sets to address issues of interest to them. This is

---

[19]   Over time, technically aircraft are becoming more fuel-efficient, but this is more than offset by the increased amount of air traffic.

[20]   Button *et al.* (1999) provides a general discussion of the usefulness of techniques such as meta-analysis in examining microeconomic issues. See also Chapter 13.

particularly so regarding the age of aircraft fleets, their geographical dispersion, technical reliability of individual types of aircraft and their safety records. Airlines provide standardized financial accounts at a national level to meet auditing requirements but since such requirements differ between countries comparability is often lacking.[21] In many countries they publish data relating to service characteristics such as delays. Further, global agencies, such as the ICAO, and regional bodies, such as the Association of European Airlines and the Cargo Airlines Association, provide readily accessible compilations of secondary data and also periodic specialized studies using data gathered from members.

Providers of air transport infrastructure are sources of network related information, the air traffic control and navigation systems providing aircraft flow data[22] while airports collect and publish data on international passenger and cargo movements through them.

The need for customs and immigration clearance at many airports provides supplementary sources of data. Periodically social and economic impact studies are conducted at individual airports, often as part of a statutory assessment procedure related to expansion programs of one kind or another. Such case studies generate insights into a variety of key parameters that become the bases for subsequent value transfer exercises.

4.4.3 The gaps and weaknesses

No single set of statistics will ever meet everyone's needs. International air transport is also a complicated sector that can make the collection and presentation of statistics difficult. While offering a summary of the strengths and weaknesses of what is available is inevitably going to be subjective, Table 4.2 provides a simplified, normative assessment of the situation. It offers an indication of where data would seem to be available to confront the main needs of users (in terms of '+'s) and where there would seem to be important gaps or weaknesses (the '−'s). The aspects of data considered are the basic ones of physical data, economic data and social data but added to this is a 'modeling' criterion reflect the types of technical instruments that are available for each need.[23]

---

[21]   There are also differences in the type of ownership of carriers and with this goes differences in the types of information that they need to reveal for auditing purposes. A state-owned carrier is generally subject to different legal accounting rules to an airline that is a publicly traded company or one that is a private company even within the same country.

[22]   In some cases this is collected mainly for long-term planning purposes but some agencies, such as EUROCONTROL, have a major revenue collecting function and data is also collected for accounting purposes.

[23]   There is clearly no intent to imply that each type of data is of equal importance for all needs.

4.4.3.1 Policy assessment

In addition to international sources of data, many countries collect and publish additional statistics for their own policy-making purposes. This has traditionally been true at the more macro level for negotiating bilateral air service agreement adjustments and more recently when considering such matters as responding to the emergence of a new strategic airline alliance (Dresner and Windle, 1996). In some instances there have been criticisms concerning the nature of this information and its usefulness. The US General Accounting Office (1995a) has been critical of the amount of suitable economic data available for conducting international bilateral negotiations.[24]

Table 4.2 A general indication of the adequacy of international air transport data

| Need | Type of data | | | |
	Physical	Economic	Social	Modeling
Policy assessment	++	+	+	+
Forecasting demand	++	+*	−	+*
Infrastructure	+	+	+	+
Costing	+	+	−	++
Safety	+	−	−	−
Environment	−	− −	− −	−

* The weaknesses here concern data availability and modeling procedures suitable for medium-term forecasting.

The initial thrust of the US's Open Skies policy, and prior *de facto* initiatives in stimulating the introduction of more liberal bilateral agreements between 1976 and 1981, were estimated by Dresner and Tretheway (1992) to have generated as much as $325 million (current prices) savings in North Atlantic fares in 1981. More global analysis along similar lines,however. was limited by lack of complete data from less developed countries. Even the routes that were included

---

[24] The US General Accounting Office (1995b) has also argued that the US policy response to code-sharing has been hindered by, '... such [things] as a lack of detailed data on foreign carriers' code-share traffic traveling to and from the United States'. Further, 'Data problems handicap DOT's efforts to place a value upon the access rights to the US market that it relinquishes to foreign governments in exchange for improved access or code-sharing.'

could only be assessed in terms of either the full economy fare or the lowest minimum fare.

The problems are not that data do not exist but that they are of limited use in addressing the types of questions under review. Physical data on passenger flows and flights are available, but these are often of only little use in addressing what are fundamentally economic questions. While there may exist an *a priori* case for freer trade in international air transportation services, bilateral negotiations are concerned with the costs and benefits of adjusting existing regulatory structures and, as we see below, data here are often lacking.[25]

Much of the data are also too aggregate in nature to address central aspects of competition and anti-trust policy. This point was made in a study of airline alliances by Oum and Park (1997) who argued that, 'Probably because of the difficulty in obtaining consistent route specific data and the difficulty of separating effects of alliances from other changes, we are aware of only four empirical studies which attempted to measure the effects of airline alliances on carriers and consumers.'

their (!)

4.4.3.2 Forecasting

Forecasting of supply and demand is important for the effective longer-term management of international air transport but the time horizons differ for the various actors. Major airlines have there own divisions responsible for making use of published statistics and for collecting and analyzing additional commercial material. The advent of computer reservation systems provides for rapid feedback and response at an individual services level. This information is the key to the dynamic price discrimination that now characterizes much of the sector. Short-term forecasts, because of this in-built, interactive data collection/ application element of CRS systems, tend to be efficient.[26] Longer term planning requires more aggregate levels of information. One source is internal market surveys and another the publicly available forecasts of aggregate trends and predictions of change by market segments. Bringing these and other data together at the airline level, however, is not easy as exemplified by the volatile cycles the sector experiences and the frequent overreaction of the airlines.

---

[25]   In strict terms, trade is about comparative advantage rather than competitive advantage in a single sector and in this sense the types of negotiations that treat trade in air transport separately from trade in all goods and services are somewhat illogical from an economic perspective.

[26]   The issues are rather ones of how much information the owner of a CRS system should be allowed to keep confidential and the extent to which airlines should be permitted to use their own systems in a competitive air transport market. Good information on revenues and prices is required for public policy and infrastructure policy formulation but equally, for competition to be effective, air carriers require to be allowed to exploit any comparative advantage that they may enjoy.

The long-term aggregate forecasts used by airlines and infrastructure providers are relatively good at pinpointing broad trends but much less reliable at foreseeing turning points in medium term cycles. One of the difficulties is the problem of predicting the main determining variables such as changes in income levels. In terms of the US domestic market, Morrison and Winston (1995) found that the high levels of excess capacity that existed in 1990–1993 were largely due to airlines finding it difficult to predict the future levels of key economic indicators such as income.[27]

4.4.3.3 Costing and productivity

The technical analysis of costing and productivity analysis of supply has advanced a long way. There is now a plethora of models that can be applied to the costing problem and a range of econometric and programming software available to conduct the empirical estimation. Problems still remain regarding the data to feed into the models. In particular, the greater commercialization of international air transport as economic regulations are lessened and airlines are increasingly privatized means that cost data are less readily available.[28] Where they are released this is often done in very broad categories.

More specific weaknesses have emerged in some recent studies. First, outside the US few countries have the information required for detailed cost analyses. In his work on international airline productivity using a total factor productivity model, Windle (1991), while having data on US carriers' fuel inputs, had to impute fuel use for non-US carriers. In other cases, even when some data are available, there is the lack of consistent time series statistics. One example is the simulation study of European air transport networks conducted by Berechman and de Wit (1996). Here only 1992 data on the distribution of business and non-business class passengers meant that a time series for 1986 to 1992 had to be synthesized. The aggregate nature of information on yield, and the fact that it was available only for US carriers on North Atlantic routes, meant that Maillebiau and Hanson (1995) had to rely on a partial data base in their log-linear estimation. They speculated this would produce an error-in-variables bias leading to underestimation of fare elasticities.

Academic debates concerning the desirability of competitive international markets are usually conducted based a set of assumptions implying that costs are divisible, demand is relatively elastic, and that suppliers all have identical U-

---

[27] This is not a problem peculiar to international air transport. In the 1960s the UK statistical authorities attempted to use a logistic curve extrapolation of car-ownership to predict future national income trends on the pragmatic basis that, whatever the intellectual problems involved, this could produce more accurate forecasts.

[28] Although it was not unknown for 'creative accountancy' to be practiced when government intervention was more widespread.

shaped cost curves. Violation of such conditions can lead to an empty core and inadequate supply (instability conditions). Button (1996b) had to rely upon a variety of proxy variables when seeking to establish whether market stability conditions existed for air transport within the EU.

The issue of capital is always a difficult one to deal with in applied analysis. Setting aside physical problems such as capacity measurements, there are inevitable difficulties in putting a monetary value on a capital stock and the opportunity costs of using it. Historic costing has now largely been abandoned in analytical work although official data often include it. Replacement costing pose particular problems in air transport where technical change is rapid. These general issues are compounded at the international level when different countries pursue different accountancy conventions for such things as depreciation.[29]

Regarding costs to air transport users there are considerable gaps in our knowledge. Yield management makes it difficult to conduct analysis beyond that of simply trying to explain average yield and its effects on demand. But, beyond this, a full analysis of user costs would embrace assessment of the 'generalized costs' of using air transport. Such a cost function would entail the monetary equivalent of the overall time costs involved. Travel time valuations are available (e.g., they are used in the US by the FAA) but they seldom reflect features such as the unreliability of the time taken for a trip or differentials for various components of a trip (e.g., travel to airport, waiting at airport, interchanging between aircraft and flight time). Different types of air traveler seek different time attributes from air services[30] and this needs to be reflected in an appropriate abstract mode model.[31] There is also a need to look at trips more holistically and to embrace movements to and from airports as part of the overall cost of trip making.

4.4.3.4 Infrastructure

Airports engage in multifaceted operations and obtaining comparable data is not easy (Doganis, 1992). There are several problems in separating the implications of international air transport movements from those of domestic traffic. The ICAO is the only agency that collects comparable financial data on airports and separation of data by various traffic types is not comprehensive. The number of countries that

---

[29]   The concept of depreciation in an expanding network industry is a complex one in itself. While there is a case in engineering terms and with respect to maintenance costs for assuming that links in a network depreciate with time or use, if the network is expanding the external benefits from being a part of that larger network mean that a link may gain in value. Its economic value is appreciating and it becomes a negative cost item.

[30]   Leisure travelers put a premium on low fares but business travelers put service quality (including frequency, duration of overall trip, etc.) as their prime concern.

[31]   For an account of the theory of abstract mode modeling, see Quandt and Baumol (1983).

participate is small and the data provided are limited.[32] Even at the national level, because airports are generally under the authority of local governments or state agencies,[33] data on key economic indicators are often lacking.

One of the practical problems with financial statistics is that airports provide a range of different services but many of these (e.g., handling of baggage, freight and aircraft maintenance) are treated as commercial activities separate from the airport itself. The degree to which these types of service are handled by individual airports differs widely. Airports also vary in terms of government involvement and control and with this come differences in the nature of data that will be disclosed. Differing national accountancy practices add to the problem of compatability. The latter is also a major problem when examining air traffic control systems. There is also the problem of deciding what financial data actually imply, the increasing trend towards privatization and corporatization means the profits trends may well reflect differing degrees of monopoly power rather than efficiency changes.[34]

There are issues concerning air traffic control and navigation systems. Many systems throughout the world are dated and technologically obsolete. Countries such as the US are attempting to update their systems and to incorporate new notions such as 'Free Flight' into the way air traffic is managed. In other areas, most notably the EU, the effort is as much on standardizing what are at present a diverse collection of national systems. Overlapping this are new initiatives for stimulating greater efficiency in the management of systems; e.g., the Canadian move to corporatizing their system and the UK's introduction of private financing. Efficient use of resources in this rapidly changing environment requires not only good physical data but also reliable models and carefully constructed financial data. The financial data are particularly important if economically based charging is to be more widely adopted both from an accountancy perspective and as assurance at the international level that there is no exploitation of systems.

4.4.3.5 Safety
Safety statistics at the aggregate level are extensive and available in long time series. There is a need for greater international consistency, especially regarding the

[32]   Within Europe, as early as 1984 the European Commission had attempted to establish indicators that would provide a basis for inter-airport comparisons as well as international comparisons.

[33]   A very small number of major international airports such as Heathrow in the UK are privately owned and here conflicts arise regarding availability of data. Commercial considerations point towards a degree of confidentiality but at the same time the monopoly power of airports such as Heathrow has led to regulation and with it the requirement of public accountability.

[34]   Total factor productivity models (e.g., involving such techniques as non-parametric index numbers) are available that can offer more useful guidance on efficiency (Hooper and Hensher, 1997).

developing nations and the former communist states of Europe, but even here the international agencies are making progress. Safety data are sparse, incidents are infrequent and increasingly, because of improved technology and regulatory controls, often unique. As a result, the emphasis tends to be on looking at conditions where there existed a potential for a serious incident but this was avoided. Data on air-misses have a long pedigree but at the international level there are definitional and reporting problems.[35] As noted above there are also major national divergences in the way that cockpit recorded data are collected and used, in part because of problems in labor relations but also because insensitive collection could lead to potential adverse feedback on cabin crew behavior. These micro data are important, however, since the strict causes of many accidents are not known or result from a series of actions that may not be immediately clear from the currently available data.

Presentation and explanations of safety data pose serious problems. It is generally agreed by economists that from a cost-benefit point of view air transport may be too safe - i.e., resources devoted to airline safety would yield a higher social return in some other use. Media coverage of incidents is part of the explanation (accidents involve a spatial and temporal concentration of deaths and injuries that make for spectacular journalism) as is a general lack of education on the nature of probabilities. How this problem could be resolved is uncertain, but public knowledge on transportation safety is, in general, inadequate.[36]

4.4.3.6 Environment
Concern about the environmental damage associated with air transport, beyond issues of noise nuisance, is comparatively recent and growing (see Chapter 13). It is not surprising that there is still considerable uncertainty about the physical links involved let alone the economic and social implications. Part of the problem lies in the need for more pure scientific analysis to ascertain how various pollutants associated with air transport adversely affect the environment. Before this issue is fully clarified it is impossible to place viable monetary values on these items.[37]

---

[35]   For example, domestically in the US, there have been periodic changes in rules of reporting with immunity from liability being given when incidents were reported between 1968 and 1971 but removed after 1971. Rates of reported incidents were found to go down significantly after 1972 (McKenzie and Shughart, 1988). There was a dramatic drop in the number of air-misses recorded immediately following President Reagan's dismissal of striking air traffic controllers in the early 1980s, possibly because the remaining controllers were difficult to find to make reports to.

[36]   The safety question is returned to in Chapter 13.

[37]   There are additional problems in that aviation fuel can be bought at various points on an aircraft's flight itinerary and hence the amount of fuel burned on any particular flight is difficult to assert.

In many ways broad criticisms regarding environmental data transcend any discussion of air transportation; many of the issues are new, the impacts are often long term and the underlying relationships are not fully understood (Button, 1993b; Levinson *et al*, 1998). The issues are often more to do with a need for basic scientific research than with large-scale data collection. What is missing, however, is a systematic effort to bring together existing knowledge and to ensure that on-going and future analysis presents findings and data in ways that allow viable synthesis. There are many ways in which quantitative information and empirical findings may be brought together but for full efficiency common reporting procedures are generally required.[38]

4.5 CONCLUSIONS

International air transport policy has changed remarkably over the past twenty years and continues to evolve. Here we have looked at some of the changes that have taken place but have been particularly concerned with informational issues. The discussion has not been comprehensive and other aspects of it are returned to later. The issue of good information at the international level has been a central theme of the chapter. Reliable statistics are important for public policy making in international air transport and for the commercial vitality of operators. The world in which air transport operates is, however, a rapidly changing one. There are major technical advances not only in aircraft but also in the information and control systems that control their use. Institutional adjustments mean that the role of government is now different to twenty years ago with market forces, privatization and commercialism playing a much stronger part in the way the sector functions. This produces new challenges in terms of information requirements.

It is not only the airlines' component of the sector that is undergoing transformation. Airports are being privatized, or being required to operate in a much more commercially orientated manner, and air traffic control is in some instances being put on a more accountable basis. Successful change requires reliable and germane data if *ex ante* policy decisions are to meet specified criteria and *ex post* operations are to be efficient. At the international level, greater transparency will inevitably be needed if liberalization is to continue and not be thwarted by concerns of market manipulations at the infrastructure level.

---

[38]   Button (1998a) provides a critique of techniques for synthesis data sets and empirical findings and offers comment on the respective merits of traditional 'literary reviews', meta-analysis and subjective quantitative assessment methods. This is discussed in more detail in Chapter 13.

What is encouraging is that international air transport statistics are in many ways improving and becoming more consistent. The coming together of national groupings (such as the EU) to develop consistent 'internal' air transport policies has necessitated this in some cases. The major international agencies in air transport, such as IATA and ICAO, have new roles to play in this respect as the traditional structure of the industry changes and as new markets, particularly in the Pacific Rim area and in Eastern and Central Europe, grow (albeit at a rather stuttering pace). The emergence of more competitive markets and greater commercialism in the sector as a whole poses additional challenges but equally stimulate actors to participate more fully in internalizing their data needs.

5   EARLY IMPACTS OF US, CANADIAN AND EU AIRLINE DEREGULATION

5.1 INTRODUCTION

While it is often intellectually exciting to think in the abstract, the bounds of reality often impose important constraints on what networks look like and the freedoms that the actors have to develop network systems. Geography and the nature of alternative transport networks are often important constraints. A variety of institutional factors also influence the ways in which networks are supplied and the ways in which they are used. In practice, air transport has always been regulated for a variety of economic reasons and for social reasons such as environmental protection and for safety. Looking at a static regulated network or at a cross section of different networks can offer some insights as to the importance of regulatory structures. The difficulty, however, is that of defining a meaningful counterfactual, free market situation for comparison and this results in the approach being of rather limited use. Examining changing conditions as liberalizing regulatory reforms occur can often prove more fruitful.

The purpose of this chapter is to examine the implications of institutional change for several important air transport networks, those of the US, Canada and the European Union (EU). These are not the only networks that have undergone important regulatory changes in recent years but they do offer important insights for a number of reasons.[1]

All of these markets have a tradition of their scheduled airlines being heavily regulated but have in the past twenty years been through a dynamic process of market liberalization. Each followed its own particular path.[2] None of the markets

---

[1]   The majority of national markets in South America have been liberalized with various types of privatization programs. Australia and New Zealand markets have also been deregulated. Additionally, the World Trade Organization (WTO) brought into play (albeit an extremely small role) a new and geographically wider policy making institution to supplement the roles already played by bodies such as the International Civil Aviation Organization (ICAO) and the International Air Transport Association (IATA). Aviation issues are also on the agenda of new regional groupings such as the Asian-Pacific Economic Council (APEC).

[2]   The US essentially followed a 'Big Bang' in that deregulation was introduced at one step, although phased in. The EU and Canada deregulations were gradual and less planned. The theoretical time paths of the costs and benefits associated with the two philosophies are stylized in the diagram below. Essentially, the shock treatment approach has high initial costs of disruption to an industry and possibly consumers but

is genuinely free in the strictest economic sense after this process. Not only are there many regulations and controls imposed for safety and environmental reasons but there are also vestiges of economic regulation that remain. These latter controls are in addition to more generic controls of an antitrust nature that transcend any particular industry.

The experiences are not designed to offer any comment on the current state of any of these air transport markets but rather they are used as case studies to examine the types of change that took place during a period of major regulatory transition.[3] Additionally, since the changes in the US and Canada largely took place some time ago many of the longer term ripple effects that inevitably accompany change have had the opportunity to work their way through. The more recent EU changes are still impacting on European markets. The difficulty is that the reforms in the US did take place in the 1970s and to compare the pre-1978 situation to that at the turn of the century is unrealistic. It is, however, difficult to make valid comparisons between the current situation and a regulatory structure

a rapid move to a higher level of total economic welfare. In contrast incrementalism has fewer initial adverse implications but the benefits of change take longer to materialize. At its simplest, this diagram below highlights the importance of the social discount factor in selecting the desirable strategy. Advocates of incrementalism implicitly have a lower discount rate. This implies less concern with the current costs of regulatory inefficiency and less interest in reaping the immediate benefits of liberalization.

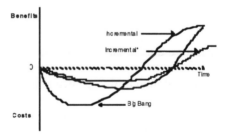

In practice reforms are seldom as straightforward as the diagram implies. For example, as we see below, Canada reforms represented a number of separate, often independent, liberalizing initiatives, not a series of pre-planned and advertised incremental changes. The diagram also implies that ultimately there is a convergence in the paths of the alternative strategies but there is no reason to anticipate this happening. The incremental path could converge on a lower asymptotic benefit level than the Big Bang curve (e.g., path Incremental* converges to a lower asymptotic benefit curve than does the Big Bang path).

[3]   More contemporary issues regarding US air transport are covered in Borenstein, (1992a), Morrison and Winston (1995) and Transportation Research Board (1999) and regarding Canada in Oum *et al.* (1991).

that would have inevitably been modified and adjusted over the intervening period. One can take the counter-factual of the pre-deregulation institutions just so far before the comparison loses much of its legitimacy. In consequence much of the attention is on the decade after deregulation. This is long enough for the main adjustments to have occurred but equally not so long that regulatory parameters become meaningless points of comparison.

5.2 THE US DOMESTIC AIR TRANSPORT REFORMS

5.2.1 Background

The 1930s were a period of considerable intervention by government in transport markets. This interventionist philosophy transcended modal and international boundaries (Button and Gillingwater, 1986). The justification for the regulation of transport came in several different forms. Much of the argument was couched in terms of a desire either to ensure safety in the rapidly expanding transport sector or to provide an institutional framework within which the new and dynamic transport modes could be efficiently expanded to integrate with the existing transport system.

Over time some skepticism has emerged about the validity of this 'public interest' interpretation of events and, for example, questions have arisen concerning the policy-making role of self-interested parties and especially operators of older, established transport modes and incumbent suppliers of the newer transport services. This 'capture' of the regulatory and policy, and especially operators of older, established transport modes (such as the railways) and the incumbent suppliers of the newer transport services, both intent on protecting their own positions, was initially highlighted by the Chicago School of Economists. The capture of the regulatory and policy making system has been seen to extend beyond the simple power of direct transport supplying firms to the unions that represent their labor and the manufacturers who supply their equipment. It has even been argued that the regulators themselves have an interest in establishing and maintaining a complex administrative structure to meet their own, especially career, aspirations.[4]

It is against this background that the US Civil Aeronautics Act was passed in 1938 establishing the Civil Aeronautics Authority – from 1940 the Civil Aeronautics Board (CAB).[5] Regarding economic regulation, the CAB was given

---

[4]   The classic theoretical works in this field are, Peltzman (1976) and Stigler (1971).

[5]   The legislation took time to emerge (there were 15 investigations to determine the need for and the best form of regulatory structure for the aviation industry between 1918 and 1937) and was modeled on the Interstate Commerce Act of 1887 and the Motor Carrier Act of 1935.

authority to:[6]

- regulate entry into the industry (interstate and foreign commerce) and to control the expansion of established operators into new and existing routes;
- control exit by virtue of operators requiring approval before cessation of service to a point or on a route;
- regulate fares on the basis of rate making provisions adopted from the Interstate Commerce Act;
- award direct subsidies to carriers;
- control mergers and inter-state agreements (providing the industry with immunization from the antitrust laws);
- investigate unfair methods of competition and trade practices; and
- exempt carriers from certain provisions of the Act.

Intra-state aviation and commuter operators (employing small, technically unsophisticated aircraft) which provide feeder services to the trunk haul routes were exempt from the rate and route controls of the CAB.

The motivation for the 1938 legislation was expressed mainly in terms of public interest arguments. It was passed at a time when memories of the Great Depression were still strong and, with them, the experiences of the excess capacity and cut-throat competition which characterized common carrier industries. The incumbent airlines were not averse to the idea of regulation, especially since the system was one of industry self-government (Altshuler and Teal, 1979). In general, the Act aimed at providing a stable, nationwide network of schedule services with the minimum of federal subsidy.

There were accepted existing operating patterns for mail services that followed broadly parallel routings with different operators providing a system of services rather than competing. This was seen as efficient and meeting the needs of the user and it was felt desirable to replicate for passenger services. This was especially so at the time because the low density of passenger traffic on most routes meant that they were essentially joint product, natural monopolies that could only be sustained by combining mail and passenger rights. Competition was seen as disruptive and controlled entry, with one carrier per route, desirable. In particular, competition was liable to erode profits earned on the more lucrative routes that were needed to supplement revenues in the thinner markets.

To meet the needs of small communities and to promote the development of the air service network, the CAB was given power to provide direct financial

---

[6]   The CAB was also initially given responsibility for the 'social regulation' of the industry and had authority over safety matters. The Federal Aviation Act of 1958 separated the social aspects of control from the economic and placed safety matters in the hands of the Federal Aviation Administration (FAA).

operating subsidies. The amounts given were initially modest, in part because of the subsidies from the US Post Office to mail services, but they rose after 1953 when the Post Office withdrew support for air mail subsidies (Eads, 1972).

Safety standards were also seen to be variable across carriers and, given the impossibility of travelers having the expertise to assess 'quality' in this respect, paternal regulation was felt necessary. Market entry controls and safety were also not seen as independent issues and as late as 1975 the CAB was arguing that, 'In the absence of countervailing measures, removal of entry and price controls would be likely to degrade safety. Any serious financial difficulties encountered would be conducive to a deterioration of safety' (US Civil Aeronautics Board, 1975).

5.2.2 The evidence on regulatory performance
The Civil Aeronautics Authority was created at a time when the US aviation industry was in its infancy and technology was far different to that today. Further, it could be argued that even then an appropriate system of contract bidding for routes would have provided a more efficient system for achieving the stated objectives than the controls initiated. Unfortunately, franchise bidding of a sort had been tried for mail contracts in the late 1920s with disastrous results[7] and this colored subsequent thinking.

There is a clear public interest rationale in giving the CAB powers to regulate fares but it is the old fashioned one of preventing monopoly exploitation of customers rather than any novel theory based on the uniqueness of the industry. Market entry controls cannot, however, easily be legitimized in this way. If fares are regulated then supply should automatically adjust and the most efficient airlines provide the services required. At the time the Federal Aviation Commission argued for certificates of public convenience and necessity on both safety grounds and because of the possibility of excessive competition (with hit-and-run entrants 'cream skimming') developing.[8]

The argument concerning excessive competition, has been attacked because, until comparatively recently, economists have found no theoretical reasons to suppose that cream skimming leads to serious problems of market instability. Work by Baumol *et al.* (1982) and others on sustainable monopolies, however, indicates that the US Congress may have been correct in acting to control market participation. If so the 1938 Act would seem to have been initiated in the public interest. This does not mean that the details of the legislation were appropriate or that its subsequent administration was in the public interest.

---

[7]   Mainly due to bid rigging in the Postmaster General's office. The bidding system adopted was also far from ideal (Levine, 1975). It is questionable whether, given the joint nature of passenger and mail services at the time, any form of franchise bidding purely for mail contracts would have resulted in anything better than efficient mail services coupled with monopoly priced passenger services (Panzar, 1980; 1983).

[8]   Safety arguments were refined when safety became an FAA concern after 1958.

Further, the external world changed and, even if the basis for the Act was sensible, reforms may subsequently have been justified.[9] One force leading to deregulation in the late 1970s was a build up of evidence that the regulatory system was no longer in the public interest. There were macroeconomic, as well as microeconomic, reasons for believing this. Further, technical changes had occurred since the 1930s and, certainly, the overall economic and political climate of the period was moving away from 'Big Government', but economic analysis of the activities of the CAB itself provided a specific basis for concern.

Whilst transport has not always attracted the detailed economic analysis reserved for many other markets, the regulatory performance of the CAB is one area where rigorous analysis was applied as early as the 1950s (Keyes, 1951).[10] These academic studies played a role both in bringing about change in the regulatory regime and in moulding the new legislative framework after 1978 (MacAvoy and Snow, 1977). The 'structure, conduct and performance industrial organization paradigm' provided the basis for early studies of aviation (Caves,

---

[9]   Critics have tended to move their academic analysis more in the direction of examining these latter features rather than the underlying rationale of the Act itself. For example, 'This modified [public interest] theory says that airline regulation was imposed by a Congress which, while attempting to act in the public interest, made a mistake' (Levine, 1981).

[10]   The following table offers a summary of some of the findings from these studies

Study	Data	Comparisons	Conclusions
Caves (1962)	CAB routes	Structure, conduct and performance	Problems with the industry's performance that required changes in the regulatory structure but did not oppose regulation
Levine (1965)	Intra-state and CAB routes	Fares	Regulation caused higher fares and resulted in lower load factors
Jordan (1970)	California and CAB routes in 1965	Fares	Regulation caused excess capacity, benefited aircraft manufacturers, labor unions and airline service suppliers
Keeler (1972)	California and CAB routes in 1968	Fares	Regulation created excess capacity that dissipated any profits from fares set at cartel level by the CAB
Douglas and Miller (1974)	CAB routes	Fares and flight frequency	Regulation resulted in high fares and sub-optimally high qualities of service
DeVany (1975)	California and CAB routes in 1968	Fares and flight frequency	Regulation protected the consumer with fares set close to output-maximizing levels
Keeler (1978)	California and CAB routes in 1974	Fares	CAB regulation led to excess charges amounting to $2.7 billion per annum

1962). Subsequent evaluation of the performance of the CAB was made possible because of the existence of some essentially unregulated markets (i.e., intrastate systems such as California, Texas and, to a lesser extent, Florida, and the commuter airlines). These provided the important benchmarks against which the implications of regulated fares and market entry could be gauged.

The methodology in many of these studies was to compare key variables (fares or profits) between regulated and unregulated services making suitable allowances for such factors as difference in route lengths and potential traffic densities. Some of the early studies employed fairly simple numerical and statistical procedures but the later ones adopted a more econometrically rigorous approach. The analytical economic model assumed varied considerably and ranged from fairly sophisticated models of cartel behavior to simple comparisons of data with no real underlying hypothesis concerning markets. The studies may be criticized because of their static nature and their avoidance of any consideration of the dynamic of market change over time although, given the circumstances and degree of agreement reached, such criticisms would seem rather pedantic.

The studies do not yield a consensus view although the vast majority of them indicated that CAB regulated services had, *ceteris paribus*, higher fares than their unregulated counterparts, although the operators themselves were not reaping higher levels of profit. Further, those studies which were initially less critical of the CAB have themselves subsequently been the subject of reassessment. Caves (1962), while accepting regulation was important, did point to weaknesses in the system and this feature of his work was a stimulus to later, more damning studies. By the mid 1970s there was a near consensus amongst economists that the regulated domestic aviation market was not, overall, serving the interest of customers (or potential customers). Who exactly was benefiting was less clear. Various theories of regulatory capture were advanced.

One approach would be to see the airlines as the capturers of the regulators.[11] Links between the regulators and the airlines must, however, be expected. The industry is a complex one and the airlines were responsible for providing technical and economic information to the CAB. The airlines were clearly not benefiting from this situation in terms of profitability; the rate of return earned in the industry was well below that of US industry in general. The CAB policy of 'cost plus' fare setting gave little scope for strict economic rent extraction and certainly, until the mid 1970s, on long haul markets the industry seldom earned what the CAB considered an appropriate return. Where the airlines did benefit was in the security of their operational environment, the CAB having stability as a primary

---

[11]   Indeed, a Senate Committee under the chairmanship of Paul Douglas had, in the early 1950s, adversely commented on the friendliness between the airlines and the CAB. Caves (1962) chronicles the history of presidential involvement in CAB activities and the indirect lobbying done through that office by the incumbent airlines.

objective. This cushioned management and allowed X-inefficiency to develop. Where competition did exist, Keeler (1972) and others argue, it was in the form of service competition leading to excess capacity. This would imply benefits to management in the form of status and personal remuneration.

Airlines cannot be viewed in isolation from industries that supply them with equipment and services or from the labor unions with whom they negotiate. In a regulatory environment based upon cost plus principles airline management had limited incentive to control its own costs. Depending on the data examined and the period covered, various stories can be narrated with each offering different interpretations of who gained from regulation at various times.[12] While one could argue that the distribution of the economic rent derived from regulation is now something of an academic matter and that the only really important thing is that, in aggregate, customers seen to have been the losers, this misses an important point. If the regulatory system had been captured then something must have happened to cause those in control to move towards deregulation from 1976.

One explanation for the change is that regulation is initiated and subsequently controlled by a 'winning coalition' of interests. The public interest theory simply becomes a special case, that of consumers dominating the winning coalition. If the interested parties are divided into groups such as leisure travelers, business travelers, incumbent airlines, potential new market entrants, aircraft manufactures, labor unions, public administrators, and environmentalists then a substantial number of potential coalitions emerge that, at various times, can form to pursue a common interest. Coalitions may change as different groups see their own particular interests can be best served in a different way or, indeed, their interests may themselves change with time.

In these ways the winning coalition of interests may capture the regulatory authorities and, for a time at least, direct policy in a self interested fashion. Panzar (1983) points to the importance of growing numbers of leisure travelers and of potential market entrants, together with dissatisfaction with the prevailing CAB policy on the part of some incumbent airlines in the late 1970s, in forming a powerful coalition favoring deregulation. Breyer (1982) extends this argument by examining how the objective of such a grouping may manifest itself in the form

---

[12]   Olsen and Traplain (1981) attempted to disentangle the elements involved to see if particular groups benefited at different periods. They took 70 domestic US city pair markets for 1971, 1976 and 1977 as 'snap shots' and tested the applicability of a profit maximizing and a sales maximizing hypothesis as the explanation for the fare structure that the CAB approved. They found that the pricing policies of the CAB have not served the interests of consumers. Estimates for the year 1971 suggest that the typical market had prices significantly above the profit maximizing level and the manufacturers of aircraft and suppliers of other inputs benefited. Prices fell, in the relative sense, after 1971 until 1977, when the markets appear to have obtained a profit maximizing solution and the distribution of benefits changed in favor of airlines.

of political power.

5.2.3   The move towards reform

The year 1974 represented something of a watershed in US regulatory history. President Ford, confronted with the new phenomena of 'stagflation' sought means of simultaneously reducing prices and stimulating economic activity.[13] Reduction of regulatory controls was seen as one way forward and a National Commission on Regulatory Reform was directed to look at ways in which federal regulations increased prices. At about the same time Senator Edward Kennedy initiated an investigation into federal regulatory bodies and the CAB was selected as the main agency for study (Breyer and Stein, 1981).[14]

The Department of Transportation in 1975, supported by the Justice Department, the Council of Economic Advisers and the Council on Wage and Price Stability, drafted a Congressional bill favoring greater air fare flexibility. The CAB simultaneously established a task force that came down in favor of deregulation with entry controls being phased out and substantial reductions in the CAB's power to regulate fares. It also began to authorize new entrants on some former monopoly routes and in 1976 relaxed restrictions on charter operations. Early in 1977, the CAB approved two innovative fare schemes (American Airlines' 'Supersaver Fare' and Texas International's 'Peanuts Fare') and had taken from it the power to control air freight activities except in Alaska and Hawaii. The movement forward in *de facto* reform in aviation accelerated towards the end of 1977 after the appointment of Alfred Kahn as Chairman of the CAB.[15] He now began moves to change the legal framework of control and, in the interim, worked within the existing system to open up the marketplace.

Even if one agrees with Levine (1987) that empirical academic studies played an important role in pointing to the shortcomings of regulation, it was a major development in theoretical economics that provided the intellectual underpinnings for the subsequent legal framework. The economic literature of the 1960s and 1970s tended to argue rather simplistically for the creation of more competition within the aviation industry. The difficulty was that neo-classical ideas of perfect

[13]   Politicians began moving towards liberalization in the early 1960s when the Department of Commerce, the Attorney General, the Council of Economic Advisers and the Office of Management and Budget all supported reform (Williams, 1993).

[14]   These hearings (US Congress, Senate: Committee on the Judiciary, 1975) pulled together studies on the effects of regulation and clarified many factual issues. The coverage for these hearings and the picture that emerged regarding the effects of regulation enhanced public support for change.

[15]   This was part of a wider policy of replacing administrators and former politicians on regulatory boards with economists and management scientists, with the aim of introducing more market orientation into their decision making (McCraw, 1984).

competition as a benchmark goal did not match an industry where many suppliers were not small and where many routes are most efficiently served by a single supplier or by a duopoly. The development of the theory of contestable markets provided the intellectual justification for the 1978 Act.[16]

The requirement of a contestable market is that entry and exit is totally free. There are no sunk costs to deter hit-and-run activities should an incumbent seek to raise prices above those required to earn normal profits. Contestable conditions arise not simply through the existence of classical perfect competition, which denies the existence of scale, density and multi product effects, but from the potential of competition. The features of a contestable market are seen in Table 5.1 and are set against the older notions of monopoly and perfect competition.

Table 5.1 Economic features of perfect competition, perfect contestability and pure monopoly

Characteristic	Perfect competition	Perfect contestability	Pure monopoly
Number of firms	Large	Whatever is efficient	One
Size of firms	Small	Whatever is efficient	Substantial
Barriers to entry/exit	None	None	Extensive
Product of firms	Homogeneous	May be diversified	Homogeneous
Profit levels	Normal	Normal	Monopoly rent
Managerial motivation	Profit maximization	Profit maximization	Normally profit maximization

Contestability offers guidance in ascertaining where intervention is justified and provides indications as to the appropriate action for regulatory bodies and legislators intent on improving economic welfare. Those concerned with the development of the theory felt that a deregulated domestic aviation industry would broadly conform to their model.[17] Ease of transferability of aircraft to different routes meant that there are negligible sunk costs involved in entering a market. Without fare and entry controls services would be provided where they were in

---

[16]   Bailey (1982); Bailey and Baumol (1984); Baumol (1982); Baumol and Willig (1986); Baumol *et al.* (1982, 1983); Panzar and Willig (1977) offer detailed outlines of the theory, McDonald (1987) is a more accessible account of the approach, and Spence (1983) and Schwartz (1986) provide rigorous critiques.

[17]   Baumol *et al.* (1982) stating that, 'it is highly plausible that air travel provides real examples of contestable markets'.

demand at the relevant minimum cost level and customers could not be exploited.

The importance of these ideas of market structure in determining the attitudes of the CAB is difficult to establish. They were only fully formalized at the end of the period of policy formulation although the general underlying approach had been understood somewhat earlier. Kahn (1988 a; 1988b) seems to have felt that there is need for actual competition to ensure fares are set equal to marginal costs and that resources are employed efficiently.[18] Despite this, CAB members, such as Bailey, and professional staff economists instrumental in developing the deregulatory program were fully cognizant of the work on contestability. As with many things in a practical world, it seems probable that it was the general thrust of the theoretical trend that was important even if the finer points of detail and the subtle nuances were passed over.

5.2.4   The 1978 legislation

De jure regulatory reform in US domestic aviation began in the freight transport sector but it is the 1978 Airline Deregulation Act that formed the centerpiece of the liberalization process. The name of the Act is a misnomer: regulation of safety and of antitrust matters still remained. It was economic regulation that was removed from scheduled passenger, inter-state aviation. Under the 1978 Act, signed by President Carter on 28 October 1978, the CAB was charged with relaxing and finally shedding controls over entry (1 January 1982), route competition, levels of service, pricing policies (1 January 1983) and exit. The Board itself would cease to operate from January 1985 (the 'Sunset Clause'). Questions involving international aviation and those concerning the social provision of air transport to small communities were to be handled by the Department of Transportation together with continuing responsibility for airline merger questions.

The staggered move to complete pricing and market entry and exit freedom was designed to minimize disruption. While it was appreciated that the eventual market equilibrium could never be accurately forecast after such a long period of federal regulation, the staggering of the liberalization process was seen as a mechanism permitting airlines to plan and, if necessary, revise their strategies as the situation evolved. By initially relaxing entry restrictions it was hoped to put less upward pressure on fares when greater fare flexibility became a reality. The CAB, in its market entry and fare setting policy, gradually relaxed its controls during the transition period. In terms of market entry the burden of proof shifted from potential entrants being required to justify the need for a service to opponents having to prove it to be against the public interest. Zones of reasonableness were

---

[18]   For example, 'The number of carriers in a market is the main factor in keeping prices down. If carriers in a city are reduced from two to one, I get worried. The possibilities that other carriers might come in is not sufficient protection for consumers', quote by Kahn (Labich, 1986).

set for fares during the transition (e.g., initially fares on trunk routes could rise by up to 10% and by up to 5% on a limited number of days of the year on thinner routes, or be reduced by up to 50% in relation to the CAB calculated fare level).

There was a fear that the changes could have potentially adverse effects for peripheral services on less profitable routes as resources would be transferred to those parts of the core network which were capable of earning higher returns. To ease the transition the Essential Air Service (EAS) Program was enacted to subsidize air services linking small towns with larger centers.[19]

5.2.5   The short-term impact

The immediate effects of the passing of the 1978 Act differed quite noticeably from those many had predicted and, also, differ very markedly from the longer-term effects which have been apparent since the mid 1980s. The divergence of the short-term impact from the longer term effects is to be expected, especially since the years immediately after 1978 were years of transition with the CAB gradually removing itself from a position of authority. The industry is also influenced by external factors. The US economy was in serious recession for much of the period following deregulation and this restrained demand. Demand for air transport services at this time was also affected in some markets by the continued regulation of other transport modes, e.g., inter-state bus services continued to be regulated until 1982 and were targeted by People Express when developing its cut price services (Button, 1987). There were also substantial rises in fuel prices between 1978 and 1981 (between November and March of these years the price of aviation fuel rose by about 240%). In 1981 there was the strike of the air traffic controllers that led to constraints on the efficient operation of the air traffic control system.

Under the service quality competition regime fostered by the CAB, airlines purchased many new wide-bodied jets. These were also suited to the non-stop services the licensing system favored. Some airlines, such as Braniff, took the view that there would be significant economies of scale in operating such fleets in a deregulated situation. The outcome was an initial bidding up of aircraft prices and book values. Subsequent experience showed this was a misguided view.[20]

---

[19]   The Transport Research Board in 1973 had estimated that by 1988 (when the system would be up for renewal) between 15% and 20% of the communities enjoying services under the EAS Program would have built up traffic levels that would cover the costs of operation. A further 30% would lose their air service but be within reasonable driving distance of a hub airport and the remaining 50% of communities would probably lose access to air services altogether.

[20]   The industry also tends to offer possibly illogical, and sometimes commercially fatal, romantic attractions to many people. Under the final years of full legal regulation airlines had also enjoyed record profits (net profits of $700 million and $1.2 billion in 1977 and 1978, respectively). The opening of the market led to a

The approaches adopted by the airlines varied. In some cases there was a belief that the non-stop style of operations which had grown up since 1938 would continue to dominate the market and that a more substantial presence in the marketplace, or a greater geographical spread of services, would result in higher revenue earning power. Trans World was the most important of these amongst the majors, although Braniff's expansion was the most pronounced. Others, for a variety of reasons but mainly stemming from a perception that their existing route pattern was sub-optimal, contracted their operations in the restructuring process.

New airlines only began to emerge on a large scale after 1981 and by September 1983 there were 22 new jet carriers providing scheduled interstate passenger services. Most of these were commuter operators but larger scale undertakings also emerged providing more specialized services.[21] In general, the new entrants offered lower fares, albeit to varying degrees, and this had knock-on effects on the incumbent carriers. The latter, to retain their market shares and, later, to expand their operations, were forced to adjust their operations and cost structures to meet the challenge of these more flexible newcomers.

In general all types of airport had more departures by 1979 with the 33 medium hubs (with 617–2500 thousand passengers enplaned annually) and the 24 larger airports (more than 2500 thousand enplanements) experiencing the biggest gains. This was a relatively short-term expansion, however, as the effects of the recession and higher fuel prices began to exert an influence. By mid-1981 about half the domestic aviation markets experienced reductions in frequencies with only the medium sized markets (the 51–200 band) recording marked expansions due to trunk and local service airlines moving into them (Table 5.2). The 142 markets losing services lost an average of five flights a day that was counteracted by an average increase of four flights a day in markets experiencing growth.

The pre-deregulation fears that small communities would suffer a serious diminution of service after reform were not borne out (Meyer and Oster, 1981). Those non hubs which had lost services tended to be more than compensated, in terms of flight frequencies, by commuter airlines moving in to replace the departing trunk and local service carriers. Table 5.3 shows that, while the capacity of the non-hub sector declined in terms of aircraft seats provided, the use of small and more suitable aircraft enabled more flights to be offered. Indeed, commuter routes in general expanded after 1978 as small companies moved into new markets and filled gaps left by jet operators exiting from routes. Between 1978 and 1980, the total growth in commuter routes served was 20.8% with about a fifth of this

number of entrepreneurs with no or limited experience in the aviation industry initiating airline operations. Many were subsequently sifted from the system.

[21]   Midway began offering a range of non-stop or one-stop business services from Chicago with fares which only slightly undercut the regulatory formula fares, while People Express and New York Air focused on cheap, no frills, basic services generally aimed at the non business traveler.

accounted for by replacement of large jet carriers (Oster and Strong, 1988).

Table 5.2 Service changes in selected markets

Market	More flights	Same number of flights	Fewer flights
1976–1981			
Top 50 markets	12(28%)	7(16%)	24(56%)
Markets 51-200	85 (61%)	10(7%)	44(32%)
Markets 201-500	66(44%)	10(7%)	74(49%)
1981–1984			
Top 50 markets	26(60%)	3 (7%)	14(33%)
Markets 51-200	43 (31%)	14(10%)	82 (59%)
Markets 201-500	108 (72%)	12 (8%)	30(20%)

Source: Meyer and Oster (1987).

Table 5.3 Changes in aircraft and seat departures, 1978-84

Airport size	Percentage change I June 1978 – 1 June 1984 in	
	Aircraft departures	Seat departures
Large hub	35	3
Medium hub	38	1
Small hub	19	9
Non hub	9	7
Total	28	9

Real terms fares fell during the period following deregulation although, given the fluctuating price of fuel and evolving route structure, it is difficult to make direct comparisons with the pre-1978 situation. Other problems emerge when trying to make comparisons. Firstly, fares had tended to fall anyway throughout the 1960s and early 1970s, primarily because technical advances in aircraft technology, and especially the adoption of jet aircraft, had considerably reduced operating costs. Most of this effect, however, had expired by the late 1970s.

Secondly, the increased use and variability of discount fares (some 60% of passengers were flying on some kind of discount fare by 1984) makes it difficult to know exactly which fares should be compared to which.

The initiation of discount services was particularly important in pulling down general fare levels when People Express entered the Newark Buffalo market in 1981 to compete with USAir which already was operating with a near 90% load factor. People's offered a $35 fare, which significantly undercut the $97 offer by USAir. The incumbent responded by matching the lower fare and significantly increasing the number of flights offered. Even so, People Express managed a load factor sufficient to enjoy a positive return on the service (Bailey, 1985).

An indication of the scale and depth of discounting that took place is seen in Table 5.4. Discounts, especially on the longer routes, existed before deregulation but they were limited in scale and qualification for them was restricted especially in the thinner markets. By 1981 substantial discounts were available, with conditions attached to such things as pre-booking periods and time of day travel, for all types of service. Linked with this was the emergence of fare structures more akin to the costs of service provision and fares reflecting the savings associated with traffic flows justifying larger aircraft on long routes (Table 5.5).

Table 5.4 Fare discounts pre and post deregulation

Market rank	Percentage of market with discount fares			Average discount fare as percentage of coach fare		
	1976	1981	1984	1976	1981	1984
Top 50	69	95	96	78	63	61
51-100	60	92	90	80	67	63
101-150	36	82	84	80	70	72
151-200	39	86	80	80	72	77
Smaller markets	30	81	72	80	74	76

Source: Meyer and Oster (1987).

The movement away from strict mileage based fares and the growth of widespread discounting make it difficult to estimate the exact level of average fare change which took place. The fact that there was already a general downward drift in fares accompanying the improvements in technology prior to deregulation serves to compound this problem. One way of looking at the issue is to examine the 'average yield' per passenger mile (or revenue per revenue passenger mile). The data reveal that average per passenger yield for trunk carriers fell appreciably after

1978 and at the very least continued the real fall seen in preceding years.[22]

Table 5.5 Airline fares as a percentage of the CAB formula (2nd quarter of 1983)

Market distance (miles)	Market size (passengers per day)			
	10–50	51–200	201–500	501–1000
1-400	114	112	95	71
401-1500	110	97	87	80
> 1500	*	75	65	60

*Too few markets to provide comparisons.
Source: Bailey (1986).

Fragmentary evidence suggests greater competition emerged in the years immediately after 1978. One way of gaining an overview is to assess the degree of rivalry for various markets that developed in the late 1970s. Comparisons of the degree of rivalry (both price and non price) on 123 large city pair markets for the periods 1974–1976 and 1978–1980 by Sandler (1988) reveal considerably more 'instability' after 1978 in all but the most concentrated markets. In other words, deregulation stimulated competitive forces.

The deregulation should also be viewed from a social perspective. One of the main reasons for the enactment of the 1938 legislation in the US was to improve aviation safety. A major concern of those opposed to the 1978 liberalization was that, despite the powers retained by the FAA, the competitive conditions created were liable to lead to much lower safety standards. The fear was that new entrants would not have the experience to operate a safe airline and that even the established operators would, if commercial pressures built up, eventually sacrifice safety considerations to cut costs.[23] Certainly, until 1978, because of improved aircraft design and traffic control systems, there had been a long term improvement in the accident record of the industry and the issue is really, therefore, whether this trend would be halted or even reversed after deregulation.[24]

---

[22]   This may well understate the post-1978 decline in yield because of the use of a consumer price index as the deflator because by 1979 the cost of aviation fuel was rising considerably faster than the general price index.

[23]   *Ex post* analysis of pre-deregulation aviation has cast serious doubt on the idea that airlines are more accident-prone as their profits fall (Golbe, 1986).

[24]   Miller (1975) provides a general discussion of safety.

Air safety poses serious measurement problems. Often different measures of safety (e.g., fatal accidents per million flights, fatal accidents per unit of capacity provided; or fatalities per unit of capacity provided) can be used to tell different stories. Short-term assessments are particularly difficult because air accidents are rare and even a single serious crash can often yield a false impression. (e.g., to say that deaths per billion passenger miles fell from 1.62 in 1979 to 0.019 in 1986 does not really tell us much). The situation is further complicated by the air traffic controllers' strike in 1981 and the subsequent dismissal of striking controllers. Nevertheless, in the five years after deregulation, when many new operators entered the market and the economic recession put a particular strain on the financial position of incumbents, the general downward trend in accident rates continued.

One particular concern was that many of the market entrants were commuter airlines using smaller aircraft, had limited navigation aids and operated from airfields with less sophisticated equipment. These airlines were small with limited financial reserves and potentially more prone to cyclical down turns in business. They also flew shorter routes making more take-offs and landings, the most dangerous phases of any flight. While these factors all point to potentially lower safety levels, some of the measures contained in the 1978 Act provided a basis for mitigating against the worst scenario. Additionally, the general safety standards applicable to operations were, following six years of study, revised by the FAA.[25]

The general downward trend in accidents continued after the initial deregulation phase. Comparing the accidents per 100 000 flight hours for the eight years pre-deregulation with the eight years from 1978, they fell by 54% and by 56% for fatal accidents in scheduled aviation and by 30% and 50% for all commercial aviation. Morrison and Winston (1988) also found that, after making allowances for such things as changes in aircraft type, and traffic control facilities there was a decline in the premiums asked by insurance companies for airframes and passenger liability after deregulation. There was a perceived reduction in actuarial risk.

Near misses, defined in the US as aircraft passing within 500ft of each other. are also sometimes seen as safety indicators. These rose from 231 in 1972 to 840 in 1985. A difficulty in assessing these data is that a near miss that is reported by air crew may not be recorded in the official statistics – the definition is only a guide line and passes at a greater distance may be recorded as near misses. The care exercised over the handling of the data also appears dependent on the state of current concern (McKenzie and Shughart, 1988). The method of reporting incidents also influences the count. Between 1968 and 1971 airlines were given immunity from liability if incidents were reported and 1 620 near misses a year were recorded. This immunity was removed in 1972 and the number of near misses fell to 231.

---

[25]   Detailed examination of the issues by Oster and Zorn (1983) indicates that the initial concerns were somewhat exaggerated and the deregulation had little influence on the safety record of carriers providing commuter services.

In 1985, the FAA changed the method of reporting again. Even with these difficulties, McKenzie and Shughart found that, between 1972 and 1986, near misses closely tracked the growth in passenger miles, suggesting that the incidents rate had remained roughly constant over the post deregulation phase.[26]

One reason for this generally improved safety record is that slightly more was now being spent by the airlines on aircraft maintenance although this is unlikely to be an altruistic gesture by the airlines. In the competitive environment that followed deregulation there was a commercial cost for an airline to be considered an unsafe carrier.[27]

5.2.6 Longer-term effects

In the slightly longer term, over a decade, the market moved on from what Frank Lorenzo, former chairman of Texas Air, called the 'new-airline phase, through the consolidation and cost-cutting phase', and into the 'megaline phase', the most noticeable feature of which was the expansion of the industry as a whole. Passenger enplanements in the US in 1987 were up by over 55% compared to 1978 and by 88% compared to 1976 and employment in the industry in 1987 was around 450 000 compared to 340 000 in 1978. Scheduled revenue passenger miles in 1987 were 62% higher than in 1978 and available seat miles nearly 65% higher. There was domination of virtually all the major airports by a single carrier or a duopoly and there were many of mergers and take-overs of airlines.

This does not mean that all the short-term trends evaporated. Fares remained lower in real terms than under regulation (Table 5.6). This, to a large degree, was due to even more discounting (90% of travelers were estimated by the Air Transport Association to be flying on discounted tickets in 1986, with the average discount being 61%). In addition, the consolidation in the industry, in terms of mergers and the advent of a hub and spoke operational strategy, coupled with tighter management practices, helped to bring airline costs down (see Chapter 3).[28]

Revealed preference shows that many airlines benefited from hubbing but others also gained. Passengers benefited from lower fares and increased frequency of service (destinations may be reached via a range of possible hubs on flights that leave at different times as well as by direct routings). Travelers also prefer single-carrier services when it is necessary to change planes because this reduces

---

[26]   The one exception was the period of the air traffic controllers' strike and the subsequent dismissals when near misses fell substantially below the growth in traffic due, possibly, to the increased difficulties of reporting incidents.

[27]   Chapter 13 goes into detail about safety considerations on an airline network.

[28]   Control of airport gates became important for carriers and where these changed hands this was often for large sums of money. In 1986, for example, Pan Am paid Texas Air $65 million for three gates at Logan International Airport (Boston) and La Guardia (New York) and 64 landing slots at La Guardia and National Airport (Washington).

uncertainty and other transactions costs (Carlton *et al.*, 1980). Not all the effects, however, are positive. Passengers incur time cost because hubbed flights involving an indirect routing take longer. A trade-off must therefore be made in assessing the overall effects of hubbing on the traveler. Estimates of 769 aviation markets by Morrison and Winston (1986) indicated that the net benefits of deregulation, at 1977 prices, amounted to about $6 billion per annum (or around $11 billion in 1987 prices).[29]

Table 5.6 Real costs of air travel between various forms of hub

Market type	Real price (cents per mile)	
	1979	1985
Large hub-large hub	4.4	3.6
Large hub-medium hub	4.7	4.0
Large hub-small hub	4.9	4.1
Large hub-non-hub	5.3	4.6
Medium hub medium hub	4.9	4.1
Medium hub-small hub	5.1	4.4
Medium hub-non-hub	5.5	5.1
Small hub-small hub	5.4	4.8
Small hub-non-hub	5.7	5.3
Non-hub-non-hub	6.2	5.8

Real price is total real revenues divided by total revenue passenger miles flown.
Source: Rastatter and Stein (1988).

Pre-deregulation, the restrictive policy of the CAB meant that in 1972 there were only 36 US domestic and international carriers with four additional airlines entering the market in 1978. After the enactment of the Airline Deregulation Act the number rose rapidly and by 1987 there were 78 airlines. As Table 5.7 shows, this simple statistic hides a complex, dynamic situation in which there were many firms entering the industry but subsequently leaving (13 certified carriers and 24 commuter airlines ceased operation or went bankrupt in 1984) or becoming a component in a merger.[30] After forty years of regulation and then a decade of fluctuating market conditions following liberalization some volatility in supply could have been anticipated. Equally, with the removal of quantitative entry

[29]   Later work indicated that these benefits would, in 1977 prices, have been $2.5 billion higher if the deregulated market had proved to be perfectly contestable (Morrison and Winston, 1987).
[30]   If 1985 had been taken instead of 1987 then there were 106 active carriers.

controls and the expansion of the industry that resulted (from 114 billion passenger miles in 1972 to 366 billion in 1986) more carriers were needed to ensure efficiency in the market.

The extent of market consolidation can be judged by the fact that between 1938 and 1978 the CAB had permitted 15 trunk and local service carriers to merge while in the two and a half years after May 1985, there were 24 acquisitions or mergers. The mergers reflected a wider change in US antitrust policy (Harris and Sullivan, 1986). With the demise of the CAB, responsibility for merger control was passed over to the Department of Transportation until at least January 1989. Its position tended to be relatively adaptable to short-term government attitudes, unlike the Justice Department that tended to take a more consistent longer-term approach. The latter was over-ruled when expressing concern over some specific mergers (e.g., Northwest with Republic and TWA with Ozark).

Table 5.7 Entrants to and leavers from the scheduled aviation market, 1978–87

	Number of US scheduled airlines
Certificated prior to 1978	36
Certificated 1978–July 1987	210
Total	246
Merged, liquidated, decertificated or not operating under certificate	168
Total operating July 1987	78

Source: James (1988).

There were criticisms of the way the Department approved airline mergers outside of the domestic market but nevertheless influential upon it. In particular, Fisher (1987) pointed to the excessive market power conferred upon United Air Lines when it was permitted to purchase Pan American's Pacific Division for $750 million in 1985. He argued that the aim of developing a powerful US international presence in a market experiencing rapid entry by foreign carriers could have been achieved by actions less restrictive on competition between US airlines. Germane to domestic US aviation, the merger caused Northwest to acquire Republic Airlines in order to strengthen its feeder services to international hubs rather than American, which may have been a more logical choice in other circumstances.

In addition to mergers of larger carriers, many of the smaller commuter airlines combined with trunk operations to offer coordinated services at key hubs, usually with common code numbers. In 1983 there were only nine agreements between the major carriers and commuter airlines to provide feeder services with a common identification, but this had risen to 19 by 1985, to 50 by mid-1986 and to 65 by January 1987. To ensure financial stability in the commuter airline industry, and thus guarantee their feeder services, the majors then increasingly bought up the small operators rather than simply reaching operational accords.

There were often sound economic reasons behind mergers and consolidation involving scale effects, complementarity, product development and the rational deployment of assets from an ailing concern. Equally, consolidation by merger or acquisition was used to cream economic rent from consumers by virtue of the creation of quasi-monopoly powers. If a market is perfectly contestable then there is no need to worry about mergers because the fear of potential competition from new carriers coming into the market ensures incumbents, whatever their industrial configuration, cannot exploit travelers. The empirical evidence, however, suggests that the aviation market is not perfectly contestable.

Morrison and Winston (1986) found that an actual competitor was three times more powerful in influencing the behavior of an incumbent than a potential competitor (although the latter was, in welfare terms, preferable to a market regulated *à la* CAB). Moore (1986) found that coach class fares were markedly lower in markets served by five or more carriers than those with fewer. Again, Bailey *et al.* (1985) found in the fares airlines charge a sensitivity to the income levels of travelers and also that incumbent suppliers moved fares down to meet competition only when a rival actually entered the market. The typical monopoly market was found to have fares 6% higher than one with two equal sized competitors and 11 % higher than markets with four equal sized competitors.

Retrospective analysis provided arguments to support these findings in the context of hub and spoke operations. There are sunk costs involved in entering a particular market (Levine, 1987) because an airline must commit non-recoverable resources to advertising and marketing outlays, aircraft time for a trial period and basic administrative services. An incumbent, especially one enjoying economies from hub and spoke operations, is likely in the short term to dissipate any economic rent being earned by matching fares offered by a new entrant. The reputation of the incumbent, though, means it can attract more traffic at any fare level than a rival. Knowing this, it is unlikely entry will take place on a piece–meal basis and some rent can be enjoyed by the incumbent. An exception is where several established, reputable airlines share a hub and one could, if excessive profits were being enjoyed by another airline, threaten to compete on some routes. Other cases would be instances where the new entrant hubs at the other end of a service. Mergers may, therefore, limit the contestability effects of the deregulation.

Concern over the consolidation effects of deregulation can be understood by considering Table 5.8. The period after deregulation saw a decline in the market share of the largest carriers (whether measured in terms of four- or eight-carrier concentration ratios) but by the late 1980s this trend had been reversed. The market had become dominated by a small number of large carriers each with its structure of hubs. This concentration was seen as offering considerable potential for consumer exploitation.

Those supporting deregulation took a somewhat different position. If the scheduled airline industry is characterized by substantial economies of scale (stemming from sheer size of operations), economies of density (from intensive utilization of capacity) and economies of scope (from operating a diverse range of services), then one would logically expect the market to be dominated by a small number of large network operators together with some specialist carriers. The point is not how many airlines serve the market but rather the degree and nature of competition which exists between them.

Table 5.8 Concentration ratios (% of domestic revenue passenger miles)

12 Months ending 30 September	Top four carriers	Top eight carriers
1977	56-8	81-7
1979	56-6	80.7
1981	54-2	74-5
1983	54.8	74-5
1985	51-7	70.7
1986	65.5	88-7

Source: *Air Carrier Traffic Statistics* (various issues).

There was evidence that more choice emerged for customers as the large carriers compete for business in a way not possible under CAB route allocation procedures (Table 5.9). There was a reduction in the number of routes served by only one carrier and a significant increase in the number served by two or more operators. Even where there was a choice before, new entrants offered further alternatives.

This latter effect is reinforced by the events that just preceded or followed the main mergers (Jordan, 1987). The commercial rationale for merger is to strengthen market power and enhance the prospects of long-term profits. This means, in general, there must be gains in terms of additional revenues from better integrated services and/or unit cost savings. It is the cost savings effect that is of most importance because if unit costs cannot be reduced down to the level of the non-merged airlines then losses will ensue. The tendency is for service points to be dropped by newly merged airlines (a situation which sometimes precedes the official linking) and these are then taken up by smaller, specialist carriers.

Table 5.9 Number of scheduled carriers serving each market

Number of carriers	Number of markets February 1978	February 1987
1	3 839	3 458
2	802	1 027
3	205	419
4	66	191
5	26	87
6	13	52
7	7	27
8	4	14
9	1	8
10 or more	2	9
Total	4 965	5 292

Source: *Official Airline Guide* (February 1978 and February 1987).

Complacency may prove inappropriate. While Table 5.9 gives an aggregate picture, there were some areas where a single carrier had rather more market power than the broad picture suggested. Northwest, for example, controlled around 80% of the capacity at the Twin-Cities of Minneapolis-St. Paul and had a virtual monopoly of traffic in that area of the Midwest. Other hubbing arrangements posed fewer problems. There were also issues concerning the nature of competition between the megalines especially in terms of computerized reservation systems and various forms of loyalty payment.

Airline costs were not only being reduced by changes in operating practices, there were major savings made in labor costs (Table 5.10).[31] The effects of this differed according to the perspective taken.[32] The situation with regard to labor conditions and remuneration fluctuated after 1978 and differed between carriers. The new entrants after 1978 had none of the encumbering labor agreements that

[31] The period immediately after 1978 often saw employees accepting straight pay cuts (workers at Braniff and Continental took a 10% cut and in 1983 those at Republic took a 15% reduction). Pilots at Western accepted a pay freeze. The ease with which such agreements were reached depended as much on the actual unions involved as on the specifics of the financial position of the airline (Lieb and Molloy, n.d.).

[32] Kahn's (1988c) view was that, 'Labor unrest and the insecurity and downward pressure on the wages of the pre-existing labor force have been an undeniable cost of deregulation. From the standpoint of the public, however, grossly monopolistic wage levels are no more acceptable than monopoly profits.'

established carriers had settled upon in the days when cost increases could be passed on to passengers. One example was New York Air which in 1981 paid pilots $30 000 per annum for flying 75 hours a month compared to the older carriers who were paying $62 000 for 55 hours of flying. The labor cost difference extended to all types of personnel (Blumestock and Thochick, 1986).

Table 5.10 Labor costs of the major US airlines, 1978–85

Airline	Annual labor expense per employee ($)		Percentage change in constant $
	1978	1985	
American	25 968	42 777	-0-3
Continental	24 168	23 205	-41-0
Delta	26 168	46 862	8-3
Eastern	26 190	41 888	-3-2
Northwest	26 301	42 617	-2-0
Pan Am	27 788	38 885‡	-15-3
Piedmont	24 676	34 341‡	-15-8
Republic†	25 274	35 093	-16-0
TWA	26 088	46 106	6-9
United	26 189	42 792‡	-1.1
US Air	25 956	44 949	4-7
Western	28 211	36 316	-22-1
Average	26 225	42 855	-1.1

† Includes North Central, Air West and Southern Airlines in 1978.
‡1984 used because of strikes at Pan Am and United and unavailability of Piedmont data.
Source: Lieb and Molloy (n.d.).

The incumbent suppliers were forced to react. In the early years of deregulation the deflationary effects of the oil price rise, followed by the air traffic controllers' strike, had forced some labor shedding (about 60 000 jobs by 1983) but unit-cost savings were required. This came about through new pay structures and the adoption of more efficient working practices. In many instances these were achieved only after serious labor disputes (e.g., TWA in 1986). In others, application of Chapter 11 bankruptcy laws was adopted to end established union positions. The 1978 Act contained an Employee Protection Program but its implementation was slow and no financial benefits were awarded.[33]

[33]   An unconstitutional clause ruled it invalid in 1984 (McMullen, 1986).

After 1984, when demand for air travel began to rise and competition between carriers intensified, wage bills were often cut by the initiation of two-tier wage structures. Employees joining after a certain date (or, in some cases, coming from an acquired airline) were on a lower pay scale. American Airlines initiated this practice in 1982 when new workers were started on wages 20% to 40% lower than incumbent employees. Republic adopted a similar type of structure in 1983, Northwestern, Western and United followed in 1984, Pan Am and US Air in 1985, and Eastern Delta and TWA in 1986. In most of the latter cases the scales were to be merged after a predetermined period. In some instances, employees negotiated stock options (e.g., Eastern, Republic and Western) or labor representation on company boards (e.g., Pan Am) for accepting such conditions.

These wage agreements helped to reduce the marginal cost of labor and had the advantage that wage bills actually declined over time as older employees left or retired. Part-time labor was also employed to maximize the flexibility of labor use. Agreement with the unions at American Airlines, for example, allowed 12.5% part-time labor from the Transport Workers Union while, from 1985, Pan Am had an agreement to use up to 15% part-time members of the same union. In total, part-time employment rose from 2% in 1978 to 9% in 1985.[34]

The airline companies after 1978 experienced mixed financial fortunes. Critics of deregulation in the early years pointed to very poor profits earned (operating losses of $0.2, $0.5 and $0.7 billion for 1980, 1981 and 1982, respectively) as indicative of unsustainable markets and possible longer term negative implications for safety. There were also some spectacular bankruptcies, most noticeably that of Braniff. In fact, these types of result did not continue beyond the transitional phase and the period of US recession and by 1984 operating profits for the industry were $2.2 billion with $1.4 billion and $1.3 billion in the following two years.

Operating profits, however, may not be the most important financial indicator. Despite early strength, with the real value of the ten trunk airlines' share remaining constant from 1976 to 1983 while the real value of all shares on the New York Stock Exchange fell 3%, there was a subsequent sharp decline in the return on equity in the industry. This partly reflected a higher debt/equity ratio. From the economic perspective it is not altogether clear that this was a problem since it did not deter investment (Kahn, 1988a).

Another way of looking at the financial performance of the industry is to consider, over relatively long periods, returns on annual total invested capital (i.e. interest on debt plus net profit after tax). Table 5.11 indicates that deregulation had little effect on this return and that the volatility of the return (as measured by its

---

[34]   Work rules were also changed. United Airlines imitated new entrants by adopting two-man flight crews for the Boeing 737, 757 and 767 aircraft, decreased away-from-home guarantees, extended flying hours, and eliminated duty rigs. The crew remaining after rationalization obtained better pay.

standard deviation) actually declined. But even on these figures the return in the industry was substantially below that of US industry in general (which was about 13.0% per annum for 1979–86). As with the return on equity, however, this does not seem to have resulted in a shortage of investment. Higher rates of return enjoyed by the more efficient operators pulling in funds may partly explain this, but the industry did seem to retain an unfathomable charisma of its own.

There were differences in the performance of different segments of the industry. Trunk airlines' profits pursued a 'U'–shaped path, with a dip after 1978, mainly due to the severe recession in the US and higher fuel prices, being followed by an up-turn as the economy picked up after 1983. The mean level of profits for local carriers was more consistent and remained positive. Bailey and Williams (1988) argued that local carriers enjoyed monopoly control of thin routes within a geographical market and around a local hub airport. They had local advantages and the trunk carriers were not, at least in the early 1980s, interested in trying to counter. At the outset, the locals, because of the nature of their pre-deregulation operations, also enjoyed the advantage of aircraft fleets suited to hub-and-spoke operations (e.g., Republic's fleet averaged 89.6 seats per plane, Piedmont's 85.8, and Frontier's 81.6; compared to United Air Lines' 157.0, Trans World's 160.4 and Delta Airlines' 151.4).

Table 5.11 Rate of return on annual total invested capital in US airlines

Period	Mean	Standard deviation
1965-1970	6.3	3.5
1970-1977	5.3	3.1
1978-1986	7.2	3.1
1979-1986	6.4	2.4

Source: Kahn (1988a).

Deregulation also impacted on aircraft manufacturers. The early years of deregulation saw airframe manufacturers suffering alongside the airlines from the international recession. Boeing, and others, introduced new leasing arrangements and initiated buy-back policies whereupon they would buy in older planes to help airlines finance the purchase of new ones. Things then changed. Setting aside external events, the aviation industry expanded, the type of aircraft required for hub-and-spoke operations is somewhat different to the wide bodies formerly used on non-stop routings, new labor agreements logically led to the use of more technically advanced aircraft and interest levels fell, stimulating new investment.[35]

5.2.7 Problems with the deregulated US market

It is difficult to think of any change in policy that has benefited all (i.e., a Pareto improvement). Inevitably there are costs that have to be borne somewhere in the system. The issue is whether the burden of costs outweighs the benefits generated. Further, there is a natural tendency when confronted by freer market conditions, especially those moving in the direction of contestability, for incumbent suppliers to try to protect themselves by developing strategies limiting the degree of competition confronting them. Several potential difficulties, such as domination of hubs, have been touched upon; here consideration is on some other issues.

Competition resulted in airlines becoming more concerned with the marketing of their products but it had become apparent by the late 1980s that many of the airlines had been overoptimistic in their claims about the services they could offer. The incidence of late flights and cancellations rose markedly. In 1987, 34 in every 1 000 flights were delayed by at least 15 minutes and in 1987 42% of consumer complaints involved delays or cancellations (compared to 21% between 1971 and 1976). Absolute numbers of consumer complaints fluctuate considerably, often depending on the amount of media attention on the subject (Rastatter and Stein, 1988), but there were indications that, after a period of reduced consumer concern from 1978, complaints about service quality rose.

Many of the delays are concentrated at eight congested airports and stemmed from airlines attempting to offer services all scheduled at peak times. The problem was reduced somewhat in the autumn of 1987 with only 20-30% of flights being 15 or more minutes late. Complaints consequently fell by about a half. The improvement came about through scheduling changes partly stimulated by informal prodding by the Department of Transportation. It was also stimulated by a new requirement that the 14 largest airlines must show on the computers used for seat booking the degree to which they failed to meet published timetables.

While this type of action helped resolve short-term difficulties, there remained the problem that, while the deregulation of airlines stimulated economic fare-setting strategies, pricing of airport services was economically primitive (Creager, 1983). Airport landing fees were generally set to recover operating costs and ignored the costs of airport buildings (which to a large extent were borne by

---

[35]   The outcome was that demand for aircraft grew. In December 1979 there were 160 jet aircraft delivered, worth (with ground equipment and spare parts) $3.2 billion, this fell to 117 ($2.9 billion) by 1982 but rose to 205 ($7.5 billion) by 1987. Perhaps more important for an industry that takes a very long-term view was the rise in the number of orders and options for aircraft from 693 ($22.1 billion) in 1979, through 855 ($33.3 billion) in 1985 to 1064 ($42.8 billion) by September 1987.

airlines leasing facilities from airport authorities) and the external costs landings impose on others, such as delays, noise and safety hazards.[36]

The FAA was responsibility for regulating landing fees and had the power to withhold federal construction subsidies if its policies were not pursued. Airports must be available for public use on fair and reasonable terms and without discrimination with fees kept at 'reasonable' levels. New landing slots were traditionally allocated at committee meetings involving the various interested airlines and the airport authorities, while grandfather rights prevailed for existing slots. At four very heavily congested airports (John F. Kennedy International and La Guardia in New York, O'Hare International in Chicago and Washington National Airport) the CAB had formed scheduling committees in the late 1960s whereby airlines agreed amongst themselves on slot allocations. Slots could not, until 1986 (except for a short period in 1983), be bought or sold although airlines could barter amongst themselves.

Strict pricing solutions to slot allocation were initially rejected, because the schemes proposed (Grether *et al.,* 1979) only took into account runway congestion and peak-load costs and this would favor larger aircraft and long distance services. Passengers using these types of service would be willing, through their fares, to bid the highest amount for a slot (there are more of them on large planes over which to spread the cost and on long flights landing costs are a small part of the total cost). This would alter the nature of many airports, and in a politically unacceptable way. This type of approach also ignored other social costs (e.g., noise and land-side congestion) that may favor the use of smaller, quieter aircraft.

Incumbent control of landing slots and gates pushes up the costs of market entry and, because of the network implications of efficient hub-and-spoke configurations, may affect the financial viability of other services (Levine, 1987). The extent of such distortions are difficult to assess but the existence of quasi-monopoly structures seems likely to have reduced overall efficiency and resulted in some economic rents being extracted from air travelers.

Empirical work has highlighted the importance of economies of density and scope in airline operations (Chapters 2 and 3). To reap maximum benefits from these economies it is not only important to hub operations but also to draw and retain passengers from diverse markets. From the mid-1980s most major US airlines employed two powerful tools to achieve this – the use of loyalty payments (in the form of bonus flights under 'frequent flyer programs') and of computerized reservation systems (CRSs).

Frequent flyer programs were initiated by American Airlines in 1980 as a marketing device. The attraction of these programs for business travelers, who do not normally pay for their tickets, is that they can accumulate 'points' that are not

---

[36]   Where an airline dominates a hub many of the problems of delays are internalized within the airline's own cost structure.

taxable returns but enable them to enjoy 'free' leisure travel. Such loyalty payments were a manifestation of the airlines' efforts to reduce actual and potential competition. They effectively tied passengers to a specific carrier irrespective of that carrier's efficiency. Overall it can lead to excessive aggregate air travel. Someone who has accumulated 100 000 miles of travel with a particular airline offering a frequent flyer program is unlikely to switch to another carrier for his/her next flight even if there is a shorter or more convenient routing. Equally, the marginal benefit from an additional flight to gain the few extra miles needed to reach a key threshold mileage can easily outweigh the time and additional costs of making such a trip irrespective of whether the journey serves any other real purpose.

The longer-term impact of these programs may be financially detrimental to the airlines and other, non-participating travelers. The costs of the free flights may eventually have to be paid, and in 1988 the outstanding retail value of the flights owed amounted to about $1 billion.[37] Of course, some of the costs will be offset by the efficiency gains that airlines reap from the economies of density and scope associated with additional travel but these are relatively small. The problem is compounded by the beggar-my-neighbor attitude that can divert traffic between carriers rather than generate a substantial amount of new traffic.

Computerization of seat reservations was initially developed to reduce paperwork but also enabled airlines to enjoy greater flexibility in fare setting and offers greater scope for tailoring services to the specific needs of customers. CRSs in the US, with the exception of the MARS-plus system, were developed by the airlines and several of the larger systems (especially American Airlines' SABRE and United Air Lines' APPOLO systems that between them had 67% of the market in 1987) were rented out by their parent company to other carriers. The importance of a good CRS can be illustrated by the fact that the main reason Texas Air acquired Eastern Airlines in 1986 was because of the latter's SYSTEMONE reservation system.

CRSs, especially combined with the use of loyal payments to travel agents, can serve to manipulate information available to potential travelers and result in favorable bookings for the controller of the system used. Before 1979 travel agents were not allowed to rebate the fixed commissions received from airlines to their customers, the intention being that travel agents could not be a weapon in the competition between airlines. The incumbent travel agents benefited because the CAB effectively allowed their trade association to decide upon accreditation. The travel agency market was deregulated in 1979 by removing rules requiring airlines and travel agents to deal with each other, by allowing rebates to be given to customers, and by the removal of antitrust immunity (Meyer and Oster, 1987).

---

[37]   Although many people never use their miles and several airlines now have expiration dates incorporated in their programs.

The impact of the deregulation was that travel agents became dealers in information, a point of importance as CRSs have become more widely used (Levine, 1987). Travel agents provided a service in linking airlines offering a wide range of diverse products to potential but generally uninformed, travelers. The result was that the number of travel agents rose from 13 000 in 1977 to over 27 000 by 1986 with the aggregate commissions paid them by the airlines going up from $527 million in 1977 to $3.34 billion over the period. The commission costs paid to agents by the major airlines rose from 4.4% of their operating expense in 1976 to 8.7% by 1986.

This change was paralleled by the adoption of CRSs – in 1979 only about 15% of agents were computerized but by 1983 this had risen to 82% and by 1988 over 95% of travel agencies were automated. In 1986 some $21.6 billion of domestic US air travel was booked through 24 693 agents using CRSs (US Department of Transportation, 1988). Initially, a direct link to an airline's CRS was through its own ticket office. Then, following United Air Line's example, the airlines allowed travel agents to subscribe to their systems.

The problem confronting policy makers was of ensuring that the customer received the most appropriate information from the agent. Fears existed that the information displayed on CRSs favored the host airline – some 80% of bookings were taken from the first page of information.[38] In addition, there were concerns about halo effects when an agent is induced to book more flights on a CRS-owning carrier's flights because of the airlines' maintenance of supportive business relations with its CRS subscribers.[39]

In 1984 in one of its last acts, the CAB set out rules, to be administered by the Department of Transportation, that attempted to remove bias from the primary

---

[38]   United Air Lines and American Airlines defended themselves against charges of exploitation before antitrust hearings on the grounds that a degree of bias was necessary for them to be able to recover their full CRS development costs and to permit travel agents' use of the systems at a reasonable cost. They claimed that the respective annual internal rates of return on their APPOLO and SABRE systems were about 5% (1975–87) and 18.8% (1976 projected to 1990), which was commensurate with the development costs and commercial risk involved (US Department of Transportation, 1988). Subsequent evaluation by the US General Accounting Office (1986) indicated these figures to be on the low side, but it could not develop better estimates.

[39]   The halo effect seems to have been substantial and was unaffected by the 1984 rules. The CRS vendors estimated that in 1986 the halo effect ranged from 15% of airline passenger revenue for SABRE to 9.1% for SYSTEMONE. Subsequent analysis by the US Department of Transportation (1988) yielded higher figures with the halo effect in 1984 ranging from 39.9% for SABRE to 12.1% for SYSTEMONE.

display of data.[40] Despite these measures the system still offered scope for airlines to gain advantages not associated with market efficiencies. By tying in with commuter airlines a major airline could still pull more traffic onto its trunk services.[41] In other cases, when services are ranked by travel time, there were cases where advertised flight times were significantly lower than recorded times and some carriers advertised very low fares to gain priority listing but only offered one seat a month at that fare.

The airlines owning a CRS had the further advantage that they could collected detailed information on travel agents and competing airlines that subscribe to their system. This enabled host carriers to make rapid and sensitive adjustments in changing circumstances and permitted almost instantaneous responses to market initiatives of rivals. In terms of contestability theory, it meant that not all airlines participating in or entering the market had access to the same technology.

Despite these problems, those who conducted detailed econometric analysis of the events after 1978 seem to find that the aviation industry in the US and its users benefited from reform. The conclusion is not quite unanimous (Brenner *et al.*, 1985 and Ruppenthal, 1987) and comparisons between what advocates of deregulation promised and what materialized indicate some divergence (Kyle and Phillips, 1985). There were concerns over the distributional consequences of the change and the longer-term dangers of an excessive concentration of market power. Nevertheless, US society seems to have enjoyed a net improvement in its welfare.

The empirical work of Moore (1986) and Morrison and Winston (1987) amongst others, however, showed that the deregulated aviation market in the US was not strictly purely contestability. This is consistent with the detailed, eco-legal analysis of Levine (1987) who argued that some of the benefits of deregulation 'have come about in spite of impediments to contestability brought about by customer preferences for market practices and product features that incidently inhibit competition'.[42]

---

[40]   For example, services listed by level of fare or travel time rather than by carrier. Subsequent moves by Congress resulted in further changes with the removal of bias from secondary screens.

[41]   This was another reason for arrangements between commuter carriers and major airlines.

[42]   Some of the strongest initial advocates of deregulation expressed subsequent reservations about the degree to which the 1978 Act created a genuinely contestable environment. For example, 'We now believe that transportation by trucks, barges and even buses may be more contestable than passenger air transportation ... trucks and buses do not face the heavy sunk costs involved in the construction of airports or the shortage of gates and landing slots at busy airports such as that which prevented People Express from acquiring even a single gate of its own at Denver's Stapleton International Airport, so it was forced instead to lease gates from other carriers, catch as catch can, during a year of flying to that airport'. (Baumol and Willig, 1986).

5.2.8 Wider lessons to be learned

The experiences of one country cannot be directly transferred to others. There are inevitably different institutional arrangements in each country which range from the degree of market organization (e.g., in terms of labor unionization and institutional financial arrangements) to the general involvement of government in the coordination of industry (e.g., in terms of controlling air space, and providing airports). Equally, in terms of basic market characteristics, demand varies considerably between countries. Nevertheless, the experiences of the US was used in debates surrounding the deregulation of aviation in Europe and the liberalization of international aviation more generally (Sawers, 1987; Button, 1997c).

The immediate effect of deregulation was that US carriers expanded their international activities. An indication of this trend is seen in Table 5.12 that sets out details of foreign gateways that were served non-stop by formerly predominantly domestic carriers in 1986 compared to their pre-deregulation numbers. This expansion was in part because of the higher relative efficiency of the US industry after 1978. A liberalization of bilateral agreements (Doganis, 1985; Gomez-Ibanez and Morgan, 1984; 1987), provided the institutional framework within which such developments could occur.[43] Equally important was the stimulus provided for domestic carriers to exploit economies of scope on an international basis. A logical extension of internal network development was for carriers to draw international traffic to their respective hubs to push greater passenger flows through their domestic networks.[44]

The implications of these trends for non-US carriers serving the US market were serious in the short term. As discussed later, European carriers operated in a more regulated environment where the possibilities of reaping economies of scope through extensive hubbing were much more limited (McGowan and Trengrove, 1986; Wheatcroft and Lipman, 1986). Attempts to circumvent this difficulty by mergers (to extend the range of services offered rather than for reasons of enhancing pure scale) and by linking in with US carriers to provide online connecting/feeder flights in America were rapidly pursued.

The period after deregulation saw an upturn in the relative international economic performance of US airlines. Passenger costs per available seat kilometer in 1983, for instance, were, according to IATA data, between 57% and 67% higher for cross-border, intra-ECAC flights than for US domestic flights. There are limitations in looking at these crude data. Average flights were shorter within

---

Despite these reservations they conclude that overall, 'in terms of the airline case we can infer that market forces through the pressures of competition, both actual and potential, have done a commendable if imperfect job in protecting consumer interest'.

[43]   From 1979 the US began liberalizing its bilateral air service agreements under its 'Open Skies' policy.

[44]   This is dealt with in more detail in Chapter 6.

limitations in looking at these crude data. Average flights were shorter within Europe, pushing up landing and take-off costs in the overall calculus. To allow for this, and for variations in the relative sizes of different market types, Sawers (1987) compared the costs of local European services with those of the US carriers Piedmont (which concentrated on business travel) and Southwest (concentrating on leisure travel) that offered services of similar length. In 1983 European carriers had costs per available seat mile of $0.142 compared with Piedmont's $0.090 and Southwest's $0.065. This type of analysis, however, is static and says little about the effects of deregulation.

Table 5.12 Foreign gateways served by selected US carriers

Carrier	1978	1986	Hubs
Delta	1	5	5
American	0	8	6
United	0	14	5
Texas Air	3	21	7
Total	4	48	23

Source: James (1988).

A more sophisticated method is to compare factor productivity. Comparing the performance of 27 non-US carriers with that of 21 US carriers for the five years to 1975 with the subsequent five years (Table 5.13) shows that while the growth in productivity of the latter continued at the pre-deregulation level, it declined by about 40% for non-US airlines.[45]

5.3 LIBERALIZING THE CANADIAN SCHEDULED AVIATION MARKET

5.3.1 Background
The interest in the Canadian air transport network lies largely in that liberalization came some ten years after the deregulation of the US passenger aviation industry. It, therefore, offers insights into what legislators learn from the experiences of

---

[45]   This type of analysis provided ammunition for those wishing to see deregulation extended elsewhere. As seen below, it was deployed in debates leading to Canadian deregulation of domestic airlines and was used within Australia to argue for liberalization of its 'two airline' policy (Starkie and Starrs, 1984).

others. Additionally, the approach adopted in Canada was also gradual and phased. The merits of such an approach are often seen in terms of minimizing short-term market fluctuations and of providing a framework in which errors of policy can be detected and allowed for as changes take place. There is also an built-in learning process as reforms proceed. The contrasting view supporting more radical and complete reform is that distortions in the market continue during a gradualist program and that operators in the market will have the chance to react and protect their positions. Further, there are inevitable regulatory lags (Archer, 1983) as legislation is framed and enacted and as markets adjust. With a succession of policy changes, overlaps in these lag structures occur making monitoring of policy impacts and the development of subsequent phases of reform difficult.[46]

Table 5.13 Average annual percentage decline in unit costs and sources of unit costs for US and non-US carriers, pre- and post-deregulation

	Pre-deregulation (1970–1975)		Post-deregulation (1975–1983)	
Sources	US	Non-US	US	Non-US
Productive efficiency				
Operating characteristics	1-6	3-3	2-2	2.4
Technical efficiency	1-4	1.2	1.1	0-4
Total productive efficiency	3	4-5	3-3	2.8

Source: Caves *et al.* (1987).

5.3.2 The development of the regulatory regime

By international standards Canadian aviation has a fairly lengthy history. From 1919 local air services were initiated but long-distance, trans-continental services were very slow to emerge. It was to provide a scheduled coast-to-coast service, without the need to go via the US. The Canadian government has a tradition of heavy involvement in the economy terms of regulation and public ownership and this applied to air transport where the provision of long-distance domestic services served as an initial justification.[47] The Crown corporation, Trans Canada Airlines

[46]   The literature on Canada, while not insignificant in volume or deficient in quality is rather less accessible than that for the US, especially outside Canada. Stanbury and Tretheway (1986) offer a bibliography.

[47]   Stanbury (1987) offers an overview of regulation in Canada. This shows that in 1980, government-regulated industries accounted for 38% of the Canadian GDP; that in 1983 government-owned or controlled enterprises account for 26% of fixed assets of

(from 1964, Air Canada) was founded under the 1937 Trans Canadian Airlines Act. The first route serving Montreal–Vancouver was initiated in 1938 and the airline subsequently became a 'preferred vehicle' government policy.

Private sector involvement in aviation was mainly on local routes – Trans Canada Airlines having a protected monopoly on transcontinental routes. In 1933, Canadian Pacific Railways bought Canadian Airways and, by mergers and acquisitions of small carriers, formed Canadian Pacific Airlines in 1942 (from 1968 CP Air). There were also regional carriers (reduced to five major regionals by the mid-1970s – Pacific Western Airlines, Nordair, Eastern Provincial Airlines, Transair and Quebecair) that gradually developed after 1945.[48] These were often started to provide services to remote communities.

Charter services began to develop in the 1950s and grew in the 1960s, especially in the international market. Entry was less regulated than for scheduled services. Constraints on charter activities, however related to such things as advanced booking requirements, minimum stay periods, non-refundable fares and rebooking fees for flight changes. These prevented strict competition with scheduled services, especially for business travel, and none of the charter carriers grew to any size.[49]

From an early stage, regulation of civil aviation was a federal responsibility.[50] Initially, control of aviation was a military responsibility and it remained so until the formation of the Department of Transport in 1936. While the Air Transport Board Act of 1919 represented the first major piece of legislation, the basis for subsequent economic regulation was the Aeronautics Act of 1922. This, with subsequent amendments, gave the federal government power over rate setting, entry and route licensing, conditions of service, mergers and acquisitions and route abandonments. In the early years, however, it was never generally exercised.

The 1938 Transport Act established the Board of Transport Commissioners with responsibility for licensing based on criteria of 'public convenience and necessity'. The emphasis was on the coordination of activities and the stability of the industry. Within this framework, the centrality of the Crown carrier was

all Canadian corporations; and that federal and provincial loans and credits accounted for 8.5% of GNP in 1980.

[48]   Mergers were particularly common under the regulated regime which existed and the five regional carriers were actually formed as a result of at least 20 mergers between 1946 and 1966 (Jordan, 1986a).

[49]   Wardair, the largest specialist charter concern, was formed in 1953 to offer services in the Northwest Territories and expanded into international charter operations in 1961. In 1979 it obtained licenses to operate domestic, non-schedule intercontinental services. Even so, by 1987 it only had seven aircraft to cover both domestic and international operations.

[50]   This differed from the situation in the US where the 1938 Civil Aeronautics Act only applied to inter–state aviation.

emphasized with other, smaller airlines operating feeder services. The board was independent of the minister, but entities with such autonomy seldom endure. The Air Transport Board was established in 1944 to replace the Commissioners. The new board had the remit of advising the minister on matters relating to the issuing of licenses and the approval of rates. The aim was to create a large network of scheduled services across Canada. Monopoly positions were protected by licensing to ensure the commercial viability of routes and to create a system of cross-subsidization. Relaxation of entry control was limited.

The early 1960s, especially following publication of the report of the MacPhearson Royal Commission (Royal Commission on Transportation, 1961), saw a change in attitude. While the main concern was the cost recovery problems of railroads, the Commission's view that 'most of the ills which beset transportation in Canada are caused by the failure of public and private attitudes to adjust to the realities of competition' led to a more general reassessment of policy.

There had been some *de facto* relaxation of entry controls between 1957 and 1963, but these were comparatively minor. In effect, the traditional forms of control continued almost unchanged until 1967 and the enactment of the National Transportation Act that created the Canadian Transport Commission.[51] The Air Transport Board was replaced by the Air Transport Committee of the Commission that had overlapping membership with boards concerned with other modes. The Committee was intended to have considerable autonomy but the federal government could still change or rescind its actions. A degree of governmental suasion could also be exercised in that the Commission was meant to adhere to government policy statements when making its decisions.

The changes came through the need to cater for the growing amount of discretionary travel. The initial response was to relax charter licensing whilst protecting scheduled services dependent on captive travelers paying high fares. Subsequent reforms in the 1970s led to a more liberal regime, with the aim of improving efficiency and reducing costs, whilst still offering some protection to scheduled carriers. Domestic charters were started in 1977[52] and, after 1979, albeit restricted by advanced booking requirements, minimum stay conditions, and rebooking fees for flight changes, charter class fares were permitted on scheduled flights. Fares had to be shown to cover variable costs.

At the regional level, the policy of balkanization, that had reached its zenith in the late 1960s dividing the market between designated carriers, began to break down. The aim was to divide the country into five regional markets each with a

---

[51]   Responsibility for safety matters is the province of Transport Canada.

[52]   In fact the first one had been initiated by Sun Tours the previous year but their service between Vancouver and Toronto operated via US airports with some connections to Canada being by a bus service!

single, regulated carrier to supplement the national networks of Air Canada and CP Air.

To ensure that the system would not require federal subsidies, the policy involved the transfer of some Air Canada and CP Air routes to regional airlines and protection of services (Stanbury and Reschenthaler, 1977). This encouraged the regional airlines to purchase jet aircraft but these proved uneconomical. The merger of the financially ailing Transair with Pacific Western in 1977 meant the beginning of the end of this policy (Barone *et al.*, 1986).

The Air Canada Act introduced further liberalization into the national market by changing the status of Air Canada. The airline was placed on a similar footing to the other schedule carriers by being put under the regulatory control of the Canadian Transport Commission. Its remit was changed to encourage it to operate in a commercial manner and to become more market oriented (Baldwin, 1975). In contrast, there was increasing public sector involvement in the control of the regional carriers.[53] While initially private concerns, the regional carriers were the subjects of considerable change in the 1970s and early 1980s. In most cases this involved a degree of either direct or indirect public sector ownership.

Overlapping the evolving regulatory structure of Canadian domestic airlines was policy regarding Canada's international air transport. International aviation is extremely important to Canada. Some 15% of scheduled and charter revenue ton miles operated by Canadian jet carriers were cross-border services with the US and a further 38% was generated by services to other countries (Jordan, 1986a). Since this aspect of aviation policy is determined through bilateral intergovernmental negotiations there are constraints over the power any one country can exercise. A key point about the Canadian stance was the attitude adopted in awarding routes to carriers once agreement on a service had been reached. From 1973 the approach involved designated 'spheres of influence'. Air Canada was awarded routes involving Northern Europe while CP Air was given routes over the Pacific. There were examples, such as when Air Canada was unable to obtain a Pacific route to Korea, when an airline was excluded from the other's sphere even if the latter did not operate the service. In terms of efficiency, this had potential to limit the development of service networks and would seem to have offered shelter behind which prices were unlikely to be minimized (Dresner and Tretheway, 1987).

5.3.3   The pressures for more rapid liberalization

The liberalization of the 1970s improved the efficiency of Canadian airlines and by the end of the decade cross-subsidization had been substantially reduced.[54] The

---

[53]   There were over 70 third-level carriers providing a range of services to smaller communities and acting as feeders for the larger carriers.

[54]   Evidence given in 1982 indicates that all the major airlines were recovering at least the variable costs of each individual route operated (Canadian Parliament, 1982).

situation was not static, however, and pressures were building for further change (Oum and Tretheway, 1984). Some of these pressures were domestic but there were also ripple effects emanating from the deregulation of fares and market entry in the US. The effects of US deregulation were, in the short term, to offer indirect competition on many routes served by Canadian carriers and, in the long term, to demonstrate that, with some caveats, there were major benefits to be derived from further liberalization.

The majority of Canadian traffic is along a narrow strip bordering the US. Consequently, the fare elasticity of demand for much of the domestic Canadian market is influenced by the possibility of using surface transport to cross the border and adopting a US carrier for the trunk haul. The effect of deregulation in the US, and the entry of new, low cost carriers such as People Express into the market, was to attract Canadians to cross the border. Air Canada was particularly adversely affected by this.[55] There were also fears of shifts in international traffic away from Canadian airports and carriers to those in the US. The Canadian airlines countered this by lowering fares on international routes to keep them in line with US competitors. This meant that on many Canadian services were priced in line with deregulated US services.

While the impact of regulatory reform in the US provided encouragement for those in Canada favoring similar moves others were less enthusiastic (Oum and Tretheway, 1984). Significant differences existed between the US and Canadian airline markets. The former was much larger and more diverse. The Canadian route structure is largely linear (east/west) and Toronto is only one major hub on a par with the large ones in the US. Linked to this is the limited number of high density routes in Canada – in 1985, 45.4% of all domestic air travel was concentrated on twenty-five markets. Additionally, the market differed in scale. The combined revenues of the main US carriers in 1982 was $35.6 billion compared to $3.1 billion for Canadian airlines (Gillen *et al.*, 1985). There are, relatively, far more 'thin' routes in Canada than in the US. The Canadian airlines were small compared to the main US carriers and the Canadian aviation industry was much more concentrated.[56] The US industry had also always been entirely privately owned. Further, public ownership in Canada extended to all the major airports whilst in the US there was considerable local government involvement.

Adding to these characteristics were the problems being encountered by the Canadian carriers as a result of macroeconomic conditions and changes in factor

[55]   The Canadian airlines were not always passive in the face of the threat of losing traffic and there were periodic sales of seats at up to 75% discount on the economy fares.

[56]   Gillen *et al.* (1985) point out that in 1982 the largest US carrier, United Airlines, accounted for 13% of the industries' revenues and 14% of its revenue tonne-kilometers, whereas Air Canada accounted for 56% and 53% respectively.

costs. Central was the fact that the Canadian economy went into recession in the early 1980s. This put pressure on Canadian airlines as demand for air travel declined.[57] The impact of depressed demand was compounded by the fact that from 1979 there had been a dramatic rise in fuel prices, by nearly 240%, between November 1978 and March 1981 and this hit the aviation industry severely.

5.3.4 *De facto* and *de jure* deregulation

The initial policy response in the early 1980s was to further relax controls over charter operators[58] and to permit scheduled operators greater freedom to match the fares of the charter carriers. It was an effort at fine-tuning the existing regime rather than any major shift in the thrust of policy (House of Commons Standing Committee on Transport, 1982).

The airlines responded to the depressed market by attempting to develop more services rather than reduce costs and concentrate on core operations. Given constraints over fare levels, there is a natural tendency to compete in terms of service and this becomes important in the quest revenue. The airlines also made use of what flexibility in fare setting they enjoyed. Air Canada, with a better timed service, tried to capture traffic from the charters by undercutting Wardair fares with seat sales (at up to 35% discount) on some routes.[59]

The moves by government and the airlines did little to remedy the mounting problems of the industry. Air transport was slow to recover from the recession and the fall in revenue passenger-kilometers did not bottom out until 1983. The scheduled airlines still faced severe competition from an increasingly efficient US industry over certain routes and the charter carriers had grown in importance. There were also other, less easily quantifiable problems. Consumer groups expressed concern about the arbitrary form fare discounting was taking. Regulators were concerned with some of the practices being adopted to capture passengers – e.g., the Air Transport Committee was concerned with the proclivity of carriers to advertise and book passengers at low fares immediately these were filed making rejection of new fares politically difficult.

---

[57]   The revenue passenger-kilometers of level-1 Canadian carriers fell from 36.1 billion in 1980, to 35.4 billion in 1981, to 32.1 billion in 1982 and bottomed out at 31.3 billion in 1983. The corresponding passenger figures were (in terms of enplaned passengers), 55.1 million (1980), 55.0 million (1981), 49.4 million (1982) and 47.8 million (1983).

[58]   In particular, this allowed Wardair greater penetration of the Canadian transcontinental market.

[59]   According to Spalding (1979), Air Canada had always enjoyed some advantages over the charter operators even prior to the changes in its regulatory control in 1977. In particular, it enjoyed fewer administrative delays in gaining acceptance of fare changes or for the provision of part charters on scheduled services.

The subsequent major shift in policy can be traced to the appointment of LLoyd Axworthy as Minister of Transport in 1983. To distance the arm of government from the airlines, and to reduce the potential for regulatory capture either by those in the industry or by civil servants, employees of Transport Canada and the Air Transport Committee had to give up their free air travel passes. He also set in train two courses of action designed to gain more information on the prospects for liberalizing Canada's domestic industry. The Air Transport Committee was to conduct hearings on air fares policy and, concurrently, a task force was given the remit to examine ways of adapting the US regime of deregulation to meet the specifics of the Canadian market (Ellison, 1984).

No consensus emerged from these deliberations and the outcome was determined by the general election of 1984. The Transport Minister initiated the 'New Canadian Air Transport Policy' aimed at introducing a degree of *de facto* flexibility into the existing legislation. Moral suasion through government statements was exercised to loosen the Air Transport Committee's policies on entry and pricing.[60] The new policy was seen as part of a longer-term process that would, over two years, give airlines freedom to reduce prices but limit rises to increases in an input price index. At the same time restrictions over discount fares would be removed. Entry to the charter markets in the south of Canada would be freed whilst exit would be easier for carriers unable to compete in the new environment. Regarding airport slots, new entrants to the scheduled market were to be treated on equal terms with incumbents. At the local level it was envisaged that the Regional Carrier Policy would be repealed, although services in the north would remain regulated for social reasons.[61] Finally, Air Canada was to relinquish Nordair (acquired in 1978) and was not to engage in deliberate competitive practices unless private carriers initiated such actions.

This period also saw changes in the regulation of transborder aviation. A bilateral agreement with the US had been signed in 1966 that agreed route schedules for both nations' carriers with one carrier from each on most routes unless mutually agreed otherwise (Haanapel, 1980). Fares had to be agreed by both countries but the airlines were left to determine their capacities on each route and the aircraft deployed. Charter operations came under a later agreement that allowed

---

[60]   The legal position was that conditions of 'public convenience and necessity' still had to be met if a new license was to be authorized, but the intention was to modify the Committee's interpretation of this. Ministerial powers of granting appeals against Air Transport Committee rulings were also exercised. The Air Transport Committee published its own findings favoring a long term aimed at 'controlled competition' whereby regulations would be relaxed but only in a limited fashion. It argued for mandatory restrictions on deep discounts and for the continuation of the Regional Carrier Policy (Canadian Transport Commission, 1984).

[61]   Broadly corresponding to the area of a line stretching from the 55th parallel on the Pacific coast to the 50th parallel on the Atlantic coast

flexibility in the way charters operated but reserved powers for negotiations should their actions interfere excessively with scheduled services or the charter operators from the other country. The idea was to have broad compatibility between the number of passengers carried by each country's charter air services and the level of traffic originating from that country. Since the majority of traffic was Canadian (trips to 'sun' destinations in the US) this meant that the Canadian charters enjoyed the largest share of the market.[62]

Changes to the regulatory regime in 1984 reflected the gradual liberalization policy that the US had been pursuing in international aviation under its 'Open Skies' initiative. One new agreement related to commuter and local services and allowed for greater ease in obtaining approval to operate new services with automatic procedures agreed for most types of service. Under a second, there was an experimental transborder program aimed at developing new services and testing the viability of new pricing systems. Access to Mirabel Airport by designated carriers operating from all but seven US airports was unrestricted and any number of the designated carriers could offer these services. Fares were not controlled unless both countries objected. As a balance, the US airport of San Jose was later designated as an experimental US airport with similar rules (Gillen *et al.,* 1988a).

Subsequent discussions between the US and Canada to further liberalize transborder services failed to achieve any consensus.[63] Indeed, while free trade in aviation services was included in the US/Canadian Free Trade Agreement of 1985, inability to reach final agreement meant its exclusion from the subsequent treaty.[64]

The return of a new administration in late 1984 ensured the continued movement towards greater domestic liberalization – e.g., Wardair began operating domestic schedule services in May 1986. *Freedom to Move* was published, setting out the philosophy behind the government's transport policy (Transport Canada, 1985). This was to be based on 'the principles of greater reliance on competition

---

[62] Rather perversely, the agreement required the US carriers to have between 25% and 40% of the market by 1978 - a figure that was never approached. In the early 1980s the Canadian charter airlines accounted for something over 90% of all transborder traffic, which contrasts with the 40% of scheduled transborder traffic that the Canadian airlines managed to capture (Dresner *et al.,* 1988).

[63] Agreements on a genuinely liberal bilateral agreement finally came in 1995.

[64] Both parties submitted proposals which would have considerably liberalized markets but they differed in their philosophy. The Canadian concept paper favored a common market approach covering both countries while the US was concerned only with deregulation of transborder traffic and adjusting the rights of Canadian airlines operating services to the US to correct for structural disadvantages. The airlines on both sides of the border, however, feared for their positions – US carriers arguing that other countries might demand cabotage rights if Canadian airlines were granted them, as under the Canadian proposals.

and market forces, a reduction of government interference and regulation, and the creation of a regulatory process that is open and accessible'.

The document had particular implications for domestic aviation (Heaver, 1987). It advocated almost complete deregulation of Canadian aviation *à la* the US. Subsequent pressure from the airlines and other interested parties, however, led to a more restrictive piece of legislation being passed as the National Transportation Act in 1987 with enactment from January 1988. In addition, in 1987 the former division of international markets between Air Canada and CP Air was ended and route trading took place allowing Air Canada to operate Pacific routes. There was also a liberal agreement reached with the UK regarding transatlantic services.

Some degree of economic regulation was retained in the sparsely populated northern part of Canada. Services were to be provided based on a 'fit, willing and able' test but subject to the caveat that new services would not 'lead to a significant decrease or instability in the level of domestic service'. In 1986 there were 25 airlines operating in the north although all but four routes were monopolized by a single carrier. The new regime was intended to introduce considerably more competition. The onus of proof was switched from the airlines needing to justify a service to objectors having to demonstrate serious potential adverse consequences. The new National Transportation Agency retained power to control such things as the routes to be followed, the areas to be served, schedules, fares and insurance requirements, and market exit had to be preceded by a period of notice. Subsidies were provided for essential services although, in an effort to maximize efficiency, these were allocated through a tendering system.[65]

Southern Canada was to enjoy a much more liberal regime, although one still subject to some control. The 'fit, willing and able' criterion still applied but any service could be provided on condition that the carrier had an operators' license, there was adequate insurance cover and there was proof of 75% Canadian ownership of the airline. In most senses the Act introduced an environment in southern Canadian markets akin to that in the US. There were, though, some differences. While fares are not controlled there was provision for the national Transportation Agency to disallow 'unreasonable' fare increases on routes where 'there is no other alternative effective, adequate and competitive transportation service'.[66]

---

[65]   Oum and Tretheway (1984) had expressed concern that, without a clear plan of compensation, subsidies for remote services could be open to abuse. Airlines running services in the north and the south might try to cross-subsidize the latter by obtaining funding for the former. Tendering was aimed at offering a partial solution to this.

[66]   Kahn would seem to have sympathy with this policy: 'I hope I do not shock anybody by observing that I probably would have been very reluctant to abandon price ceilings entirely had I the choice. All [US] studies of airline pricing since deregulation confirm that reluctance: market concentration does matter; and their general trend over time has been towards the conclusion that it matters a great deal' (Kahn, 1988).

The rules on mergers were also modified to require due notice of change of ownership and, if there were objections, the National Transportation Agency was left to determine whether the action was in the public interest. The Competition Act of 1986 was less strict than this but because of the earlier decision of the Supreme Court of Canada in BC *Law Society* v. *Jabour* in 1982 there was some ambiguity as to the applicability of the Act to aviation (Stanbury and Tretheway, 1987). The Act was, however, invoked in the context of CRSs.

A final strand in the deregulation process was the privatization of Air Canada. The objective was to remove any advantage a Crown corporation may have in the marketplace.[67] In addition, privatization took place at a time when Air Canada wanted to replace its aging fleet of Boeing 727s and DC9s. It was felt that privatization offered a method of ensuring sufficient funds were available for reinvestment at a time when the government wished to reduce its expenditure. The program of privatization, with a 10% limit on individual share holdings (but with the state retaining, at least in the short term, a majority 55% holding) was aimed at ensuring a spread of equity with no dominant, controlling interest. Counter to this is the power exercised by the so-called 'technostructure'[68] in companies with such diversified ownership. Whether the airline had sufficient market power to survive operating at less than maximum efficiency for any length of time would depend upon the degree to which it could shelter itself from the full forces of competition.

5.3.5 Impacts of the pre-1988 changes in regulation

Since airlines were given considerable warning of the impending legal deregulation, and indeed a phased *de facto* liberalization preceded it, there was time for them to adjust to what they thought the new conditions would require. The airlines essentially adopted proactive strategies in an effort to gain the best position when the market became fully deregulated. There was increased concern from the established scheduled carriers over the effects of the expanding competition on the high-density routes by admitting Wardair. The spate of mergers of small carriers that occurred during the mid-1980s added to this competitive environment. In an effort to maintain market share, an increasing amount of traffic began to be carried on discount fares. In 1978 less than 15% of the two major carriers' revenue came from discount fares but by 1985 this had risen to 60%.

---

[67]   It has been suggested, for example, that government ownership may mean a lower cost of capital and that this in turn may make the costs of predatory behavior lower – see Gillen *et al.* (1988b).

[68]   The term applies to the management and advisers in a company who are freed from the rigors of the marketplace to pursue their own, not necessarily commercially optimal, objectives because of the lack of effective control which accompanies dispersion of ownership (Galbraith, 1967).

One long-term feature of US deregulation was the large number of mergers and acquisitions that ultimately took place. Mergers in Canada had a somewhat longer tradition than in the US and were employed as a means of handling airlines' financial difficulties under the regulatory system when exit from loss-making routes was not permitted. After 1984 there were major changes in the nature of these mergers, with the market share of the two largest carriers considerably enhanced   (Table 5.14). In particular, the formation of Canadian Airlines International through mergers meant a genuine competitor to Air Canada existed on all major routes.[69]

Table 5.14 Share of the domestic Canadian aviation market, 1987

Airline	Domestic market share (% revenue)
Air Canada	50–55
Canadian Airlines International	35
Wardair	7
Small regionals	Remainder

The important mergers and acquisitions prior to 1988, were CP Airlines' acquisition of Eastern Provincial Airways Inc. in 1984 and the subsequent merging of the two into Canadian Pacific Air Lines two years later. The company then acquired a 99% holding in Nordair by mid-1986 with a formal merger coming the following year. In turn, Canadian Pacific Air Lines was purchased by Pacific Western Airlines (PWA) Corporation and the undertakings merged in 1987. As a product of the earlier merger with Nordair, this gave Canadian Airlines International Ltd. a 35% share in Quebecair, which the conducted business as Inter-Canadien with links to Nordair- Metro and Quebec Aviation. *En route* to this conglomerate, a number of third-level carriers were taken over, e.g., Canadian Pacific Air Lines acquired Air Atlantic in 1986, while Air Canada acquired Air BC and a majority shareholding in Air Ontario and Austin Airways in 1986.

The airlines attempted to form themselves into hub-and-spoke style operations similar to those that dominate US domestic air transport. The aim of the mergers was to ensure a powerful market position with good feeder services to their main hubs, and to try to exploit economies of density to the maximum. In particular, acquisition of local airlines was seen as a quick means of attaining control over the vital feeder services (Table 5.15).

---

[69]   The merger of the two airlines in 2000 ended this.

Empirical evidence on the costs structure of the Canadian industry confirmed it to be similar to that of the US. Very limited economies of scale emerged, but that there are marked economies of density up to quite large traffic volumes. There were indications that Air Canada was at about the minimum efficient traffic density prior to the mergers in the mid-1980s but that CP Air still had scope for expansion of traffic density – its subsequent mergers effectively enabled it to achieve them according to these calculations (Gillen *et al.*, 1986).

Table 5.15 Major airline affiliations, 1988

Air Canada		Canadian Airlines International	
Affiliates	Relationship	Affiliates	Relationship
Air Ontario	75% Ownership	Inter-Canadian	35% Ownership
Air BC	100% Ownership	*(includes Quebecair*	
Air Nova	49% Ownership	*Quebecair Inter*	
Air Alliance	75% Ownership	*Nordair Metro)*	
Northwest Territorial	90% Ownership	Ontario Express	49% Ownership
Air Toronto		Time Air	46% Ownership
(Commuter Express)	codesharing	*(includes Nomanair)*	
		Air Atlantic	45% Ownership
		Calm Air International	45% Ownership
		Air St Pierre	codesharing

Source: Transport Canada (1988).

Whether the mergers proved successful is difficult to assess given the on-going process of change that subsequently took place. Evidence from the US shows many mergers, albeit after deregulation rather than in an intervening period of gradual liberalization, were misguided (Jordan, 1988). The argument is that successful mergers have involved combining airlines with similar operating features, and even here short-term problems arise and a high degree of rationalization is often required to reduce operating costs to pre-merger levels.[70] Many of the demand side advantages of mergers (e.g., common identity and

---

[70] This is very much in line with the findings relating to the economic rent enjoyed by US carriers although the conclusions stem from a different starting position. Bailey and Williams (1988), using the competitive-spectrum approach, broke down a seemingly oligopolistic market and considered the possibility of earning local monopoly rents by exercising regional monopoly power. In the case of airlines, product differentiation permits there use of limit pricing and is akin to local monopoly power in spatial markets. Diversification is unlikely to generate additional profits.

economies of information dissemination) can be obtained by means of shared designation codes, linked frequent flyer programs and integrated time-tabling without actual merger. Hence the merger between Pacific Western and Transair – two regional carriers with similar types of operation – in 1979 only saw a slight and temporary fall in profits *vis-à-vis* other carriers. However, the resultant network of points served by acquisition of Eastern Provincial by Canadian Pacific and their subsequent merger did little to improve the latter's financial position that deteriorated from a small profit in 1986 to losses immediately after the acquisition.

This raises the question of whether the gradual deregulation in Canada allowed the necessary rationalizations after mergers to be completed with minimal disruption. In the US, mergers occurred after deregulation when the shelter enjoyed by airlines had been removed. The Canadian situation was different in that the main mergers took place during the transitional phase and the subsequent period did not see the financial difficulties some merged US carriers experienced. There had been time for errors and mistakes to be at least partly rectified.

The mergers resulted in duopolies on most major routes with Wardair gradually building up as a third force. US evidence is that the existence of actual competition on a route tends to be preferable to the weaker forces of potential competition. The findings suggest that competition limited to two carriers (or three where Wardair was active) was still not a strong force for low fares.

Airport capacity problems in Canada, with the marginal exception of Toronto's L.B. Pearson Airport, were not severe. There were, however, peaks in demand and slot allocations can be important at these times. In all cases there were Schedule Coordinating Committees consisting of representatives of the main users and these allocated slots. Normally, either Air Canada or Canadian Airlines International took a 'strong leadership' position in these Committees (Gillen *et al.*, 1988b). There was thus scope for incumbents to limit the availability of prime take-off/landing slots to potential entrants. The major airlines often enjoyed 'grandfather' rights to favorable terminal gates or even (as at Vancouver International Airport) to allocate gates. Entrants were confronted by problems in gaining the use of adequate and suitable gates. Finally, the dominant airline at a terminal often provided ground facilities (fuelling, aircraft maintenance, etc.) and sold these to other users with the potential that a high price would be extracted.

As with the US, Canadian airlines attempted to protect their individual markets by using of frequent flyer programs. The Canadian programs began in 1987 and virtually all airlines operated one, either in their own right or, on payment of a fee, as a member of one of the majors' schemes. Linked with this was the increase in designator code sharing that helps to protect the flow of feed traffic to the majors and at the same time ties the smaller airlines to them.

While these practices were adopted in many countries, in Canada Air Canada and Canadian Airlines International combined in a fashion that appears to have offered mutual protection of their duopoly. They joined in 1987 to establish a single CRS. About 80% of air tickets were sold through travel agents in Canada and most of these made use of CRSs. Air Canada's 'Reservec' system had formerly dominated the market, with 85% of automated travel agents linked to it, while Canadian Airlines International's 'Pegasus' had 15%. Many Canadian Airlines International tickets were sold through Air Canada's system, giving the latter advantages in information collection, but also the Reservec system was biased against Canadian Airlines International's services because its information on the latter's flights was forty-eight hours old. When in 1987 the two airlines combined their systems they formed 'Gemini' which was soon used by about 90% of agents, the remaining 10% share going mainly to 'Sabre'. Because Gemini did not provide Sabre with details of Air Canada's and Canadian Airlines International's last minute seat availability many travel agents subscribed to both systems. The merging took place despite the Canadian government implicitly assuming two competing computer reservation systems would remain when accepting the creation of Canadian Airlines International. In the early part of 1988, hearings were called before the federal Competition Tribunal. Wardair was offered the chance to join the Gemini system but declined, possibly because of unfavorable terms. Instead it became a 'participating carrier' in the system and a hosted carrier in SYSTEMONE of the Texas Air Corporation. Such arrangements put the operator at a serious competitive disadvantage in the scheduled services market.[71]

5.3.6 The lessons of Canadian gradualism

The changes in Canadian aviation policy during the 1980s in the southern part of the country created an industry akin to that found in post-1978 US. There were differences but these were mainly in the way the deregulation was achieved. It was by gradualism. Whether this is to be preferred to the more dramatic shift in US policy is not easy to assess; after all the Canadian reforms were enacted with the experiences of the US. Some general points do seem to emerge and to indicate differences in the short- and long-term effects of the two strategies.

Gradualism gave the opportunity for Canadian airlines to adjust their fleets in a systematic fashion rather than be confronted with the types of shortage that many US airlines encountered after 1978. The hub-and-spoke style of operations that emerged as the most efficient form of providing aviation services necessitated a change from the wide-bodied jets being used on the linear routing structures that

---

[71]   The importance of controlling CRSs is not only that they provide an important source of revenue to the vendor (it was anticipated that Gemini would generate about $150 million per annum in revenue) but that there is the opportunity for protecting the vendor's operations from market entry or from the full rigors of competition from incumbent carriers. Even where, as in the Canadian case, measures were adopted to remove the most obvious forms of bias that can be incorporated in a system, there still remain the 'halo' effects which, it has been suggested from the US experiences discussed above, can be quite substantial.

the CAB had imposed on the US industry. Many airlines misjudged this and met with difficulties in keeping their costs down. Others had serious problems acquiring sufficient narrow-bodied jets to operate their hub-and-spoke systems efficiently. The mergers and changes in Canada, in contrast, were exploited to free aircraft to meet the needs of a gradually liberalized market with purchases of additional equipment used to complement the process.

When airlines encountered financial problems the distribution of that impact differed between the US and Canadian. US airlines declared bankruptcy and passed the incidence of failure onto shareholders, or forced concessions from workers who consequently bore the burden. In Canada, to avoid serious disruptions to the market, there was either direct subsidization of ailing carriers or they were taken and stripped of their profitable services (e.g., Eastern Provincial in 1984). The tax payer or air traveler bore the cost (Jordan, 1986a). The desirability of the options is a normative judgment, but certainly the impacts of the two policies differ.

A major initial benefit of deregulation in the US was the entry of new carriers into the national market. These provided innovated services and stimulated response from the incumbent carriers. In Canada there was no such entry. Incumbent carriers modified their activities in response to reform but it is difficult to speculate what the outcome may have been with a significant new entrant into the market. Wardair in some ways represented a scheduled new carrier, albeit from a base of established charter operations, and if its actions were indicative of the impact a new carrier would have exercised on the market the implications are of a conservative kind. Rather than initiate new domestic types of operations, Wardair began to act like the two majors, and to purchase aircraft to operate services.

New entrants were also instrumental in undercutting many high cost practices in the US. The situation in Canada during the move to deregulation was less clear-cut. The Canadian aviation industry was heavily unionized and in the period 1979–85, while the number of strikes per annum fell compared to 1975–78, they were of considerably longer duration (i.e., 64.9 days compared with 19.5).[72] Whether air travelers actually benefited is, thus, really a matter of judgment.

It would appear that some of the innovative energies that burst forth after the US reforms were missing in Canada but this may not be a serious criticism. The US industry had no one to mimic when it was deregulated and was forced to experiment. There was little point in a more gradualist approach than that adopted – it would only have led to a longer period of uncertain adjustment. In a sense Canadian airlines benefited from the US industry bearing the R&D costs of operating in a deregulation environment. It was able to move up the learning curve

---

[72]   Although the ability of airlines to continue functioning during a strike improved during the later period, mainly due to high levels of unemployment, and this may have stiffened the resolve of management in the industrial conflicts (Jordan, 1987).

quite rapidly and with less of the friction that was experienced in the US. The remaining problems were similar to those in the US, namely mergers, the use of computerized reservation systems, and the deployment of frequent flier programs.

It is difficult to separate the effects of the gradualist reforms in Canada from the advantages policy makers and airlines enjoyed from been able to observe US experiences. There are indications that gradualism can help smooth transitional difficulties in an industry where equipment is expensive, specialized and durable. It provides policy makers with a wider range of options in deciding which groups should bear the costs of reform. The reactions of incumbent airlines also reflected the advantages they had from having time to protect their position during a phased liberalization. In many cases their reactions were at least as much the result of lessons learned from their US counterparts and from the liberal attitudes in Canada with respect to such things as CRS policy and mergers policy as from the reaction periods they enjoyed. Perhaps the major lesson of the Canadian experience is that, while gradualism has benefits, there are still inherent problems in any liberalization process due to the natural inclination of incumbent suppliers to devise mechanisms to blunt the effects of any actual or potential competition.

5.4   REFORM IN THE EUROPEAN UNION

5.4.1 The regulated market
The European Union air transport differs from either the US or Canadaian markets in that a large part of the traffic is international. While there has been a Common Transport Policy since the signing of the Rome Treaty in 1957, aviation was initially excluded from EU policies. Countries regulated their own domestic aviation and a bilateral system of agreements, evolved from the Chicago Convention of 1944, governed international air transport within the Union, as well as outside it. Policies were concerned with the regulation of scheduled fares, service provision and market entry. Coupled with this was the growth of a very large European charter market that met north–south tourist traffic demands. This market was less rigorously regulated and served by low cost operators.

The EU has also never had a single regulatory body with responsibility for international air transport like the former CAB in the US. The bilateral air service agreements that emerged after the 1944 Chicago meeting were piece–meal arrangements, although common motivations often led to standard features[73]. They

---

[73]   Articles 1, 6 and 17-20 of the Chicago Convention were particularly important in recognizing each contracting state's complete and exclusive sovereignty over the airspace above its territory, the requirement that aircraft should have a nationality by being registered in one particular state, and the consequence need for aircraft registered in any state to obtain the permission of a state in order to operate air services to or from its territory.

were generally restrictive and often allowed only one airline from each country to operate a route.[74]

Within the EU, overlapping philosophies and approaches to economic regulation extended into the supply of aviation services and make the creation of a unified policy difficult. The patchwork of controls over such things as market entry, fares, and conditions of operation that existed in 1957 grew with time. To a large extent, they were initially a reflection of these differences. Countries such as France, Spain and Greece, where domestic aviation is relatively important, have a tradition of heavily regulating entry and fares, and this has extended to their views of international aviation policy.

This degree of regulation was frequently justified by governments in terms of serving the public interest by ensuring market stability, maintaining safety standards, protecting the public from monopoly exploitation and providing a comprehensive network of services. The controls also served as important instruments for the protection of other aspects of the national interests by maintaining flag carriers that meet wider economic and military criteria.

Exporting aviation services can also represent an important element of 'invisible' earnings from foreign trade. In addition, there was the question of status and market presence. In some countries (e.g., Greece), aviation was provided through statute by national, state-owned airlines. Such direct controls not only influence provided air transport services but can also be deployed to regulate the purchase of aviation equipment which can also form a major item in foreign trade accounts.

Such a regime of *ad hoc*, state-based regulations is unlikely to generate the most efficient air transport system for Europe. While some countries may have benefited because of their bargaining position or through historical accident, overall it tended to protect inefficient operations and distort the overall pattern of services provided. It acted as a restraint on trade and had associated with it the same undesirable economic implications as tariffs. The problem was that countries with well-entrenched systems of market controls, even if appreciative of the probable adverse implications of this for the overall welfare of the Union, still effectively cushioned their airlines from competition and found it difficult suddenly to compete in a more market-oriented environment.

Change came slowly and came in several ways.

---

[74]   While this type of restriction may be similar to the CAB's entry policy to US inter-state routes prior to 1978, the European situation was more stringent; over 90% of bilateral agreements involved controlled capacity with obligatory 50:50 revenue pooling. Some 900 of the agreements excluded fifth freedom rights. The two countries involved agreed on the airfare, and competitive pricing was excluded. Many of the airlines were state owned 'flag' carriers and received substantial state subsidies.

5.4.1.1 Domestic reforms
There were reforms of domestic policy within a number of EU members. Some, such as in the UK, were *de facto* changes and did not entirely free up the market. They saw the national regulatory agency being more liberal in the allocation of licenses and acceptance of fare flexibility (UK Civil Aviation Authority, 1988). Other countries such as France, Spain, Italy, and Germany were less inclined towards unilateral domestic liberalization.

Reforms were gradually accompanied by greater private sector involvement in the provision of aviation services. In some instances (notably British Airways), there was complete privatization of former state companies at an early stage. More common (in Germany and the Netherlands) was a gradual selling off of stock.[75] Airports and other fixed infrastructure, outside the UK where the main airports were privatized as the British Airports Authority in 1987, have tended to remain in the public sector.

5.4.1.2 Reforming bilateral air service agreements
Since the mid-1980s, there has been a move to liberalize bilateral agreements between some members. In 1984 the UK and the Netherlands concluded an agreement that significantly relaxed the rules covering traffic between the two. The main features were that any airline (based in either country) could fly between the two signatories and that tariff freedom was established: there was no compulsory consultation with other airlines and fares were to be set by the airline of the country from which a flight originated. The capacity offered was left to the airlines. In 1985 the countries introduced a double disapproval system. Previously fares had been subject to approval by the country of origin. But from 1985 airline were free to modify fares unless both countries disapproved.

Subsequently the Anglo-German (1984), Anglo-Belgium (1985), Anglo-Luxembourg (1985), Anglo-Italian (1985) and Anglo-Irish (1988) agreements all embodied varying degrees of liberalization. Whilst these developments were a step forward, what was still lacking was a Union-wide act of deregulation. This was something that could only be accomplished by the Council of Ministers.

The changes did initiate liberalization into fragments of the EU international market. It encouraged new entrants and brought response from incumbents. Evidence from Irish–UK routes point to lower fare levels and benefits estimated in 1989 at £24.9 million for the 994 000 existing passengers and £16.2 million for 1.3 million additional passengers generated post-liberalization (Barrett, 1990). The

---

[75]   Studies of these different approaches to privatization (albeit in terms of looking at British Airways and Air Canada) suggest that complete private sector ownership has distinctly positive implications for aviation markets (Eckel *et al.*, 1997). Prodromidis and Frangos (1995) offer further empirical evidence of the greater efficiency of private airlines.

impact of the Anglo-Dutch liberalization was more muted which can be in part be explained in terms of its timing in the trade cycle and the fact that the existing bilateral was not excessively restrictive.

5.4.1.3 'Open Skies' agreements

Not all liberalizing measures were exclusively within the Union, such as the Anglo-Swiss bilateral free access capacity provisions with limited tariff constraints. Of particular importance are agreements involving the US whose 'Open Skies' policy, since 1979, has attempted to develop liberal bilateral air service agreements with individual EU states. The bilateral agreements between the US and individual EU countries had traditionally varied by country but in general were relatively restrictive on capacity and entry points as well as fifth freedom rights. There was a gradual change in the 1990s but, to date, the only long-standing liberal agreement is with the Netherlands.

In 1994, however, the US initiated liberal bilateral agreements with a number of European countries, although none has been a major international airline. In 1996, an interim arrangement was reached with Germany amounting to an Open Skies agreement. The impact of both types of development and stance the US has taken is to help bring European aviation closer to the global marketplace.[76]

A longer standing issue, in the context of an EU air transport policy, is whether it is still appropriate for individual member states to engage in such bilateral arrangements or if a common EU negotiating position should be taken (Association of European Airlines, 1999). In 1996, EU states gave over some soft-negotiating rights to the Commission but major players in the trans-Atlantic market, and especially the UK, have resisted relinquishing their individual negotiating rights.

5.4.1.4 EU air transport policy

The development of the EU's air transport policy requires to be put into context.[77] The foundations of the regulation of scheduled air passenger services were laid in and shortly after the Chicago Convention. Inter-state services in Europe were no exception. The Convention gave rise to a United Nations agency – the ICAO –

---

[76]   The liberalization of the North Atlantic has not been entirely painless in the short term. Between 1984 and 1990 the six countries with the most liberal bilateral air service agreements with the US (Belgium, Denmark, France, Germany, Spain and the Netherlands) lost market share while those with more restrictive agreements (Greece, Denmark, Italy, Portugal and the UK) gained market share. Over the same period, overall the US carriers took a larger proportion of the fast-growing non-US citizens traffic on the Atlantic.

[77]   For more details, see Button and Swann (1992); Vincent and Stasinopoulos (1990); Stasinopoulos (1992; 1993); Doganis (1994); Borenstein (1992b); McGowan and Seabright (1989); Pelksman (1986); Good *et al.* (1993) and Stevens (1997).

that was largely concerned with technical standards, the collection of statistical data, etc., rather than detailed economic regulation. Discussion at the Convention was dominated by governments claiming absolute sovereignty over the airspace above their territories. The underlying hope was that those signing would grant to all other signatories freedom of access to this airspace and to airports beneath them. Failure to achieve this resulted in a system of bilateral air services agreements.

Bilateral agreements involving EU members were inevitably not uniform, but there were typical features.

- Access to the market was not free but was indeed severely restricted. Often only one airline from each country was allowed to fly on a particular route. This was referred to as single designation. As late as 1987, out of 988 routes within the Union air services network only 48 had multiple designation, i.e., more than one airline from either side.
- Fifth freedom competition was the exception – of the 988 routes only 88 allowed fifth freedom rights. The capacity offered by each bilateral partner was restricted. Generally each state enjoyed 50% of the traffic between countries.
- The division of the market was often accompanied by pools in which the airlines shared the revenue in proportion to the capacity employed. Thus even if one airline obtained 54% of the revenue and the other thus enjoyed only 46% they would nevertheless split the proceeds equally.
- Fares were approved by the regulatory bodies of bilateral partners and there was no competition on price, as opposed to service.
- The airlines designated by each country had to be substantially owned and controlled by the country designating them, or by its nationals.
- In some cases airlines, many wholly or partially government owned, enjoyed competition distorting state aids.

The 1957 Rome Treaty, effective from January 1958, originally involved West Germany, France, Italy, the Netherlands, Belgium and Luxembourg. Subsequently it was enlarged – in 1973 the UK, the Ireland and Denmark became members. In 1981 Greece was admitted and in 1986 the Community was enlarged to include Spain and Portugal. Sweden, Austria and Finland are now members. The Treaty required free competition across frontiers calling for the removal of all protective tariff, quota and non-tariff barriers to the free circulation of goods. The Treaty envisaged free competition across frontiers for services. Around the free trade area there was to be a common external tariff. The EEC envisaged free factor mobility.

Three features of this arrangement had potential for undermining the system of air transport regulation. First, in Article 3 of the Treaty laying down the objectives of the EEC one of the key aims is seen as the creation of conditions of undistorted competition. The system of airline regulation was anti-competitive and fundamentally at variance with the competitive ethos of the Treaty. Secondly, the requirement to abolish non-tariff barriers applied not merely to goods but also to services. Antitrust-type restrictions constitute such a barrier and the European Communities Commission could ban cartel arrangements, The price-fixing and revenue-pooling arrangements of the airline regulatory system appeared to be extremely vulnerable to attack. Thirdly, a key feature of the bilateral agreements was the restriction on access to routes. They were at variance with the idea of freedom to supply services.

Whilst the Rome Treaty appeared to threaten the system, the Community made only limited progress in removing the restrictions on the free movement of goods, services and factors.[78] An explanation of how deregulation emerged requires identification of the players and forces at work.

The European Commission is charged with the task of ensuring that the aims of the Union are achieved. It makes proposals for Union law and plays an executive role. The power to make Union law lies with the European Communities Council of Ministers. The legislative players in this area are the member state governments. Their ministers of transport make up the Council of Ministers (on transport matters) and as the Union's lawmakers, are in a position to undo the regulatory knot that had been tied on an intergovernmental bilateral basis. The European Court of Justice has the power to uphold or overturn the actions of the institutions and to render preliminary judgments on issues of European significance arising in national courts. The airlines were a diverse group including national scheduled flag carriers and regional and charter carriers. There is a collection of bodies including user groups and individual investigators. They have had the capacity to expose the regulatory system to criticism and to mobilize public opinion. Finally, there were autonomous forces.

At the outset, the balance of forces favored the existing regulatory system. While the Commission was charged with the implementation of a treaty that clearly embraced a pro-competition philosophy, the competitive rigor of the Commission's policy was conditioned by the prevailing orthodoxy. Moreover the Commission was faced with some uncertainty over the position of air transport under the Treaty. This provided for a separate regime for transport – a Common Transport Policy (CTP) – that could be somewhat different from the rest of the Treaty. However, whilst the Rome Treaty was sparing when it came to spelling out the detailed nature of a CTP, the provisions that were revealed were liberalizing. Moreover when the Commission came to put policy flesh on the

---

[78]   This shortcoming explains the signature in 1986 by the then 12 member states of the Single European Act. This recognized the Union's failure to complete the Single European Market and set the end of 1992 as the target date for its completion.

Treaty it chose to adopt a competitive stance. However, the CTP only applied to road, rail and inland waterway – air and maritime transport were not included.[79]

Other players were also favorable to the *status quo* or were relatively quiescent. Member states had created the regulatory system and the prevailing orthodoxy plus inertia did not dispose them to undo it. Scheduled flag carriers enjoyed the protection of the system and were unlikely to deviate from the position taken by their governments. Free and intensified competition carried with it the possibility of losses that would fall upon national exchequers. The non-scheduled airlines were carving out a role for themselves but they had not gained enough confidence to mount a direct assault on the preserve of the scheduled carriers. It was only as air travel grew that users became an increasingly significant pressure group.

In 1974 the first significant change occurred. In the *French Merchant Seamen* case the European Court of Justice declared that the general rules of the Treaty, and by implication those relating to competition, applied to sectors such as air transport. This appeared to open up air transport regulation to attack. However, this was not so for various reasons. The Treaty allowed the Commission to prohibit activities such as collusive price fixing and abuses of dominant positions but even if applicable to air transport there was still the problem that the Commission lacked powers to directly implement these rules. Article 87 enabled the Council of Ministers to confer implementing powers on the Commission. This the Council did not do in the case of air transport, and the Commission had to rely on the implementing provisions of Articles 88 and 89. These required the Commission to investigate infringements only in collaboration with the Member States. The Commission also lacked powers to directly impose penalties.

In 1981 attempts were made to take the Commission to task for not applying competition rules to fare-fixing restrictions. The Commission replied that fare fixing was an autonomous act of government whilst the competition rules applied to enterprises. A further difficulty arose in connection with designation. Licensing often only allowed one airline from each bilateral partner. This appeared to conflict with the freedom to supply services. However, Article 90, which covered public enterprises and enterprises to which member states grant special privileges, said that the rules of the Treaty should not be applied if their application would obstruct these enterprises in the tasks assigned to them. Members could therefore declare that their national flag carriers were enterprises granted special privileges and that strict licensing principles were essential.

---

[79]   Technically, the Council of Ministers was left with the power to decide what provisions should be made for air and sea transport: '[t]he Council may, acting unanimously, decide whether, and to what extent and by what procedure appropriate provisions may be laid down for sea and air transport'.

Ultimately, the changing climate of opinion and the US example had an effect. The Commission took a bolder line in 1979 encouraged to take a bolder line and issued *Civil Aviation Memorandum No. 1*. It made rather modest proposals.

- Increased possibilities of market entry and innovation were desirable but full freedom of access was a long-term prospect
- There was a need for the introduction of various forms of cheap fare.
- There was also a need to develop new cross-frontier services connecting regional centers within the Community – this was acted on later.
- An implementing regulation applying Articles 85 and 86 directly to air services was essential – a proposal on these lines was made in 1981.
- Increased competition emphasized the need for a policy on state aids.
- Whilst the right of establishment applied directly to airlines, Council action was necessary since practical and political obstacles would otherwise still exist.

In 1984 came *Civil Aviation Memorandum No. 2* that moved on to more specific liberalization proposals.

- Fares should be subject to a zone of flexibility system. A reference fare level and a zone of reasonableness around it would be arrived at on the basis of official double approval – i.e., both sides would have to agree. Having thus determined the scope for flexibility, airfares within the zone of flexibility would be subject to country of origin approval or double disapproval.
- The dominance of national flag fliers within the bilateral system was to remain relatively undisturbed except for allowing other carriers to enter and take up any unused route operating rights.
- In the case of the 50/50 division of traffic between the national flag carriers, state A could not oppose a build up of traffic by state B until state A's share had fallen to 25%.
- Inter-airline agreements should be subjected to control. Capacity agreements would be permissible provided airlines were free to withdraw. Revenue sharing pools might be exempted if their revenue redistributing effect was minimal.

The European Civil Aviation Conference (1981) showed the restricted nature of competition in European aviation. It indicated that only on 2% of city-to-city routes was there more than one airline operating per state. On 93% of routes there were apparently limitations on the number of flights that airlines could put on. Revenue pooling arrangements covered between 75% and 85% of total ton-kilometers flown. Inevitably comparisons were made between air fares in Europe and those in the US. According to the UK House of Lords, certain fares were double the US fares for similar distances, although the differences for return fares were much less marked. Other studies emerged supporting the view that European air fares were significantly higher. The Commission of the European Communities (1981) also carried out investigations. Just as scholars in the US had been able to compare the free competition fares of California with the CAB regulated rates, so it was possible in Europe to compare bilateral regulated rates with those offered by the competitive charter sector.[80]

There were two final precipitating factors. In 1979, the European Parliament was for the first time directly elected rather than being representatives of national parliaments. This enhanced its authority and it put forward a far-reaching draft Treaty of European Union. This led to an intergovernmental conference. Whilst the member states did not agree to go along with Parliament's scheme, they recognized the need to revive the idea of closer economic union. This led to the 1986 Single European Act a key feature of which was the economic commitment to complete the internal market by the end of 1992. Part of the program involved the need to address the continuing restrictions in air transport.

The final push came from the European Court of Justice and centered around the *Nouvelles Frontières* case which concerned the air fare-cutting activities of, amongst others, a French travel agent. Tickets had been sold below the officially approved price – a violation of the *Code de l'Aviation Civile*. The resulting legal proceedings in France in turn generated an appeal for a ruling from the Court of Justice as to the conformity of the *Code de l'Aviation Civile* with the law of the European Community. The result of the judgment was to encourage the Commission in the view that its powers to attack fare-fixing activities were greater than the lack of an implementing regulation might suggest. The Court said that if the Commission, or an appropriate national authority, was to pronounce adversely on an airline restriction, then a national court would have to take account of that fact. A party with standing might therefore bring an action against such a restriction in a national court and the restrictive arrangement in total might fall.

This forced the Council of Ministers to act although there were differences between Members on the desirability of competition. The Commission decided to increase pressure and to instigate proceedings against certain airlines. The Council decided that the best way to regain control was to agree to introduce deregulation but of a kind, and at a pace, of its choosing. Hence the 1987 deregulation package – the 'First Package'. The basic philosophy of these measures was that deregulation would take place in stages – evolution rather than revolution being the watchword and workable competition being the objective.

---

[80] Barrett (1987) reviewing the Commission's conclusions based on cascade studies, draws attention to the Commission's observation that 'it would appear that only a relatively small proportion of the difference between scheduled and charter costs cannot be attributed to inherent differences between the two modes of operation'.

A regulation was adopted enabling the Commission to apply the antitrust articles directly to airline operations.[81] Whilst this enabled the Commission to attack agreements restricting competition (and abuses by firms in a market-dominating position) another regulation was introduced that allowed airlines to continue to collude in certain matters.[82] This enabling regulation allowed the Commission to exempt *en bloc* three categories of agreements:[83] concerning joint planning and coordination of capacity, revenue sharing, consultations on tariffs and aircraft parking slot allocation; relating to computer reservation systems; and about ground handling services.

The Council also adopted a directive designed to provide airlines with greater pricing freedom. Whilst airlines could collude, the hope was that they would increasingly act individually. The degree to which competition emerged was recognized as depending on the degree to which airlines exhibited a competitive spirit in their approach to airfare applications made to national civil aviation authorities. The directive declared that member states shall approve fare applications provided they were reasonably related to the long-term fully allocated costs of the applicant air carrier, while taking account of other relevant factors. They had to consider the needs of consumers, the need for a satisfactory return on capital, the market situation, including the fares of other air carriers operating the route and the need to prevent dumping. State authorities were not allowed to keep price competition at bay by refusing to approve a fare application simply because it was lower than that offered by another carrier.

The new arrangements did not constitute free competition. Whilst conditions were laid down that reduced the national authorities' room for maneuver in rejecting airfares, they could still do so. If, however, there was disagreement on a fare the disagreeing party lost the right of veto because a right of arbitration was provided for and under this the disagreeing party could have its case overturned.

The key fares in the approval procedures were economy fares. The directive provided scope for discounts. Provided certain travel conditions are met fares could be reduced below the benchmark by varying amounts. Discounting and deep discounting were automatic rights. There was an additional degree of flexibility for fares which, when the directive was introduced, already fell below the bottom of the deep discount zone. Fifth freedom operators could match these discounted fares.

---

[81]   Only inter-state operations were covered; the intra-state services and services to third countries were not affected by this measure. Certain technical agreements were also left untouched.

[82]   Article 85, which attacks agreements, is not based on the *per se* principle. Rather, it prohibits but holds out the possibility of exemption when certain defined benefits can be brought forward in defense.

[83]   This block exemption power was of limited duration – it had to be revised by July 1990 and Commission regulations made under it expired by February 1991.

The 1987 package also made a start on liberalizing access to the market. A decision was adopted that provided for a deviation from the traditional air services agreement's 50/50 traffic split between the two countries. Member states were required to allow competition to change the shares up to 55/45 in the period to 30 September, 1989 and thereafter to allow it to change to 60/40. Fifth freedom traffic was not included in these ratios and was thus additional. There was also a provision in which serious financial damage to an air carrier could constitute grounds for the Commission to modify the 60/40 limit.

The decision additionally required members to accept multiple designation on a country pair basis by another member state. A member state was not obliged to accept the designation of more than one air carrier on a route by the other state (i.e., city pair basis) unless certain conditions were satisfied. These conditions become progressively less restrictive over time. The decision also made certain fifth freedom rights automatic but these were hedged around with safeguards. Flights had to be extensions of a service from the state of registration or a preliminary of a service to the state of registration.[84] Additionally, one of the airports had to be a category-two airport – this prevented competition on the key routes between main airports. The above example by involving Birmingham (category two) and Brussels (category one) met the condition. There was also a ceiling on the proportion of passengers that could be in the fifth freedom category – on an annual basis not more than 30% of the people carried could be in the Brussels to Birmingham category.[85]

In December 1989 the Council of Transport Ministers returned to the issue of deregulation. A 'Second Package' involving more deregulation was entered into by the Union.

- In respect of the freedom of airlines to make competitive fares, from the beginning of 1993 a system of double disapproval was accepted. Only if both civil aviation authorities on a route refuse to sanction a fare application could an airline be precluded from offering it to its passengers. The regulation essentially provided for a revised system of discount fares based on a reference fare within which all fares meeting the specified criteria were approved automatically.[86]

---

[84]   An example of the latter would be that Aer Lingus might already have a right to fly between Birmingham and Dublin. It could now enter the Brussels to Birmingham route normally reserved for UK (and Belgian) bilateral operators, i.e., it could drop off in Birmingham passengers picked up in Brussels on a flight en route to Dublin.

[85]   Both the fare directive and the access decision represented minimum degrees of liberalization that had to be accepted by all member states. More flexible arrangements were permitted.

[86]   The zones based on the reference, standard fare were 95% to 105% (normal economy), 80% to 94% (discount) and 30% to 79% (deep discount).

- The old system of setting limits to the division of traffic between the bilateral partners was to totally disappear in a phased manner.
- Member States endorsed the principle that governments should not discriminate against airlines provided they meet safety and technical standards and are run economically.[87]
- The Council agreed to address the problem of ownership rules. An airline typically had to be substantially owned by a European state before it could fly from that country. The Council abolished this rule over a two-year period. The implication was that airlines could enjoy fifth freedom rights provided they are registered in the Community.
- Air cargo services were liberalized so that a carrier operating from its home state to another member country can take cargo into a third member state or fly from one member state to another and then to its home state. Cabotage, or operations between two free-standing states, was not liberalized.

The final, 'Third Package' came in 1992 to take effect from the following year. This initiated a phased move that, by 1997, resulted in a regulatory framework similar to US domestic aviation although important questions remain regarding the EU's role with respect to international aviation outside the Union.

- The measures removed significant barriers to entry by setting common rules governing safety and financial requirements for new airlines.[88] Since January 1993, EU airlines became able to fly between member states without restriction and within member states (other than their own), subject to some controls on fares and capacity.
- National restrictions on ticket prices were removed with only safeguards if fares fell too low or rose too high.
- Consecutive cabotage was introduced allowing a carrier to add a 'domestic leg' on a flight starting out of its home base to a destination in another member state if the number of passengers on the second leg did not exceed 50% of the total in the main flight. Starting in 1997, full cabotage was permitted, and fares are generally unregulated.
- Foreign ownership among EU carriers is permitted, and they have, for EU internal purposes, become European airlines. This change does not apply to extra-EU agreements where national bilateral arrangements still pertain.[89]

---

[87] This was reported to be a response to a case made by UTA, the French overseas airline, which lobbied the Commission because the French civil aviation authorities refused to allow UTA to compete on European routes served by Air France.

[88] Charter operators are also allowed to set up in any European market and can sell tickets to private individuals on a seat-only basis at both ends of a service.

[89] One result has been a considerable increase in cross-share holdings and a rapidly expanding number of alliances (UK Civil Aviation Authority, 1994).

Early analysis of reforms by the UK Civil Aviation Authority (1994) indicated that the reforms of the 1990s produced, in terms of multiple airlines serving various market areas, greater competition both on EU domestic routes and on international routes within the Union (Table 5.16). Similarly, Schipper (1999) looking at 34 inter-city pair markets between 1988 and 1992 found that on fully liberalized routes, the standard economy fare had fallen by 34% and the departure frequency had increased by 36%.

Table 5.16 Changes in competition on selected EU scheduled routes

| | Proportion of round trip flights with two or more competitors | | | |
| | Domestic routes | | International routes | |
	December 92	December 94	December 92	December 94
Austria	0%	0%	12%	12%
Denmark	0%	4%	8%	11%
Finland	9%	9%	7%	0%
France	10%	9%	26%	35%
Germany	36%	40%	10%	15%
Greece	0%	0%	0%	16%
Ireland	0%	0%	36%	46%
Italy	28%	26%	7%	15%
Netherlands	0%	0%	20%	18%
Norway	27%	38%	0%	9%
Portugal	47%	35%	14%	37%
Spain	0%	60%	14%	20%
Sweden	47%	47%	12%	12%
UK	43%	56%	40%	45%
Total	26%	36%	19%*	25%*

* Includes Belgium and Luxembourg.

The changes varied but countries such as Greece and Portugal increased the number of competitive international services within the EU area considerably. Many routes, however, because either multiple services were simply not technically sustainable or institutional impediments still limited market entry remained monopolies in 1994.

More recently, the Commission of the European Communities (1996), in examining the impact of the Third Package, found evidence of important consumer benefits. These included, a rise in the number of routes flown within the EU from 490 to 520 between 1993 and 1995. Additionally, some 30% of Union routes are now served by two operators and 6% by three operators or more, 80 new airlines had been created while only 60 had disappeared, fares had fallen on routes where there are at least three operators and overall, after allowance is made for charter operations, 90%–95% of passenger on intra-Union routes were traveling on reduced fares, a caveat being that there were quite significant variations in the patterns of fares charged across routes.[90]

There had been little change in fares on routes that remain monopolies or duopolies. The number of fifth freedom routes doubled to 30 between 1993 and 1996 although this type of operation remained a relatively small feature of the market and seventh freedoms were little used. Indeed, much of the new competition has been on domestic routes where routes operated by two or more carriers rose from 65 in January 1963 to 114 in January 1996 with the largest expansions in France, Spain and Germany. The charter market has also continued to grow and in some countries accounts for more than 80% of traffic. Table 5.17 offers selective data on changes in scheduled air fares where competition has emerged.

Table 5.17 Scheduled airfares from Brussels (Belgian Francs)

Return fares From Brussels to:	January 1993			January 1993		July 1995	
	IATA	SN	BQ	IATA	SN	BQ	IATA
Madrid	14 570	11 230	4 600–9 000	14 500	8 490	4 600–9 000	14 500
Vienna	16 290	17 790	5 600–9 000	17 790	6 990	5 600–9 000	17 790
Rome	18 730	9 990	5 600–9 000	20 170	5 600	5 600–9 000	20 170

Source: Commission of the European Communities (1966).

A recent UK Civil Aviation Authority (1998) study has also looked at the evolving market. It finds some indication that the dominance of the major carriers has declined somewhat with reform (Table 5.18) with regional carriers enjoying a larger market share. The only country, however, where the traditional national carrier does not still control more than 70% of the market is Ireland where Ryanair has 60%. Underlying this, however, is evidence that much of the growth has been in short haul markets, with the larger carriers strengthening their positions on inter-continental routes.

[90]   Mandel (1999) found that found that routes with three or more competing airlines (about a third of the total in terms of passengers carried) fares have fallen.

Table 5.18   Capacity of air system (total number of seats available in thousands) on scheduled return flights within the EU

	December 1992	December 1997
All carriers	12 232	16 893
Flag carriers	9 929	11 355
Regional carriers	2 303	5 538
Share of flag carriers	81%	67%

The study also looked at changes in fares between 1992 and 1997 for four markets (Amsterdam/London, Brussels/Rome, Madrid/Rome and Madrid/Milan) and found a mixed outcome. Fares had not fallen dramatically and, for some classes, especially business classes, there had been a rise. This simple statistical analysis does not, however, reflect changes of patronage between classes or the effects of frequent flyer and other benefits.

The series of EU reforms also seem to have influenced the size of aircraft flown in Europe; Table 5.19 shows the slow decline in the average number of seats. This is in the face of increased infrastructure capacity problems (see Chapter 9). This pattern can in part be explained by the tendency of airlines to compete in terms of service quality in a less regulated environment. Passengers put a premium on a high frequency of services. Linked to this, experiences from the 1978 US deregulation also suggest that hub-and-spoke operations can lead to the use of smaller aircraft. The growth of alliances has also provided the potential for carriers to make more efficient use of their fleets.

More recently, the EU Commission has switched its attention to the matter of the relationship between EU air transport policy and external relations (Mencik von Zebinsky, 1996). The traditional right of governments to negotiate bilateral air service agreements with non-EU states has been brought into question by the Commission.[91] The adoption of the offer of Open Skies policies by the US and the *de facto* granting of anti-trust immunity to the airlines of countries that follow this course have led to divisions in the EU. In particular, the UK has traditionally

---

[91]   This does not mean the EU Commission has not previously been involved in negotiating aviation agreements with third countries. The early agreement between the EU, Norway and Sweden that extended the scope of the EU air transport legislation to the latter countries is an example. The EU Commission was given permission in 1996 through the majority voting procedure to negotiate on behalf of all EU countries on soft issues regarding aviation but did gain the unanimous support for taking over responsibility for hard rights.

opposed giving up negotiating rights with the US, given the domination of Heathrow as the main trans-Atlantic hub. The issue has been complicated by the development of global alliances that fall within the remit of the EU's competition agencies as the Transport Directorate.

Table 5.19 Average size of aircraft used by AEA members on European and domestic air services

Year	Average number of seats	Year	Average number of seats
1973	106.5	1983	137.0
1974	109.5	1984	135.0
1975	113.0	1985	135.5
1976	120.0	1986	134.5
1977	124.0	1987	134.0
1978	123.0	1988	135.0
1977	125.5	1989	135.5
1978	131.5	1990	134.0
1979	136.0	1991	133.0
1980	139.0	1992	133.0

5.5 CONCLUSIONS

The different paths of air transport market deregulation open to governments confronted them with the types of choices that are not easy to make. The US deregulated its domestic passenger market relatively rapidly and in a predetermined manner. There were some external lessons from deregulation of other sectors in other countries, such as that of UK trucking, but they were limited and have never been really analyzed in any detail. Canada and the EU, for somewhat different reasons, pursued gradualist approaches that really had no preconceived pattern underlying them. The latter had the clear advantage that those responsible knew from the US experiences what to expect in broad terms from liberalization. Their institutional arrangements and market structures, however, were somewhat different.

The US domestic market also evolved for some time after deregulation as both internal adjustments were made following learning experiences and as external forces changed. Indeed, the airlines are still testing alternative hubbing structures, seeking the configuration that provides a preferred combination of costs and revenue. There are also on-going policy debates in the US over such issues as how to handle potential market failures such as predatory behavior and how to provide air transport infrastructure most efficiently.

In all cases, the network regulatory reforms seem to have generated important net consumer benefits. Some groups gained more than others, especially geographically, and there were unquestionably some losers but in aggregate the effects seem to have been positive. There were some losers amongst the owners of carriers that lost market share or were forced to cease trading. The implications for labor have been mixed. The slower changes in Canada and the EU do not, however, seem to have reduced the costs of transition and may even have increased them in terms of the uncertainties that were introduced. What also seems to emerge is that there are economies of experience in network activities gained by actors having been in the market for a length of time. In most cases incumbent carriers tended to fare better than new entrants.

6   FILLING INCOMPLETE NETWORKS: INTERNATIONAL AIR TRANSPORT

6.1   INTRODUCTION

There are a number of microeconomic reasons, for example to do with nature of market structures, why airline networks even in market conditions may not be complete and the following chapter looks at some of these in detail. Here attention is on problems of missing elements, either links or nodes, that are a function of institutional factors and especially of government actions in the market. In particular, attention is paid to the problems of international air transport markets where institutional arrangements, often seen as a mechanism by individual governments to protect their own short term interests, have led to incomplete networks. This is not to say that in the absence of the current regimes other institutional structures would have proved tractable, but rather the objective is to consider ways in which the system of international agreements could be advanced to stimulate greater economic efficiency in air transport.

Air transport networks suffer from a variety of missing links and the attention here is purely on missing international services. There may be missing domestic links but these are less common as deregulation permeates most national markets. The focus is also on the problems of international agreements.[1] Gaps may also occur for other reasons that are only touched upon. Inadequate or inappropriate air traffic control can lead to the non-provision of services that would otherwise be economically justified. Since air traffic control is largely publicly owned and controlled this is another form of intervention failure. Airport capacity or location is influential in determining the air services that are supplied and, again, public policy can distort leading to sub-optimal networks and missing links.[2] Of course, in some cases excessive investment in airports or sub-optimal airport pricing policies can also lead to an excessively large network.

Transitioning from the current position of missing elements in the international air transport system to something closer to the optimum is unlikely to be costless and will inevitably impose a burden on some operators.[3] This is

[1]   Developments in the EU are a special case of recent developments in multilateral policy and were covered in more detail in Chapter 5.

[2]   Chapter 8 looks in more detail at airport issues.

[3]   It also implies a reduced requirement for negotiators and other administrators which, following some schools of economic thought, does not encourage public servants interested in their own welfare from rigorously pursuing reform.

essentially a political issue but one that cannot, in practice, be ignored. The chapter looks at some of the possible ways in which efficiency could be improved and at least some of the gaps in the international network filled.

6.2 CAUSES OF INTERNATIONAL AIR TRANSPORT GAPS

The Chicago Convention of 1944 established the bilateral system of air service agreements covering international air transport that have since governed relations between most countries.[4] These have the advantage that limiting the effects of agreements to specific bilateral partners permits experimentation with change on a piece-meal basis. They can, however, as experience has shown, prove to be very restrictive and inflexible whenever one partner wishes.

The issue of missing international air transport links is not, though, strictly one of the bilateral regime *per se* but rather relates to the ways in which it has often been implemented. Bilateral air service agreements can have the considerable merits of flexibility and can be tailored to meet the requirements of specific markets. There are, for instance, bilateral agreements such as those between the US and the Netherlands, the US and Canada, and the more recent US–German agreement that are relatively liberal. Further, the geographic limitations of specific bilateral agreements may be partially circumvented either by a web of more liberal ones or through the use of sixth freedom rights. The traditional types of restrictions on entry and exit inherent under bilateral arrangements may, however, impose limitations on the development of the industry.

The major underlying weakness of the bilateral system is that it cannot accommodate complex international network traffic flows, which are multilateral in nature. The terms of the bilateral agreement reflect the negotiating power and current aviation policies of the countries involved as well as national interests including trade and tourism. It also takes time to time to renegotiate bilateral agreements and this often means the institutional structure lags behind market and management trends. With the more restrictive bilateral agreements, productivity was usually low in the protected airlines and costs were high. High fares resulted from the exclusion of new market entrants and the division of the predetermined market size among the incumbents. The prices for international air services have largely been ceded by national governments to the airlines themselves organized under the auspices of the IATA. The control of output to predetermined levels was a precondition of the high fares charged. The protected carriers created by regulatory

---

[4]   Chapter 4 provided a more detailed account of the history of international air transport regulation.

bans on new entrants produced too little and charged too much, compared to a market- determined system.

There are also implications of the bilateral system for multi-country operations that require a series of bilateral agreements. Equally, the ICAO and others have pointed to the lack of adequate dispute resolution procedures that can lead to protracted disputes. They are also *ad hoc* in their nature and consequently must be treated in the context to which they apply. Again, this makes assessment of their efficiency difficult. Notwithstanding the liberalizing changes that have occurred, there is normally the requirement that designated airlines are effectively owned by nationals of the states involved. Whilst fifth freedom rights are increasingly being granted, these are of no practical use unless they are also embraced in the bilateral agreement with the third country involved. Even when this is available the impact can be quite small, as found with the fifth freedom liberalization in the EU's Third Aviation Package.

Liberal bilateral agreements also do not free up domestic cabotage rights, which can limit the opportunity to develop genuine international hub-and-spoke operations. There are ways in which airlines can circumvent some of these difficulties (e.g., by becoming involved, either financially or through operating arrangements, with national carriers) but these, although they can generate various forms of benefit, may not be as efficient as possible and are themselves the subject of government impediments.

There are important links between air service agreements and ownership of airlines. There are differences in national laws on foreign ownership and, despite the gradual process of privatization that is occurring, many international airlines are still publicly owned or have a major government shareholding. In other cases there are restrictions that prevent or limit foreign investment in a country's aviation industry. While there is some variation in the limits, most stipulate that control of an air carrier must reside with citizens or residents of the nation, and that foreign ownership of a carrier is restricted to a percentage, often in the range 25% to 49% of the voting common stock. Where nations do not have formal legislative limits on foreign ownership, there may be *de facto* restrictions.

Under the bilateral system each country is free to decide exactly what is meant by the term 'substantial ownership'. The trend in the past has been to favor national ownership,[5] although this is being modified. The EU's Package sets no limit on the stake a Union national or Union airline can hold in an airline registered in another EU state. Restrictions on non-EU shareholdings, however,

---

[5]   More rarely there is joint ownership, as is the case with the participation of Norway, Sweden and Denmark in SAS.

remain and, with a few limited exceptions non-EU, investors cannot hold a majority stake in a EU airline.[6]

In the US, foreign shareholding of up to 49% of equity under certain circumstances and 25% of the voting stock is now possible. The government also imposes *ad hoc* control tests to determine whether a foreign shareholder, irrespective of equity held, could exercise substantial influence over decision making. Australia's privatization measures have also seen British Airways taking up an ownership position in Qantas, through a trade sale, while privatization of Air New Zealand in 1989 saw a consortium of Qantas, Japan Airlines and American Airlines purchasing 35% of the share issue. In Japan, aircraft registration by foreign nationals is restricted and foreign ownership of airlines exceeding a third of voting interest is prohibited. The pattern is for restrictions on foreign ownership and involvement to slowly recede. However, the pattern is not even across regions and markets. Moreover, with the change has come further developments in the system of international air service agreements.

6.3 ISSUES OF STRUCTURAL ADJUSTMENT IN INTERNATIONAL AVIATION

Air transport industries in different countries have distinguishing features, which means any process of structural change will not commence from the same starting point. Some of the variation relates to inherent differences in comparative advantage, and this forms the very basis of desirable trade. Not all is market-based, however, but rather stems from institutional arrangements (involving such things as subsidies and legal monopolies). Reforming these arrangements is not easy because, as Levine (1995) points out, choices are limited by history, geography, infrastructure and commercial realities.

International aviation is not a homogeneous industry. Airlines, for a variety of historical, institutional and commercial reasons, differ in size and structure. In some cases, these differences arise from the interaction between the economies of domestic aviation and the economies of international aviation. For example, the large domestic market in the US has fostered the creation of particularly large hub structures and network carriers. Airlines from smaller countries do not have the benefits of operating in a large domestic market, which may put these carriers at an initial disadvantage in providing networks of services. However, some small-

[6]   Further, investment, if it is felt to exercise a decisive influence over an airline, can be disallowed. There is the possibility of a more liberal exchange of equity between EU airlines and non-EU investors if the latter are from countries that themselves have liberalized their rules on foreign investment in their airlines.

country operators, such as KLM and Singapore Airlines, seem to have largely overcome this shortcoming by developing extensive sixth freedom rights.

Airlines of different countries also vary in their cost structures. Part of the variation in operating costs may be the effect of the level of currency exchange rates; another part may be explained by the nature of the markets involved (e.g., in terms of length of haul). But even when due allowance is made for such features, significant differences in economic efficiency between airlines remain (Distexhe and Perelman, 1994). Some of these variations can be explained by factors such as economies of experience or be due to economies of market presence, but others stem from institutional factors, such as the availability of subsidies and the protection afforded by ownership. Additionally, there are disparities in the level of management efficiency, often the result of inadequate commercial incentives. These institutional differences can pose political problems for restructuring since they inevitably mean that any rapid contraction in demand or change in the institutional framework may result in some airlines contracting or ceasing to exist. These are, however, problems common to all dynamic situations.

Institutional arrangements differ across international markets. Although the emergence of airline alliances has reduced the impact of these variations, there are still differences between markets that are subject to multilateral arrangements (such as the international market among EU members) and those where bilateral agreements continue. But even within the latter, bilateral air service agreements exhibit wide variations (e.g., in terms of the number of airlines designated and capacity allowed) and, in many cases, contain confidential agreed minutes. This makes it difficult to integrate various regional and local airline markets.

Regulatory frameworks also interact with longer-term market trends. Aircraft markets, for instance, have been swinging from periods of glut, with many aircraft available on the market, to periods of scarcity. In recent years aircraft manufacturers have sometimes significantly reduced production lead times; nevertheless, long lead times and the inability to forecast demand accurately make such swings likely. The situation is aggravated if operators are regulated to prevent them from varying frequency or capacity. Such regulations often lead to airlines deploying sub–optimal aircraft fleets.

It is often easier to bring about change during high points in the trade cycle when resources for compensation and to cover transitional costs are most freely available.[7] The financial health of air transport is, however, particularly prone to cyclical effects. For example, although the later years of the 1990s saw many airlines making record profits, commercial aviation as a whole suffered major financial losses in the early 1990s. The ICAO reported net profit margins for the world airline industry of -2.2% and -1.8% for 1990 and 1991, respectively. The US scheduled carriers as a group accounted for a combined operating loss of $2.5

---

[7]   In other words it may be possible to achieve a genuine Pareto improvement.

billion in 1992, which should be set in the context of a worldwide loss of only $1.5 billion experienced by ICAO airlines (International Civil Aviation Organisation, 1994). While a significant part of the losses was in domestic aviation, international markets also suffered. The IATA estimated, for example, that its members lost $15.6 billion between 1990 and 1993, with only a token profit of $1.8 billion in 1994. The financial situation varied by routes and by carrier. Many airlines have suffered from cash flows that have not been sufficient to cover self-financed investment. This does not, of course, mean that all airlines experienced losses over the period. Some, such as British Airways,[8] Air New Zealand, and Singapore Airlines, have tended to be consistently profitable. Equally, some airlines such as Lufthansa, KLM or Northwest Airlines, while showing poor performance in the beginning of the 1990s, managed to effect a much quicker turn-around than others.

The severe losses suffered in the beginning of the 1990s typify some of the factors that affect airline markets. They were largely attributed to the worldwide economic recession and the impact of special factors such as the Gulf War. The difficulties were compounded by over-optimistic investments undertaken by many airlines in the late 1980s. However, while cyclical swings and special circumstances have been important determinants, it appears that, in recent history, market peaks and troughs have become more pronounced. For the period 1960-90, for example, yields dropped by 2.2% per annum for passenger traffic and by 3.4% per annum for freight, whilst unit costs only fell on average by 1.9% per annum. The upturn in the world economy since the mid-1990s, coupled with internal efficiency improvements, has eased the financial position of many airlines, although there are still very pronounced differences in the performance of individual carriers.[9]

Even allowing for this, the sector has only enjoyed an annual surplus of less than 2% over the past twenty years, even allowing for the very high profits of the late 1990s. An important consideration is whether this situation is sustainable. The International Air Transport Association (1992) has estimated, for example, that an operating surplus (before interest and taxes) of 6% per annum on international services is needed to finance future requirements.[10]

---

[8]   Although making a significant loss at the beginning of 2000.

[9]   The Asian economic crisis added to this problem and was particularly detrimental to carriers with significant activities in that region and with limited scope for transferring their aircraft to other spheres of operation.

[10]   The operating surplus of international operations of IATA members was only 4.8% in 1994 and, although a surplus of 7.8% was earned in 1995, the long-term trend is well below that needed to match the returns IATA feels are adequate for a sustainable airline industry. The ability of an industry to meet its long-term investment needs is also determined by the structure of its financial liabilities. Declining operating margins of many airlines have led to a significant rise in debt–equity ratios over past

The complexity of the situation is compounded by the need for the industry to retire old aircraft (*inter alia*, in the light of stricter environmental norms regarding noise levels) and to invest in new capacity to meet projected demand. While estimates suggest that improvements in load factors and aircraft utilization, combined with the projected use of larger aircraft, mean that fewer planes will be required to cope with any given future traffic level - e.g., it is predicted that by 2005 the 1990 volume of traffic could be handled using 37% fewer aircraft - this must be set against the fact that the total volume of business will increase significantly. Boeing forecasts that nearly 12 000 aircraft will be delivered over the next twenty years at a total cost of $857 billion (1992 prices), and the ICAO has produced a figure of $800 billion for the period 1991-2000.

To some extent the financial problem has been cushioned in the short term by developments in the wider aviation market. Aircraft manufacturers' progress in cutting production lead time, for example, has increased the flexibility of airlines in placing aircraft orders. There is also an increased division between ownership of hardware in the sector and the provision of aviation services. Many airlines now lease rather than purchase aircraft, and aircraft manufacturers themselves now often provide tailored financial packages to facilitate the purchase of their products.

A further problem has been the financial difficulties encountered by the aircraft leasing companies, which have made them more cautious in their leasing practices to airlines. This poses particular problems in the longer-haul market where, because larger aircraft are less easily redeployed, leasing companies tend to charge a premium. A sound financial foundation clearly increases air carriers' scope for undertaking structural change. The concern is that this does not exist at present in international aviation.[11]

The structural adjustments airlines are making to allow them to operate in less regulated markets is being undertaken within a framework of national competition policies. Many of the world's leading international air carriers, however, now

years. For US carriers the debt–equity ratio more than doubled between 1978 and 1992. Although these data suggest that in the past access to credit has not been a major problem for the airline industry, it is questionable whether in the future debt financing would be available to the same extent. In the longer term, high debt–equity ratios are only tolerated in industries with relatively stable cash flows and little temporal change in their earnings performance. This is not the situation with regard to international aviation. Capital markets are increasingly perceiving the inherent risks as witnessed by the development of US airline shares, which in early 1996 were traded at a 55% discount to the general market index.

[11]   The Comitè des Sages for Air Transport (1994), for instance, pointed to a possible 35% funding gap between the flow of finance into the European industry and the cost of restructuring, even if traditional modes of financing were to be improved. The situation differs in other geographical markets because of variations in the organization of their financial institutions.

operate almost exclusively in international, not domestic markets. Even carriers with large domestic markets, such as Air Canada and Qantas, still derive significant revenues and traffic from international routes. At the domestic level, many nations have a regulated conduct exemption for air transport from the application of competition law, or certain elements of the law. The rationale is that, in some instances, directed regulations will deal more effectively with aviation specific competition matters. This exemption is to prevent needless duplication of regulatory authority. Similar exemptions also may apply in nations using government ownership of enterprises as a policy tool.

With domestic liberalization, the process of transition can be relatively straightforward. When passing the relevant deregulation legislation, the new law either makes clear the precedence of existing competition laws, or alternatively simultaneously modifies the competition laws to make clear their applicability to the now deregulated industry.[12] With liberalization of wider international markets, applicability of competition law is often less clear. This is a generic problem of applying competition law to international enterprise, that is not specific to air transport. A number of nations, such as the US, take the view that their competition law applies to conduct outside their territory if it affects their international or domestic markets. Many other states, however, do not recognize this form of extraterritorial power. Some nations' general competition laws specifically exclude applicability to multinational enterprises while others have ambiguity in their laws and have either chosen not to test the law in court or have not had the opportunity to do so.

Unclear and conflicting competition rules may create uncertainty regarding the extent to which cooperative activity is lawful thereby compromising the efficiency of the restructuring process. Compliance with two or several sets of rules can expose airlines to substantial additional cost, in particular when they affect the formation of international alliance networks and the development of code-sharing operations.

6.4 NOTIONS AND CHALLENGES OF TRANSITION

There is growing experience concerning the alternative ways in which transition may be approached as the lessons of new international bilateral arrangements are learned and regional multilateralism has taken place in some markets. The

---

[12]   Where agency jurisdictions overlap, this is clarified. In the US, airline merger review under the 1978 Airline Deregulation Act was assigned to the Department of Transportation until 1989, at which time it was phased out in favor of the Justice Department review under general antitrust laws. In Canada overlapping jurisdiction still prevails, with merger reviews being conducted separately by the National Transportation Agency and the Bureau of Competition Policy.

experiences of domestic transitions also provide guidance to the merits of different strategies (see again Chapter 5).

As we have seen in the context of domestic reforms, from the broadest perspective, there are a variety of ways of approaching transition. To some extent all have been partially adopted in different markets, including international aviation markets, over recent years. By broad perspective is meant the overall strategy and implementation of the transition process rather than the details of the changes which take place. At one extreme, there is what may be thought of as the 'Big Bang' approach with reforms suddenly being initiated in a single package. Another approach is to have a predetermined phasing-in of change, whereby the overall set of institutional reforms is initiated according to a clearly defined timetable. Alternatively, change can be evolutionary, with each stage in the process being developed from the experiences of previous phases. There are, as discussed in Chapter 5, several detailed variants on these theories.

6.4.1 The overall strategy

The 'Big Bang' approach, whereby there would be a sudden and comprehensive change in the institutional framework governing international aviation, is an extreme case. The main advantage of this approach, as we have seen, is that it removes a number of the first-mover advantages that some airlines may enjoy in a phased change. The approach may also. in some cases, involve lower transaction costs, as players need only adjust to the new position once. The disadvantages stem mainly from the possibility that the institutional changes may be flawed and consequently seriously damage the development of the sector. It also imposes heavy burdens on those in the sector who - for a variety of reasons, e.g., relating to existing institutional frameworks - start from a more disadvantaged position than others. Finally, there are difficulties because of variations in national legal systems that impinge on aviation but are of a broader nature and cannot be readily changed to meet developments in any individual sector.

In practice, given the multidimensional nature of issues surrounding aviation, the 'Big Bang' approach in its pure form is an unlikely option. A more realistic approach is that of phased change. Phasing-in of measures has the advantage of allowing airlines and others to plan their strategies. Phasing can also be developed in such a way as to address carriers' fears arising from different competitive starting points. Predetermined gradualism does, however, have the disadvantage that it may not keep pace with changes in the market system. It may also provide time for entrenched interests to develop strategies to protect their positions in the new institutional environment.

An important variation of the gradual approach is phased institutional change with no clearly pre-defined sequence of changes - the learning-by-doing approach. This, for instance, was the pattern adopted by the EU, whereby there were three main packages of measures each in themselves independent and not fully preplanned. This has the advantages of the more formally phased approach, and additionally allows for learning effects derived from the experiences of previous packages. It does, however, introduce a degree of uncertainty about the nature and timing of subsequent changes, and problems may arise over the implementation of each stage. It also provides scope for game-playing by those involved as they lobby policy makers for particular types of change in each package.

A further dimension to this issue is the way transition in international aviation fits within the more general transition arrangements that are taking place in world trade. International aviation services have been embraced as an annex to the General Agreement on Trade in Services but only in a very limited way (Katz, 1995).[13] At present the annex includes no hard rights and only covers three doing-business issues: aircraft repair and maintenance services, the selling and marketing of air transport services, and CRSs. In practice even these elements have not been fully adopted in the short term, and of the first 26 nations to sign GATS, 25 asked for 'Most Favored Nation'. exemption regarding selling and marketing, 24 have done so for CRS and three for repair and maintenance. Further, GATS is not permitted to reduce or affect a member's obligations under bilateral or multilateral agreements already in effect, and GATS dispute procedures cannot be invoked until those under existing ASA arrangements have been exhausted.

The advantage of a GATT/GATS-style strategy on transition in international aviation is that developments in aviation can be combined with those in other sectors. This offers the opportunity in international trade negotiations to move forward on a much broader front and to improve efficiency across a range of sectors. Countries, for example, which have traditionally pursued the protectionist approach to aviation policy may be willing to adopt a more liberal approach regarding this sector provided that they expect an overall increase in welfare from the liberalization across several sectors. The trade-off may involve commodities as well as other services.

Where there are practical difficulties with GATS, as seen by the claims for exemption from its civil aviation elements, is with, in particular, the Most Favored Nation principle. This states that a signatory must extend the trading rights afforded in its most liberal agreement with another country to all other signatories. This does not involve reciprocity; therefore, if a country negotiates an extremely liberal bilateral ASA with another, then other signatories may freely enter this market without any corresponding relaxation of entry or other controls over their own skies.

In economic terms it potentially poses a free rider problem. Countries that are in a strong bilateral bargaining position will, therefore, be reluctant to bring civil

---

[13]   International air transportation has a 'unique sectorial exclusion' under the GATS, a situation arrived at unanimously by the 108 delegates at the Uruguay round of negotiations in 1995. But the situation is required to be reviewed every five years.

aviation under a GATS framework. Additionally, there may be serious problems with the National Treatment principle, whereby a trading partner must accord to service suppliers of other countries treatment no less favorable than that which it accords its own service suppliers. This could imply the opening of national aviation markets to cabotage. This would probably prove unacceptable to larger countries unless there was a wider liberalization of international markets. In addition to these problems of general obligations, there are specific commitments in the GATS framework, such as might relate to market access and rights of establishment, and these can be applied in a variety of ways. States are effectively confronted with a matrix of options as to the modes of supply in meeting these commitments. The potentially large number of possible options can make the process unwieldy and may reduce the prospects for liberalizing international air transport within the GATS framework.

While GATS has to date had minimum effects on international aviation, over the longer term it may prove to have a useful supplementary role in helping to expand liberalization initiated through bilateral and 'regionalateral' structures to a larger number of countries. It also fits into an established framework of international arrangements that have enjoyed success in liberalizing trade in goods and, to it more limited extent, services. A number of detailed possibilities for this future role of GATS exist. For instance, the development of reciprocity within the aviation sector, possibly through more liberalized and harmonized bilateral air service agreements, could subsequently be extended to embrace conditional applications of National Treatment principles. Following from this could be the automatic implementation of the National Treatment principle and an extension of this regime from the aviation sector framework to a multi-sector framework, and from a bilateral structure to a wider geographical approach.

6.4.2 Pragmatic options

At the detailed level, the institutional arrangements covering international aviation embrace a number of key areas. As shown in the earlier chapters, each set of institutional arrangements involves its own set of issues and characteristics. Equally, each of these areas provides scope for a variety of transition paths, and these are outlined in turn below.

Some of the main options, together with the pros and cons, are as follows.

* *Existing regimes of bilateral agreements* can be modified where there is considerable diversity in the nature of the arrangements across routes, and where not all details are always transparent. This is an established system that has evolved since the Chicago Convention over 50 years ago. It has the advantage of being flexible in its implementation and allows countries to retain traditional controls over their airspace. In practical terms it is a system countries are familiar with, and one in which change is generally relatively

straightforward since it does not entail a large number of consenting parties. However, since the system has tended to focus on individual routes or small sets of routes, it can lead to difficulties in arriving at a high level of efficiency over networks of international aviation services.

- *Liberalization within the `bilateral frameworks* whereby, when bilateral agreements are renegotiated, specific provisions using defined standard terms may be incorporated. Such provisions might include open route exchanges, multiple designation, capacity freedom, fare freedom complete third and fourth freedom rights, and so on. This type of approach enjoys the benefits of introducing a degree of uniformity into the existing, quite disparate, system of agreements without disrupting their basic structure. The problem is that there may be few common concepts of practical importance which all or a significant number of countries would accept.

- A *lead sector approach* whereby specific markets, such as cargo or charter services, are liberalized first, with these providing a basis for subsequent liberalization of other services.[14] The advantages here are those of improving efficiency in fields where there is some common ground for agreement, and in providing demonstration effects for a subsequent widening of the liberalization process. In particular, with the increasing blurring of the distinction between charter and scheduled services and the strong growth in air freight traffic, liberalization of charter and cargo markets could have significant add-on effects.

- *Restrained liberalization.* A variation on the lead sector approach can be to introduced partial forms of liberalization for specific types of service, possibly for a limited period. An illustration of this in the past was the approach to cabotage within the EU with a limited form of such operations being deployed prior to the final opening of domestic markets to foreign carriers. This enables change to embody a degree of gradualism and also allows confidence to be built regarding wider reforms.

- *Allowing reform by indirect means* is a passive option and unlikely to be fully effective. This may involve governments allowing the continued growth and development of strategic airline alliances and other commercially driven cooperative arrangements between international airlines. Such actions allow airlines to enter markets to which they have no direct legal access (e.g., US airlines outside of the US–UK bilateral code sharing services into London Heathrow). By its nature this approach is second best because many actions are precluded but it can offer short-term mechanisms for circumventing institutional obstacles.

---

[14] The OECD, for example, from the late 1990s, been focusing on looking at ways to liberalize air cargo markets. This approach centers on standardization of bilateral ASAs.

- *Corridor liberalization.* Under this approach participants over one or more major corridors – such as the North Atlantic – seek to liberalize that particular market. This can be seen as a spatial variant of the lead sector approach, but has the added problem that it may involve agreement across a number of countries. It is also difficult to envisage mechanisms whereby liberalization of one corridor extends to others, apart from indirect demonstration effects.
- *Region-to-region arrangements.* These entail negotiations between groups of countries that have common interests in international aviation, e.g., NAFTA countries and EU Members, to bring about a single localized aviation market.[15] This would allow groupings of nations to come together and exploit more fully the liberalization that has already occurred inside the groupings. There is, though, the potential problem that it could result in large regional blocs excluding countries which are outside regional groupings.
- *Open skies agreements.* This is where airlines of the contracting parties may compete openly for international traffic. This may itself take several forms, ranging from the more limited bilateral 'Open Skies' policies currently being pursued by the US to completely free access among a group of countries. This general type of approach has the strength of allowing domestic markets to be regulated independently of international markets.
- *Phased multilateralism (plurilateralism).* This involves a gradual branching out from a single core of states which initiate open skies-type transport markets - new members either needing the agreement of existing participants or joining simply by agreeing to the terms in place. It would allow like-minded member states to come together fairly quickly and avoid forcing reluctant states into a rapid change in policy. The latter could join whenever they feel it is appropriate. It has the disadvantage that the states involved may not be contiguous, causing difficulties with non-participating neighbors. Further, given the economics of international aviation, non-member countries might find it difficult to develop sufficiently their own airline industry to join the core states at a later stage.
- *Full multilateralism.* Here, in every participating country it is possible for an airline to compete for passengers regardless of its nationality. This would entail the opening of cabotage to all carriers as well as freedom to supply services in international markets. This is the ultimate free market situation that may yield maximum economic efficiency but would be politically

---

[15]   This is essentially an idea articulated most recently by the Association of European Airlines (1999) in a policy statement in 1999 where it argues for a Transatlantic Common Aviation Area. It also has a basis in EU air transportation policy. The Council of Ministers, in 1996 mandated the Commission in the long term to establish a 'Common Aviation Area' where airlines on both sides of the Atlantic could 'freely provide their services in the EC and US on the basis of commercial principles.

difficult to introduce globally in the near future because of the loss of sovereignty that it entails and the probable unequal spread of benefits that would result. In the longer term there are also practical problems in attaining changes to any large-scale multilateral agreement once it is reached. The experiences of recent GATS negotiations highlight some aspects of this difficulty.

The various approaches are not mutually exclusive. Combinations of, for example, phased mulilateralism, regional arrangements and more liberalized bilateral agreements could offer the possibility of more rapid change. One could see the existing regional arrangements extended to current non-members (such as with expansion of the EU arrangements, which already include Norway and Iceland, to other non-EU countries) while at the same time permitting the experiences accumulated to be harnessed for liberalization across the regional groupings. Those outside of these structures would then have the opportunity, if not wishing to participate fully to negotiate bilateral agreements in the form they wish. The key point is perhaps the need to avoid doctrinaire solutions but rather to seek pragmatic ways forward.

While liberalization removes some of the requirements for complex and potentially rigid administrative structures, a policy embracing a more flexible institutional structure may eventually require new approaches to conflict resolution. The existing bilateral arrangements that, for example, cover much of the international aviation market do not require extensive and sophisticated conflict resolution facilities - the states concerned reach mutual agreements. ICAO, which has been given a role as arbitrator in the Chicago Convention, has hardly been used in the past in case of disputes. A more liberal market, whereby various forms of multilateral agreements are emerging, could present new challenges in this area.

At present there is no agreed mechanism or institution which has been established to deal with conflicts which may emerge. The institutions which do exist (e.g., within the EU) are regional in their coverage, and there are clear problems in the ways in which, for example, relations with countries outside the region are handled. The question that emerged in 1995 of who has jurisdiction over the external aviation policy of EU member states illustrates this.

Matters relating to ownership in international aviation are important in three distinct ways. These concern issues of public/private ownership, regulations governing levels of foreign ownership of airlines, and potential problems that could stem from flags-of-convenience operations.

The possibility of changes in ownership may be important in ensuring that greater flexibility is introduced into future international aviation. In addition, ownership controls over airlines can have important implications for countries' aviation policies. There is a tendency for countries to be protective of carriers that are based in their territories and to direct their international policy on matters such as ASA negotiations and subsidies accordingly.[16] There is a trend towards more private ownership of major international airlines to reap the efficiency benefits which this can achieve (e.g., the privatization of British Airways in 1987, the public sale of shares in Qantas and Lufthansa in 1995 and the large number of small private airlines now offering scheduled international services).

6.4.3   Ownership and control

As we see later in Chapter 8, air transport infrastructure has also been the subject of limited privatization in a number of countries. The main airports in the UK were privatized, for example, in 1987 and there are initiatives in, for instance, Canada and Germany to transfer at least some airports to the private sector. In Canada, the federal government has attempted to ensure airports meet local needs by passing many of them to provincial control. Equally, privatization of ATC systems has recently been considered in the UK (with some changes being initiated) and in the US and been moved to become a Crown Corporation in Canada.

Such policy reviews have been motivated by a desire to enhance the management efficiency of existing infrastructure, including the setting of clearer objectives, and to provide additional resources for financing investment in new infrastructure. Allowing more private ownership in the international air transport sector is likely to facilitate the restructuring process. Privatization increases the general efficiency of international aviation and removes many of the channels of intervention based on public ownership that have traditionally been used by governments to support favored carriers. The economic benefits through enhanced decision making on the basis of commercial criteria will, however, only arise if privatization does lead – in addition to increased private shareholding in international transport companies – to the effective transfer of control to private investors.

Privatization also provides a mechanism permitting higher levels of foreign investment in international carriers. A number of countries, while seldom allowing majority foreign ownership, are now gradually transforming their laws regarding the extent to which airlines registered in their country can enjoy a degree of foreign ownership. Within the EU there is no limit on the level of foreign ownership although practical considerations regarding extra-EU ASA agreements acts as aconstraint. More open capital markets not only allows for a more efficient flow of international investment but it is also an important concomitant to other changes, for example with regard to ASAs, aimed at reducing trade barriers in the market for international air transportation services.

---

[16]   The US, for instance, has an interest in ensuring that its civil airlines have sufficient capacity to meet any demands placed on them at times of military crisis (the need to meet CRAF commitments).

Relaxation of foreign ownership rules would, in the context of strategic alliances, even when mergers are not desired, allow network synergy effects to be more completely exploited. Further, with a relaxation of foreign ownership rules and more bilateral ASAs, there is the possibility of airlines' adopting 'flags of convenience' akin to a large part of the world's mercantile marine. Carriers may theoretically opt to register in states that offer low taxation regimes and where they can acquire labor and other factor inputs at the lowest cost. The emergence of markets offering wet-leasing of aircraft and crew provides a particularly flexible way for flag-of-convenience carriers to operate; the creation of 'virtual airlines'. Airlines could pursue flag-of convenience registration strategies to minimize airlines' costs following the evidence that the costs of ships sailing under such flags are lower than for ships with other registrations.

6.4.4   Social and environmental issues

Greater liberalization of ownership rules may raise safety, environmental and social issues as well as the concern on the part of non-flag-of-convenience countries that they will lose revenue. In some cases matters of sovereignty and the prestige of having an air carrier registered in the country are also important to nations, although this is a diminishing consideration. Some of these problems, such as tax revenue dilution, are common to a wide range of industries and pose problems to policy makers that extend beyond international aviation. Others, for example those related to safety, security and the environment, are more specific and may require coordinated international policy initiatives.[17]

The institutional challenge for international air transport is to develop ways to allow for the benefits of the international mobility of capital, which, at the same time, avoids flag-of convenience problems. Regarding safety and the environment, a more liberal environment does not mean that countries forgo the possibility of ensuring that adequate standards are maintained. Countries enjoy sovereignty over their airspace and can use this to enforce internationally agreed standards as developed by ICAO. Further, the tax haven problem is one that is not peculiar to international aviation but extends across a wide range of service sectors (e.g., international finance) and could be handled within a wider institutional structure.

Subsidies have in the past been widespread in the aviation sector. Some remain in the form of restructuring subsidies (such as within the EU), cross-subsidies (such as the Fly America Program to encourage airlines to participate in the Civil Reserve Air Fleet Program) and social subsidies for remote communities. Infrastructure, such as airports, and surface transport access also often benefit from central or local government subsidies. While they vary in their

---

[17]   This is considered in general terms in Button (1993b) and is discussed in aviation terms in Chapter 13.

intensity and form, the general potential of market distortion is well understood and, as a basic economic principle, subsidies should only be adopted to meet very specific objectives where no better alternatives exist.

The current, generally *ad hoc*, structure of subsidies does little to foster overall efficiency and, in many instances, does not seem to achieve the desired sector-specific objectives. As liberalization takes place the social and political pressures for restructuring subsidies grow as some airlines encounter financial problems. The finance for restructuring often offered by government differs from commercial finance in that there is no default risk attached to it. In many cases it is awarded to nationalized carriers on the proviso that they meet set criteria These are, though, by definition bureaucratically determined objectives rather than those of the commercial sector. In some cases, such as with aid in the EU, the intention is that restructuring finance should not distort competition. It is difficult, however, to establish situations where, in an economic rather than a legal sense, injections of aid on a non-commercial basis, and to selected actors in the market, do not affect aggregate supply or relative market share.

One option in these circumstances is to continue with the *status quo*. This is, however, inefficient and politically divisive, as government subsidies run the risk of allowing airlines to put off the necessary restructuring decisions.[18] Maintaining the *status quo* has the merit that as the trend towards privatization continues the role of government in some countries as lender of last resort to airlines will naturally diminish. Privatized airlines are disciplined by the market in terms of their day-to-day operations and in their long-term planning. Further, where subsidies are still given for restructuring purposes, there is evidence of more stringent monitoring by governments over how moneys are used and the increasing imposition of sunset provisions is reducing the prospects of subsidies continuing.

An important alternative transition option is to accelerate the process by which subsidy levels are reduced and to limit those that remain to be provided on the condition that certain restructuring targets are met within a predetermined time frame. To achieve this would initially involve agreement on definitions of subsidies, the development of an acceptable method of quantification of their scale, and an accepted method for allocating and managing remaining subsidies. This type of transition arrangement could be particularly relevant in the context of other initiatives designed to further privatize airlines and liberalize ASAs. There may be a small number of cases where services provided on a non-commercial basis can be justified on social cost–benefit criteria such as the provision of minimum levels of service to remote communities.

---

[18]   For example Olympic Airlines continued to receive subsidies from the state after an initial restructuring agreement in 1994 and had to be subjected to a more rigorous, EU imposed regime in 1998.

An efficient system of meeting these, and similar, objectives may require that there is uniformity in the criteria applied. Common codes remove high transaction costs of multiple compliance. Specific policies, however, have the advantage that they can be directed at the targeted issue, but by virtue of their specificity they can conflict with the objectives of the more general competition policies of a country. They may, for example, lead to alternative modes of transport to aviation being put at a competitive advantage or disadvantage. There are also questions regarding onus of proof. One option is to let that be with the industry, but this may stifle development in a dynamic sector, such as air transport, and be costly to administer on a case-by-case basis. The alternative is to place the burden on government. This reduces the possibility of intervention failures occurring but can pose problems in specifying legal details to restrain anti-competitive practices.

6.4.5   Competition and antitrust policies

There are national variations in general competition policies that apply to the aviation sector. In many cases international air transport, and often transportation more generally, is exempt from national competition laws. They are subjected to specific legislation. For example, EU competition rules apply in the UK but air transport in that country is nonetheless excluded from laws on restrictive agreements – although it is possible for the relevant Secretary of State to make reference regarding monopoly considerations. In Germany, prohibitions on price recommendations do not apply to associations of enterprises providing certain services in airports. The US has a tradition of imposing its anti-trust laws extra-territorially. It has a tradition of being reluctant to embrace multilateral agencies in this process.

While there has been, since 1986, a simple exchange of notifications regarding actions in this field and a number of bilateral agreements have been signed, rules are still lacking at the international level. Procedures, time limits and the criteria for taking decisions vary considerably. These are broad problems with international competition laws that add to the costs of trade in general.

There are several possible options for transition. One is to allow the present process to continue. An alternative is to encourage its more rapid progress and to seek additional means to foster convergence of competition rules across states. This could involve, initially, a clearer definition of responsibilities regarding specific issues of competition policy. Additionally, increased transparency regarding the criteria to meet antitrust regulations, but also in respect of the actual implementation of national competition rules, may help increase the consistency of competition policies across countries. One path to this longer-term situation may be through the initial deepening of regional arrangements and their subsequent widening through the admittance of non-members and through interregional agreements. Another possible path would be a multilateral one building upon existing codes and practices (such as those relating to CRS displays).

6.4.6 Infrastructure access

Even when air service agreements allow services to be provided, infrastructure capacity and access constraints can still prove an impediment to the efficient provision of air services.[19] While airports, air traffic control systems and other key elements of infrastructure are being expanded and modernized, and techniques for managing their use are being improved, from an institutional perspective, there still exist limitations on their efficient use. A number of initiatives have been developed to improve the institutional arrangements for accessing infrastructure – e.g., the runway slot allocation criteria of the EU and the slot sales that have been allowed at some major US airports – but problems remain.

Focusing on airport slot allocation several possibilities exist. The *status quo* could be maintained. The continuation of the existing self-regulation system of airport scheduling committees that operates at most airports outside the US has the advantage that it directly involves the major players and allows airlines the opportunity to coordinate their landing/take-off needs across a network of airports. Limitations in the system arise because it often limits scope for new entry. Some airports minimize this problem by ensuring that some gates are available for new entrance or for smaller operators at the airport to expand their activities. Additionally, since it is not a market-based approach, the negotiated procedure involved does not adequately take into account the cost of slots.

The administration of slot allocation by a regulating authority seeking to meet wider social or economic objectives than airlines is a possibility. This would involve establishing an autonomous agency and providing it with terms of reference. On the operational side, a major difficulty is one of information and management. The airline industry provides a complex network of services that are dependent on the decisions of more than one airport. It would require a large bureaucracy to operate such a system given the vast details of the flight needs required. The airlines effectively internalize and minimize many of these costs under, for example, a regime of scheduling committees (Doganis, 1992).

The development of uniform codes of conduct for airport scheduling committees combines the self regulation approach with that of an administrative structure. It permits the costs of runway slots to be more fully integrated in decision processes, Most committees already operate under the IATA criteria (e.g., regarding periods of use of a slot, 'use it or lose it' and grandfather rights). In Europe, the EU has additional rules, notably Council Regulation (EEC) 95/93 aimed at helping new entrants into a market.[20]

---

[19]   The economic of airports are dealt with in more detail in Chapter 8 and Chapter 9 concerns itself explicitly with EU airport policy.

[20]   The evidence from airports such as Gatwick and Heathrow, however is that there is scope for developing these codes further to allow more freedom of effective entry (UK Civil Aviation Authority, 1995).

The greater use of economic pricing to allocate scarce slots would encourage the more efficient use of scarce capacity.[21] Peak load premiums and charges which are more strictly related to economic, rather than accountancy, costs form a key element of this. In general, runway costs are related to aircraft movements and terminal costs to passenger throughput, and this should be reflected in an economic pricing system. The difficulty is one of defining the appropriate costs in the context of airports and of developing a pricing regime which allows for the particular needs of airlines offering services across a number of time zones and for which windows for departures and arrivals are small. In practical terms, more efficient pricing may also need combining with an administered system. We return to the topic of airport pricing in later chapters.

The introduction of auctions for slots (the property right approach) would involve bringing the allocation of infrastructure capacity more nearly within a competitive framework. There are a number of methods for slot auctioning that would reduce some of the inherent problems of banking (the long-term holding of little-used slots) which is often seen as a potential problem with auctions and would permit the matching of slots at origins and destinations. The problems of the non-divisibility of slots remain, however, and any auction process would inevitably also entail a relatively complex set of operational criteria.

Secondary slot trading involves the buying and selling or exchanging of pre-allocated slots. In some instances, as with the system introduced to a number of US airports in the 1980s, there may be restrictions on the types of trade permitted. Slot trading allows for more efficient use of slots, especially among those enjoying grandfather rights, and permits some scope for new entry. Limitations of trading stem from the possibility of incumbents sitting on slots to prevent a new entrant or another incumbent rival acquiring them, although 'use it or lose it' requirements may be used to reduce this. Technically, there may be difficulties in that trading of slots would seem to contravene the Chicago Convention, which requires that access to airports should be open to all on an equal basis.

6.5   DEVELOPING MARKETS

International aviation extends beyond the confines of the major industrialized countries, and many carriers operate in a global marketplace. Equally, more developed economies are important markets for airlines from developing nations. For those reasons, transition within the more economically advanced nations cannot be treated in isolation from what is occurring outside. A difficulty for policy coordination stemming from these patterns is that, while there are a number

---

[21]   Many studies have indicated that from an economic perspective current landing fees at lost airports are inefficient (Morrison, 1983).

of dynamic aviation nations outside, for example, the Organisation of Economic Cooperation and Development countries, many other aviation markets, notably in Africa, tend to be developing less rapidly.

Where there is a rapid expansion, as for example in China, it is often from a much lower base level. Further markets, such as those in the former communist states of Europe, are going through a major restructuring phase, the outcome of which remains unclear (Smith, 1995). In the former Soviet Union, for instance, the end of the Aeroflot monopoly in the early 1990s quickly produced some 220 airlines, of which 195 are based in Russia. Some are elements of the old Aeroflot, but there were also new start-ups such as Transaero. A number of these countries have a proclivity to protect their aviation industries through their approach to the bilateral air service agreement system, often on the grounds of fostering an infant industry. They also may wish, for political reasons, to reensure their sovereignty over their airspace and to use flag-carriers as a mark of national identity. They may be willing to do this even if there are substantial economic costs involved. They are often, therefore, opposed to rapid liberalization measures.[22]

These features of many aviation markets outside, for example, the OECD grouping distinguish them from the international airline markets involving the majority of the main industrialized countries. This means that it is unlikely that policies such as global multilateralism will become a reality in the foreseeable future. What is important for a global industry is that transition within the developed block of countries is undertaken in such a way that the airlines of other nations may be in a position to participate fully in any agreements if and when they are interested in doing so.[23]

There are a number of transition mechanisms that would allow this to come about. As to which will ultimately be adopted, that will depend as much on the individual designs and aims of the countries involved as on the actions of the developed countries. One possibility is that, as regional agreements among the developed countries develop, features such as standard principles could be embraced by other nations and thereby integrated into a wider workably competitive market. In some cases, such as in South America and among some Pacific nations, regional groups are already developing which in themselves may provide the basis for ultimate harmonization and coordination with regional arrangements among some groups of developed countries. The growth of strategic airline alliances is one mechanism that is likely to foster this type of development.

---

[22]   E.g., as witnessed at the ICAO 4th Conference on Air Transport in 1994.

[23]   The ability to absorb new members is one the features of the proposed multilateral structure put forward by the Association of European Airlines (1999).

7   ISSUES OF MARKET STABILITY

7.1   INTRODUCTION

Air transportation is not the only network industry that has attracted particular attention in recent years. There has been a recent upsurge of interest in the economics of network industries more generally. In part this can be explained by the dynamic technology and dramatic growth that has been experienced in the telecommunications industries, a process that is strongly supported by dynamic network externalities and the efficiency increases accompanying information and communications technology (ICT) networks. Less dramatic, but nevertheless important, has been the increased demand for transport services as incomes have risen, new logistics philosophies such as just-in-time production have gained acceptance and barriers to international trade have been reduced. On the supply side, there has been increased interest in the role that investment in network infrastructure can play in both helping to stimulate spatial convergence of economic development and, at the macro-level, leading to increased aggregate production.[1]

Institutionally, the European Union, in particular, has taken an increasing interest in the provision and use of networks as instruments in industrial, regional and trade policy. The Single Market initiative of the early 1990s has resulted in a phased removal of economic regulatory controls over most modes of transport and the Trans-European Networks (TENs) initiative has begun a process aimed at stimulating more investment in new international infrastructure and greater overall co-ordination in policies.

This chapter is less concerned with the enlargement and improvement of network infrastructures and more concerned with their use. In particular, it looks at issues of network stability and economic integration. Within this domain it focuses, therefore, on a number of particular themes and is selective in its coverage. In terms of exclusion, for example, it does not attempt an assessment of the strict importance of network availability for economic development or for economic integration. Topical and important as these themes are, they are largely ignored in our analysis. Nor is any new econometric work presented, but rather reliance is placed on looking at the evidence of previous work, the basic characteristics of modern networks and on insights gained from 'case study information.

---

[1]   An interest recently stimulated by the empirical work of Aschauer (1990).

What we are concerned with is the extent to which the increasingly liberalized markets in network industries are likely to be stable in economic terms and if instability is a possibility then what the policy response should be.[2] In homing in on these issues assumptions regarding the role of networks in regional integration are inherent. Essentially, the very fact that potential economic instability in some network markets has been seen as a threat justifying a policy response by the EU authorities implies that stability is in itself an important goal for those concerned with spatial economic integration. There is little point, for example, in extending or improving physical networks if they are not subsequently used optimally.

7.2 FEATURES OF NETWORK REGULATION

As we have seen in Chapter 3, networks exhibit a number of distinguishing features that affect their economic performance. The characteristic that has, perhaps, attracted the greatest attention in recent years have been that of network synergy whereby positive externalities are generated as a network is expanded (Capello and Rietveld, 1997). A large bus network, for example, everything else being equal, offers far more options of route and destination choice than does a smaller network. Equally, joining a telephone network has more value if there is a large number of other users to make and receive calls.

From an economic regulatory perspective, however, the nature of many networks means that they can pose a series of specific economic problems.

Physical communications networks are composed of a combination of fixed infrastructure such as rail track and mobile plant such as trains. A key issue is the extent to which one can and should separate the regulation and ownership of the network infrastructure from the plant that makes use of it. A number of options are available but the issues involved are often complex. In some network industries, such as road transport, much of the infrastructure is relatively flexible in terms of its use and is of such a general kind that there is little direct immediate interaction between decisions regarding its supply and use and the decisions of those operating the mobile plant. This is less true of some other network industries where for technical reasons there is a closer link between infrastructure and operations. With rail transport, for example, overtaking is not easily done and coordination of infrastructure use across the various potential users is often seen as important.[3]

---

[2]   Instability in this context in its extreme form would mean under or zero supply because a rational supplier would not enter a market knowing that by doing it would result in sub-normal profits being earned at the new level of aggregate supply.

[3]   This does not, however, mean that there is any agreement on how to treat track and operations in the railway industries (Brooks and Button, 1995)

Network infrastructure also seldom exhibits the classic characteristics of non-excludability and non-rivalness and so for its efficient use some mechanism for limiting access is required. A number of possible options are available that range from charging regimes through to physical controls and rationing. One of the particular difficulties with many networks is to develop a tractable access policy that is sensitive to the use made of the infrastructure. For example, in many countries access to road transport infrastructure is limited in the sense of high annual license fees being in place but these do not reflect actual use of the system or provide incentives for its efficient use. There may, however, be high transaction costs associated with direct usage charging when jointness of supply imposes technical problems in defining appropriate prices and then imposing them on users.

In differing circumstances networks can overlap and either compete with or complement each other. For instance, local urban bus networks interact to support inter-urban rail networks, telecommunications networks act to support the operation of air transport networks but equally motorway networks compete with inter city rail networks and postal networks compete with telecommunications networks. Given this interaction, insensitive regulatory structures can distort the synergy effects that can stem from complementary infrastructure or, alternatively, lead to misallocation of use when there is potential competition.

Regulation of any individual network, therefore, must take into account the interactive effects that may spill over to other, either competing or complementary networks. Linked to this are the interactive effects within networks that means that any interventions influencing the performance of a particular link or node in a network can have repercussions on other, often distance, elements of the network. For example, subsidies given to a particular bus route may have implications for competing rail services but may also impact, by altering travel behavior, on other bus services. Slot allocation measures at one airport may have system-wide implications for all network users.

Networks may provide suppliers with cost economies by allowing them to enjoy combined benefits of density and scope. The hub-and-spoke operations practiced by many airlines is an example of this. Equally, from the users' perspective, larger networks generally offer more choice; e.g., being linked into a large telecommunications system is generally much more useful than belonging to a smaller one. There are also economies to suppliers resulting from market presence that facilitates more effective advertising and consumer awareness.

Indivisibilities exist in many industries but often pose particular types of problems for networks industries offering a predetermined level of service. A scheduled train service, for example, offers a fixed number of seats but demand for these seats can be variable both in a fairly predictable way (for instance daily peak/off peak demands) and also in a less certain way (for instance, due to variations in the weather).

Most manufactures, and even agricultural products, are relative durable in the sense that if they are not consumed at the moment of production they can be kept for a period of time to be consumed later. Most network services, in contrast have to be consumed at the point of production or they are lost forever. An airline seat, for example, has to be taken at the time of departure or that particular service will not be available again. They are not unique in this respect, seats in a theatre have identical non-durable features, but such products do result in pressures for suppliers to reduce prices to short-run marginal costs with the prospect that full costs are not recovered. This issue is of particular importance to the existence of a core that is the focus of later discussions.

7.3   ISSUES OF ECONOMIC STABILITY

The 1980s and the 1990s have been characterized as a period of regulatory reform as the use of command-and-control instruments to steer industry has been liberalized. There has also been a generally shift away from state ownership of manufacturing and services sector activities, especially in the European economies. These changes have come about both because of quasi-practical concerns expressed by economists such as Stigler and Posner that state interventions were often far from perfect and because of shifts on the intellectual side as ideas of economists such as Schumpeter and van Hayek that even perfectly executed policies limiting immediate monopoly power can delay and distort innovation. While the economic analysis that has been done generally shows these changes to have enhanced the efficiency of production, the issue of long-term stability in more competitive markets has received less attention.

Concerns over the economic stability of competitive markets is an old one although one that seems to attract only periodic interest. Edgeworth (1881) addressed the subject in his analysis of unrestricted competition for pure exchange with recontracting. In terms of industrial applications, Viner (1931) produced a seminal paper on stability issues when identical firms producing a homogeneous product have U-shaped average cost curves and increasing marginal costs. He defined Pareto optimal conditions when competition exists between a large number of traders and coalitions. The emergence of game theory in the late 1940s revived intellectual interest in market stability and, more recently, Scarf (1962) and Scarf and Debreu (1963) used this in developing the modern theory of the 'core' including giving a limit theorem for the core of an economy.[4] Linked with this,

---

[4]   The underlying idea of the core is relatively straightforward. A simple economy can be modeled as a set of economic actors who produce goods and services and transact with one another. An allocation of goods and services is said to be in the core when there is no group within the economy that could be better off by trading

but tackling the issue from a somewhat different angle, has been the development by Baumol and others of theories concerning the contestability of markets and their potential sustainability (Baumol *et al.*, 1982).

More recently Telser (1978; 1987; 1990; 1991; 1994; 1996) has resurrected the topic and has done so in a way particularly relevant for the deregulated network industries that have emerged in the past two decades.[5] The economic analysis has largely been led by theoreticians and much of it is of a highly technical nature.[6]

amongst itself. Intuitively, the concept of the core of such an economy is related to the notion of equilibrium or the absence of further gains from trade. For an outcome in the core no further gains from trade are possible for any group or sub-group.

As a hypothetical example, suppose there are three customers **B1**, **B2** and **B3** each wishing to travel between two the same points. **B1** is prepared to pay $100, **B2** $80 and **B3** $75 for the trip. There is an airline **A1** that can carry up to passengers. The airline can provide this service at a cost of $140 whether it carries zero, one or two passengers. All of the outcomes in the core have the property that **B1** and **B2** travel on the airline while **B3** fails to make a contract. The outcomes in the core differ in the fares that **B1** and **B2** pay for the journey the outcome depending on their negotiations with **A1**. For example, the allocation in which **B1** and **B2** both make the trip and pay athe same fare of $75 is in the core. In all the outcomes in the core, the airline **A1** always makes profits of at least $10. If the airline lowered the fare below $75 **B3** would also wish to use the airline, potentially disturbing the coalition of **A1**, **B1** and **B2**. There would be an excess demand at this rate and **B1** and **B2** would bid the fare up..

Not all economies have a core. If another identical airline, **A2**, with a capacity of two seats and the same costs, enters the market the model now has no core. Because the two airlines are identical, and because in the core their owners must receive the same profit (otherwise the airline with the lower profit could simply negotiate with the customers of the other airline to carry them at a slightly lower fare and steal all the business) there is not enough demand to sustain both carriers. One of the airlines must always be idle earning zero profit otherwise, since the two carriers must earn the same profit, both would earn zero profit. There are no outcomes in the core in which suppliers earns zero profit.

[5] The evidence on the implicit concern with the possibility of market instability in liberal network industries over the years, although couched in somewhat different terms can be illustrated by a whole range of measures. These include the controls introduced into the UK bus and trucking industries in the 1930s; the banning of 'jitney' operations in the USA in the 1920s; the arguments in the EU in the 1960s and 1970s for the need for a lower fork on trucking rates; the acceptance by most countries of international cartel arrangements in shipping and aviation; and the adoption by the EU in the 1990s of the ability to limit market entry and control minimum air fares.

[6] Telser (1994) offers a general introduction to the theory of the core but a much more accessible account is that of Smith (1995) in the particular context of the aviation market. Sjostrum's (1989) paper is also less technical and offers a practical approach to considering whether a market is likely to prove inherently unstable or not.

The analysis of the early papers related mainly to general exchange conditions issues while the initial applied work was not specifically directed at the peculiarities of network industries (Bittlingmayer, 1982; 1985). The situation has changed somewhat recently with an empirical literature emerging concerned with issues involving shipping (Pirrong, 1992; Sjostrom, 1989; 1993) and aviation (Button, 1996).[7]

Telser (1996) highlights the types of situation where a core may be empty: 'With relatively large fixed costs, avoidable (set-up) costs, indivisibilities, or network effects, unrestricted competition cannot bring about a stable efficient outcome' and adds 'Many public utilities, transportation industries, and some manufacturing industries ... seem to have cost conditions in which a stable, efficient equilibrium is possible only by means of a suitable restriction on competition'.[8]

The general conclusions reached from Sjostrom's synthesis of the theoretical work on core issues are:

- the greater the variation in suppliers' minimum average costs are, the more likely there will be a competitive equilibrium;
- there is more likely to be an empty core when demand is less elastic;
- the larger is a supplier's capacity relative to the market, the more probable the core will be empty;
- agreements to create a core are more likely during an economic recession;
- wide variability in demand or costs increases the probability of agreements;
- agreements are less likely when there are legal restrictions on entry.

To complicate empirical analysis, however, several of these conditions are also consistent with collusion for rent seeking purposes. Table 7.1 provides a summary of situations where this holds.[9] Hypothesis testing is, however, possible in those cases where there are differences in direction of the relationship. For example, if demand conditions are relatively inelastic then collusion is more likely for reasons of avoiding the problems of an empty core than for rent seeking motives.

[7]   Button and Nijkamp (1998) offer a more general examination of the relevance of core theory to network industries. It should be noted that the non-existence of a network service that is thought important for social reasons to do with, say, policies of access or income distribution does not imply the lack of a core.

[8]   One should note that a core may not be unique but that there may be a number of potential outcomes that can constitute a core. Telser (1978) is particularly relevant for network industries and many of the main arguments surrounding core issues are set out in the context of a simple aviation market example.

[9]   More details of the various conditions under which an empty core may pertain are seen in Section 7.4.

The notion that the core may be empty can also provide insights into the nature of the equilibrium in more familiar economic models of oligopoly competition. In addition, some of the limitations of the core concept can be highlighted by comparing predictions of core models with conventional economic models of monopoly. The simple examples highlight a general economic principle that is frequently overlooked in conventional economic models of oligopoly. In the presence of a minimum efficient scale (i.e., when entry must be at a minimum scale to be profitable) and free entry, then often no equilibrium will exist unless restrictions are imposed on the ways in which economic actors can transact with each other. In standard models of contestable markets or monopolistic competition, an equilibrium will only exist under assumptions about the ability of entrants to negotiate with potential customers.

Table 7.1. Differing conditions for rent seeking and stability collusion

| | Chance of Collusion | |
	Cartel	Empty core
Heterogeneous supply	Low	Low
Less elastic demand	Low	High
Small numbers case	High	High
Industry in slump	Unclear	High
Variable supply/demand	Low	High
Legal restrictions	High	Low

Suppose that the minimum of the average cost for each firm occurs at a unique quantity Q and the minimum average cost corresponds to a price p. Suppose further that the quantity demanded at the minimum average cost is $D(p)$. It would be fortuitous if the price corresponding to that minimum average cost corresponded to a simple multiple of the efficient scale for each firm (i.e., that $D(p)= nQ$ for some n). In the more likely case, the demand at the price corresponding to the minimum average cost $D(p)$ will lie between nQ and $(n+1)Q$ for some n. In this case either production will be efficient (i.e., at a simple multiple of Q) and there will be excess demand, or there will be no excess demand and production will occur at a price in excess of minimum average cost.

Consider models in which the normal equilibrium has the property that production occurs at the minimum average cost, such as models of Bertrand competition or contestable markets. There will typically be excess demand at a price equal to minimum average cost. A question then arises as to how those customers who do not receive service at the market price should be treated. Most of these customers will be prepared to pay a little more than the market price for service. This provides an opportunity for profitable entry by new a entrant who offers supply at more than the market price to these customers and the same price to other existing customers.

The concept of the core, therefore, illustrates that in the presence of a minimum efficient scale of entry, Bertrand[10] or contestable market models only have a meaningful equilibrium under assumptions about the ways in which entrants can contract with the customers who do not receive service in the normal equilibrium.

Further, in standard models of monopolistic competition the equilibrium outcome features production at a level of output insufficient to achieve full economies of production and the market price lies above the minimum average cost. Although markets clear in this model, the question arises why a new entrant or an existing player cannot undercut the market price and expand output to the efficient scale. As long as a new entrant can attract sufficient business by cutting its price, the market price cannot be sustained above the minimum average cost. The standard monopolistic competition equilibrium is, again, meaningful only under assumptions about the manner in which entrants can contract with existing consumers.

There are other ways in which the concept of the core yields predictions that are in conflict with some conventional economic wisdom. Specifically, the concept of the core conflicts with standard economic analysis of market power. An outcome that is in the core can never have the property that there is exploitation of market power. The core concept predicts that an efficient outcome will always occur, even in the extreme case of a pure monopoly.

The intuition behind this result is that within the core all opportunities for gains from trade have been exploited. As is sometimes pointed out, however, there remain opportunities for gains from trade. Gains from trade are only exhausted when the output of the monopolist is such that the price is equal to the monopolist's marginal cost. At this price overall social welfare is maximized. As long as the level of output is such that the monopolist's price remains above marginal cost the monopolist can sell an extra unit at a price which leaves both the customer and the monopolist better off.

To illustrate, suppose a monopolist can produce output at a constant marginal cost of $5 and that there are 3 consumers, willing to pay $10, $8 and $6 for the good. If the monopolist sets a price of $10 he sells one unit for a profit of $5. If he sets a price of $8 he sells two units with a profit of $6. If he sets a price of $6 he sells three units for a profit of $3. Clearly the profit maximizing output is to

---

[10]   The late nineteenth century French mathematician Joseph Bertrand suggested that in duopolies and similar markets, sellers can set prices but do so after making assumptions about the prices rivals will charge.

set a price of $8 and sell 2 units. This outcome, however, is not in the core. The monopolist can, after selling those units, sell an additional unit to the 3rd customer at a price of 6 and increase his profit to 7. This is an illustration of the general principle that an outcome that is in the core can never have the property that there is a welfare loss due to the exercise of market power.

This result on the efficiency of outcomes in the core can be generalized further. The Coase Theorem (Coase, 1990) asserts that in the absence of transactions costs, the outcome of transacting in an economy will be efficient whatever the assignment of property rights and whatever the assignment of legal rules, even in the presence of conventional market failures such as externalities and public goods.[11] It provides an argument for a very limited role for government. The core concept essentially assumes zero transactions costs - all trades between members of the economy are feasible. The core concept, therefore, does not just rule out welfare loss from monopoly power, in addition, it rules out welfare loss from all other forms of market failures.

7.4 THEORETICAL CASES OF 'EMPTY CORES'

For Adam Smith's 'invisible hand theory' to eliminate dead-weight loss, and for prices to guide individuals to outcomes that maximize economic welfare a number of states of the world must hold. It is necessary that the aggregate industry production function must be superadditive. The sum of the outputs of two separate organizations does not exceed the total output that would result from their merger and the aggregate industry production function must have non decreasing returns to scale. Telser and others have added to these two conditions in order to embrace the problems of empty cores. Notably, 'One feature [of] empty cores is that the firms' total costs resulting from the factor prices generated by unfettered competition among them for the factors of production exceed the total revenue so that none can survive, although there is a net benefit to the public from having these commodities' (Telser, 1996).

Work on situations when an empty core can arise has tended to be highly abstract and is often difficult to access. The following provides a verbal and graphical description of the some of the types of market situation when an empty core can emerge. It is not intended to be comprehensive but rather to offer a degree of theoretical support for some of the policy discussion later in the Chapter. For example, empty core problems, in addition to those outlined in the body of the text, can potentially arise because of government failures as well as resulting from market features. In the context of US domestic air transportation the Chapter 11

[11] Aivazian and Callen (1981) discuss the interaction of core theory and the Coase Theorem. See also Coase's response, Coase (1981).

bankruptcy laws would seem to have the potential for generating instability. Airlines performing poorly financially have the incentive to restructure and reduce their debts by seeking 'Chapter 11' protection in the courts. This subsequently allows then to compete with lower costs and puts pressure on other carriers. These latter airlines may then find themselves needing bankruptcy protection. In the longer term, as this spreads across airlines, it will prove impossible for carriers as a whole to earn sufficient to recover full industry costs.

7.4.1   The Viner case

The simplest and most cited situation where an empty core may arise is the Viner (1931) case. This non-core situation can be illustrated by taking two identical airlines on a route each with standard U-shaped average cost curves. In other words, there is an assumption of fixed costs. Marginal cost on the route is a discontinuous function of total airline output and is equal to the minimum average cost of the aircraft at two points in Figure 7.1, namely Q_1 and Q_2. Market demand is represented by D.

In this situation if one airline operates a flight then excess profits will be earned. Expansion to two aircraft as the second carrier is attracted to the market will result in both making a loss since competition will lead to them operating at a price equal to marginal cost. Only if by chance the demand curve intersects the average cost curve at a point coincidental with the marginal cost curve will a stable outcome emerge. Increasing the number of firms does not affect the outcome until the number becomes very large, at which point the Pareto-optimal number of undertakings is reached.

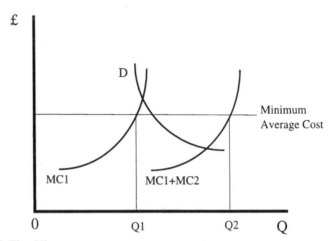

Figure 7.1 The Viner case

7.4.2 Non-identical firms

It is possible for an empty core to emerge if the assumption of airlines being identical is relaxed; for example, they may have different minimum average costs as the evidence of Oum and Yu (1999) would suggest. In Figure 7.2 the air service industry supply curve (moving from one to three carriers) is both discontinuous and upward sloping. The core is empty in this case when the market demand curve goes between the segments of the supply curve. The more homogeneous the suppliers are, and the more their minimum average costs differ, so the more likely that the market demand curve will pass through a gap (with perfect homogeneity one has the Viner case) and, hence, the higher the probability that there will be a non-core situation. This type of situation may occur when airlines each with different types of aircraft fleets compete.

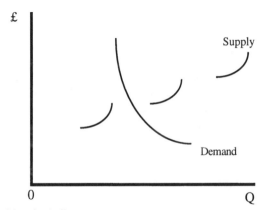

Figure 7.2 Non-identical firms

7.4.3 Low elasticity of demand

Figure 7.3 illustrate a situation where suppliers are not homogeneous but each has a vertical supply curve. A section of the industry supply curve is depicted as VWXY. D_1 and D_2 represent possible, vertically parallel market demand curves. For the market to have a core the market demand must lie between Y and X. What one can see is that, at any price, the less elastic is demand the more likely it is to fall into a gap in the supply curve, e.g., between X and W. At the extremes, when demand is perfectly elastic the probability of an empty core is unity but with a perfectly elastic demand curve a core must exist.[12]

---

[12] This would suggest a greater potential for an empty core problem to emerge in business travel markets rather than leisure travel markets.

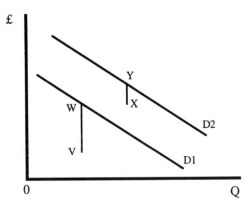

Figure 7.3 Low elasticity of demand case

7.4.4   The market is in a slump

The state of the total market can influence market supply when there are fixed costs involved. If individual suppliers have U-shaped cost curves, implying an element of fixity in costs, then they may remain in the market for a period even if their average total costs are not completely covered, as would be the case at costs between C_1 and C_2 in the left-hand image in Figure 7.4.

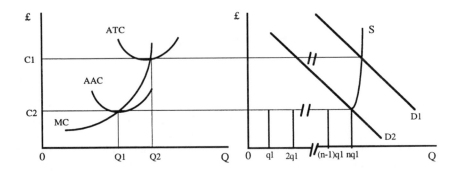

Figure 7.4 The situation with market slumps

In the market with n supplying undertakings, shown on the right in the figure, if demand rises slightly above D_1 there will be no market entry because a newcomer of minimum scale q_1 would drive the price down below C_1. Equally, a small drop in demand would not cause exit because of the fixed cost factor. In terms of core theory the core is not empty either for a small rise or fall in demand. If, however, demand falls below D_2 then an empty core situation does emerge because the market cannot support all the n suppliers in the market. From a pragmatic perspective, therefore, the core is more likely to be empty when an industry is in a slump. A shift up in the avoidable cost curves confronting firms has a similar implication.

7.4.5 Fluctuating and uncertain demand

Linked to the above, variability in demand can lead to an empty core. Where there is a U-shaped long run cost curve, as in Figure 7.5, with substantial fluctuations in demand (between D_1 and D_2 at the extremes), then establishing a fixed price at the competitive equilibrium, q, will result in losses at all times other than when demand coincidentally cuts the LRAC at the minimum point. Perfect market adjustments to allow prices to vary as demand fluctuates would remove this problem but with the provision of scheduled services, where service output and prices are set in advance, there is very limited scope for this. With this information airlines will not enter the market unless they can be assured of prices across the range of demand fluctuations that ensure normal profits may be earned in the long-run.

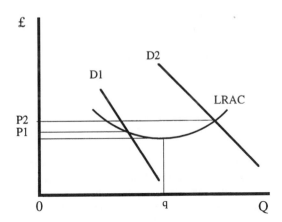

Figure 7.5 Demand fluctuations

7.5 EMPIRICAL EVIDENCE

While liberalization of network markets is an on-going process,[13] there are, nevertheless, an increasing number of experiences that may be drawn upon to

[13]   For example, Button and Keeler (1993) offer an account of recent developments in the transport sector.

assess the empty core hypothesis. These, however, must be taken as indicative of the possible existence of an empty core and to-date no rigorous method of testing for empty cores has been devised. They are largely outside of civil aviation but can offer some insights to that sector.

Sjostrom's own analysis, which essentially follows a structure, conduct, performance type of approach, looks at conditions pertaining in shipping conference markets to explore the extent to which the existence of these cartels conform to situations consistent with either a monopoly rent-seeking or an empty core scenario. In particular, given the data available, he seeks to see if there are legal restrictions on entry (making the core theory for collusion less likely) or severe temporal variations in demand and costs (making the core theory more likely). He concludes from data relating to 24 shipping conference routes operating to and from the West Coast of the US in 1982, that the cartel theory can be rejected and there is some support for the theory of the core.[14]

Pirrong's approach, again looking at shipping cartels, is complementary to Sjostrom's in that it puts its emphasis on exploring costs.[15] In particular, he looks at the relations between cost, demand and market organization. Pirrong

---

[14]   Because the quantity shipped by a conference depends partly on the effectiveness of the cartel, Sjostrom used a two-stage estimation of the general form:

$$CON = f[Q, SD, P, REST]$$
$$Q = f[CON, LDC, EXP, IMP]$$

where:
CON =   conference's share of liner shipments on its route,
Q =   quantity shipped on liners,
SD =   standard deviation of liner shipments on the route,
P =   average value of goods shipped on the route by liner ships,
RES =   dummy variable isolating Latin American, Indonesian and Philippine routes,
LDC =   dummy variable isolating routes to and from less developed countries,
EXP =   total exports of the country in which the liner cargo originated,
IMP =   total imports of the region of the cargo's destination.

The equations estimated using two-stage least squares yielded:

$$CON = 3.37 - Ln0.22Q + 1.53E\text{-}6SD + 0.03P - 0.54REST$$
$$LnQ = -0.24 + 2.98CON - 0.73LDC + 0.49EXP + 0.48 IMP \qquad n = 24$$

The signs of the coefficients of the SD and REST variables are consistent with the existence of an empty core.

[15]   The potential existence of an empty core has also been explored by examining cost function in the context of experimental economics as well as the more conventional procedures discussed below (Van Boening and Wilcox, 1992).

isolates conditions where the demand structure is finely divisible and the cost curves are non-homogeneous as describing the circumstances under which competition is not feasible. The evidence, he concludes, is consistent with Sjostrom's findings and suggests collusion and coalitions in the shipping market serve to ensure market stability and avoid competitive chaos. Whether the exact nature of the collusion is efficient could not be judged.

These developments in empirics also provide a basis for looking at the situation in aviation markets. While one would not like to take the analogy too far, interestingly there are important parallels between the shipping conference system and the aviation market. As with scheduled aviation, shipping lines provide regular, scheduled services that increasingly involve, through the use of electronic data interchange systems, crude yield management procedures (Brooks and Button, 1994). Tramp shipping is akin to the charter services operated in aviation and hub-and-spoke patterns of shipping service are emerging. Deferred rebates and other loyalty payments offered in some conference markets have similar implications to frequent flyer programs. The move towards consortia in liner shipping has similarities to code-sharing in aviation markets. Shipping berth allocation has much in common with that of airport slots and there are differential handling charges according to line in both cases.

While there is implicit recognition of the potential for an empty core situation to arise in the reformed European aviation market, the topic has only partly been explored. Comparative analysis is possible and a number of studies have pointed to inherent similarities and differences between the pre-liberalized European scene and the post-1978 deregulated US domestic market but they do not go beyond this (e.g., Button and Swann, 1992). For instance, despite the considerable out-flow of work on the efficiency of US domestic aviation very little econometric analysis has been attempted on market stability – Sandler (1988) being an exception.

Button (1996), making use of the general analytical framework established by Sjostrom and Pirrong, examined the European internal international aviation market for signs of potential instability. The study took 1990 data covering 106 international routes within Europe. The results, based upon the Sjostrom market entry approach, provided indicative, but certainly not conclusive, evidence of the possibility that the increasing number of collusion arrangements emerging in European aviation markets may be coming about due to the existence of an empty core but they do not go beyond that.[16] The statistical associations, although

---

[16]   The general formulation of the model employed in Button (1996) was;

$$SE = f(AD, LR, NC, CR, TF, PL, NR, DV)$$

where:

generally in the direction that would support this hypothesis, are extremely weak. The direct application of Pirrong's cost function approach to aviation is difficult because of data limitations but the general nature of the costs functions exhibited by airlines (see Chapter 2) would seem, from other empirical analysis, to offer the potential for an empty core condition to exist.[17]

7.6 POLICY OPTIONS

If some competitive network industries are potentially prone to instability why has this appeared to manifest itself so infrequently in practice? One purely theoretical answer to this, that is consistent with the theory of the core, is that suppliers will not exist in such markets and thus the hypothesis is not empirically refutable. In practice, however, the extreme conditions required for non-supply are unlikely to exist and instability would more logically manifest itself in terms of very rapid market entry and exit of suppliers and users and in violent price

SE =   percentage of traffic on a route carried by airlines from countries at either end of the route,
AD =   distance between airports in kilometers,
LR =   acts to reflect the nature of the legal environment and is a dummy variable taking a unitary value if the route is the subject of a liberal bilateral,
NC =   number of carriers on the route,
CR =   Dummy variable taking a value of unity if the route serves north-south traffic to reflect possible competition from charter services,
TF =   total flights,
PL =   average load factor,
NR =   dummy variable taking the value of unity if there was no service in 1985,
DV =   annual variability of demand between 1985 and 1990 expressed as the coefficient of variation in annual passengers carried on each route included in the analysis.

For estimation, the specification of the dependent variable is in terms of a log-odds transformation to allow for it being bounded in its natural form. The OLS estimated equation was:

$$Ln[SE/(1-SE)] = 8.855 - 0.001AD + 0.538LR - 2.002NC + 1.512CR + 0.001TF$$
$$+ 14.630PL + 5.101NR + 2.200DV \qquad n= 106, \ R^2 = 0.50$$

The results offer some tentative support for the possible existence of empty core conditions.

[17]   More specifically, the types of condition one is looking for are summarized by Pirrong (1992) as 'if the cost functions of individual plants contain regions of both increasing and decreasing returns, demand is variable, and if plants serve several customers simultaneously, the core is almost always empty.'

fluctuations. There may be either natural market feedback reactions to this or implicit institutional factors that limit the problem.

In practice, as noted earlier, the core concept has been used to justify a variety of regulatory interventions, such as regulatory restrictions on quantity and antitrust exemptions from cartel behavior. In this respect there are two very important points to recognize:

- The first is that where the core is non-empty, the outcomes in the core all have the property that welfare cannot be improved. In other words, where the core is non-empty, regulatory intervention cannot lead to a more efficient outcome.[18]
- The second, is that when the core is non-empty without additional information we can say nothing about welfare implications. The reason is that in order to conduct welfare analysis we first need a model that can predict outcomes. Once we have such a model we can compare outcomes on the basis of some welfare criterion. In the absence of a prediction of outcomes we can make no such comparison.

Conducting any form of welfare analysis on outcomes that arise when the core is empty, therefore, needs some additional elements to the model further specifying the outcomes that will arise in the context of an empty core. In the numerical examples given earlier, the core was empty because the incumbent was earning positive profits in equilibrium, thereby attracting new entry which attracts customers away from the incumbent, thereby destabilizing the existing equilibrium. If it is assumed that all potential suppliers have full knowledge of the situation then there is no incentive for them to enter the market because they realized that all will earn zero profits – this lack of supply is conceptually associated with market instability.

There are, however, theories of how incumbents respond to new entry in ways that raise barriers to entry. One of the results of such theory is that the incumbent may be able to deter entry by developing a reputation for 'toughness' and for not yielding any customers to the entrant. Foreseeing this possibility, the entrant forecasts that the market price will drop sufficiently post-entry so as to make entry unprofitable and, therefore, chooses to forego entry. There may also be other simple contractual arrangements that the incumbent can enter into with his clients that produce the same outcome without having to invest in a reputation for toughness. The incumbent included include a 'price-matching' or 'most-favored nation' clause in its contracts which guarantees the customer the best price offered

---

[18]   Indeed, under broad assumptions, regulatory intervention will not even be able to change the outcome - since the parties can negotiate they will typically be able to offset any attempted public policy change through private agreement.

elsewhere, or there may be deferred-rebates offered (e.g., frequent flyer points). Such contracts essentially ensure the loyalty of the customer to the incumbent, preventing the entrant from bidding the customers away. The entrant foresees that entry will be unprofitable and so entry will not be attempted.

There may be still other approaches for ensuring the loyalty of customers. One might involve a form of vertical integration between the incumbent and customers. In the earlier example, if **A1** vertically integrates with **B1**, then even in the presence of a second airline, the core is non-empty. This model offer potential stability because it is harder for a competing coalition to attract the business of **B1** away from **A1**. This arises because the successful ship airline makes profits of at least $10. Thus, any outside coalition must be able to offer the **A1-B1** alliance at least $10 as a reward for breaking up and taking business elsewhere.

In terms of welfare effects, provided the incumbent is prevented from pricing below minimum average cost (perhaps by competition restrictions), entry is only deterred when there is insufficient excess demand at the price of minimum average cost to allow entry at the minimum efficient scale. Entry is not deterred when there is sufficient excess demand for the entrant to enter at the minimum efficient scale. Moreover, provided there are a sufficient number of competing incumbents, standard competitive pressures ensure rates cannot rise very far above minimum average cost. In other words, standard models of entry and entry deterrence provide one means of resolving the empty core problem. Provided the entry deterrence is not anti-competitive, the resulting market outcomes are entirely consistent with full efficiency.

Since there seems a *prime facie* case for suspecting that at least some network industries such as air transport may, if left to pure market forces, will be confronted by empty core and instability problems, what should be the appropriate policy response? There are essentially four broad ways in which policies can be developed to counter-act market instabilities in network industries or, to put it in technical terms, for 'resolving' an empty core;

* the situation may be deemed unimportant and no action taken,
* policies may be instigated with the aim of manipulating the role of markets,
* policies may be instigated involving institutional measures that involve direct provision of networks,
* policies may allow actors in the market to tackle the problem internally through the adoption of coalition or other measures.

As seen above, leaving the situation to market forces may prove the most effective approach when, because of precise knowledge of the mechanisms at work or distrust of the suitability of the remedial policies at hand, intervention failures are likely to outweigh the market failure of instability if the latter is not severe. In general it is difficult to be precise about the existence of an empty core and even more difficult is the design of policies to ameliorate the problems associated with the market failure.

One approach is to directly intervene to limit the degree to which actors can price down to marginal cost or saturate the market. As Telser (1994) says, 'a general method of resolving an empty core requires imposition of suitable upper bounds on the quantities that may be sold by certain sellers. Such bounds always exist.'

The EU, for instance, has implicitly exhibited concern about the potential for empty core problems regarding both trucking and aviation. For example, regarding trucking, policies in the 1970s were aimed at deriving a system of 'forked tariffs' with upper and lower limits, the latter to prevent excessive competition. Equally, Council Regulation 2408/92 allows for freezing capacity when the aviation market is fundamentally unbalanced and Regulation 2409/92 allows for intervention to prevent downward spirals on air fares. At the more localized level, it is normal for taxicab markets to operate under a regime of regulated fares and, in some cases, with market entry controls.[19]

The difficulty with such direct actions, however, is to determine the appropriate price floor or capacity ceiling, a difficulty which is particularly pronounced in a network setting. The issue becomes one of weighing the potential of the costs of market failures because of the implications of the empty core against those of the resources costs of intervention failures where parameters are misspecified. The problems are a mirror reflection of the challenges of specifying appropriate antitrust and monopoly regulations where one is dealing with suppliers' efforts to gain a high degree of market power.

Since the main problem of an empty core is insufficient or, at the extreme, no supply then government may intervene to directly provide capacity. This approach has been one of the arguments used in the past to justify the nationalization of networks. The evidence is that, in general, the removal of market incentives leads to reduced efficiency and higher unit costs of provision especially where policies mean that cross subsidies are deployed. It has also been found difficult in practice to isolate circumstances where there is a genuine empty core problem from instances where the demand curve for the network services lies entirely within the cost curve and, *ipso facto*, no capacity could be justified on positive economic criteria. Examples of the latter situation would seem to involve situations where there may initially have been grounds for public provision to meet an empty core problem but where subsequent shifts in either costs or demand no longer justify such actions. Closures of rail links often seem to pose this type of problem.

---

[19] The medallion system operated in New York is the most famous of the quantity control regimes.

The final alternative is to allow those in the market to tackle the problem of a potentially empty core themselves. In other words, to develop managerial approaches and market strategies that circumvent the instability implications inherent in many network industries. If we take aviation as an example, one can explain such things as the advent of frequent flier programs in terms of retaining customer loyalty and keep fares above short-run marginal costs in a volatile market.[20] Further, airline mergers, such as the wave that followed shortly after the introduction of the 1978 deregulation of US domestic markets (see Chapter 5), strategic alliances[21] and franchising can be seen as methods of controlling some aspects of supply, and yield management techniques can be viewed as a mechanism to price discriminate and generate maximum revenue.[22]

In some ways this type of approach has been implicitly accepted in some policy areas. It has been the approach pursued in the domestic US aviation market where mergers policy, in the hands of the Department of Transportation, was comparatively lax in the twenty years following deregulation and devices such as the frequent flier program were developed. Equally, EU aviation policy has effectively both allowed mergers provided that certain concessions are made (e.g. the relinquishing of designated routes) to limit resultant market power, and provided block exemptions from elements of competition policy. Further, frequent flyer programs have not been attacked under EU competition policy and these provide a mechanism for retaining customer loyalty across periods of fluctuating demand. At the international level, the IATA has in the past enjoyed the power to influence fare levels and, more recently, anti-trust immunity has been afforded by some governments to the strategic airline alliances that have emerged.

The policy challenge in this case is to ensure that if such devices are used then their potential costs in terms of the possible monopoly power that can result do not exceed the benefits of avoiding potential empty core situations. This is particularly difficult in network industries where conventional antitrust policies pose problems in implementation, not least because appropriate markets over

[20]   For example, Telser (1996) argues the general case thus: 'Participants in a market lacking a core do contrive arrangements that will suitably restrict competition.... Long-term contracts between suppliers and their customers such as the take-or-pay contracts in natural gas are arrangements that restrict competition insofar as they eliminate some spot markets.'

[21]   These can take a variety of forms but often include related frequent flyer programs, code-sharing and coordinated schedules; they can also embrace equity swaps.

[22]   Similar types of argument have been used successfully to maintain the system of shipping conferences and parallels to aviation can be found in the form of deferred rebates and the development of consortia.

which legal judgments can be made are difficult to define.[23] The complexity of cost allocation over networks also poses serious potential problems of regulatory capture.

7.6   CONCLUSIONS

The economic evidence is that the recent phase of market liberalization has in general enhanced both the technical and dynamic efficiency of network industries such as air transportation. Markets, however, are not static entities and there are inevitable shifts over time on both the demand and supply sides. In normal circumstances this may not pose any serious problem but, given the basic characteristics of network industries, there is the possibility that instability may result with, in the extreme condition, no supply being provided despite the net economic benefits that exist. In other words many network industries may be characterized by an empty core if competition is fostered.

While the numerous cases exhibiting the extremities of an empty core are unlikely to emerge in practice, the features of many network markets do mean that volatility may be high, with services being provided on an intermittent and unreliable basis. This raises issues about the appropriate government response to such conditions. Policy may take a number of courses but it is unlikely that their is any ideal approach to handling the problem of empty cores. Much depends on the ability of policy makers and their analysts to identify instances where empty core problems are likely to exist and their possible order of magnitude. But even beyond this, different policy approaches will have associated with them a variety of transactions costs issues and may well involve complex distributional questions.

There seems no straightforward *a priori* approach to policy formulation but rather more empirical analysis is required to provide a more stringent set of criteria upon which the inevitable *ad hoc* sectoral policies can be developed. If, though, the considerable investments which are now going towards developing infrastructure networks are to achieve their primary goal of enhanced spatial economic integration, it is important that the most effective policies for tackling empty core problems be devised.

[23]   This problem is exemplified by recent debates over international airline alliances where policy makers must decide if it is a service, a route, a set of routes or a wider network that forms the basis of the market under review.

8   AIRPORTS: PRICING AND ACCESS

8.1   INTRODUCTION

The efficient provision of airports and the use of their capacity are vital to the overall efficiency of air transport networks. Airports, like most forms of infrastructure where indivisibilities, high costs of investment, extensive externalities and the potential for the creation of a natural monopoly are seen as serious threats to their economic use, have been the subject of both widespread public ownership and regulation. This is true of local airports as much as major international hub airports although here local governments have often been more active.

Airports take up a large amount of land and inevitably there is public concern about investments in new infrastructure. There are now fairly well developed methods of handling this from a public policy perspective. In recent years, with the growth of hub-and-spoke operations, however, it is the pricing of capacity at hubs that has attracted the most attention. The ways in which prices are set at nodal points and the access that is allowed to potential users of nodes influence the way in which the entire air transport network functions.

While the practice of airport pricing is relatively crude in most cases, often being founded on a combination of crude engineering and accountancy principles, the economic theory of how airports should be priced is, despite the complexities involved, fairly well developed. This is largely because the features of airports are not significantly different to those associated with many other forms of infrastructure although there are some nuances that have to be considered. The conventional economic wisdom on the subject is dealt with at the outset, although in a fairly brief and general way.

The practice of how airports price and make investment choices is very different from the economic ideal and this is also looked at in this Chapter. The coverage is to some extent stylized because there is variation between airports, especially those offering only domestic services. The situation is also a fluid one and there are significant changes taking place in the ownership of airports and the ways that their services are being priced.[1] To provide a more complete and detailed

---

[1]   In Canada and the UK there have, for instance, been important measures of privatization. In the UK the British Airports Authority (BAA) was formed and floated on the stock exchange. It operates Aberdeen, Edinburgh, Glasgow, Gatwick, Heathrow, Prestwick and Stansted, as well as some smaller facilities.

picture of some of the developments that are taking place, the following chapter looks particularly at what has been taking place in Europe.

8.2   AIRPORT PRICING THEORY

8.2.1   The non-peak situation

The oft-cited problem with pricing airports is that there are important divergences between the short run costs associated with the use of an existing level of capacity and the long run costs of varying that capacity. Since the accepted first best public sector pricing strategy in the absence of any form of budgetary constraint is marginal cost pricing this raises issues of defining the appropriate cost function to be adopted.[2]

The generally accepted position is that the long run average costs (LRAC) of airport capacity initially fall but then flatten out (Figure 8.1). Given the problems of finding suitable locations for new airports or gaining public acceptance for expanding existing ones, with very high traffic volumes one may expect that this curve will eventually turn up, although this is not depicted in Figure 8.1. This means that in general smaller airports have higher unit costs that larger ones, although the costs at mega-airports begin to rise – which is one explanation why many cities have several large facilities rather than one single, massive airport.

Where exactly the LRAC curve flattens out is to some extent contextual and would seem to shift out and down with time as improved technology and innovative management techniques improve efficiency. Evidence from the UK from the 1980s indicates that the flattening begins at around 1.0 to 1.5 million passengers per annum and that there are very few additional economies after about 3 million passengers per year.

The short run average costs (SRAC) of airports are more immediately U-shaped because they reflect the costs of congestion that build up as more traffic uses the fixed technical capacity available. The indivisibilities inherent in such ventures as building a new terminal or runway mean that the LRAC curve envelope is not continuous in the standard neo-classical economic sense but is a set of discontinuous scallops (following the lowest path of $SRAC_1$, $SRAC_2$, $SRAC_3$, etc. in the diagram. $SRAC_1$ may be seen as a situation with one terminal

---

[2]   The strict Coasian approach to the problem is to allow markets to develop for airport capacity. To some extent this is what happened at some congested US airports (John F. Kennedy, La Guardia, O'Hare and Washington National) where slots for domestic flights have been traded between carriers since 1986. Those holding the slots prior to the introduction of the system retained them and could sell them. If slots are not used, however, they are returned to the FAA. There are also a number of supplementary rules, for example to encourage new market entry. There is also a distinction between slots for commuter carriers and air carriers.

and a single runway, $SRAC_2$, with the addition of extra terminal capacity and $SRAC_3$ when an additional runway is added. All are tangential to the LRAC curve, although only $SRAC_1$ and $SRAC_2$ touch it at their minimum points.

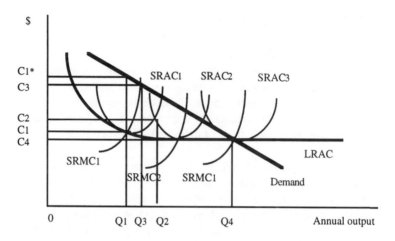

Figure 8.1 The long- and short-run costs of airport provision

The optimal price and capacity will depend on the level of demand as well as cost considerations – Pareto optimality requiring marginal utility to equal marginal costs. Here it is assumed that demand does not fluctuate with time of day or with season. In reality there are considerable fluctuations in the demand for air services.

If there is a single terminal and one runway then the long and short run curves coincide at Q_1. With the demand depicted a price equal to C_1 would lead to excess demand and a premium of $C_{1*} - C_1$ is required to suppress this. This premium reflects the marginal congestion costs at this output level. The utility generated makes it desirable to take more traffic at the airport and to move out along the $SRAC_1$ curve until demand is equated to $SRMC_1$ (i.e., at an output level Q_3).[3]

Since the price is above the LRAC costs super-normal profits are being generated. The existing terminal and runway could be used up to the point where $SRAC_1$ meets the demand curve and a break-even situation is attained. But adding an extra terminal and moving to a new set of cost curves is more efficient because of the additional benefits generated *vis-à-vis* the additional costs. An expansion of capacity is thus justified and since revenues exceed costs then this can be done

---

[3]   The pricing and output options considered here reflect notions of social optimality. If pure profit maximization was the goal then the airport authorities would seek pricing levels where marginal costs and marginal revenues are equated and this would be to the left of Q_3.

without the need for subsidies. In fact, because of indivisibilities, if only financial costs are being considered, then the capacity expansion should take place only after an annual output of Q_2 has been attained.[4]

In our example, the additional terminal associated with $SRAC_2$ will not be sufficient to meet the demand level prevailing unless a congestion charge is added. The optimal long-term situation is at output level Q_4 with prices set at C_4. Here there is equality between the various cost curves and demand and no super-normal profits are being earned.

Of course the argument is a simplification. There may, because of indivisibilities be no point where short run marginal costs are coincidental with demand and long run marginal costs. The simplification assumes that there are no external costs of the type normally associated at airports, such as noise, and focuses on the single objective of social welfare maximization. Nor does it consider second best factors such as the policies being adopted by competing airports or by competing modes of transport.

There are also wider institutional factors, such as international agreements, that determine the rates that can be levied on some groups of users. The policy makers often use airports as part of wider social and development strategies rather than being interested in their narrower economic efficiency. Added to this, an airport does not provide a single service but rather a basket of services ranging through landing fees to concessions and this multi-product mix makes the idea of a single price for airport use rather simplistic.

8.2.2 The peaked demand situation

As we have seen, the basic economic principles of marginal cost pricing suggest that welfare is maximized where prices are set equal to long-run marginal cost. As with economies of scale, under economies of scope, price will be below average costs with this marginal cost pricing prescription. As Kahn (1988d) points out, the traditional legal criteria of proper public utility rates have always borne a strong resemblance to the criteria of the competitive market in long-run

---

[4]   There is often the mistaken view that marginal cost pricing in the face of indivisibilities is not practical because a new capacity is added at a time when it is initially underused in an engineering sense. It is justified because the short run marginal costs of adding more capacity are lower than using new capacity more intensively. This could be interpreted to imply that the marginal user's marginal cost is the entire cost of the new investment. In fact, the marginal cost related to any individual user should be seen as a probabilistic function. For example, user Q_2+1 has a marginal cost associated with her embracing not only the cost of using the exiting terminal and runway but also the probability that the trip will require an additional terminal multiplied by the cost of so doing. This produces a meaningful finite cost but is clearly way below the construction costs of actually providing the extra terminal.

equilibrium. The principal benchmark for 'just and reasonable' rate levels has been the cost of producing, including the necessary return on capital.

The rule that individual rates not be unduly discriminatory has similarly been defined in terms of the respective costs of the various services. However, it is short run marginal cost to which price should be equated because it is the short run marginal cost which reflects the social opportunity cost of providing the additional unit that buyers are at any time trying to decide to buy. Marginal costs look to the future not the past, since it is only future costs that can be saved if production is not undertaken. In the presence of competition, it is long run and not short run costs which should set the floor. If capital costs are to be included in price, then it should be clear that those capital costs are those that will have to be covered over time in the future if service is to continue to be rendered.

The issue then arises as to whether all users should pay the price, which includes the capacity costs. The demand for air transport, both passenger and cargo, is not uniform through the day or week, or across seasons. The demands of leisure travel, for instance, is much higher during some parts of the years than at others and there are variations in the destinations preferred at various time of the year.

Kahn argues that the off-peak users should not pay these costs since they do not impose these costs on society once their demand is sufficiently slight and inelastic that even at a zero cost, no congestion occurs at the time when they use the facility. The customers impose the necessity for expansion at the peak hours. If the same type of capacity serves all users, capacity costs should be levied only on utilization at the peak. This peak responsibility pricing is not discriminatory between peak and off-peak users (that discrimination implies that the price differences are not based on cost differences); rather, it reflects the fact that there is a genuine increase in the costs of supplying users at the peak compared with the off-peak. The proposal then is to reflect the cost difference in respective prices.

When infrastructure is built far in advance of total need (because, for example, of economies of scale), charging depreciation in equal instalments imposes a disproportionately heavy burden on customers in earlier years, when much of the capacity lies idle. This idle capacity is of benefit to future, not present, customers. Economic efficiency suggests concentrating capital charges in the later years.

Finally, in situations of economies of scale or scope, where price set equal to marginal cost will yield a loss, Ramsey prices eliminate the deficit while minimising the loss in welfare that results. Ramsey prices maximize social welfare but also require revenues to cover costs: the resulting prices achieve as great a level of social welfare as possible in the presence of realities that prevent the use of marginal cost prices.

Of the alternatives, demand management techniques can be either administrative, where an executive body make decisions and directly allocates runnway capacity, or involve pricing techniques, whereby operators make choices on the basis of their willingness to pay. Table 8.1 summarizes the literature on runway congestion management techniques under these two headings, and presents the advantages and disadvantages associated with both sets of approaches.

Regarding the relationship between marginal cost pricing and investment, Vickrey (1971) suggests a pattern of pricing over time when investment is lumpy. This is illustrated in Figure 8.2. In the top part of the figure, demand is increasing over time. When demand grows from D_1 to D_2, in the short run, the marginal cost price rises from P_1 to P_2. As new capacity is added, and demand continues to grow, prices fall to P_3. The increase in price prior to the expansion of capacity rations the capacity at its initial supply level. The pattern continues over time as illustrated, with short-term increases in price when each successive level of capacity is reached. With additional capacity being added the price reduces to the level of the marginal cost.

Vickrey's pricing pattern is somewhat different: as demand grows, price should rise for a period before the new capacity is available. The increase in price should be sufficient to curtail demand to the existing level of capacity. When the new capacity comes on stream, the price should drop sharply to the point where the new capacity is fully utilized. Once again the price should increase as demand grows so as to keep consumption within the limits of the available capacity.

Issues arise regarding who should pay the higher short run charges as demand increases and also which costs are fixed and which are variable in this scenario. Small *et al.* (1989) provide a detailed analysis of the application of such a pricing and investment policy to the management of road infrastructure, given different categories of road users, differing levels of deterioration in existing pavements, and differing levels of investment requirements for new and existing facilities. They also suggest a simplified policy application, given the likely public and government reaction to constantly changing prices.

Small *et al.* suggest two sets of charges. The first are wear charges and the second congestion charges. The wear charges suggested would encourage firms to use less damaging vehicles and use roads most suited to heavy trucks. The charges would ideally be applied to all categories of heavy vehicle, whether publicly or privately owned. The proposed congestion charges would replace traffic management measures and should be determined on the basis of their impact on specific sections as well as on competing sections.

For airports, that have the facility to expand capacity, the funding for this capacity and planning regulations are the key issues needing to be addressed. The decision regarding the expansion is inevitably a public decision involving planners, residents and other interested groups. This process has become increasingly more involved and lengthy as environmental regulations in particularly have become a far more prominent issue in the public consultation process. The weights attached to each environmental effect and the extent these effects should be set against narrower, more traditional economic benefits is inevitably a subjective judgement.

Table 8.1 Approaches to runway congestion management

Technique	Option	Advantages	Disadvantages
Administrative techniques	Restrictions of aircraft operations (quotas and bans)	*Quotas:* Simple method; attractive to airport authorities *Bans and quotas:* Prompt and direct means Can meet variety of objectives (efficiency; social; environmental; regional development) Effective at controlling peak period traffic	May not result in economically efficient allocation Mix of categories may not be efficient or reasonable May require constant monitoring and revision
	Allocation of access rights by airline scheduling committee	Encourage certainty in airline route planning Encourages continuity of scheduled service	May be anti-competitive, biasing slots towards incumbents Reduces contestability of industry May make inefficient allocations Less workable as gap between demand and supply increases
	Allocation of slots by lottery or partial allocation	Unbiased allocation mechanism May promote competition by allocation to new entrants	Difficult to build schedule on random allocation May not be sufficient to develop network schedules May not be efficient allocation May provide windfall gains to operators
Pricing or market based techniques	Peak period pricing	Straightforward to administer Access open to all potential operators based on willingness to pay Helps remove or reorient low value operators to uncongested facilities non-discriminatory Revenue raised may be used for expansion	May still require administrative strategy during peak period Determination of appropriate MSC prices is impossible – prices determined based on demand suppression effect Charges continually vary upwards based on increasing demand Low cross-elasticity of demand between peak and off-peak: may be difficult to spread the peak period Inequitable system favoring large higher revenue airlines
	Auctioning airport slots	If prices is the sole means of allocation, will establish true market value of slots Increase contestability of industry - open to all operators	Bidders may lack adequate information on value of slots Auction format may significantly influence success or failure of process Long term implications of selling access rights to airport users need to be fully appreciated

Sources: Bureau of Transport and Communications Economics (1996); Balinski and Sand (1985); Brander *et al* (1989); UK Civil Aviation Authority (1993); Doganis (1992); Fawcett and Fawcett (1988); Fisher (1989); Hamzawi (1992); Kearney and Favotto (1993); Mills (1990); Morrison (1987); Reed (1992); Swoveland (1980).

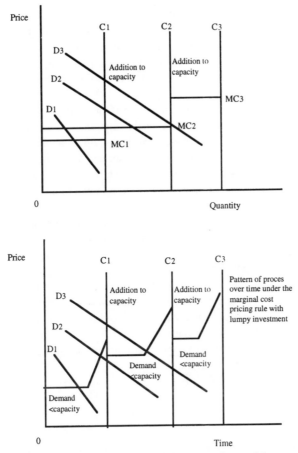

Figure 8.2 Marginal cost pricing with shifting capacity and increasing demand

The extent to which hearings and inquiries may delay or halt the process of expansion needs to be addressed from a policy point of view, since the uncertainty over the ultimate decision has significant cost and route-planning implications for airport users. The timing of investment decisions should be closely linked with an airport's pricing policy. The greater the degree of uncertainty in the timing of new capacity, the more difficult will be an appropriate pricing and management policy.

8.3 AIRPORT PRICING IN PRACTICE

The most common approach to allocating airport capacity is not through the price mechanism but rather through various forms of rationing. IATA has laid down widely used guidelines for this in its *Scheduling Procedures Guide*. This places considerable emphasis on grandfather rights (the retention of slots by incumbent users). There are variants on the basic model and the EU, for instance, has adopted measures that have sought to stimulate new market entry by reallocating slots in certain circumstances, for instance when they are little used by the incumbents (see Chapter 9).

The strict Coasian approach to allocation (Coase, 1961), that allows markets to develop for airport capacity, is not easily implemented but there are instances where trading is permitted. To some extent this is what happened at congested US airports (John F. Kennedy, La Guardia, O'Hare and Washington National) where slots for domestic routes were traded between carriers from 1986. Those holding the slots prior to the introduction of the system retained them and could sell them. If slots are not used, however, they are returned to the FAA. There are also a number of supplementary rules, for example to encourage new market entry. There is also a distinction between slots for commuter carriers and air carriers.

The outcome has been an initial period of intense activity with a sorting out of slots but then a gradual stabilization as more leasing emerged. The users of larger aircraft subsequently had a greater tendency to lease slots whilst the commuters airlines are more prone to buy and sell. Some 83% of transactions in 1988 involved leases of less than six month, and 8% of more than six months whilst with commuter carrier transactions only 17% in total involved any form of leasing. There was new entry into commuter markets but most trade for air carrier slots was between existing operators.

The pricing of airport facilities by public agencies is determined more by accountancy and institutional considerations than by economic theory, although there have been some changes in recent years.[5] A key issue in the way in which

---

[5]   A simple diagram shows the accountancy and economic approaches.

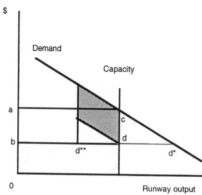

To limit runway use to its capacity the airport would impose an economic rationing price of ab above the accountancy cost of 0b. The airport would then earn a profit of

prices are determined involves the ways airlines are financial linked to airports; this largely determines the framework upon which many pricing decisions are founded. There are broadly four different arrangements that in practice determine the compensation that airlines must pay airports for the services enjoyed.

- The residual cost approach has the airlines agreeing to make up any shortfall in revenue in the running of the airport that cannot be allocated to other users or recovered from non-airline users.
- The widely adopted compensation approach has the airport operator taking the major financial risk and charging airlines fees and rentals for facilities.
- The hybrid approach combines the residual and compensatory approaches. Profits (or losses) are shared between the airport authorities and the airlines. It is, for example, the approach of the airports in the Washington area.
- Privatization involves stock ownership, with the airport financed in line with any other, comparable private undertaking.

Airports, irrespective of their financial structure, have two main sources of revenue (aside from any form of subsidies from the state or local government). These sources are fees for air-side and land-side services. The latter are often used as a means of off-setting costs before setting land and other fees and are based on what the market will bear. This offers scope for cross-subsidization, including that from non-aviation activities such as retailing to air transportation activities.

Focusing on air-side revenues, which are most closely linked with the running and operations of an airport, concerns the use of operational areas, leased areas and grounds. Landing fees in most countries, including the US and Europe, are largely based on aircraft weight although there may be some differentiation by time of day

abcd. Without this price the quantity demanded, d*, would exceed the available capacity of the facility. If the airport does not impose such a charge but simply allocates capacity on an administrative basis, then airlines will still have to contain the demand for the seats they can offer so that runway use stays within capacity. To do this they will charge fares of 0a (or with yield management, discriminatory fares down the demand curve to the point where capacity is fully utilized). Airlines holding slots thus enjoy the scarcity rent, abcd, that would go to the airport with effective slot charging. The fact that there is a capacity shortage also means that the slots are not well used.

The extreme case can be illustrated by considering the dd* shortfall in capacity would have been used by marginal services if it had been available. If these services are instead still provided as part of the administered allocation (i.e., d**d is set equal to dd*) then there would be an efficiency loss equal to the shaded area. In other words, less demanded services would be replacing more demanded services. The illustration is an extreme one since the carriers with runway output d**d would have an incentive to make good use of it although there may be some other institutional constraints preventing this being completely realized.

(partially reflect congestion factors) and by type of aircraft (reflecting noise differences). The standard US model differs from that found in most European countries. It normally involves contractual agreements between the airport and regular users (use agreements). Some of these agreements are vey long term. Capital and operating costs are booked according to explicit accountancy rules and divided by aircraft weight to give a simple charge per tonne landed. Passenger facilities are dealt with by space rentals and the like that are directly cost related. The US is almost unique in having major publicly owned airports that have privately owned and managed terminals

In continental Europe the fee is more often based on landing weight with an additional component for each passenger with a contribution for aircraft parking. The fees are not normally directly related to costs but are adjusted to meet overall budget needs. This essentially weight-based approach is, however, often seem as a reasonable approximation to costs when an airport is underutilized, but does not otherwise reflect full economic costs (Vasigh and Hamzaee, 1998).

Major private airports have traditionally been rare in the world although this is changing (Hooper and Hensher, 1997). The British Airports Authority (BAA) provides an example of how commercially driven pricing at private airports within the constraints of national regulations (in this case a price-capping regime imposed over the system of BAA airports) and international codes (those of ICAO and IATA[6]) is being adopted. The effort here has been to try to develop an economically based marginal-cost pricing structure. Initial attempts at peak pricing during the pre-privatization phase in 1979 came about through the need to generate

[6]   These bodies vary in the way they think airport charges should be applied.

ICAO	IATA
1. Should be simple	Agree
2. No discrimination against foreign airlines or between them	Agree
3. Landing fees based on weight	Agree
4. No differentiation for international flights or by stage distance	Agree
5. A single charge where possible	Agree
6. Landing fee covering lighting and radio aids	Agree
7. Passenger charges acceptable but collected from airline	May be economic necessity but collect from passenger
8. Security charges only to cover relevant costs and if non-discriminatory	Not justified; it is government responsibility
9. Noise surcharge only to cover noise-alleviation measures	Not justified
10. Fuel throughput charge to be considered as concession fee	Only if covering costs of fuel facilities; not justified as concession fee
11. ?	Peak-period surcharges not justified

additional revenues. Peak users had their prices pushed up most within an overall rise of 40% at Heathrow. The move was also linked to the longer-term need to finance investment in a new terminal. Further price rises and restructuring came in 1981 and the system stayed much the same for the next decade.[7]

An important modification made over time was the move away from weight-based fees and by 1985 BAA had completely phased out rate based landing fees and replaced them with a fixed charge per aircraft at peak times. The impact of this was a dramatic fall in the number of commuter aircraft using Heathrow, with the percentage under 16 tonnes using the airport declining from 3.5% in 1984/5 to 2.5% in 1988/89 and to 0.01% in 1992/3, the simple economics being that the flat rate landing fee of £156 for a Shorts 360 was equivalent to £5.00 per seat compared to £0.40 for a Boeing 747.

Some airlines objected to this structure, in particular the peak period users, necessitating a detailed analysis of costs. This analysis provides information important for subsequent, more cost-sensitive pricing.[8] The evidence showed peak load policy was effective in shifting traffic between peaks and off-peaks (Table 8.2). The charges, however, were not based on strict cost estimates and posing problems for BAA which was charged with discrimination, in part because there was some negotiation between it and the carriers when arriving at fares. Legally, the notion of peak pricing was accepted, but the mechanisms were seen as potentially unfair. Consequently, while the basis for charging has been retained, fine-tuning has been initiated in response to these criticisms.

In addition to the pricing of slots, airlines pay for a variety of other airport services. A variety of mechanisms are used for setting these prices. Ground handling is a term that is often used generically. IATA, however, in its Standard

---

[7] From May 1981 there was a landing charge of £120 + £4.8 per ton over 50 tons (with a winter rebate), a peak period international departure charge of £10.10 per passenger and £4.80 per domestic peak period passenger, an off-peak charge of £1.60 per passenger and a parking charge of £0.22 per hour, with each minute counting as 4 minutes during peak periods.

[8] The table below provides a summary of the cost-based rates estimated for Heathrow at 1983 price levels. The high peak/off-peak differential is explained by the high costs of adding additional terminal capacity compared to taking more traffic at existing terminals during the off-peak periods.

Per passenger	Off-peak	Peak
International departure	£1.66	£13.40–£15.50
International arrival	£0.46	£6.71–£7.85
Domestic departure	£1.25	£7.59–£8.66
Domestic arrival	£0.18	£2.00–£2.15

Ground Handling Agreement, isolates specific components: ground administration and supervision; passenger handling; baggage handling; cargo and mail handling; ramp services; cleaning; fueling; aircraft maintenance; flight operations and crew administration; service transport; and catering services. The costs to airlines of using the ground services at airports in Europe have traditionally differed considerably between terminals and these variations cannot be explained away purely in terms of differences in national labor costs (Button *et al.,* 1998). They have also tended historically to be considerably higher than those found in the US – a DC-9 handled at Atlanta in the early 1990s cost about $700 and an A320 cost $800 compared with $3 175 and $4 762, respectively at Paris CDG.

Table 8.2 Movement in flight departure times following changes in the pax peak period at Heathrow

Peak period (GMT)		1986 (1000–1449)	1987 (0900–1529)	1988 (0900–1529)
British Airways	BA215 Boston	1515	1600	1600
	BA600 Vienna	0900	0855	0850
Air Algérie	AH2055 Algiers	1500	1530	1530
Cyprus Airways	CY327 Larnaca	0900	0900	0830
El Al	LY316 Tel Aviv	1515	1530	1545
JAT	JU231 Rijeka	1500	1615	1610
Olympic Airways	OA264 Athens	1520	1520	1545
Royal Air Maroc	AT915 Casablanca	1515	1515	1615
TWA	TW755	0955	0930	0855

The historically higher cost airports found within Europe were generally associated with monopolies over ramp handling (i.e., Athens, Bilboa, Faro, Frankfurt and Madrid). The AEA estimated that in the past costs were about 30% higher at airports where there was no competition. Because of local market conditions and the nature of individual airports, the form of service offered differs between airports, as do the input costs involved, but it seems unlikely that this can explain the generally higher costs found at monopolized terminals (Table 8.3).

As competition in the industry has grown, so has the ability of airlines to secure what they regard as proper standards of handling. Airports usually restrict these rights, often on the proposition that space is too restricted to allow for the levels of equipment that would accompany unlimited handling rights or for reasons of security. Often the result has been that it has become restricted to one company, frequently the national carrier or the subsidiary or associate of the airport operator.

In the UK, this problem has been diminishing. There has long been a number of competing handling companies, both airside and landside, at Heathrow and Gatwick. Following the intervention of the UK's Monopolies and Mergers Commission, multiple airside handling will be in both terminals at Manchester. Given this precedent, it is highly probable that multiple handling will be introduced, when necessary, at airports where it is absent. Elsewhere in the EU, the tradition of monopoly handling has tended to continue. This is despite efforts by the Commission to open up ground handling to competition in the mid-1990s.

Table 8.3 Airport and handling charges (1993 ECU) for a scheduled A320-100 service

Airport	Airport-related	Handling costs per turn-around adjusted to reflect labor cost differences	Airport-related charges and handling cost per turn-around
Amsterdam	1 953	1 372	3 325
Athens	2 003	2 815	3 629
Bilbao	847	1 883	2 463
Brussels	1 612	1 611	3 210
Dusseldorf	1 671	1 582	3 389
Faro	1 391	4 468	3 124
Frankfurt	2 052	2 656	4 936
London Gatwick	1 145	1 030	2 160
Madrid	986	2 053	2 748
Manchester	1 952	943	2 881

In the wake of the conclusion of the Comité des Sages (1994) that 'ground handling services at European airports must be fully liberalized as soon as possible', the European Commission produced a Consultation Paper followed by a Ground Handling Directive. The legal basis for the latter is Article 84(2) of the Rome Treaty. The underlying principle being that full liberalization should be focused on ground handling activities that come into some sort of contact with passengers with partial liberalization of other services.[9] The reason for this was the diversity of services involved and the concern that the primary focus should be on areas where an airline's brand-image seemed to be important.

[9]   Liberalization is to be phased in until 2003 with larger airports being the early movers. Self-handling will be liberalized less rapidly than third party handling.

9   EUROPEAN AIRPORTS POLICY

9.1 INTRODUCTION

As seen in the previous chapter, an airport represents a multi-service networked industry with significant monopoly control in the provision of many of its services. The main aim here is to examine the current capacity of the EU's airport infrastructure and the key factors determining that capacity.[1] The increasing levels of congestion experienced in the 1990s, particularly at the largest airports, indicate that there is insufficient capacity. The nature and causes of delays at airports are examined and the ways of alleviating or reducing delays are outlined.

Airport infrastructure capacity constraints are crucially important in determining the long-term development of the air transport sector. While the airline industry has been liberalized extensively through the implementation of the EU's 'Third Package' of aviation liberalization measures (see Chapter 5), control over the industry continues to be exercised indirectly or directly by governments through their control of airport capacity allocation. Airport pricing policy is of great significance in affecting economically efficient allocations of existing capacity and in signaling where and when expansion of capacity is necessary and justified.[2] The pricing policy will, among other things, influence the average size of aircraft at airports, the relative importance and emphasis on short- versus medium- or long-haul services, and the distribution of all EU traffic across the airports system. These factors in turn have important implications for airline network structures - a key competitive tool for carriers in a deregulated market.

9.2 THE CAPACITY OF AIRPORT INFRASTRUCTURE

9.2.1 The nature of airport services
The basic functions of an airport are to provide access for aircraft to the national airspace, to permit easy interchange between aircraft and to facilitate the consolidation of traffic. In order to perform these functions, the airport must have

---

[1]   For a more detailed assessment of the development of EU airport policy see Reynolds-Feighan and Button, 1999).
[2]   European airports vary in the economic efficiency but work by Pels (2000) using data envelopment analysis suggests a high level of average inefficiency.

several basic infrastructure elements present[3] such as runways, taxiways, aprons ('airside infrastructure') and airport ground resources for passengers or cargo. The ground resource elements as well as airside infrastructure capacity dictate the airport's air traffic capacity.

Traditionally, European and US airports have been in public ownership by local, regional or national governments or some combination of government tiers. Approximately 160 airports received scheduled international air services in the EU in 1991. This number has been expanding recently with the growth in services to regional airports encouraged by air transport liberalization. The largest EU airports are owned by a combination of city, regional and national governments, with the exception of the London airports, The London airports are privately owned and operated by BAA plc. In the US, the airports that are used by scheduled air carriers are virtually all publicly owned facilities run by an agency on behalf of the state or local government. There are a small number of publicly owned airports which are managed and run by private companies who receive a management fee for their services. No US airports have been privatized to date.

The EU has taken substantial steps towards liberalizing the air transport sector, particularly with the provisions in the 'Third Package' of liberalization measures (see Chapter 5). One of the cornerstones of these regulations is that there be free entry to international markets. As Hardaway (1991) noted, access to airport gates and terminals is critical in permitting effective competition to take place and 'Denial of access serves as an absolute barrier to entry'. The constraints on existing airport capacity have been identified in several studies as one of the main

---

[3]   The following distinction between aeronautical and non-aeronautical uses is made in *Policy Regarding Airport Rates and Charges* [Federal Register: June 21, 1996 (Volume 61, Number 121)] [Notices]: 'The [US] Department [of Transportation] considers the aeronautical use of an airport to be any activity that involves, makes possible, is required for the safety of, or is otherwise directly related to, the operation of aircraft. Aeronautical use includes services provided by air carriers related directly and substantially to the movement of passengers, baggage, mail and cargo on the airport. Persons, whether individuals or businesses, engaged in aeronautical uses involving the operation of aircraft, or providing flight support directly related to the operation of aircraft, are considered to be aeronautical users. Conversely, the Department considers that the operation by US or foreign air carriers of facilities such as a reservations center, headquarters office, or flight kitchen on an airport does not constitute an aeronautical use. Such facilities need not be located on an airport. A carrier's decision to locate such facilities is based on the negotiation of a lease or sale of property. Accordingly, the department relies on the normal forces of competition for non aeronautical commercial or industrial property to assure that fees for such property are not excessive.'

elements that will determine the extent to which competition actually develops in the liberalized EU market.[4]

The larger European and US airports often have a monopoly position in relation to terminating or originating traffic (i.e., hinterland traffic) but face competition for connecting or transferring traffics from other airports. In many large cities, there are two or more airports supporting air transportation and thus competing for the hinterland traffic as well as transferring traffics. The economic rationale for public ownership and operation is usually that some type of market failure exists and government regulation or direct involvement is required.[5]

Concerns are often whether these issues are relevant to all of the services provided at airports or, if users would benefit and efficiency would be improved if some airport services were competitively provided and, for services which remain in public ownership, what forms of economic regulation will optimize efficiency and capital investment? Concerns in the US about privatization have highlighted two issues: first, that privatized airports may not be able to fund long-term maintenance and capacity expansion programs; second, that access for certain carriers as well as for general aviation users may be problematic under a privatized system, particularly if capacity constraints exist or are likely to exist in the future.

Juan (1995) suggests, on the basis of evidence from the relatively small scale private sector participation in airport ownership, that the quality of service and investment commitments have significantly improved. This is when the private sector has a significant participation in management and ownership. The effect of airport privatization on airport pricing policies is difficult to measure although some observations are possible. First, airside charges have not variied much in terms of their average level but the charges pricing mechanisms have become more complex. Second, airside charges are now the subject of price-cap economic regulation. Finally, there has been intense development of high revenue yielding non-aeronautical commercial airport revenue.[6]

---

[4]   These include, Balfour (1994), Comite des Sages (1994), Doganis (1995), Association of European Airlines (1996).

[5]   The main types of market failure and other arguments for public ownership of airports are (Button,1993; Kahn,1988d) the containment of monopoly power, the control of excessive competition, the regulation of externalities, the provision of public goods, the provision of high costs infrastructure, the integration of transport into wider economic policies, the improvement in transport coordination, the importance of the facility nationally, that the facilities may be natural monopolies, and that competition simply does not work well.

[6]   At present, there are few constraints on a private developer building car parks or hotels on lands adjacent to a large number of European airports and competing with the airport authority in the provision of these services. If airside capacity is required however, constraints exist because of the airport authority's ownership of most of the land tracts adjacent to the runways and taxiways.

Figure 9.1 gives a schematic representation of the categories of airport services typically found at European and US airports. The services are grouped according to; whether the airport service is an 'aeronautical use' or non-aeronautical use , whether there is general public access or access only for those travelling by air, and whether or not there is direct airside access.

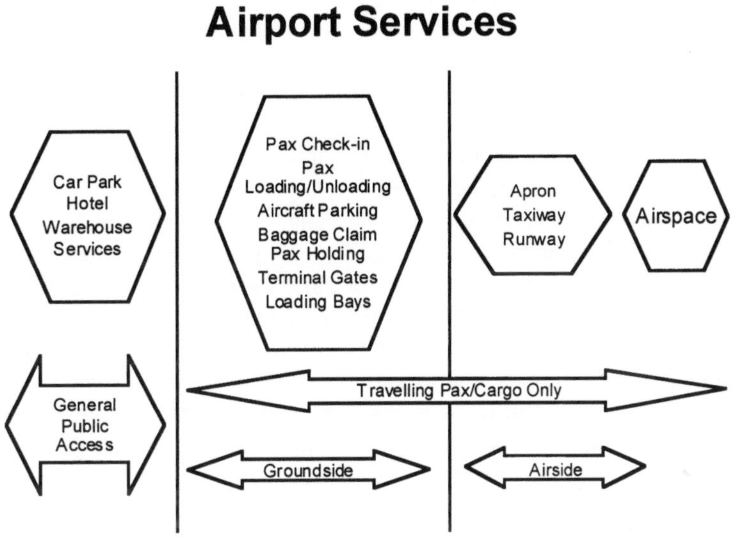

Airport Services

Figure 9.1 Nature of airport services

For airside facilities, it can be argued that duplication of runway, taxiway and apron facilities is not advisable. These infrastructural items require substantial capital investments and should generate fees sufficient only to cover replacement costs. They have significant planning requirements in terms of zoning of adjacent lands, and surface transport access. Finally, these facilities have merit good characteristics and have non-economic potential benefits or insurance aspects. For reasons of defence or growth and development, it may be necessary to provide excess capacity or facilities of a higher technical standard than are actually required to meet current demand with current technology.

Groundside facilities can be provided in a number of ways: e.g., through continued public ownership by a single airport company; through franchised arrangements with public or private management/operator companies; through mixed public/private ownership by multiple companies; and through privately owned terminal companies, which have airside access. From an economic standpoint, the main issue is whether competition in the provision of these services is necessary, feasible and can be justified in terms of keeping rates and costs low and producing a reasonable standard of service quality. While the costs and benefits of each alternative approach need to be assessed for particular facilities, European airports offer an increasing range of services and facilities to their different customer groups. Retail franchising and duty free sales are very lucrative areas for the airports and have allowed for investment and expansion of the airports' suite of services and facilities. The airports have maintained a dominant or monopoly position for this suite of services. In many instances, landing fees have been kept low because cross-subsidization has taken place.

Many companies doing business at an airport pay rental for the space that they occupy and a gross receipts fee based on their turnover at the airport. In computing carrier fees, some airports take these concessionaire revenues fees into account. There are two methods for computation of air carrier fees, the residual and the compensatory methods. With the former, the airport deducts all revenue earned from non-airline sources from its total annual budget. The airlines then pay the residual. With the latter, the airport is divided into various cost centres and the airlines pay their fees based on the measures of airport services or facilities which they use – e.g., parking and terminals. If competition is permitted in the provision of terminal and groundside services, then this cross-subsidisation is unlikely to continue. With competition in groundside services, revenues for infrastructure use can be collected either by billing carriers separately for each service or by imposing collection requirements on a single agent.

The provision of basic airside infrastructure requires significant capital investment as well as having substantial planning requirements. In addition, the merit good characteristics and insurance aspects provide strong argument for continued public sector ownership and involvement. However in relation to the other types of airport services, a wide range of possibilities exist for raising the level of private sector involvement and imposing competitive or efficiency conditions on the production of services.[7] Generally speaking, the US airports offer a narrower range of services and facilities to airlines and passengers and have exercised greater flexibility in permitting private sector development and use of publicly owned airport lands.

9.3. THE DETERMINANTS OF AIRPORT CAPACITY

9.3.1 Defining airport capacity
'Capacity', in an engineering sense, refers to the ability of a component in the airport system to handle aircraft and is usually expressed in terms of operations per

---

[7]   A World Bank report (Juan, 1995) gives examples of a variety of circumstances and contexts.

hour (arrivals or departures).[8] This hourly capacity is the maximum number of operations that can be handled in a one hour period under specific operating conditions relating to such things as ceiling and visibility, air traffic control, aircraft mix, and the nature of operations. Engineers think in terms of the 'ultimate' or 'saturation' capacity which gives the maximum number of aircraft that can be handled during a certain period under conditions of continuous demand. Runway capacity is usually the controlling element of the airport's system capacity. The main factors influencing it's capacity are:

- *Air traffic control:* EUROCONTROL specifies minimum vertical, horizontal and lateral separations of aircraft in the interests of safety. These minima depend on aircraft size, availability of radar, sequencing of operations and runway occupancy time. Capacity can be increased by inserting departures between pairs of arrivals, since the minimum separations of both operations limit the total hourly capacity of a runway. Arrivals on final approach are typically given absolute priority over departures where the latter are permitted when suitable gaps occur in the flow of arrivals.[9]

- *Demand characteristics:* Runway capacity depends on aircraft size, speed, maneuverability and braking capability as well as human factors such as pilot skills. Aircraft size impacts on approach and touchdown speeds and wing-tip vortices. Slower speeds reduce the runway capacity; the generation of wing-tip vortices by larger aircraft creates maneuverability problems for smaller aircraft and therefore requires greater separation between larger and smaller aircraft for reasons of safety. Often, practical separations are longer than the regulated minima in order to allow for a mix of fast and slow, large and small aircraft. The runway occupancy time required by arriving aircraft varies depending on speed, braking capability and ground maneuverability. This influences the availability of suitable slots for departing aircraft. Furthermore, the mix of arrival and departure operations will affect the runway capacity.

- *Environmental factors:* Visibility, runway surface conditions, winds and noise abatement requirements are the most important environmental factors influencing runway capacity. As visibility conditions worsen, longer separations are required for reasons of safety. When visibility falls below certain thresholds, instrument flight rules (IFR) are required, which passes

---

[8]   Economists treat capacity as that point at which it is more cost-effective to add additional units of supply than to use the existing units more intensively.

[9]   Although separation minima are the dominant ATC factor affecting capacity, other ATC factors include length of the common path from ILS (Instrument Landing System) gate to the threshold, sequencing strategy used by controllers for aircraft travelling at different speeds (e.g., first- come first-served versus speed-class sequencing), probability of violation of the separation rules, and technology and the degree of sophistication of the ATC system

control of spacing to the air traffic controller from the pilot. Wet or slippery conditions may force longer runway occupancy times as braking, for example, may take longer. Crosswinds or tail winds may require the imposition of restrictions on the use of multiple runways. Noise abatement regulations affect capacity by limiting or restricting the use of one or more runways at particular times of the day.

*   *Design factors:* Layout and design of the runway and taxiway system are important influences on the runway capacity. The factors that are important are the number, spacing, length and orientation of the runways, the number, locations and design of exit taxiways and the design of ramp entrances.[10]

9.3.2   Measuring capacity and delays

The main sources of data used to look at European airport delays and indications of congestion come from the Association of European Airlines (AEA) and the Centre for Delay Analysis (CODA) at EUROCONTROL (the European Organisation for the Safety of Air Navigation). The AEA has conducted a regular survey among its members at a nineteen of the larger EU airports since 1986, aimed at monitoring, on a monthly basis, the extent and reasons for delays on intra-European departures. The data are obtained from between ten and thirteen reporting airlines. The AEA use IATA's standard delay codes and categories in collating their results and annually present two summary figures in their yearbook. These data are highly sensitive commercially and confidentiality clauses constrain them from making more information publicly available. IATA detail very precisely the situations giving rise to delays in airline departures and conduct their own survey among sixteen airlines annually.[11]

The AEA survey showed relatively high levels of delay in the late 1980s, with improvements generally in the early 1990s, up to 1994. Since 1994, there has been a gradual rise in departure delays as measured by the percentage of flights delayed by 15 minutes or more. In 1997, there was a 4% increase in average delay per aircraft movement for all reasons compared with 1996. In 1997, 54% of all flights were delayed for any of the above causes, compared with 59% of all flights

---

[10]   The relationship between each of these factors and runway capacity is discussed in Ashford and Wright (1992).

[11]   Departure delays in the AEA and IATA surveys are based on real recorded delays compared with the CODA measure of delay which is based on the difference between the scheduled off block time and the calculated off block time, taking into account slot time and estimated taxi time. The standard delay codes used by both IATA and the AEA fall into internal airline problems or schedule discrepancies, passenger and baggage, cargo and mail, aircraft and ramp handling, technical and aircraft equipment, damage to aircraft and EDP automated equipment failure, flight operations and crewing, weather, airport and government authorities (including air traffic control) reactionary, and miscellaneous (e.g., industrial action).

in 1996, with the average delay per movement being 11 minutes. The majority of delays were related to airport and air traffic control difficulties, which accounted for roughly 60% of all delays in 1995 and 1996. Figure 9.2 shows the monthly trend in European departure delays. For 1996, the distribution of delays shows a less obvious seasonal pattern than in previous years.

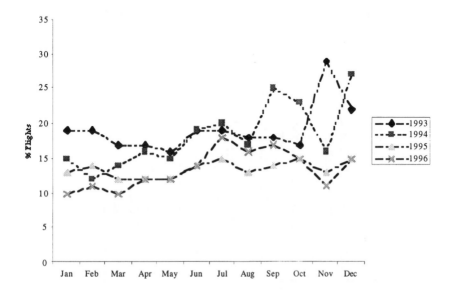

Source: Association of European Airlines Yearbook (1997).

Figure 9.2 European departure delays (flights delayed more than 15 minutes), 1993-7

In 1996, air traffic flow management over Europe was centralized within EUROCONTROL which resulted in a wider distribution of delay. While the move helped to alleviate delays in the worst affected sectors but introduced delays in sectors which had previously operated with minimal delay. The European air traffic control system remains fragmented with 49 European ATC centres, 31 national systems, 18 hardware suppliers, 22 operating systems and 30 programming languages under the European Civil Aviation Conference (ECAC) organizational umbrella (Association of European Airlines, 1997).

In monitoring the charges for ATC services, the AEA demonstrate that both en route charges and ground handling charges are the two main infrastructure costs which have increased most significantly on European routes since the implementation of the Third Package in January 1993. On average, landing charges have remained unchanged since 1993, with ground handling increasing by 6.2% and en route charges increasing by 6.4% between 1993 and 1995. These costs vary significantly across the ECAC states as demonstrated in Figure 9.3 that shows the en route costs in US dollars to overfly European states for a standard aircraft type and distance of 850km. Aircraft and passenger handling delays have increased in significance in the most recent period, reflecting internal airline procedures as well as airport ground facilities and terminal conditions.

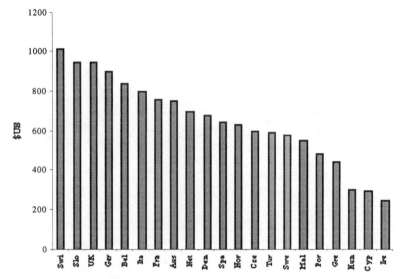

Source: Association of European Airlines (1997)

Figure 9.3 Costs to overfly Europe: Airbus A320 in 1997 for the average AEA airline's flight of 850km.

In 1997, the Centre for Delay Analysis at EUROCONTROL began producing monthly delay reports using data collated from several sources, the main three being, AEA data, Air Traffic Flow Management data reported by the Central Flow Management Units within EUROCONTROL and data supplied by the IATA, which are based on sixteen reporting airlines.[12]

---

[12]   The Centre produces its *CODA Delay Indicator*, which gives an overview of the overall delay experience. The CODA analysis provides more detailed breakdowns of the causes of delays and gives route specific analysis of average delays in minutes, based on CFMU data. The main trends reported in the most recent CODA reports are outlined below and pertain to 1996 and 1997. First quarter results for 1998 were also available and have been included where relevant. The data obtained from the AEA are

ECAC traffic grew by 6% in 1997 over 1996 traffic levels. Despite this growth, CODA claim that the amount of delay caused by the imposition of air traffic flow management measures of the CFMUs has remained relatively unchanged since 1996. The number of flights delayed by more than 15 minutes decreased between 1996 and 1997, with longer delays of greater than 30 minutes decreasing by 15% between 1996 and 1997, amongst flights subject to ATFM restrictions. The ATFM restrictions were put in place to protect congested airports, which faced problems associated with lack of capacity, parking difficulties, low visibility procedures etc. Airports particularly affected by these restrictions include London Heathrow, Athens, Barcelona, Milan and Amsterdam (Centre for Delay Analysis, 1997).[13]

Summary statistics for ten worst departure and ten worst destination airports are presented in Table 9.1. The departure airports with the worst average delay per movement in 1997 were Athens, Madrid, Palma, Nice, Düsseldorf and Geneva. For all of these airports more than 25% of flights were delayed and the average delay per movement exceeded 4.9 minutes. For the ECAC area as a whole, the percentage of delayed flights was 15% in 1997, with an average delay per movement of 2.9 minutes. The destination or arrival airports with the worst average delay per movement were Athens, Milan/Linate, Barcelona, Madrid/Barajas, London/Heathrow and Paris/Charles de Gaulle.

The data were combined with the Airports Council International (ACI) traffic data and correlations with growth rates are also presented. The ACI data cover the years 1995, 1996 and 1997 and give breakdowns of traffic for 38 European countries, 341 European cities and 359 European cities in 1997.[14] Tables 9.2a;b and 9.3a;b present traffic statistics for the busiest city in each European state, for the period 1995-7.[15] Of the 341 European cities examined, eight are served by two airports, three by three airports and London is served by five airports.

presented in CODA reports in far more detail than they appear in the AEA's yearbook, but are only available since the beginning of 1997.

[13] The CODA report presents data for ECAC airports with more than 30 000 movements (departures and arrivals separately) annually and gives the following for each airport: total number of flights, total number of delayed flights; total delay in minutes; number of flights delayed an hour or more, average delay per delayed flight, and average delay per movement.

[14] Traffic statistics cover aircraft movements (distinguished by passenger, combination and all-cargo air transport aircraft as well as detailing general aviation movements), passenger volumes (distinguished by domestic and international terminal passengers and transit passengers) and cargo (differentiated by domestic and international cargo, and by mail and all other freight).

[15] This is in line with US analysis by the Federal Aviation Administration using its hub classification, which analyses air traffic patterns for cities or metropolitan areas as single entities.

Table 9.1 Summary statistics for the ten worst departure and the ten worst destination airports

Most penalized destination airports (with more than 30 000 flights)

Ranked by average delay per movement

Airport	Total flights	Delayed flights	% Delayed flights	Total delay '000	Flights delayed 60 min	Average delay	Average delay per movement
Athens	67 790	19 336	28.52	561	1 566	29.06	8.29
Milan/Linate	91 829	32 857	35.78	655	841	19.96	7.14
Barcelona	107 139	33 608	31.37	680	745	20.25	6.35
Madrid/Barajas	131 659	45 197	34.33	791	837	17.52	6.01
London/Heathrow	218 132	65 221	29.90	1 308	2 459	20.07	6.00
Paris/Charles deGaulle	200 538	53 899	26.88	1 100	1 554	20.41	5.49
Paris/Orly	122 318	33 996	27.79	615	676	18.11	5.03
New York	30 418	7 830	25.74	151	123	19.34	4.98
Nice	63 932	15 017	23.49	296	274	19.75	4.64
Tenerife Sur/Reina Sofia	27 055	5 987	22.13	120	88	20.07	4.44

Most penalised departure airports (with more than 30 000 flights)

Ranked by average delay per movement

Airport	Total flights	Delayed flights	% Delayed flights	Total delays '000	Flights delayed 60 min	Average delay	Average delay per movement
Athens	68 102	27 064	39.74	802	2 333	29.64	11.78
Madrid/Barajas	132 350	43 493	32.86	897	1 500	20.63	6.78
Palma De Mallorca	74 123	18 758	25.31	391	378	20.85	5.28
Nice	64 014	16 276	25.43	316	325	19.42	4.94
Düsseldorf	91 386	25 778	28.21	448	315	17.42	4.91
Geneva	62 592	15 846	25.32	294	357	18.59	4.71
Lyon/Sartolas	50 394	12 164	24.14	226	244	18.60	4.49
Marseille/Provence	46 751	10 854	23.22	207	220	19.09	4.43
Barcelona	106 866	23 460	21.95	471	673	20.11	4.41
Brussels	134 942	33 831	25.07	590	497	17.44	4.37

Table 9.2a Traffic statistics for the busiest city in each European state

Country	City	Number of airports	Total air transport movements '000			Total passengers '000		
			1995	1996	1997	1995	1996	1997
Austria	Vienna	1	143	154	155	8 546	9 140	9 738
Belgium	Brussels	1	221	241	254	12 600	13 520	15 935
Bulgaria	Sofia	1	23	22	22	1 212	1 095	1 084
Croatia	Zagreb	1	21	23	25	902	1 008	1 080
Cyprus	Larnaca	1	34	34	35	3 777	3 648	3 797
Czech Republic	Prague	1	68	73	77	3 211	3 798	4 359
Denmark	Copenhagen	1	237	265	279	14 678	15 860	16 837
Estonia	Tallinn	1	11	13	17	366	431	503
Finland	Helsinki	2	113	121	136	7 140	7 689	8 471
France	Paris	2	558	605	632	55 009	59 089	60 349
Germany	Frankfurt/Main	1	372	380	387	38 179	38 761	40 262
Greece	Athens	1	121	123	139	10 480	10 411	11 090
Hungary	Budapest	1	44	50	55	2 909	3 314	3 619
Ireland	Dublin	1	110	121	134	8 024	9 091	10 333
Italy	Rome	2	219	248	259	21 857	23 815	25 845
Latvia	Riga	1	14	14	15	504	505	535
Lithuania	Vilnius	1	9	9	11	355	370	410
Luxembourg	Luxembourg	1	36	37	40	1 235	1 262	1 413
Macedonia	Skopje	1	9	6	7	583	422	440
Malta	Malta	1	27	26	27	2 589	2 518	2 704
Monaco	Monaco	1				109	117	131
Netherlands	Amsterdam	1	290	321	349	25 355	27 794	31 569
Norway	Oslo	2	152			10 552		
Poland	Warsaw	1	44	50	55	2 735	3 090	3547
Portugal	Lisbon	1	69	73	76	6 476	6 580	6 817
Romania	Bucharest	2	38	24	26	2 089	1 468	1 470
Russian Fed.	Moscow	3	69	182	198	4 362	12 922	14 355
Slovac Republic	Bratislava	1	8	8	8	213	273	300
Slovenia	Ljubjana	1	17	17	14	638	668	713
Spain	Madrid	2	219	242	252	19 956	21 856	23 601
Sweden	Stockholm	2	231	245	267	14 362	15 052	16 111
Switzerland	Zurich	1	209	224	241	15 340	16 226	18 268
Turkey	Istanbul	1	131	148	158	12 074	13 506	14 801
Ukraine	Kiev	1	30	28	30	1 307	1 280	1 375
United Kingdom	London	5	716	772	815	83 304	88 401	94 934
Yugoslavia	Belgrade	1	16	18	20	976	1 191	1 379
Average			132	141	149	10 945	11 560	12 449

Note: Blanks indicate data not available.

Source: Airports Council International (1998).

Table 9.2b Recent traffic statistics for the busiest city in each European state

Country	City	Total freight '000 tons			Percentage international passengers			Percentage transit passengers	
		1995	1996	1997	1995	1996	1997	1995	1997
Austria	Vienna	98	101	113	93.7	93.8	94.6	2.0	1.4
Belgium	Brussels	441	464	530	99.2	98.7	99.2	0.7	0.7
Bulgaria	Sofia	11	10	10	91.9	92.3	92.6	0.0	0.0
Croatia	Zagreb	8	7	7	62.3	65.8	65.5	0.5	1.0
Cyprus	Larnaca	29	28	29	95.5	95.6	96.7	4.4	3.2
Czech Rep.	Prague	30	19	24	97.4	95.7	92.1	1.3	6.4
Denmark	Copenhagen		337	387	79.2	80.0	82.2	2.4	1.3
Estonia	Tallinn	2	3	5	99.2	98.9	98.8	0.0	0.1
Finland	Helsinki	91	97	99	65.3	65.1	63.6	8.7	9.3
France	Paris	1 220	1 241	1 309	66.4	66.4	67.9	0.7	0.3
Germany	Frankfurt/Main	1 461	1 497	1 514	79.2	80.0	80.5	1.8	1.4
Greece	Athens	104	84	119	63.9	63.6	61.5	2.2	0.0
Hungary	Budapest	23	23	27	100.0	100.0	100.0	0.0	0.0
Ireland	Dublin	66	74	92	94.0	94.1	94.3	0.5	0.9
Italy	Rome	298	308	298	57.3	55.3	54.5	1.8	1.4
Latvia	Riga	3	3	4	97.3	98.2	99.2	2.6	0.7
Lithuania	Vilnius	9	6	5	100.0	99.9	99.8	0.0	0.0
Luxembourg	Luxembourg	286	281	340	97.9	99.1	99.2	2.0	0.7
Macedonia	Skopje	9	2	4	99.6	99.3	97.7	0.3	2.2
Malta	Malta	11	11		98.1	97.0	96.7	1.8	3.2
Monaco	Monaco								
Netherlands	Amsterdam	1 019	1 124	1 207	97.4	97.4	97.6	1.9	1.7
Norway	Oslo	71						0.7	
Poland	Warsaw	34	41	51	88.9	88.0	88.4		
Portugal	Lisbon	99	100	110	77.0	77.5	78.1	3.6	2.7
Romania	Bucharest	31	19	13	70.2	95.6	96.1	5.2	3.8
Russian Fed.	Moscow	27	120	131	6.9	60.6	58.7	0.5	1.2
Slovac Rep.	Bratislava	2	3	2	79.8	84.7	87.5	12.6	4.9
Slovenia	Ljubjana	6	5	5	99.9	99.8	98.6	0.0	1.2
Spain	Madrid	253	267	282	47.6	46.7	46.6	1.4	2.0
Sweden	Stockholm	130	145	146	53.7	55.4	57.3	1.7	1.5
Switzerland	Zurich	344	340	355	91.0	91.1	91.6	2.7	2.1
Turkey	Istanbul	139	140	178	67.2	68.5	66.4	1.2	1.3
Ukraine	Kiev	16	17	12	64.5	67.8	94.0	0.7	1.0
UK	London	1 488	1 570	1 713	87.2	86.7	87.1	0.6	0.6
Yugoslavia	Belgrade	5	6	8	67.0	76.2	74.8	0.0	0.0
Average		231	24	268	76.0	78.7	79.4	1.8	1.6

Note: Blanks indicate data not available.
Source: Airports Council International (1998).

    The data demonstrate the international nature of European traffic; Moscow, Stockholm, Madrid and Rome are distinctive by their high share of domestic traffic. The percentage of transit traffic is generally low. The tables give two measures of average passenger per aircraft movement: the most useful uses average passengers per air transport movement rather than per total movements (which includes general aviation), but in many instances data on air transport movements alone were not available. The main trend seen is the significantly lower number of passengers per movement in the former Soviet Union/Eastern European states.

    As one might expect, the average passengers per movement are highest at the main hubs in the UK, Germany, France and Italy, that tend to have the most congested airports. Rates are also high in the Southern European tourism oriented cities of Larnaca (Cyprus), Malta, Madrid and Istanbul. Indeed, congestion may in some ways be more of an issue here due to seasonal peaking of traffic. The growth rates in passenger volumes has generally been higher than growth rates in aircraft movements. The highest growth rates have been experienced in the former Soviet Union/Eastern European states. Significant declines in traffic were also most significant among these states, a reflection of the poor performance of their economies during the transition to more market based institutional structures. More modest growth rates are recorded for Paris, Frankfurt and Athens.

Table 9.3a Passenger traffic for the busiest city in each European state

Country	City	Average passengers per passenger/combi movement			Average passengers per total movements		
		1995	1996	1997	1995	1996	1997
Austria	Vienna	60.6	60.1	63.7	59.6	59.2	62.4
Belgium	Brussels	62.6	61.7	69.7	56.8	55.9	62.5
Bulgaria	Sofia	54.3	51.2	52.5	51.0	47.8	48.7
Croatia	Zagreb	42.3	42.3	42.7	42.3	42.3	42.7
Cyprus	Larnaca	109.5		107.7	108.6	106.0	107.5
Czech Republic	Prague				46.8	51.4	56.3
Denmark	Copenhagen	65.5	62.9	63.6	61.8	59.6	60.2
Estonia	Tallinn	32.3	31.5	32.4	32.2	31.3	29.1
Finland	Helsinki				63.1	63.2	62.0
France	Paris	103.2	102.1	100.3	98.5	97.5	95.4
Germany	Frankfurt/Main	108.3			102.4	102.0	103.9
Greece	Athens				86.0	84.6	79.3
Hungary	Budapest				65.0	65.3	65.7
Ireland	Dublin	79.7			72.5	74.7	76.9
Italy	Rome	105.0			99.5	95.8	99.7
Latvia	Riga	35.2	33.8	34.7	35.1	33.8	34.7
Lithuania	Vilnius	38.8	38.4	36.6	36.8	37.1	36.2
Luxembourg	Luxembourg	39.9	39.2	41.6	33.8	33.5	35.0
Macedonia	Skopje	64.4	63.0	61.6	59.6	61.0	60.5
Malta	Malta	97.1	95.3	99.2	94.7	94.0	97.4
Monaco	Monaco						
Netherlands	Amsterdam	90.8	90.0	93.8	87.2	86.3	90.3
Norway	Oslo	71.8			69.2		
Poland	Warsaw	61.4	61.4	63.8	61.4	61.4	63.8
Portugal	Lisbon	94.2	90.8	89.5	92.7	89.9	88.7
Romania	Bucharest				53.8	60.9	55.1
Russian Fed.	Moscow	65.6	72.0	78.2	62.3	70.8	72.1
Slovac Republic	Bratislava	31.0			25.4	30.5	33.8
Slovenia	Ljubljana	38.2	39.8	54.3	36.2	37.2	48.4
Spain	Madrid				90.9	89.9	93.4
Sweden	Stockholm	63.6	63.7	62.1	61.9	61.3	60.2
Switzerland	Zurich	73.4	72.3	75.6	73.3	72.3	75.6
Turkey	Istanbul				91.7	90.6	93.4
Ukraine	Kiev	44.2	47.2	47.1	42.5	44.6	44.8
United Kingdom	London	123.1	117.9	119.8	116.1	114.5	116.4
Yugoslavia	Belgrade	59.9	66.6	66.9	58.7	66.0	66.7
Average		53.2	39.0	43.2	64.7	63.1	64.4

Note: Blanks indicate data not available.

Source: Airports Council International (1998).

Table 9.3b Traffic growth for the busiest city in each European state

Country	City	Traffic growth - passengers			Traffic growth – movements		
		1995/6	1996/7	1995/7	1995/6	1996/7	
Austria	Vienna	6.9	6.5	13.9	7.7	1.0	8.8
Belgium	Brussels	7.3	17.8	26.4	8.9	5.4	14.8
Bulgaria	Sofia	-9.6	-0.9	-10.5	-3.5	-2.7	-6.2
Croatia	Zagreb	11.7	7.1	19.6	11.7	6.1	18.6
Cyprus	Larnaca	-3.4	4.0	0.5	-1.0	2.6	1.5
Czech Rep.	Prague	18.2	14.7	35.7	7.5	4.7	12.6
Denmark	Copenhagen	8.0	6.1	14.7	11.9	5.0	17.6
Estonia	Tallinn	17.7	16.5	37.2	21.0	25.1	51.5
Finland	Helsinki	7.6	10.1	18.6	7.4	12.2	20.6
France	Paris	7.4	2.1	9.7	8.5	4.3	13.3
Germany	Frankfurt/Main	1.5	3.8	5.4	1.9	1.9	4.0
Greece	Athens	-0.6	6.5	5.8	1.0	13.6	14.7
Hungary	Budapest	13.9	9.2	24.4	13.2	8.6	23.0
Ireland	Dublin	13.2	13.6	28.7	10.0	10.4	21.4
Italy	Rome	8.9	8.5	18.2	13.1	4.3	18.0
Latvia	Riga	0.3	5.8	6.1	4.3	2.9	7.3
Lithuania	Vilnius	4.1	10.8	15.5	3.2	13.7	17.4
Luxembourg	Luxembourg	2.1	11.9	14.3	2.9	7.1	10.3
Macedonia	Skopje	-27.5	4.3	-24.3	-29.1	5.2	-25.4
Malta	Malta	-2.7	7.3	4.4	-2.0	3.6	1.5
Monaco	Monaco	7.8	11.2	19.9			
Netherlands	Amsterdam	9.6	13.5	24.5	10.7	8.6	20.2
Norway	Oslo						
Poland	Warsaw	12.9	14.7	29.6	12.9	10.5	24.8
Portugal	Lisbon	1.6	3.6	5.2	4.6	4.9	9.8
Romania	Bucharest	-29.7	0.1	-29.6	-37.8	10.5	-31.3
Russian Fed.	Moscow	196.2	11.0	229.0	160.8	9.0	184.3
Slovac Rep.	Bratislava	27.7	10.1	40.6	6.1	-0.5	5.5
Slovenia	Ljubjana	4.7	6.7	11.8	1.9	-17.9	-16.3
Spain	Madrid	9.5	7.9	18.2	10.7	4.0	15.2
Sweden	Stockholm	4.8	7.0	12.1	5.8	9.0	15.3
Switzerland	Zurich	5.7	12.5	19.0	7.3	7.5	15.5
Turkey	Istanbul	11.8	9.5	22.5	13.1	6.3	20.3
Ukraine	Kiev	-2.0	7.4	5.1	-6.7	6.9	-0.2
United Kingdom	London	6.1	7.3	13.9	7.6	5.6	13.7
Yugoslavia	Belgrade	21.9	15.8	41.2	8.4	14.4	24.1
Average		10.4	8.4	20.2	8.4	5.9	15.2

Note: Blanks indicate data not available.
Source: Airports Council International (1998).

Tables 9.4a;b and 9.5a;b present statistics for the top 40 European passenger airports in 1997. London, Frankfurt, Paris and Amsterdam had the six busiest airports, with the top four dominating in both passenger throughput and aircraft movements. Over 80% of passenger traffic is international for these four airports, while for the group ranked from sixth to eighth serve as important domestic airports (i.e., Paris/Orly, Rome/Fiumicino and Madrid/Barajas). As might be expected given the cost structure of air transport operations, the busier airports generally have higher average passenger numbers per movement. London's Heathrow and Gatwick airports have substantially higher rates again compared with the other top ranked airports. Heathrow's rate has increased significantly in the last two years reflecting the constraints, which this facility faces.

Table 9.4a Traffic statistics for the top 40 European airports, 1997

Rank by 1997 movements	Rank by 1997 passengers	Country	Airport	Total air transport movements '000			Total passengers '000		
				1995	1996	1997	1995	1996	1997
1	1	UK	Heathrow	418.8	426.9	429.2	54 452	56 037	58 142
3	2	Germany	Rhein/Main	372.6	380.0	387.5	38 179	38 761	40 262
2	3	France	Charles deGaulle	325.3	360.6	395.5	28 355	31 724	35 293
4	4	Netherlands	Schipol	290.7	321.8	349.5	25 355	27 794	31 570
13	5	UK	Gatwick	192.0	211.0	229.3	22 549	24 337	26 961
12	6	France	Orly	232.7	245.4	237.1	26 653	27 365	25 056
11	7	Italy	Fiumicino	209.2	236.5	245.7	21 091	23 035	25 001
9	8	Spain	Barajas	219.0	242.8	252.4	19 956	21 856	23 601
7	9	Switzerland	Zurich	209.0	224.4	241.5	15 340	16 226	18 268
8	10	Germany	Munich	201.9	211.7	246.4	14 867	15 686	17 894
5	11	Denmark	Copenhagen	237.4	265.8	279.3	14 678	15 860	16 837
26	12	Spain	Palma de Mallorca	119.9	127.3	142.8	14 728	15 377	16 557
20	13	UK	Manchester	148.9	143.7	148.5	14 982	14 670	15 950
6	14	Belgium	Brussels	221.8	241.5	254.7	12 600	13 520	15 935
18	15	Germany	Düsseldorf	166.5	161.7	168.8	15 146	14 422	15 532
10	16	Sweden	Aralanda	215.7	227.9	246.2	13 540	14 221	15 197
14	17	SP	Barcelona	152.8	177.7	208.0	11 727	13 434	15 065
16	18	Turkey	Ataturk	131.6	148.9	158.3	12 074	13 506	14 801
17	19	Italy	Linate	132.6	156.9	165.7	10 827	12 563	14 271
27	20	Greece	Athenai	121.8	123.0	139.7	10 480	10 411	11 090
22	21	Ireland	Dublin	110.6	121.7	134.3	8 024	9 091	10 333
19	22	Austria	Vienna Int.	143.2	154.3	155.9	8 546	9 140	9 738
31	23	Russian Fed.	Shermetyevo		116.3	117.6		8 572	9 384
29	24	Germany	Tegel	112.5	117.2	117.5	8 271	8 374	8 731
21	25	Germany	Hamburg	118.0	119.9	124.7	8 201	8 194	8 648
25	26	Finland	Helsinki Vantaa	113.0	121.5	136.4	7 140	7 689	8 471
49	27	Spain	Gran Canaraia	76.8	76.3	78.9	7 877	7 890	8 160
85	28	Spain	Tenerife Sur	52.1	51.8	52.8	7 398	7 293	7 580
15	29	France	Nice–Côte d'Azur	122.6	141.5	173.7	6 142	6 604	7 373
56	30	Spain	Malaga	55.7	59.5	65.1	6 311	6 652	7 270
28	31	Germany	Stuttgart	85.3	96.2	95.3	5 158	6 515	6 910
46	32	Portugal	Lisbon	69.9	73.1	76.8	6 476	6 580	6 817
86	33	Turkey	Antalya	39.8	44.9	49.0	4 727	5 592	6 687

23	34	Switzerland	Genève	99.2	102.1	100.6	6 207	6 118	6 117
40	35	UK	Glasgow	74.9	75.6	80.1	5 528	5 591	6 115
37	36	UK	Birmingham	75.0	77.4	80.5	5 333	5 472	6 030
30	37	France	Marseille	72.4	79.4	86.9	5 106	5 401	5 473
35	38	UK	Stanstead	66.1	77.5	84.4	3 920	4 865	5 426
24	39	Germany	Cologne Bonn	111.4	120.2	136.2	4 740	5 227	5 308
38	40	France	Satolas	75.5	85.3	94.1	4 432	4 967	4 944

Table 9.4b Cargo and international passenger traffic at the top 40 European airports

Rank by 1997 passengers	Country	Airport	Total freight '000 tons			Percentage international passengers			Percentage transit passengers	
			1995	1996	1997	1995	1996	1997	1995	1997
1	UK	Heathrow	1 125.6	1 140.8	1 260.1	85.9	86.1	86.9	0.6	0.5
2	Germany	Rhein/Main	461.3	1 497.2	1 514.3	79.2	80.0	80.5	1.8	1.4
3	France	Charles deGaulle	929.0	979.0	1 072.2	90.0	90.3	89.3	1.2	0.5
4	Netherlands	Schipol	1 019.3	1 124.7	1 207.3	97.4	97.4	97.6	1.9	1.7
5	UK	Gatwick	245.9	294.0	287.4	91.3	90.5	90.4	0.7	0.6
6	France	Orly	291.2	262.3	237.2	41.4	38.7	37.7	0.2	0.1
7	Italy	Fiumicino	291.3	300.1	288.2	56.1	54.1	53.2	1.8	1.4
8	Spain	Barajas	253.6	267.7	282.4	47.6	46.7	46.6	1.4	2.0
9	Switzerland	Zurich	344.0	340.1	355.3	91.0	91.1	91.6	2.7	2.1
10	Germany	Munich	100.2	110.9	123.5	59.8	61.6	61.8	1.6	1.5
11	Denmark	Copenhagen		338.0	387.7	79.2	80.0	82.2	2.4	1.3
12	Spain	Palma de Mallorca	19.1	21.1	24.9	74.4	73.7	74.2	0.6	0.6
13	UK	Manchetser	54.7	83.8	99.0	80.6	82.4	83.6	2.9	1.4
14	Belgium	Brussels	441.3	464.0	530.7	99.2	98.7	99.2	0.7	0.7
15	Germany	Düsseldorf	62.1	62.9	71.4	72.9	73.4	73.9	0.8	0.8
16	Sweden	Aralanda	130.1	145.0	146.1	56.9	58.6	60.6	1.8	1.6
17	Spain	Barcelona	74.6	86.0	85.4	38.9	39.8	41.5	3.5	3.3
18	Turkey	Ataturk	139.3	140.3	178.7	67.2	68.5	66.4	1.2	1.3
19	Italy	Linate	79.0	78.1	75.6	56.7	54.9	53.8	1.0	0.0
20	Greece	Athinai	104.1	84.3	119.9	63.9	63.6	61.5	2.2	0.9
21	Ireland	Dublin	66.6	74.2	92.0	94.0	94.1	94.3	0.5	0.0
22	Austria	Vienna	98.6	101.6	113.7	93.7	93.8	94.6	2.0	1.4
23	Russian Fed.	Shermetyevo	33.4	77.8	79.3	38.6	76.7	76.0	1.0	1.7
24	Germany	Tegel	59.6	36.3	37.1	57.7	41.2	41.3	1.1	1.2
25	Germany	Hamburg	91.3	57.3	53.8	65.3	58.2	57.5	8.7	1.1
26	Finland	Helsinki	37.6	97.2	99.2	66.0	65.1	63.6	3.2	9.3
27	Spain	Gran Canaria	11.1	40.6	43.8	81.3	66.1	67.1	2.2	2.8
28	Spain	Tenerife Sur	26.7	12.0	11.6	36.1	81.9	83.2	1.2	1.8
29	France	Nice-Côte d'Azur	7.5	26.9	27.4	72.5	36.1	39.6	0.9	0.9
30	Spain	Malaga	31.3	7.4	8.4	60.7	71.8	71.9	1.4	1.0
31	Germany	Stuttgart	99.2	35.6	34.1	77.0	65.0	64.8	3.6	2.3
32	Portugal	Lisbon		100.7	110.6		77.5	78.1		2.7

33	Turkey	Antalya	3.8	3.7	3.3	87.4	88.6	89.2	3.1	2.0
34	Switzerland	Genève	78.1	72.8	73.6	82.7	82.7	82.8	1.9	1.7
35	UK	Glasgow	17.0	15.7	14.8	50.5	47.8	46.9	2.5	2.0
36		Birmingham	22.6	21.0	21.4	79.7	80.1	80.3	4.5	2.5
37	France	Marseille Provence	61.0	64.3	58.6	27.8	27.8	28.0	0.7	1.1
38	UK	Stanstead	102.3	116.9	141.8	78.4	77.3	77.5	1.5	1.3
39	Germany	Cologne Bonn	308.1	344.2	398.5	50.2	53.2	51.5	3.1	2.5
40	France	Satolas	32.5	35.0	38.2	49.0	50.1	51.2		

Table 9.5a Pasengers at the top 40 European airports

Airport	Average passangers per pax/combi movement			Average passengers per movement		
	1995	1996	1997	1995	1996	1997
Heathrow	131.1	132.4	136.6	130.0	131.2	135.4
Rheim/Main	108.3			102.4	102.0	103.9
Charles deGaulle	93.6	94.7	96.4	87.1	87.9	89.2
Schipol	90.8	90.0	93.8	87.2	86.3	90.3
Gatwick	120.6	118.2	119.8	117.4	115.3	117.5
Orly	115.9	112.2	106.4	114.5	111.5	105.6
Fiumicino	105.0			100.8	97.4	101.7
Barajas				91.1	90.0	93.5
Zurich	73.4	72.3	75.6	73.3	72.3	75.6
Munich	74.6	75.2	73.7	73.6	74.0	72.6
Copenhagen	65.5	62.9	63.6	61.8	59.6	60.2
Palma de Mallorca				122.7	120.8	115.9
Manchetser				100.6	102.1	107.4
Brussels	62.6	61.7	69.7	56.8	55.9	62.5
Düsseldorf	91.7	89.9	92.4	90.9	89.1	92.0
Aralanda	64.6	64.9	63.8	62.7	62.4	61.7
Barcelona				76.7	75.6	72.4
Ataturk				91.7	90.6	93.4
Linate	82.4	80.4	86.4	81.6	80.0	86.1
Athinai				86.0	84.6	79.3
Dublin	79.7			72.5	74.7	76.9
Vienna	60.6	60.1	63.7	59.6	59.2	62.4
Shermetyevo		75.1	81.0		73.6	79.7
Tegel	74.3	72.0	75.0	73.5	71.4	74.3
Hamburg	70.0	69.2	70.2	69.1	68.3	69.3
Helsinki				63.1	63.2	62.1
Gran Canaria				102.5	103.4	103.4
Tenerife Sur				142.1	140.7	143.4
Nice-Côte d'Azur	50.9	47.4	43.1	50.1	46.6	42.4
Malaga				113.4	111.8	111.6
Stuttgart	62.0	69.6	74.7	60.4	67.7	72.5
Lisbon	94.2	90.8	89.5	92.7	89.9	88.7
Antalya				118.6	124.6	136.4
Genèva	63.2	60.7	62.2	62.6	59.9	60.8
Glasgow	75.7	75.4	77.6	73.8	73.9	76.3
Birmingham	72.3	71.9	75.8	71.0	70.6	74.8
Marseille Provence	78.1			70.5	67.9	62.9
Stanstead	69.4	71.6	73.7	59.3	62.7	64.2
Cologne Bonn	58.1	58.9	52.9	42.5	43.4	38.9
Satolas	6.3	64.4	58.4	58.7	58.2	52.5

Table 9.5b Changes in traffic at the top 40 European airports

Airport	Traffic growth – passengers			Traffic growth – movements			Percentage all-cargo movements		
	1995/6	1996/7	1995/7	1995/6	1996/7	1995/7	1995	1996	1997
Heathrow	2.9	3.7	6.7	1.9	0.5	2.4	0.8	0.8	0.8
Rheim/Main	1.5	3.8	5.4	1.9	1.9	4.0	5.4	0.0	0.0
Charles deGaulle	11.8	11.2	24.4	10.8	9.6	21.5	6.9	7.1	7.4
Schipol	9.6	13.5	24.5	10.7	8.6	20.2	3.9	4.0	3.7
Gatwick	7.9	10.7	19.5	9.9	8.6	19.4	2.6	2.5	1.9
Orly	2.6	-8.4	-5.9	5.4	-3.3	1.8	1.2	0.6	0.6
Fiumicino	9.2	8.5	18.5	13.0	3.9	17.4	4.0	0.0	0.0
Barajas	9.5	7.9	18.2	10.8	3.9	15.2	0.0	0.0	0.0
Zurich	5.7	12.5	19.0	7.3	7.5	15.5	0.0	0.0	0.0
Munich	5.5	14.0	20.3	4.8	16.4	22.0	1.3	1.4	1.4
Copenhagen	8.0	6.1	14.7	11.9	5.0	17.6	5.6	5.2	5.3
Palma de Mallorca	4.4	7.6	12.4	6.1	12.2	19.0	0.0	0.0	0.0
Manchetser	-2.0	8.7	6.4	-3.5	3.3	-0.2	0.0	0.0	0.0
Brussels	7.3	17.8	26.4	8.9	5.4	14.8	9.3	9.4	10.3
Düsseldorf	-4.7	7.7	2.5	-2.8	4.3	1.4	0.8	0.9	0.4
Aralanda	5.0	6.8	12.2	5.6	8.0	14.1	2.9	3.9	3.2
Barcelona	14.5	12.1	28.4	16.2	17.0	36.1	0.0	0.0	0.0
Ataturk	11.8	9.5	22.5	13.1	6.3	20.3	0.0	0.0	0.0
Linate	16.0	13.5	31.8	18.3	5.6	24.9	1.0	0.5	0.4
Athinai	-0.6	6.5	5.8	1.0	13.6	14.7	0.0	0.0	0.0
Dublin	13.2	13.6	28.7	10.0	10.4	21.4	9.0	0.0	0.0
Vienna	6.9	6.5	13.9	7.7	1.0	8.8	1.5	1.4	2.0
Shermetyevo		9.4			1.1			1.9	1.6
Tegel	1.2	4.2	5.5	4.2	0.2	4.4	1.1	0.8	1.0
Hamburg	-0.0	5.5	5.4	1.0	4.0	5.1	1.3	1.2	1.3
Helsinki	7.6	10.1	18.6	7.5	12.2	20.6	0.0	0.0	0.0
Gran Canaria	0.1	3.4	3.6	-0.6	3.4	2.7	0.0	0.0	0.0
Tenerife Sur	-1.4	3.9	2.4	-0.4	1.9	1.5	0.0	0.0	0.0
Nice-Côte d'Azur	7.5	11.6	20.0	15.4	22.7	41.6	1.6	1.6	1.6
Malaga	5.4	9.2	15.1	6.8	9.5	17.0	0.0	0.0	0.0
Stuttgart	26.3	6.0	33.9	12.8	-0.9	11.7	2.4	2.7	2.9
Lisbon	1.6	3.6	5.2	4.6	4.9	9.8	1.6	1.0	0.9
Antalya	18.3	19.5	41.4	12.6	9.2	23.0	0.0	0.0	0.0
Genèva	-1.4	-0.0	-1.4	3.0	-1.5	1.4	1.0	1.3	2.2
Glasgow	1.1	9.3	10.6	1.0	5.8	6.9	2.5	2.0	1.6
Birmingham	2.6	10.2	13.0	3.2	3.9	7.3	1.7	1.7	1.2
Marseille	5.7	1.3	7.1	9.7	9.4	20.0	9.7	0.0	0.0
Stanstead	24.1	11.5	38.4	17.3	8.9	27.7	14.5	12.4	12.8
Cologne	10.2	1.5	11.9	7.9	13.2	22.2	26.7	26.2	26.3
Satolas	12.0	-0.4	11.5	13.0	10.3	24.6	8.8	9.7	10.1

The ACI data and the CODA data can be combined to compute correlations between traffic and delay characteristics and these are seen in Table 9.6. The table highlights the fact that traffic levels have the greatest association with overall delay (i.e., departure plus arrival delays) with an R-squared between traffic level and delay of 0.82. There is, however, very little statistical association between traffic growth rates and average delay per movement – the correlation between total delay and average passenger/movement being 0.37. This provides an opportunity at the congested airports which experience the greatest delays to increase their passenger throughput by encouraging the utilization of larger aircraft.

Table 9.6 Simple correlations using combined ACI and CODA air traffic statistics

	%change in passenger volume 1995-7	Average passengers per movement, 1997	Total delay per movement, 1997	Total delay in minutes, 1997	Average % delayed flights	% change in movements, 1995-7	% change in movements, 1995-6	%change in movements 1996-7	Total passengers, 1997	Total air transport movements, 1997	Total flights	Total delayed flights	Total delayed movements
%change in passenger volume 1995-7	1.000												
Average passengers per movement, 1997	-0.060	1.000											
Total delay per movement, 1997	-0.160	0.050	1.000										
Total delay in minutes, 1997	-0.013	0.370	0.205	1.000									
Average % delayed flights	-0.103	0.160	0.385	0.735	1.000								
% change in movements, 1995-7	0.154	-0.373	-0.188	-0.323	-0.138	1.000							
% change in movements, 1995-6	0.145	-0.360	-0.185	-0.084	-0.161	0.964	1.000						
%change in movements 1996-7	0.614	-0.143	-0.160	-0.098	0.020	0.392	0.253	1.000					
Total passengers, 1997	-0.111	0.593	-0.057	0.820	0.330	-0.149	-0.144	-0.205	1.000				
Total air transport movements, 1997	-0.056	0.350	-0.099	0.305	0.366	-0.004	-0.015	-0.116	0.932	1.000			
Total flights	-0.019	0.375	0.024	0.863	0.392	0.008	0.007	-0.125	0.928	0.986	1.000		
Total delayed flights	0.001	0.406	0.147	0.951	0.635	-0.076	-0.082	-0.073	0.853	0.840	0.856	1.000	
Total delayed movements	0.001	0.407	0.171	0.960	0.643	-0.084	-0.090	-0.043	0.847	0.828	0.840	0.856	1.000

Table 9.7 Air passenger traffic between EU countries (million passengers, 1994)

To:	B	D	DK	E	F	GR	I	IRL	L	NL	P	UK	A	FIN	S	EU15
B		0.91	0.26	1.69	0.91	0.48	0.86	0.13	0.04	0.26	0.33	1.75	0.16	0.10	0.22	8.10
D	0.91		1.01	12.50	3.12	4.83	3.08	0.36	0.15	1.59	1.38	6.16	1.68	0.47	0.60	37.84
DK	0.23	0.99		0.56	0.53	0.52	0.38	0.02	0.02	0.34	0.09	1.18	0.16	0.30	1.63	6.98
E	1.70	12.61	0.74		2.97	0.22	2.74	0.51	0.22	1.94	0.69	17.31	0.63	0.40	1.00	43.68
F	0.94	3.34	0.54	3.27		1.10	3.65	0.44	0.08	1.24	1.20	7.45	0.46	0.19	0.43	24.33
GR	0.47	5.28	0.59	0.19	1.04		1.26	0.07	0.04	1.01	0.02	4.92	0.75	0.23	0.74	16.61
I	0.83	3.02	0.37	2.72	3.39	1.30		0.14	0.05	0.90	0.35	4.03	0.35	0.08	0.16	17.69
IRL	0.11	0.36	0.08	0.52	0.44	0.08	0.14		0.00	0.16	0.11	4.98	0.03	0.00	0.01	7.02
L	0.04	0.16	0.02	0.21	0.11	0.04	0.05	0.02		0.05	0.06	0.16	0.00	0.00	0.00	0.92
NL	0.31	1.60	0.39	1.96	1.16	1.03	0.94	0.15	0.04		0.53	4.03	0.31	0.14	0.48	13.07
P	1.88	1.26	0.05	0.63	1.16	0.03	0.38	0.11	0.06	0.53		2.45	0.06	0.03	0.09	7.16
UK	0.16	6.26	1.28	17.65	7.26	4.96	4.19	5.12	0.16	4.01	2.69		1.14	0.42	1.12	58.14
A	0.10	1.71	0.17	0.64	0.44	0.77	0.37	0.03	0.01	0.31	0.08	1.14		0.05	0.13	6.01
FIN		0.47	0.30	0.40	0.19	0.23	0.08	0.00	0.00	0.14	0.03	0.42	0.05		0.73	3.14
S	0.22	0.51	1.26	0.78	0.34	0.42	1.09	0.06	0.00	0.43	0.08	0.64	0.10	0.73		6.66

Source: Eurostat (1997).

CODA also present detailed data on average delays per movement for routes/city pairs with 3,000 or more flights per annum. City pairs with either London or Paris as the destination airport dominate the list of the worst affected routes. These cities are critically important hubs in the European air traffic system as Table 9.7 demonstrates. These data from Eurostat show the volumes of air traffic between EU countries in 1994 and the dominance of London can be appreciated.

9.4 THE EU POLICY

The EU's framework for an airport charging policy (Commission of the European Communities, 1995) was slow to be negotiated. In draft form it demanded transparency and non-discrimination in the application of charges to operators. The directive also allows for willingness-to-pay and Ramsey pricing mechanisms, which, by their nature, are discriminatory.[16] Further, the directive permits the charges to be related to the airports overall costs or indeed to a regional system of airports' overall costs (Reynolds-Feighan and Feighan,1997). Unfortunately this 'bundling' of services creates problems when trying to relate charges for particular services to their costs: the pricing signals become obscured.

The airline industry in some parts of Europe has experienced the growth in new products initiated by low–cost scheduled operators, who have been to the fore in driving change in the regions in which they operate. These low–cost carriers have played an important role in bringing about changes to the European air transport sector. The needs of these carriers were explicitly considered by policy makers when planning infrastructure developments. The low–cost carriers have tended to focus their operations on under-utilized secondary airports close to the key European metropolitan areas.[17]

It is helpful for policy development to examine the management and traffic distribution in Europe from a system perspective and deal with issues of strategic infrastructure planning from this network point of view. For airports that do not have the ability to expand, because of land constraints or planning regulations, the

---

[16] Ramsey pricing is designed to cover full costs by differential pricing according to a combination of marginal cost considerations and willingness to pay. It adjusts the relative prices for different services according to their costs and the associated elasticities of demand (ε). If an airport offers two types of service, say peak and off-peak with different associated marginal costs (MC), then Ramsey pricing implies the prices (P) for each should be determined as follows;

$\{(P_{peak} - MC_{peak})/\varepsilon_{peak}\} = \{P_{off\text{-}peak} - MC_{off\text{-}peak})/\varepsilon_{offpeak}\}$

[17] For example, Ryanair, the Irish carrier, focused its services around Paris (Beauvais), Brussels (Charleroi) and London (Stansted and Luton airports).

issue of long term rationing of their fixed capacity and the diversion of traffic needs to be addressed from this wider viewpoint. The issue of re-distributing traffic is contentious and critically linked to the role and level of investment funding for airports. The issue needs to be addressed in order for the changes in the economic regulation of airlines to have optimal effect. On the one hand individual services need to be costed as precisely as possible, but that these specific items be viewed as part of a network or system of facilities. For example, in allocating European airport runway slots, consideration would need to be given to pavement damage and congestion effects of particular categories of users at individual facilities. These charges then have to be considered in the context of their impacts on other airports in the network, and the possibilities for expansion.

There are also legal constraints, partly linked to the pricing principles ICAO has established for international operations, associated with introducing congestion taxes and then using the revenues to provide capacity elsewhere in the system or in the economy more generally. From an investment perspective, while Europe may have sufficient airport infrastructure overall, that capacity is often in the wrong place, with congestion levels growing at the key hub centers. The expansion of capacity is not a straightforward process even if there is land available for further development at existing airports. Environmental regulations and issues related to funding of investment can have a significant impact on the timing and final outcome in the expansion of infrastructure. Air transport has always been a component in multimodal journeys for passengers and freight. Passengers need to get to and from airports, as does freight, so the issue of airport access is an integral part of airport planning and development.

A major factor that could prevent enhancement of the interoperability of the aviation sector is the infrastructure constraints and associated delays at airports. Many of the large airports in Europe now have, or have in plan, substantial rail stations at the airports, with direct links to regional and metropolitan centres. Several airports have sought to integrate high-speed rail interchanges at the airports. These kinds of developments will help to boost air traffic growth.

One option is the development of secondary airports in Europe. The developments at this category of airport by low cost operators has already been discussed. Economic forces will encourage the larger airports to increasingly substitute long haul services for short haul services, since this will allow for increases in passenger numbers without an accompanying increase in movements. The pattern is already seen at places such as Heathrow. The problem is that all airports rely on the combination of locally originating and transfer passengers to support their air services. So the feasibility of separating out point-to-point traffic and concentrating it at secondary airports is limited.

The evidence from the US suggests that deregulation allowed for significant growth in air traffic and carriers initially serviced the increased demand through interactive multiple hub network systems (see Chapter 5). Point-to-point operators at a certain stage can then enter certain markets where it is possible because of the increased volume to offer direct service. The viability of secondary airports in Europe will depend on the extent of traffic growth, the extent of competition from other surface transport modes and the characteristics of the traffic, particularly the extent of high yield business traffic. These airports will need to offer a certain threshold level of service on routes served since passengers will choose more frequent service (at primary airports) over less frequent service.

9.5 CONCLUSIONS

This chapter has focused on the airport infrastructure capacity of the European air transport sector and the measurement of factors influencing its supply of services. Initially, the multi-service network of activities, many of which are not specifically related to aeronautical uses, was examined. This has implications for the practical pricing of the air transportation activities because it has relevance for the cross-subsidization or cross-crediting of revenues which is an important issue in European competition policy. Airport infrastructure services, such as runway use and passenger terminal use, needs be costed separately, allowing the pricing mechanism to signal when expansion or rationing is required.

The definition and measurement of airport capacity is important if optimal investment and pricing strategies are to be pursued. In the context of economic assessment, capacity refers to the ability of a component in the airport system to handle aircraft and is usually expressed in terms of operations per hour (either arrivals or departures). This hourly capacity is the maximum number of operations that can be handled in a one-hour period under specific operating conditions, in particular, ceiling and visibility, air traffic control, the aircraft mix and the nature of operations. Capacity is therefore a measure of supply.

The nature of airport delays was examined and in particular the current distribution of traffic in greater Europe and the causes and levels of delay at the busier airports were considered. There were relatively high levels of delay in Europe during the late 1980s, with improvements up to 1994. There has been a gradual long term rise in delays at departure airports since then. In 1996, air traffic flow management over Europe was centralized within EUROCONTROL and this helped to alleviate delays in the worst affected sectors but introduced delays in sectors which had previously operated with minimal delay.

The general thrust of this chapter has been to argue for better use of market-based management and investment strategies. It is suggested that an airport system-wide approach to traffic management and investment would need to be considered. This is because several of Europe's larger and more congested airports are not, for a portfolio of environmental, social and economic reasons, in a position to expand capacity and the appropriate pricing across thye airport system would assist in the reallocation traffic. At the same time it is important to cost or price specific services independently, since this allows the pricing mechanism to signal optimal timing, scale and location of new capacity.

10 THE ECONOMICS OF BEING A HUB CITY

10.1 INTRODUCTION

Air transportation is not normally an end in itself but is demanded for the services that it can afford companies and individuals.[1] Transportation of all kinds is an important input into modern industry allowing rapid personal interaction between those in the business community and also opening up a wide number of locations for leisure activities. It also serve an every expanding role in providing premium service for package and freight movements that are needed in modern production management.

The pattern of air services that is supplied can, therefore, have important implications for the geographical distribution of population and for the location and growth of industry. Over the past twenty years since the enactment of the Airline Deregulation Act, the major US domestic carriers have developed hub-and-spoke structures for their operations. These have been instrumental in helping to reduce the overall costs of air travel to the US public and to increase the travel options that are available. This hubbing effect also means that the quantity and quality of air services varies quite considerably between cities in the country.

This chapter examines the benefits that accrue to a city or geographical region that is host to an airline hub. In particular, it considers the advantages that are enjoyed by business travelers who live close to major hub airports in the US and the advantages for local employers in locating in regions with a hub airport.

The approach adopted is initially to examine the basic nature of hubs. It then moves on to some of the issues involved in evaluating the costs and benefits of living in regions with hub airports, paying particular attention to matters of measurement. It then looks in very broad terms at the nature of the benefits that those located near hub airports can enjoy in terms of the direct gains from the activities associated with an airport and the advantages companies enjoy from being able to make use of one.

One element of the methodology is to look at the multiplier implications, via an input-output analysis, of a major hub. A second element involves taking a macro perspective to see if hub cities in the US perform better economically than those without hubs. Finally, it conducts a number of case studies to examine in more detail the situation at two hub cities and three non-hub cities. Not only does this work look at correlations between local economic prosperity and proximity to a hub airport, but it also considers the underlying causal linkages involved.

---

[1]   Although there are an increasing number of private flier, including those who undertake aerial acrobatics, who take to the air for pure pleasure.

10.2 BACKGROUND

The deregulation of the domestic US air cargo market in 1977 and the scheduled passenger airline sector from 1978 brought with it considerable benefits for both users and carriers.[2] In terms of the passenger sector, this has led to consumers enjoying lower overall fare levels and a greater choice of airlines on many journeys. This has been achieved with no diminution in safety levels. These gains seem to be largely enduring despite important subsequent technical and structural changes that have occurred in the sector.[3]

The new market conditions and resultant commercialism that accompanied deregulation, together with innovative managerial thinking, have been important in changing the ways that airline services are supplied. Indeed, many of these changes have been necessary for the benefits of deregulation to be realized.

One important change has been in the growth of hub-and-spoke operations.[4] These entail a scheduled airline feeding into large airports, banks of flights that come from a variety of origins and then consolidating passengers onto outward flights to a range of destinations.

While this may entail passengers taking longer over any trip than would be the case with a direct flight, it generally means that users have a much wider selection of services to choose from. The airlines can also offer lower average fares because of the economies of scale, scope and density that they can reap.

Hub-and-spoke operations *per se* were not strictly a result of the Airline Deregulation Act. Prior to 1978, many services did hub on particular airports. The differences are in terms of the scale of operations and the fact that they are provided by individual airlines. Before 1978, hub airports were often served by a multiplicity of airlines; the Civil Aeronautics Board took little account of network considerations when issuing route licenses. The result was that passengers frequently had to interline and change carriers when no direct flights were available. This meant that ticketing was more cumbersome and services were very often not as conveniently coordinated.

10.3 WHAT IS A HUB AIRPORT?

What exactly constitutes a hub airport is not clearly defined. There is no hard or fast economic or legal definition of a hub. As a general rule of thumb, however, many academic studies have thought a hub to entail carriers feeding three or more banks of traffic daily through an airport from some 40 or more cities.

---

[2]   The US's Opens Skies policy from 1979 has, as seen in Chapter 4, been effective in gradually liberalizing international traffic. This opening up of international routes has implications for hubbing because of the feed traffic needed to make many international services viable.

[3]   Appendix A of the US Department of Transportation Statistics (1996).

[4]   The major hub-and-spoke operators include American, United, Delta, US Airways, Continental, TWA and Northwest. Southwest's network is generally held up as the most important non-hub-and-spoke (or linearly) organized system.

In previous work, the US General Accounting Office assumed a concentrated hub to be an airport which was one of the 75 busiest in the nation in terms of enplanements and which where one carrier accounted for at least 60% of enplanements or two carriers combined accounted for at least 85%. Airports falling into either category but were not in the 48 contiguous states were excluded, as were those in cities with more than one airport.

The Federal Aviation Administration has classified communities into a four-class scheme depending on the total percentage of US passenger enplanements in all services and operated by US certified carriers within the 50 states and other designated areas (e.g., a large hub has 1.00% or more, a medium hub has 0.25 to 1.00%, and so on).

For practical purposes, when looking at concentration of airline activities, hubs are normally treated as airports that have a large preponderance of flights operated as part of an essentially radial network by one carrier. In a few rare cases there is a general recognition that a hub has two main carriers but this only applies to a few major airports.

As we have seen in Chapters 3 and 4, the benefits of hub-and-spoke operations accrue to both airlines and passengers (US Federal Aviation Administration, 1991). Airlines' gains in terms of economies of scale, scope and density have been heavily researched. Attention has also been paid to the demand side and economies of market presence. These involve the positive implications a large network can have on the patronage and revenue flow enjoyed by a carrier. User benefits have also been looked at in general terms. What has received somewhat less attention are the benefits that an urban area can reap from being a hub city.

The major US network carriers that deploy hub-and-spoke operations do so for both costs and revenue reasons. The costs saving comes from their ability to feed high volumes of traffic through a large terminal on banks (or complexes) of flights from a variety of origins and with passengers destined for a variety of other cities. Normally there are between three and five banks a day but there may be as many as twelve. Economies of scope come from the ability to spread costs across this range of services and economies of density from the high utilization of infrastructure that is possible. There is also the opportunity to enjoy cost savings from fleet standardization.

Placing exact figures on the various economies is difficult. Early analysis indicated, for instance, that due to economies of density, a 1% rise in the number of passengers an airline carried resulted in a 0.8% reduction in total costs, although more recent analysis indicates savings could be greater (Bruecker and Spiller, 1994).

Put another way, looking at the importance of traffic levels on a hub-and-spoke system, work conducted at the University of Illinois showed that in 1985 a major carrier such as Delta out of Atlanta carried about 36 000 passengers per quarter on an average spoke route, a medium size carrier such as US Air out of Pittsburgh carried 24 000, and a low density network such as Ozark out of St. Louis carried about 12 000 passengers. This gives comparable marginal costs of $107; $113 and $134 respectively for each additional passenger flown (i.e., it is 25% higher to carry an extra passenger on a low density route). Pushing the maximum volume of traffic through a hub, therefore, reduces costs.

In terms of passenger benefits enjoyed as a result of airline hubbing, the outcome for the US domestic market was dramatic (Morrison and Winston, 1978). Summarizing the data in Chapter 5, in the decade after the 1978 deregulation and largely as a result of the hub-and-spoke structure of operations that emerged, the number of passenger enplanements rose by 55% to over 140 million per annum, with revenue passenger miles rising by over 60%. The real costs of air travel fell by about 17% on the major routes, although by somewhat less on routes involving smaller markets. Linked to this the number of city pairs served only by a monopoly carrier fell by 10% with 651 additional routes being served by more than one carrier. Overall it has been estimated that air travelers benefited by some $15 billion (in 1998 dollars) from the Airline Deregulation Act, due to the more frequent flights and choices available to passengers.

In addition linear services of the type operated by Southwest and others offer direct services and can be lower cost mainly because they are self-contained services operated independently of flight banks and can enjoy a faster turn round time at airports.[5] This allows for high aircraft utilization that is an important ingredient in keeping overhead costs low. These non-hubbing carriers, through their threat of market entry, are one element in ensuring that larger hub-and-spoke operators do not exploit any potential market power they may have and, indeed, a recent feature of many US scheduled air transport markets is the creation of low cost subsidiaries by the majors to compete with the direct service airlines (e.g, Metroliner by US Airways).

A balanced picture does mean that the possible problems of hub-and-spoke operations require a mention. Besides potential periodic congestion, the banking of flights at hubs was traditionally seen as posing few economic problems. But it can lead to considerable periods of idle time when the number of banks per day is relatively small. Ground staff and other resources are left with little to do, and aircraft are used much less effectively.

Now it is recognized that, although airlines may enjoy economies of network presence from having large-scale hub-and-spoke operations, diseconomies need to be considered in some cases. It is for this reason that some major carriers, such as American, Northwest and Continental, truncated or withdrawn services at smaller, secondary hubs in the mid-1990s. Sophisticated accounting procedures revealed that marginal revenues generated by higher traffic volumes attained from these elements of their operations are more than offset by the fixed costs of the structure (Treitel and Smick, 1996).

Further, the provision of air services following the passing of the deregulating legislation is now by and large through market forces. This has meant that the impacts of deregulation have not been geographically uniform.[6] Indeed, some small and medium sized communities in the east and upper Midwest have experienced higher fares and/or a reduction in services. This is in part, though, due

---

[5]   Most of these services are linear rather than strictly point-to-point in the sense they serve routes A to B, B to C, C to D. Hence many passengers (e.g., from A to C) do not enjoy a non-stop service.
[6]   The continuation of the Essential Air Services Program offers a buffer from market forces for some small communities.

to the slower economic growth enjoyed in these regions (US General Accounting Office, 1998).

Hubbing also means a concentration of traffic at some airports with associated environmental intrusion for those living in the region (Button, 1998b). Regulations governing aircraft noise levels combined with careful flight path controls have greatly reduced the problem and, in general, noise levels are now lower than before the Airline Deregulation Act.

The overall conclusion is that, while not creating a perfectly competitive market and not necessarily ideal in terms of all of the distributional implications, the 1978 reforms have resulted in a situation of workable competition (Keeler, 1990), a situation whereby market forces, largely within a hub-and-spoke network structure, are generating higher levels of overall welfare than had the previously regulated structure. Care should, thus, be exercised in intervening in such a situation.

The prime concern that has been voiced about hubbing is that it confers monopoly power on the major carrier at a hub airport (US General Accounting Office, 1990). The carrier is then in a position to charge high fares to those captive to that airport. In particular, since business travelers are generally less sensitive to fare levels (i.e., less price elastic) because of their wider view of the generalized costs of making any trip, this group is potentially a soft target for hub airlines.

This is, however, rather a narrow way of looking at the situation. All market prices are the result of the interactions of supply and demand. In this case there are a number of factors that can potentially explain any premium that hub originating business traffic pays other than the exercising of monopoly power.

- There are statistical difficulties in measuring comparable fares.
- There may be additional costs of providing services for hub residents.
- Living near a hub airport increases the opportunity to accumulate frequent flyer miles on a single carrier and offers more potential destinations for which they may be used or for upgrade purposes.
- The market for air transport services may be excessively competitive in the sense that over time it is unstable. In economic terms there may exist an empty core (see Chapter 7).
- There may be major benefits to hub originating traffic that are not enjoyed by other air travelers.

Teasing out the potential importance of these different factors is not easy and the focus here is mainly on benefit issues. One or two comments on other items, however, seem pertinent.

Simply looking at fares charged by traffic originating from a hub airport compared with other non-hubs can be misleading. Full allowance must be made for a variety of factors, including the following.

- On average, yield (i.e., fare per mile) falls with distance traveled reflecting the importance of take-off and landing costs in the overall costs of air travel. The differing average flight lengths from airports need controlling for.

- Carriers offer different levels of service, and strict comparisons should therefore compare the fares of a carrier at a concentrated hub with fares of the same carrier elsewhere.
- Flights can involve a number of segments (even if a passenger is originating from a hub) and this should be allowed for.
- When comparing airports, it is important to look at the type of competition a carrier is confronted with; e.g., have any of the airports got services by low-cost carriers such as AirTran or Southwest?

The demand for airline services is highly volatile. The mid-1990s have seen high levels of profit earned by airlines, but only a few years earlier there was public concern about the long-term financial viability of the industry (US National Commission to Ensure a Strong Competitive Airline Industry, 1993). There is an inevitable catching up effect in fares over the business cycle, and short-term calculations can be misleading.

Taking full cognizance of all these factors is difficult in statistical analysis, but efforts have been made to move away from crude averaging. The indicators are that fare structures across hub and non-hub airports are complex and there is no simple pattern.

Business travelers are generally much less price-sensitive but exhibit more demands on quality of service (e.g., in terms of time and frequency of flights, availability of lounge facilities and frequent flyer bonuses). This is a reflection of the importance of generalized costs in their decision making. Survey evidence indicates, for example, that schedule convenience (especially frequency) is by far the most important factor for business travelers' choices of airline and is the second most important feature for leisure travelers (Ostrowski and O'Brien, 1991). By offering flexible tickets, comfortable on- and off-plane amenities and scheduling convenient to business needs at a premium price, carriers can attract these users, but this does cost the airlines money.

In terms of these additional costs, many cost items are joint across the provision of various types of service, and isolating them is problematic and is not attempted here. This does not mean that they may not be important. Hub airports are often provided with executive lounges, separate ticketing/check-in facilities and other attributes that benefit local travelers but that are not costless.

As indicated above, frequent flyer programs are popular and most regular business travelers are members of at least one program. Residing near a hub airport where a single carrier serves a wide range of destinations allows a more rapid accumulation of miles and a larger choice of how these ultimately may be used. If many carriers serve a hub, then accumulation can become piecemeal and utilization of the miles much less convenient.

While the benefits of competition have long been recognized, economists have always placed caveats around the conditions that allow these advantages to be fully enjoyed. It has long been recognized that there are some circumstances where the market can lead to excessive competition that in turn results in undersupply. This, as we have seen, is in technical economic jargon where there is an empty core.

10.4 BEING A HUB CITY

Airports essentially have four potential types of impact on the economy in their region. Primary effects are the benefits to the region of the construction or expansion of the facility – the design of the facility, the building of the runways, the construction of the terminals and hangers, the installation of air traffic navigation systems and so on. The direct effects involve the local employment required in the construction process and the work done by local contractors. Indirect effects include the benefits to the region of the wages and other incomes these workers and companies subsequently spend in the area.

These are clear gains to the local community and the local economy but are short term and may be rather limited in their order of magnitude. It is a once for all effect. Also, airport construction involves a degree of specialist skill, manpower and equipment that may not be available locally and this leads to leakages away from the immediate area.

In general, while airport development can have beneficial short-term effects, save in cases where there is a policy imperative to create jobs in the very short term, these are not really the key concerns. Indeed, even if there is a desire for immediate job creation, as the English economist John Maynard Keynes said, you may as well have one group of workers bury some money and have another dig it up again. This has the same short-term benefits, indeed possibly even larger since leakages are likely to be smaller than when building an airport.

Secondary effects are longer-term effects and are associated with the local economic benefits of running and operating the airport – the employment in maintaining the facility, in handling the aircraft and passengers, in transporting people and cargo to and from the terminal and so on. Again there are direct effects stemming from the immediate jobs that are created at the airport and immediately associated with it. There are also indirect effects due to the on-going flow of income that the airport's operation puts into the local economy.

These secondary effects can be extremely important to a local economy in terms of employment, income and, for local government, taxation revenue. The actual size of the secondary effect will vary between airports dependent upon the nature of their operations. As an example of the potential scale of these effects we take Washington Dulles International Airport for analysis below.

Tertiary effects stem from the stimulus enjoyed by a local economy as the result of firms and individuals having air transport services at their disposal.[7] While most forms of business activity now involve considerable use of transportation, high-technology companies make particular use of air transportation. Companies in this general area conduct activities requiring considerable interpersonal contacts. These contacts are only possible with high-quality transport. From a local development perspective it is often these types of firm that form the basis for economic growth because they are usually geographically mobile and represent a major growth sector. These effects are considered in detail at the end of the chapter.

---

[7]   Rietveld (1997) estimates that Schiphol Airport in the Netherlands generates about 85 000 jobs for the country on this basis.

The types of commercial scheduled air service enjoyed by those living in cities with airport hubs differ somewhat from cities that are a spoke on a network or that have no major carrier.[8] In particular, the following features typify the hub city when compared to urban areas with airports offering other forms of air transport services.

- More frequent flights (Morrison, 1997).
- More direct flights. One study found that in 1996, and after controlling for population size, hub airports offered non-stop flights to nearly twice the number of cities as non-hub cities with 25% more daily departures per city served.[9]
- More opportunities for same day return flights.
- Greater likelihood of international flights.
- Services geared to local market needs (e.g., serving destinations attractive to residents).
- The ability to send packages on scheduled passenger services on flights leaving after the major courier services have finished their daily pick-ups.
- At the same time, residents of hub cities have the same opportunities of linking to other major hubs as do those living in non-hubs.

These are important features for business travelers. The cost of the average business trip is not assessed purely in terms of air fares but rather in terms of generalized costs. Generalized costs embrace, among other things, air travel time, time spent in terminals, time spent getting to and from airports, air fares, money costs of getting to and from airports, costs of overnight stays and costs of time wasted due to infrequent flights. As the old adage goes, 'time is money' and time considerations are often far more important to business travelers than fares.

High levels of hub utilization by a single carrier have, however, been a recurrent theme of concern since the development of large-scale hub-and-spoke operations in the 1980s. This is not surprising when it is regularly reported that, at airports such as Atlanta, Minneapolis and Pittsburgh, the main carrier is responsible for more than 80% of the airport's traffic.

There are two types of traffic that use hub airports. There are transit passengers who pass through when changing aircraft. These passengers, which generally form the largest group of travelers at hubs, originate from other airports and are destined for other airports. Given the number of alternative air transport networks available in the US, these passengers normally have a choice of whether to take a direct flight or to transit through one of several hubs. The fact that a hub is dominated by a single carrier does not constitute a monopoly position because

---

[8]   Indeed some companies locate in certain cities because of the services that an airport provides; e.g., one of the reasons Toyota took its North American headquarters to Cincinnati was because of its airport hub.

[9]   It has been estimated that the disutility of having to make a transfer, irrespective of the additional overall duration of an indirect flight, was about $22.5 in 1987; see Oum and Tretheway (1990).

people can opt for alternative routings. The hubs effectively compete with each other for this type of traffic.[10]

The main debate revolves around whether the second group of travelers, those residing at a hub airport city, are open to exploitation. They have no choice in terms of using the hub as an origin and return destination for their trips; they are in a sense captive. The concern is whether direct fares to and from hub airports are excessively high due to the lack of competition with other hub based airline networks.

The empirical evidence does seem superficially to indicate that some fares at hub airports levied by a dominant carrier can be higher than for other airlines. Empirical work at the Brookings Institution using carefully constructed data, however, indicates that this premium in 1993 was only about 5% and that it represented less than 2% of the estimated annual benefits of deregulation (Morrison and Winston, 1995).

There are also strong grounds for arguing that any premiums charged at airports where one major carrier has a large market share are much more the result of natural demand conditions than of monopoly exploitation. In particular they reflect the need to meet the requirements of local business travelers.

The importance of frequent flyer programs for retaining airline customer loyalty is well documented and this loyalty is enhanced when convenient travel to a host of destinations is possible on a particular carrier. The value of frequent flyer mileage is greatest for residents of a city that serves as the hub for a large hub-and-spoke network because it translates into convenient free travel to a multitude of destinations.

Essentially, the users of such a carrier are paying for what is seen as a superior package of services. Additionally, business travelers generally value a large service network more than do leisure travelers and again are willing to pay for this additional service factor. It reduces their generalized costs of travel. Residents living in the region around a hub airport enjoy the advantage of having a range of destinations open to them that exceeds those in comparable regions without a hub.[11] In economic terms, residents enjoy external benefits from having transit passengers passing through their local airport that allow them access to a major scheduled air transport network.

The idea of perpetuity effects reflects an increasingly widely accepted school of thought that argues economic growth, once started in a region, becomes self-sustaining and may accelerate.[12] Linked to this, there is also empirical evidence that infrastructure investment can act as a catalyst for higher economic growth in an area; essentially it can act as a kick-start mechanism (Aschauer, 1990). The construction of a new airport or the major enlargement of an existing facility may

[10]   Kanafani and Ghorbial (1985) have also argued that this traffic does little for the local economy although this tends to ignore the wider range of services that can be provided to local residence and companies by an airport with significant amounts of transit traffic.

[11]   As the FAA has argued, 'For people who live close to the hub airport, hubbing is beneficial because many non-stop flights are available to many cities that would not otherwise be able to support such service'. (US Federal Aviation Administration, 1991).

[12]   This is known as 'endogenous growth theory'.

act, therefore, to set in progress a much larger and longer term development process in a region.

This perpetuity effect is in addition to the tertiary effects that relate to the immediate migration of firms to an area with good air transport services. It is longer-term and affects the dynamics of an area. By initially attracting undertakings to an area in sufficient numbers, airport development can lead to the crossing of important thresholds in terms of economies of scale, scope and density. In particular, in the context of 'new economy', high-technology activities, an area can acquire a vital knowledge base that fosters local research and development and makes the region quasi-independent of others. The regional economy can feed on this to further its high-technology activities and hence to accelerate its growth.

This type of dynamic economic impact of an airport is the most abstract and the most difficult to quantify. It has been little researched. It is long term and involves the interaction of an airport with all other aspects of the local economy. It is, nevertheless, potentially a very real and important benefit that may be enjoyed by a region with high quality air services.

✔ 10.5 DIRECT EFFECTS ON THE LOCAL ECONOMY

The concern here is to look at what we have defined as the secondary effects of a major airport, namely the jobs and income that an area enjoys as the result of the activities within an airport. All airports are different and their impacts on the local region are correspondingly variable. Washington Dulles International Airport is taken as an example of the importance that the operations of a hub can have for the local region.[13]

The economy of the Northern Virginia region is one of the fastest growing in the US and has a strong focus on information based activities that require good transport and communications infrastructure. Its location close to the nation's capital also means that it has strong ties with government activities and, linked to this, is involved in extensive international activities. Dulles Airport is a part of this region's infrastructure and has grown steadily until reaching its current traffic level of some 13 million enplanements per annum. With 2.7 million international passengers using Dulles in 1996, it is also now one of the nation's top ten international gateways. It represents a significant economic core in itself with the airport being a major local employer providing, in 1997, 9 773 full-time jobs and 3 588 part-time jobs. It has recently engaged in a major program of enlargement.

Since 1981, the perimeter and high density rules have been the foundation upon which the physically limited capacity of Ronald Reagan Washington National Airport has been allocated in order to create balanced use of the Washington region's three airports, and in particular balanced use between Washington Dulles International Airport and National Airport. The perimeter rule at National Airport requires nonstop scheduled airline flights from that airport to

---

[13]   See Button *et al.* (1999) for a more detailed assessment.

serve destinations within a 1,250-mile perimeter.[14] The high density rule defines the number of flight operations permitted each hour; both rules are used in combination to balance use of Washington's airport resources. The perimeter rule prioritizes use of the downtown airport to the short haul traveler for whom ground segmentation is a significant portion of total journey time. The perimeter and high density rules are designed together to direct growth to Dulles Airport and to limit the environmental impact of flight operations on communities forming the city's inner core

Proposals have been initiated to relax these rules selectively with the intention of allowing longer-haul services from National Airport, particularly to the west coast. This relaxation would have some immediate implications for the other two airports in the region but also opens the inherent issue of the ultimate total removal of National Airport's perimeter rule.

The relaxation of the perimeter rule will affect the mix of traffic using the Washington area airports with the likelihood of long distance, domestic flights moving into National Airport at the expense of the other two airports. This in turn has implications for international traffic since many passengers use Dulles Airport as a hub for transcontinental movements.

This study focuses on the implications for the local economy served by Washington Dulles International Airport of the possible relaxation of the perimeter and high density rules. It develops an analytical framework that links the probable loss of airline services at Dulles with the implications for employment in the region. The analysis has a static element in terms of looking at the immediate, short-term effects of relaxation and a long-term element, in that forecasts are made of the probable trends in the use of the airport until the year 2010 with and without the perimeter and high density rules in place. Because it is unrealistic, if not impossible, to offer precise forecasts involving such a dynamic sector as air transport, the analysis also offers some sensitivity calculations to reflect broad boundaries within which outcomes are likely to fall.

10.6 THE ECONOMIC IMPORTANCE OF DULLES AIRPORT

The analysis involves contrasting a counterfactual forecast of how traffic and employment at Washington Dulles International Airport would develop over the next decade with the existing perimeter and high density rules intact against the alternative hypothesis that the perimeter rule would be completely abandoned in 1998. The implications of this are then related to the broader economic impacts on the region's economy.

To undertake this quantitative analysis a combination of techniques embracing, scenario analysis, expert judgment, econometric modeling and input-

---

[14]   This contrasts to the Wright Amendment controlling activities at Love Field Airport in Texas, where the limitations are on states that can be served rather than on flight distances. There are also proposals to reform these regulations.

output analysis is used.[15] The modeling exercise is sequential and involves a number of stages. It is also conducted appreciating the uncertainty of any forecasting exercise of this type by incorporating a sensitivity analysis. This permits a number of alternative future scenarios to be examined rather than simply relying on one 'best estimate'.

10.6.1 Overall model

Changing the perimeter rule at National Airport will have a series of interrelated implications. To reflect this and to provide a viable method of assessment, the analysis consists of a number of stages that are outlined in Figure 10.1. While ideally one would like to have a fully integrated model this broad type of sequential modeling has been widely used in many areas of analysis and has proved to be robust.

The first stage of the sequence involves looking at past time trends in terms of the ways in which Dulles and National airports have developed. The historical perspective is important not simply to provide quantitative inputs into the subsequent numerical analysis but also to explore how trends have developed over time.

This historic information is the basis of the analysis in the second and third stages of the sequence where expert judgments are made regarding the implications for air traffic until the year 2007 of:

•   retaining National Airport's perimeter rule,
•   totally abandoning the perimeter rule at National Airport.

The analysis does require some simplifying assumptions regarding the way the regulations can change. In practice, it seems likely that, while the changes made to National Airport's perimeter rule initially involve some modifications to the flight length rules (namely some exemptions) that this will subsequently result in its complete abandonment of the restrictions. Modeling this is impossible without insights into the exact time path of change and so the once-for-all assumption is adopted; essentially a comparative statics type of framework rather than any form of dynamic model. In quantitative terms this means there is likely to be some small over-prediction of the employment consequences of change.

[15]   For static, more general models that have assessed the importance of Washington Dulles International Airport see, Simat, Helliesen and Eichner (1986); Martin O'Connell Associates (1989); Martin Associates, (1997).

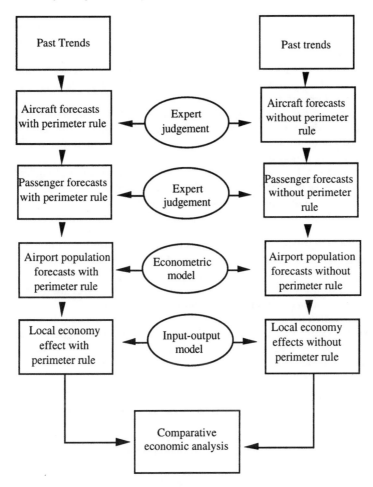

Figure 10.1 The Series of stages in the assessment of the impacts of relaxing the perimeter rule on Dulles Airport

The main expert judgments are:[16]

- Washington Dulles International Airport would lose 2.2 million to 3.3 million passengers a year (a drop of 16% to 24%) and much of its wide-body cargo lift.
- National Airport would gain 800 000 to 1 million passengers a year.
- National Airport would become the region's primary airport for transcontinental services, essentially reversing the domestic roles of Dulles and National airports.

[16]   The judgments stem from studies initiated by the Washington Airports Task Force.

- Without transcontinental connecting passengers, Dulles would lose service in six to nine international markets and international passenger use would drop by up to 63%.
- To provide slots for high value West Coast markets, 24 lower value markets at National Airport would be vulnerable to loss of all or some of their current nonstop flights to the nation's capital.
- The long term air traffic growth at Washington Dulles International Airport is assumed to be 3.75% per annum with National Airport's perimeter rule intact but falling to about a 0.5% annual traffic growth rate if the perimeter rule were to be abandoned.
- Since National Airport is already operating near to its landing/take-off capacity it is assumed that the job creation effects, and *ipso facto* regional employment consequences, will be relatively small as passenger traffic is diverted there.

The analysis, therefore, links the change in air traffic using Washington Dulles International Airport to the number of passenger movements at that airport. This is, in part, done by using expert judgment in assessing the types of traffic involved, the origins and destinations of traffic and the types of traffic most likely to transfer to National Airport if there were no distance constraints.

Once predictions of the airlines' responses to any change in the perimeter rules have been made, these then need to be linked to the number of passengers that will be switching between the region's main airports and adjustments made to allow for international flights that may relocate outside the region.

Stage 4 of the modeling sequence involves linking the passenger traffic through Dulles to the airport population. The model used involved developing a time series econometric model based upon a distributed lag framework. This took the actual data on passengers using Dulles Airport between 1976 and 1997 and related them to the number of people, both full and part time, employed at Dulles Airport. Table 10.1 sets out the details of the previous levels of enplanements and employment at Dulles Airport.

A time lag specification was introduced into the econometric model to reflect the fact that airport employment takes time to adjust and to grow as new air services are introduced or existing ones modified.

The exact details of the econometric model and the calculated parameters are seen in Equation 10.1.[17] The econometric model can explain 99.5% of the variations in airport employment growth at the airport over the period 1976 to 1997. For predictive purposes the model is fed with forecast information concerning the future growth of passenger traffic at Dulles Airport as assessed at Stages 1 and 2.

$$LnTE_t = -4.317 + 0.723 \, LnTP_t - 0.213LnTP_{t-1} + 0.334TP_{t-2} \qquad (10.1)$$

R-Squared	0.995	Mean dependent variable	8.827
Durbin-Watson	2.648	F statistic	1270.518

[17]   The model was estimated using the ordinary least squares element of the *Econometric Views* software package.

Adjusted R-squared   0.994   S.D. dependent variable   0.574

where TE_t is employment in year t and TP_t, TP_{t-1}, TP_{t-2} are passengers in years t, t-1, t-2 respectively.

Table 10.1 Use of Washington Dulles International Airport, 1977-97

Year (January)	Enplanements	Airport Population
1977	2 707 133	3 528
1978	3 022 084	3 594
1979	3 338 552	3 612
1980	2 457 049	4 062
1981	2 161 406	3 320
1982	2 465 191	3 526
1983	287 474	3 159
1984	3 403 454	3 761
1985	5 076 593	3 955
1986	8 962 346	5 791
1987	10 784 767	8 098
1988	9 516 707	9 008
1989	1 078 671	9 542
1990	10 236 350	10 684
1991	10 790 217	10 974
1992	11 331 215	11 704
1993	10 799 380	11 591
1994	11 518 711	11 652
1995	12 443 657	12 026
1996	12 893 294	13 040
1997		13 361

The alternative forecasts of passenger movements at Dulles Airport are translated into information about the implications for the local economy in Stage 5 of the sequence. This involves the use of an economic input-output framework developed specifically for the region and thus designed to allow for the particular economic features of the area.[18] Input-output tables provide for the multiplier effects of a change in the scale of activities in one part of the economic system to be traced through to other sectors.

[18]   The Northern Virginia Econometric Input-Output Model was initially developed in 1994–5 and has led to the development of the National Capital Regional Economic Input-Output Model (NCREIM). The model is useful for conducting impact assessments, forecasting and for decision support activities for government and industry. George Mason' University's Center for Regional Analysis   worked closely with the Chicago Federal Reserve Bank and the University of Illinois Department of Regional Analysis and Planning in developing the models. As a derivative, a near term forecasting system for the National Capital region as well as for Fairfax and Loudoun counties using leading and coincident indices was refined.

10.6.2.1 Passenger forecasts

The annual passenger forecasts for Dulles Airport with the National Airport perimeter rule still in place, together with those based on the assumptions of an initial 2.2 million or alternatively a 3.3 million drop in passengers and a subsequent 0.5% annual growth, are seen in Table 10.2. They are compared with forecasts developed by the Metropolitan Washington Airports Authority[19] of what it projects would have happened with the continuation of the existing regulations at National Airport.

The implications of the change are seen as a once-for-all shift in the number of passengers using Dulles Airport that is followed by a gradual increase as it takes a share of growth traffic. The initial decline in traffic would, however, be followed by much slower growth than would otherwise be anticipated as Reagan National Airport attracts the majority of the generated domestic traffic that is likely to emerge in the future and as new international passenger traffic is carried to alternative gateways.

10.6.2.2 Airport population

The details of the forecasts produced from the econometric model when considering the number of people working at Washington Dulles International Airport to the year 2010, without the Reagan National Airport perimeter rule in place, are set out in Table 10.3. These forecasts are based upon an assumed growth rate of 0.5% in passenger traffic at the airport contrasted with employment that the Washington Airports Task Force have predicted would have taken place if the regulatory structure were to remain unchanged.

The econometric model predicts that, while passenger traffic at Washington Dulles International Airport will return to 1997 levels before the year 2010 if the perimeter rules are removed, employment at the airport will still fall short of the 1997 level. This is true regardless of the initial impact scenario adopted. It is explained by the fact that the airport enjoys some degree of economies of scale and is continually improving its labor productivity – a factor indicated by the parameters estimated for the econometric model set out in Equation 10.1.

---

[19]   The Metropolitan Washington Airports Authority (MWAA) is the regional body that operates Dulles and National airports under a lease from the Federal Government.

Table 10.2 Implications for airport use

Year	2.2 million passenger loss	3.3 million passenger loss	MWAA
1972	2 319 615	2 319 615	na
1973	2 504 177	2 504 177	na
1974	2 428 543	2 428 543	na
1975	2 393 891	2 393 891	na
1976	2 691 485	2 691 485	3 528 000
1977	2 707 113	2 707 113	3 594 000
1978	3 022 084	3 022 084	3 612 000
1979	3 338 552	3 338 552	4 062 000
1980	2 457 049	2 457 049	3 320 000
1981	2 161 406	2 161 406	3 52 6000
1982	2 465 191	2 465 191	3 159 000
1983	2 874 748	2 874 748	3 761 000
1984	3 403 454	3 403 454	3 955 000
1985	5 076 593	5 076 593	5 791 000
1986	8 962 346	8 962 346	8 098 000
1987	10 784 767	10 784 767	9 008 000
1988	9 516 707	9 516 707	9 542 000
1989	1 0178 671	1 1078 671	10 684 000
1990	10 236 350	10 236 350	10 974 000
1991	10 790 217	10 790 217	11 704 000
1992	11 331 215	11 331 215	11 591 000
1993	10 799 380	10 799 380	11 547 000
1994	11 518 711	11 518 711	12 026 000
1995	12 443 657	12 443 657	13 040 000
1996	12 893 294	12 893 294	13 361 000
1997	13 198 803	13 188 803	13 814 000
1998	*11 259 421*	*10 133 357*	*14 102 250*
1999	*11 526 215*	*10 373 468*	*14 584 400*
2000	*11 799 331*	*10 619 269*	*15 134 190*
2001	*12 078 918*	*10 870 895*	*15 696 040*
2022	*12 365 130*	*11 128 482*	*16 283 150*
2003	*12 658 124*	*11 392 174*	*16 888 680*
2004	*12 958 060*	*11 662 113*	*17 49 9000*
2005	*13 265 104*	*11 938 449*	*18 125 260*
2006	*13 579 422*	*12 221 332*	*18 808 280*
2007	*13 901 189*	*12 510 919*	*19 499 410*
2008	*14 230 580*	*12 807 367*	*20 236 750*
2009	*14 567 776*	*13 110 840*	*21 001 970*
2010	*14 912 962*	*13 421 504*	*21 796 130*

Note: Italics represent forecasts.

Table 10.3 Impact on employment at Dulles Airport

Year	2.2 million decline in passengers	3.3 million decline in passengers
1976	3 528	3 528
1977	3 594	3 594
1978	3 612	3 612
1979	4 062	4 062
1980	3 320	3 320
1981	3 526	3 526
1982	3 159	3 159
1983	3 761	3 761
1984	3 955	3 955
1985	5 791	5 791
1986	8 098	8 098
1987	9 008	9 008
1988	9 542	9 542
1989	10 684	10 684
1990	10 974	10 974
1991	11 704	11 704
1992	11 591	11 591
1993	11 547	11 547
1994	12 026	12 026
1995	13 040	13 040
1996	13 361	13 361
1997	13 814	13 814
1998	*11 932*	*11 056*
1999	*12 535*	*11 878*
2000	*11 844*	*10 836*
2001	*11 894*	*10 882*
2022	*11 944*	*10 928*
2003	*11 945*	*10 974*
2004	*12 045*	*11 020*
2005	*12 096*	*11 067*
2006	*12 147*	*11 113*
2007	*12 198*	*11 160*
2008	*12 250*	*11 207*
2009	*12 302*	*11 255*
2010	*12 354*	*11 302*

Note: Italics represent forecasts.

10.6.2.3 Impact on the regional economy
The Northern Virginia region's economy is highly focused on the new economy service sector that, in turn, makes extensive use of air transport services. The input-output analysis, therefore, separated out these key sectors for particular attention. Table 10.4 lists the Standard Industrial Classifications (SICs) into which the input-output analysis divides employment in the region. The three broad

groupings of industries that are particularly important to the region's economy are information based industries, tourism and service industries.[20]

Table 10.4 SICs constituting high technology industry

Label	Title	SIC
01	Agriculture	01–09
02	Mining	10–14
03	Construction	15–17
04	Food and kindred products	20
05	Printing and publishing	27
06	Chemicals and allied products	28
07	Other non-durable manufacturing	21–23, 26, 29–31
08	Stone, clay and glass products	32
09	Fabricated metal products	34
10	Machinery and computer equipment	35
11	Electronic equipment excluding computers	36
12	Transportation equipment	37
13	Instruments and related products	38
14	Other durable manufacturing	24–25, 33, 39
15	Trucking and warehousing	42
16	Transportation by air	45
17	Transportation services	40, 47
18	Other transportation	41, 43–44, 46
19	Communications	48
20	Electric, gas and sanitary services	49
21	Wholesale trade	50–51
22	General retain	52–57, 59
23	Eating and drinking places	58
24	Financial services	60–62, 67
25	Insurance carriers, agents, brokers and services	63–64
26	Real estate	65
27	Hotels and motels	70
28	Personal services	72
29	Business, engineering and management services	73, 87, 89
30	Repair services	75–76
31	Amusement and recreational services	79
32	Health services	80
33	Legal services	81
34	Educational services	82
35	Social services	83
36	Membership organizations and household services	84, 86, 88
37	Motion pictures	78
FGE	Federal government enterprise	
SLGE	State and local government enterprise	

[20]   At this level of data aggregation, the industries that are normally considered to form the information based component of the region's economy are Electronic Equipment excluding Computers Instruments and Related Products, and Business, Engineering and Management Services; those comprising tourist-related activities embrace General Retail, Eating and Drinking Places, Hotels and Motels, and Amusement and Recreational Services; the more general service industries are Financial Services, Insurance Carriers, Agents, Brokers and Services, Real Estate, Personal Services, Repair Services, Health Services, Legal Services, Educational Services, Social Services, Membership Organizations and Household Services, Motion Pictures.

The employment impacts of reforming the perimeter rule are calculated for each of these Standard Industrial Classifications and are shown under two scenarios in Tables 10.5 and 10.6. The exhibits express the number of job changes in thousands. The scenarios are that the initial impact of reform would be either a 2.2 million passenger emplanement loss at Washington Dulles International Airport or a 3.3 million loss (Table 10.6). It is assumed that growth at Dulles Airport after this initial shock would be at 0.5%.

Table 10.5 The employment implications by high-technology classifications of scenario one

Year	1998	1999	2000	2001	2002	2003	2004	2005	2006	2007	2008	2009	2010
Other	-3.05	-3.37	-5.21	-6.25	-7.22	-8.20	-9.20	-10.22	-11.33	-12.48	-13.72	-15.05	-16.42
01	-0.01	-0.02	-0.02	-0.03	-0.03	-0.04	-0.04	-0.05	-0.05	-0.06	-0.06	-0.07	-0.08
02	0.00	0.00	0.00	0.00	0.00	0.00	0.00	0.00	0.00	0.00	0.00	0.00	0.00
03	-0.04	-0.04	-0.07	-0.08	-0.09	-0.10	-0.11	-0.13	-0.14	-0.16	-0.17	-0.19	-0.21
04	-0.01	-0.01	-0.02	-0.02	-0.02	-0.02	-0.03	-0.03	-0.03	-0.04	-0.04	-0.04	-0.05
05	-0.05	-0.06	-0.09	-0.11	-0.13	-0.15	-0.16	-0.18	-0.20	-0.22	-0.25	-0.27	-0.30
05	-0.01	-0.01	-0.01	-0.01	-0.01	-0.01	-0.01	-0.02	-0.02	-0.02	-0.02	-0.02	-0.02
07	-0.01	-0.01	-0.01	-0.02	-0.02	-0.02	-0.03	-0.03	-0.03	-0.04	-0.04	-0.04	-0.05
08	0.00	0.00	0.00	-0.01	-0.01	-0.01	-0.01	-0.01	-0.01	-0.01	-0.01	-0.01	-0.02
09	0.00	0.00	0.00	-0.01	-0.01	-0.01	-0.01	-0.01	-0.01	-0.01	-0.01	-0.01	-0.02
10	0.00	0.00	0.00	0.00	0.00	0.00	0.00	-0.01	-0.01	-0.01	-0.01	-0.01	-0.01
11	-0.02	-0.02	-0.03	-0.04	-0.05	-0.05	-0.06	-0.07	-0.08	-0.09	-0.10	-0.11	-0.12
12	0.00	0.00	0.00	0.00	0.00	0.00	0.00	0.00	0.00	0.00	0.00	0.00	0.00
13	0.00	0.00	0.00	0.00	0.00	0.00	0.00	0.00	-0.01	-0.01	-0.01	-0.01	-0.01
14	0.00	0.00	0.00	0.00	-0.01	-0.01	-0.01	-0.01	-0.01	-0.01	-0.01	-0.01	-0.01
15	-0.01	-0.01	-0.02	-0.03	-0.03	-0.03	-0.04	-0.04	-0.05	-0.05	-0.06	-0.06	-0.07
16	-2.27	-2.15	-3.44	-3.98	-4.54	-5.12	-5.71	-6.32	-6.98	-7.65	-8.37	-9.11	-9.89
17	-0.08	-0.07	-0.11	-0.13	-0.15	-0.17	-0.19	-0.21	-0.23	-0.26	-0.28	-0.30	-0.33
18	-0.01	-0.01	-0.02	-0.02	-0.02	-0.02	-0.03	-0.03	-0.03	-0.04	-0.04	-0.04	-0.05
19	-0.05	-0.05	-0.08	-0.10	-0.11	-0.13	-0.15	-0.16	-0.18	-0.20	-0.22	-0.24	-0.26
20	-0.02	-0.02	-0.04	-0.04	-0.05	-0.06	-0.06	-0.07	-0.08	-0.09	-0.10	-0.11	-0.12
21	-0.02	-0.02	-0.04	-0.04	-0.05	-0.06	-0.06	-0.07	-0.08	-0.09	-0.10	-0.11	-0.12
22	-0.03	-0.03	-0.05	-0.06	-0.07	-0.08	-0.09	-0.10	-0.11	-0.12	-0.13	-0.15	-0.17
23	-0.31	-0.32	-0.50	-0.59	-0.68	-0.78	-0.87	-0.96	-1.07	-1.18	-1.29	-1.42	-1.55
24	-0.21	-0.22	-0.34	-0.41	-0.47	-0.53	-0.59	-0.65	-0.72	-0.79	-0.86	-0.94	-1.03
25	-0.05	-0.05	-0.08	-0.10	-0.12	-0.13	-0.15	-0.16	-0.18	-0.20	-0.22	-0.24	-0.27
26	-0.05	-0.05	-0.08	-0.09	-0.11	-0.12	-0.12	-0.14	-0.16	-0.17	-0.18	-0.20	-0.22
27	-0.02	-0.02	-0.03	-0.03	-0.04	-0.05	-0.05	-0.06	-0.06	-0.07	-0.08	-0.09	-0.10
28	-0.03	-0.04	-0.06	-0.07	-0.08	-0.09	-0.11	-0.12	-0.13	-0.14	-0.16	-0.17	-0.19
29	0.00	-0.41	-0.48	-0.73	-0.88	-1.02	-1.16	-1.30	-1.45	-1.61	-1.77	-1.95	-2.14
30	-0.04	-0.05	-0.07	-0.08	-0.10	-0.11	-0.12	-0.14	-0.15	-0.17	-0.19	-0.21	-0.23
31	-0.02	-0.03	-0.04	-0.05	-0.06	-0.07	-0.08	-0.09	-0.10	-0.11	-0.12	-0.13	-0.14
32	-0.17	-0.19	-0.30	-0.37	-0.43	-0.50	-0.57	-0.64	-0.72	-0.81	-0.90	-1.01	-1.12
33	-0.03	-0.03	-0.05	-0.06	-0.07	-0.08	-0.10	-0.11	-0.12	-0.13	-0.14	-0.16	-0.17
34	-0.03	-0.04	-0.06	-0.07	-0.08	-0.10	-0.11	-0.12	-0.14	-0.15	-0.17	-0.18	-0.20
35	-0.06	-0.07	-0.10	-0.13	-0.15	-0.18	-0.21	-0.24	-0.27	-0.31	-0.35	-0.40	-0.45
36	-0.04	-0.04	-0.06	-0.08	-0.09	-0.10	-0.11	-0.12	-0.14	-0.15	-0.16	-0.18	-0.20
37	-0.01	-0.01	-0.01	-0.01	-0.02	-0.02	-0.02	-0.02	-0.03	-0.03	-0.03	-0.03	-0.04
FGE	-0.01	-0.02	-0.03	-0.03	-0.04	-0.04	-0.05	-0.05	-0.06	-0.06	-0.07	-0.08	-0.08
SLGE	-0.01	-0.01	-0.01	-0.01	-0.01	-0.01	-0.02	-0.02	-0.02	-0.02	-0.02	-0.03	-0.03
Total	-3.84	-4.25	-6.56	-7.86	-9.08	-10.56	-11.56	-12.84	-14.23	-15.67	-17.22	-18.90	-20.62

The employment figures for the region reflect the difference in jobs that would materialize with the realization of the Metropolitan Washington Airports Authority's projection of future employment at Dulles Airport assuming the regulatory *status quo* against those that are forecast to occur following the removal of National Airport's perimeter rule. The bottom rows of each table (denoted as

NCNTOT) provide an indicator of the aggregate, across sector impact of removing the National Airport perimeter rule.

Table 10.6 The employment implications by high-technology classifications of scenario two

Year	1998	1999	2000	2001	2002	2003	2004	2005	2006	2007	2008	2009	2010
Other	−4.31	−4.51	−6.84	−7.97	−8.97	−9.97	−10.98	−12.01	−13.13	−14.30	−15.55	−16.90	−18.29
01	−0.02	−0.02	−0.03	−0.04	−0.04	−0.05	−0.05	−0.06	−0.06	−0.07	−0.07	−0.08	−0.09
02	0.00	0.00	0.00	0.00	0.00	0.00	0.00	0.00	0.00	0.00	0.00	0.00	0.00
03	−0.06	−0.06	−0.09	−0.10	−0.11	−0.12	−0.14	−0.15	−0.16	−0.18	−0.19	−0.21	−0.23
04	−0.01	−0.01	−0.02	−0.03	−0.03	−0.03	−0.03	−0.03	−0.04	−0.04	−0.04	−0.05	−0.05
05	−0.07	−0.08	−0.12	−0.14	−0.16	−0.18	−0.20	−0.22	−0.24	−0.26	−0.28	−0.31	−0.33
06	−0.01	−0.01	−0.01	−0.01	−0.01	−0.02	−0.02	−0.02	−0.02	−0.02	−0.02	−0.02	−0.03
07	−0.01	−0.01	−0.02	−0.02	−0.02	−0.03	−0.03	−0.04	−0.04	−0.04	−0.04	−0.04	−0.05
08	−0.01	−0.01	−0.02	−0.02	−0.02	−0.03	−0.03	−0.04	−0.04	−0.04	−0.04	−0.05	−0.05
09	0.00	0.00	−0.01	−0.01	0.01	−0.01	−0.01	−0.01	−0.01	−0.01	−0.01	−0.02	−0.02
10	0.00	0.00	−0.01	−0.01	−0.01	−0.01	−0.01	−0.01	−0.01	−0.01	−0.01	−0.02	−0.02
11	0.00	0.00	0.00	0.00	0.00	−0.01	−0.01	−0.01	−0.01	−0.01	−0.01	−0.01	−0.01
12	−0.03	−0.03	−0.04	−0.05	−0.06	−0.07	−0.08	−0.08	−0.09	−0.10	−0.11	−0.13	−0.14
13	0.00	0.00	0.00	0.00	0.00	0.00	0.00	0.00	0.00	0.00	0.00	0.00	0.00
14	0.00	0.00	−0.01	−0.01	−0.01	−0.01	−0.01	−0.01	−0.01	−0.01	−0.01	−0.01	−0.02
15	−0.02	−0.02	−0.03	−0.03	−0.04	−0.04	−0.04	−0.05	−0.05	−0.06	−0.06	−0.07	−0.08
16	−3.18	−2.83	−4.50	−5.04	−5.61	−6.19	−6.78	−7.39	−8.06	−8.73	−9.46	−10.21	−10.99
17	−0.11	−0.13	−0.15	−0.17	−0.19	−0.21	−0.23	−0.25	−0.27	−0.29	−0.32	−0.34	−0.37
18	−0.01	−0.01	−0.02	−0.02	−0.03	−0.03	−0.03	−0.03	−0.04	−0.04	−0.04	−0.05	−0.05
19	−0.07	−0.07	−0.11	−0.13	−0.14	−0.16	−0.17	−0.19	−0.21	−0.23	−0.25	−0.27	−0.29
20	−0.03	−0.03	−0.05	−0.06	−0.06	−0.07	−0.08	−0.09	−0.09	−0.10	−0.11	−0.12	−0.13
21	−0.03	−0.03	−0.05	−0.06	−0.06	−0.07	−0.08	−0.08	−0.09	−0.10	−0.11	−0.12	−0.13
22	−0.04	−0.04	−0.06	−0.07	−0.08	−0.09	−0.10	−0.11	−0.13	−0.14	−0.15	−0.17	−0.18
23	−0.40	−0.43	−0.66	−0.76	−0.85	−0.94	−1.03	−1.13	−1.24	−1.34	−1.46	−1.59	−1.72
24	−0.29	−0.29	−0.45	−0.52	−0.58	−0.64	−0.70	−0.76	−0.83	−0.90	−0.98	−1.06	−1.14
25	−0.07	−0.07	−0.11	−0.13	−0.14	−0.16	−0.18	−0.19	−0.21	−0.23	−0.25	−0.27	−0.30
26	−0.07	−0.07	−0.10	−0.12	−0.13	−0.15	−0.16	−0.17	−0.18	−0.20	−0.21	−0.23	−0.24
27	−0.02	−0.03	−0.04	−0.04	−0.06	−0.06	−0.06	−0.07	−0.07	−0.08	−0.09	−0.10	−0.11
28	−0.05	−0.05	−0.08	−0.09	−0.10	−0.11	−0.12	−0.14	−0.15	−0.16	−0.18	−0.19	−0.21
29	0.00	−0.57	−0.64	−0.95	−1.12	−1.27	−1.41	−1.56	−1.70	−1.86	−2.03	−2.21	−2.40
30	−0.06	−0.06	−0.09	−0.11	−0.12	−0.14	−0.15	−0.16	−0.18	−0.20	−0.21	−0.23	−0.25
31	−0.03	−0.04	−0.06	−0.07	−0.07	−0.08	−0.09	−0.11	−0.10	−0.12	−0.13	−0.15	−0.16
32	−0.24	−0.26	−0.40	−0.47	−0.54	−0.61	−0.68	−0.75	−0.84	−0.93	−0.−1.02	−1.14	−1.25
33	−0.04	−0.05	−0.07	−0.08	−0.09	−0.10	−0.11	−0.13	−0.14	−0.15	−0.16	−0.18	−0.19
34	−0.05	−0.05	−0.08	−0.09	−0.10	−0.12	−0.13	−0.14	−0.16	−0.17	−0.19	−0.21	−0.22
35	−0.08	−0.09	−0.14	−0.17	−0.19	−0.22	−0.25	−0.28	−0.32	−0.35	−0.40	−0.45	−0.50
36	−0.05	−0.06	−0.08	−0.10	−0.11	−0.12	−0.13	−0.15	−0.16	−0.17	−0.19	−0.20	−0.22
37	−0.01	−0.01	−0.01	−0.02	−0.02	−0.02	−0.02	−0.03	−0.03	−0.03	−0.04	−0.04	−0.04
FGE	−0.02	−0.02	−0.03	−0.04	−0.04	−0.05	−0.05	−0.06	−0.07	−0.07	−0.08	−0.09	−0.09
SLGE	−0.01	−0.01	−0.01	−0.01	−0.02	−0.02	−0.02	−0.02	−0.02	−0.02	−0.03	−0.03	−0.03
Total	−5.42	−5.67	−8.71	−10.02	−11.27	−12.53	−13.79	−15.09	−16.50	−17.96	−19.53	−21.22	−22.96

If the removal of the perimeter rule results in passenger traffic through Dulles falling initially by 2.2 million then by the year 2010 this means that the region would have employment levels 20 620 lower than would have been expected with the continuation of the rule. If the passenger fall were 3.3 million then potential job loses would be nearly 23 000.

These potential job loses are not spread evenly across all of the sectors of the regional economy. In terms of the sectors most adversely affected, employment directly associated with air transportation would suffer most severely. Under both the 2.2 million initial passenger loss scenarios, there would also be significant potential losses of employment in Business, Engineering and Management Services, in Financial Services and in Eating and Drinking Places.

10.6.3   Overall assessment

The perimeter and high density rules were introduced at National Airport as a device to assist in the integrated development of the Washington DC airport system. The perimeter rule has served to facilitate the development of Washington Dulles International Airport and as a mechanism for limiting the environmental intrusiveness of air transport on the nation's capital. Removing the regulation governing the geographical markets served by National Airport will have implications for other local airports and for the vitality of several elements of the local economy.

The study, making use of expert judgment, econometric modeling and input-output analysis, develops a counterfactual forecast of what would happen if National Airport's perimeter rule were retained in its present form. Against this are set a number of alternative scenarios reflecting the potential impact of removing the perimeter rule on passengers and employment levels at Washington Dulles International Airport and the wider economic implications of this on the regional economy.

Much of the impact will depend upon the extent to which airlines will divert their long range, domestic services to Reagan National Airport as a result of the ending of the perimeter rule and the degree to which Dulles Airport will lose international traffic.

At the micro level the analysis indicates that it could take past 2010 for the airport population at Washington Dulles International Airport to return to its 1997 level of activity. At the macro level, the multi-staged, sequential modeling process indicates that as many as 5 420 jobs could be lost in the short term to the regional economy as a result of traffic diverting from Dulles to National Airport, a figure that rises to 22 960 by the year 2010. The sectors most likely to be affected include those concerned with the tourist industry and service sector companies, especially in the information technology sector.

These calculations only take into account the direct effects of the possible complete relaxation of Reagan National Airport's perimeter rules. These calculations do not embrace jobs lost as a result of firms feeling that inadequate air transport services in the Dulles area make it a much less desirable site for their offices and plant. In other words, they do not allow for any disincentive effects that a diminished quality of airline services may have on firms that may have considered location in the Northern Virginia region or on the implications for existing firms that may think about the need to expand in the area.

10.7 THE WIDER SPATIAL ECONOMIC EFFECTS

The main focus in this analysis is on the demand side for air transportation and on the additional welfare benefits that those living in a hub city enjoy from the air transportation services provided and the degree to which these services attract additional employment (the tertiary effect). Quantifying the benefits users enjoy from residing in a hub city is a difficult process. There are two basic methods that can be employed.

Direct, stated preference methods are gradually emerging in economics. They have their background in market research and are particularly useful for some types of forecasting. At one level these simply involve asking affected parties about the role that an airport plays in their commercial decision making (e.g., regarding location, markets served and scale of activities) and the air travel that is undertaken.[21]

More advanced stated preference techniques, through a series of carefully structured questionnaires related to a series of scenarios, provide information about what residents want from their local airport in the context of what they are willing to pay. Comparisons can then be made with what is actually taking place.

Designing the questionnaire with this approach is a difficult task, and there are potential problems in selecting an appropriate sample. There is always an inherent danger that respondents will try to manipulate their answers to their advantage rather than give a genuine reply. For example, businessmen may try to manipulate their responses to obtain lower fares but at the same time try to get better services at the expense of other air traveling groups.

More common in economic and business analysis are revealed preference techniques. These techniques seek to explore benefit levels by looking at what is actually happening and the way the local economy is responding to current conditions. This involves the use of statistical procedures that can become complex, but it is based upon hard data and is a well-tried approach. It is the revealed preference approach that is adopted for the empirical work here.

The revealed preference method can be applied at the level of the individual but this requires large samples and is costly. These problems can be circumvented by looking one stage farther down the line at the economic performance of the region or city in which a hub is located. Essentially, if being close to a hub airport means higher incomes for the area or more employment, this is a mirror image of the travel benefits enjoyed by individuals and companies.

10.7.1 An overview picture

One method of assessing the benefits of being a hub city is in terms of directly contrasting the economic performance of cities that have hub airports with those that do not. One would expect, all other factors being taken into consideration, that hub cities would enjoy a superior economic performance as a result of the superior services enjoyed by their business travelers.

This macro-level analysis can offer useful insights but it also has its limitations. In particular, there are many things that influence the economic performance of a city other than simply the nature of its links with the scheduled air transport system. It is possible, by using standard statistical procedures, to make adjustments for many of these factors and to tease out some information concerning the role of hubs. In doing this it is helpful to pay particular attention to those aspects of cities' economies that are likely to be most tightly tied to the availability of high quality scheduled air services.

---

[21] An example is Coley/Forrest Inc. (n.d).

Air transport is used by all categories of business but has become particularly important for those engaged in new economy high-technology activities.[22] It has been estimated that those employed in the high-technology sector fly over 1.6 times as much as those in traditional industries.[23] Companies in this general area conduct activities requiring considerable interpersonal contacts. These contacts are only possible with high quality transport.

To examine the benefits for any areas in terms of job creation in these more dynamic sectors, the analysis examines the new economy employment in large US cities as it is linked to the provision of scheduled air transport services. Defining high-technology industries is not simple. Here a revised version of the well tested Armington index is deployed. This is a fairly broad definition but has been widely used in industrial analysis (Stough *et al.*, 1996).

This index looks at clusterings of new economy employment. In consequence, it avoids the often distorted picture that can be drawn when reference is made to the role of a single dominant high-technology company in a region. From a longer term planning perspective there are also advantages of not being a 'company town.'[24]

A multiple regression model is employed that takes variations in high-technology employment across all 321 US Metropolitan Statistical Areas (MSAs) in 1994 as the phenomenan to be explained. It is found that the location of a hub airport (as defined by the Federal Aviation Administration, there are 56 hubs) in these areas provides a positive and statistically significant explanation for that variation. In other words, it appears that, as a generalization, having a hub airport close by attracts and facilitates new economy high-technology jobs in a metropolitan area.

The calculations enable a rough calculation of the high-technology job stimulus that being close to a hub airport provides. Put into concrete, quantitative terms, the calculations indicate that the existence of a hub airport in a region increases that region's new economy employment by over 12 000. This does not, of course, mean that all hub regions benefit by this amount but it is an average across hub cities.

In doing this analysis, allowance was made for differences in the population sizes of the areas, number of Fortune 500 companies with headquarters, housing values, highway density, per capita defense expenditure and percentage of employment in business services. The model set out in Equation 10.2 explains over 64% of the variation in high-technology employment across metropolitan areas.

---

[22]   Evidence from earlier studies indicates that good transport is a necessary but not always a sufficient attribute to attract high technology industry to an area; see Button (1987a).

[23]   Simat, Helliesen and Eichner Inc.

[24]   For example, Gateway is based in South Dakota some way from a major hub. This clearly does not affect its performance but equally does not affect any wider argument about the importance of hubs. The key point is that not all high technology undertakings require proximity to hubs to be successful, but rather that many do.

Ln high-technology employment = 5.407* + 0.503 hub airport* + 0.033 Fortune
500 companies* + 0.115 ln housing values +
1.354 ln highway density* + 0.141 ln defense
expenditure* + 2.845 ln service employment*
+ 1.405 ln population size*   (10.2)

*denotes statistical significance at 99% confidence level; n = 303; R^2 = 0.643.

Further support for the strength of these findings is that other variables in the
model behave in ways consistent with broader studies of new economy high-
technology developments. Employment in the sector is found to be related
positively to defense expenditure in the urban area and to the quality of the local
highway system. It also rises with the number of corporate headquarters located in
a city.

10.7.2   Case study analysis

Macro studies are useful in looking at the general picture, but to gain more
detailed information regarding the benefits of being a hub city it is helpful to
conduct case studies. This involves examining developments in a limited number
of locations in more detail. The results of this may not have complete
applicability elsewhere, but careful selection of the cases can minimize this
problem.

For comparative purposes five medium-sized airports (two of them generally
recognized as hubs and three as non-hubs[25]) were selected for more detailed
scrutiny. The airports were chosen so that they serve similar, medium-sized urban
communities. The hub airports had only one major carrier; this criterion was to
simplify the analysis, but the general conclusions that are subsequently drawn
would seem at least as applicable to a multiple airline hub airport city.

The hub airport cities chosen are discussed below.

10.7.2.1 Cincinnati

The Cincinnati metropolitan area includes Ohio, Kentucky, and Indiana. The
region is approximately 100 miles southwest of Ohio's capital, Columbus. With a
population base of 1.6 million, Cincinnati is ranked 31st among the 315
metropolitan areas in the US. Per capita personal income for the region was
estimated to be $25 359 in 1996, ranking it 65th in the country, approximately $1
000 above the national average. The average annual growth rate of per capita
personal income in Cincinnati over the past 10 years was 5.3% compared to the
national growth rate of 4.9%.

Earnings contributed 65.7% of the total personal income which was estimated
at $40.4 billion in 1996. Earnings of persons employed in Cincinnati increased
from $16.7 billion in 1986 to $30.1 billion in 1996. The largest industries in
1996 were services, non-durable goods manufacturing, and durable goods
manufacturing – a structure that has remained consistent over the last decade.

---

[25]   Although Nashville was a mini-hub for American Airlines for part of the time
period and has, thus, been treated differently in the analysis to the other cities.

Manufacturing of durable goods was the slowest growing industry between 1986 and 1996 (increasing at an approximate average annual rate of 2%) while the finance, insurance, and real estate sector grew at the fastest rate with an average annual growth rate of 10.1%. This sector contributed 7.6% of earnings in 1996.

In 1994, the metropolitan region had 12% of its workers employed in the high-technology sector. Employment in business services was 37% of the total employment. It appears that the combination of the service and technology sectors provide high potential for future growth. The regional unemployment rate was moderate at 4.8% in 1994–5.

Cincinnati-Northern Kentucky International Airport handled some 10.1 million enplanements in 1997. It is a major Delta Air Lines hub with the carrier (jointly with subsidiary Comair) being responsible for some 95% (9 625 377) of enplanements in 1997. About 22% of enplanements and 32% of deplanements involved business travelers. The airport went through a period of major new construction during 1992 to 1994. The airport was estimated to be directly responsible in 1996 for some 10 000 jobs and a further 60 000 full- and part-time jobs in the community (Center for Economic Education, University of Cincinnati, 1997).

10.7.2.2 Pittsburgh

The Pittsburgh metropolitan area is located in the foothills of the Allegheny Mountains and is about 100 miles south of Lake Erie. The city of Pittsburgh was historically built on deposits of rich bituminous coal. The population of the Pittsburgh metropolitan region is 2.4 million, ranking it 19th in the nation. In 1996, the per capita personal income in Pittsburgh was $25 359, ranking it 65th in the US. In 1986, the per capita personal income of Pittsburgh was $14 900 and ranked Pittsburgh 99th in the US. The average annual growth rate of per capita personal income in Pittsburgh over the past 10 years was 5.5%.

Total personal income in 1996 was estimated to be $60.2 billion. While total personal income rankings are not the best instrument for comparing economies as they are not normalized by population or employment, they still provide a good picture of the regional economic structure. Pittsburgh was ranked 23rd in the nation on the basis of total personal income. Earnings contributed 61.6% of total personal income, dividends, interest, and rent were 18.2%, and transfer payments were 20.2%.

Earnings of persons employed in Pittsburgh increased from $24.1 billion in 1986 to $40.2 billion in 1996. The largest industries in 1996 were services, 32.6% of earnings; durable goods manufacturing, 13.0%; and retail trade, 9.2%. This structure has remained consistent even though the contribution of each sector has undergone some change. Construction was the slowest growing industry from 1986 to 1996 (average annual growth rate of 2.4%) while finance, insurance, and real estate, with 7.1% of earnings in 1996, grew the fastest at an average annual growth rate of 8.2%.

In 1994, the metropolitan region had over 8% of its workers employed activities associated with new economy activities. Employment in business services was 43% of the total employment. The regional unemployment rate was 6.3% in 1994–5.

Pittsburgh International Airport has a new airport terminal located 16 miles from the downtown area which opened in 1992. This airport is a long-standing and a major hub of US Airways with the carrier responsible for 90% (9,341,875) of the enplaned passengers in 1997. The second carrier, Delta Air Lines, had 6% of enplanements. The airports, located in a city of 2.37 million residents, had total enplanements of 10.4 million in 1997. Of the 20,760 thousand passengers passing through the airport in 1997, some 70% were in transit.[26]

The three non-hub airport urban areas are:

10.7.2.3 Nashville

The Nashville metropolitan area is located on the Cumberland River in the northwestern corner of the Nashville Basin. The population of the metropolitan region is 1.15 million ranking it 49th in the nation. In 1996, Nashville had a per capita personal income of $26 262, ranking it 51st in the US. Per capita income grew at an average annual rate of 5.6% over the past 10 years, being $15 220 in 1996 (ranking Nashville 82nd in the nation).

In 1996, total personal income was $29.3 billion ranking Nashville 49th in the US. The average annual growth rate of total personal income over the past 10 years was 7.6% in Nashville, compared to 5.9% for the nation. Earnings were 73.1% of total personal income; dividends, interest, and rent were 14.4%, and transfer payments were 12.5%.

Total earnings of persons employed in Nashville increased from $11.3 billion in 1986 to $23.3 billion in 1996. The largest industries in 1996 were services, 33.3% of earnings; retail trade, 10.9%; and durable goods manufacturing. Among the industries that accounted for at least 5% of earnings in 1996, the slowest growing was construction, which increased at an average annual rate of 4.6%, and the fastest was services, which increased at an average annual rate of 10.6%.

In 1994, the metropolitan region had 39% of its total employment in the business sector. The regional unemployment rate was 3.2% in 1994/5.

Nashville's airport handled 3.82 million enplanements. Southwest had nearly 32% (1 212 649) of enplanements in 1997 with American Airlines having 16% (632 033) and Delta Air Lines 15% (599 342) of the market share. In the recent past (1985–94) Nashville had been a secondary hub for American Airlines.

10.7.2.4 Milwaukee

The Milwaukee-Waukesha metropolitan area is located on the west shore of Lake Michigan, 80 miles north of Chicago. The population of the Milwaukee-Waukesha metropolitan region is 1.45 million, ranking it 38th in the nation. In 1996, Milwaukee-Waukesha had a per capita personal income of $27 202, ranking it 38th in the nation. Per capita income has grown at an average annual rate of 5.2% over the past 10 years.

Total personal income in Milwaukee-Waukesha was estimated at $39.5 billion in 1996 (this ranked it 34th in the US). Total personal income grew at an average annual rate of 5.7% over the past 10 years compared to 5.9 for the nation.

---

[26]   This estimate is derived from the USDOT 10% ticket sample and may be an underestimate because it does not capture passengers who hub at a city but are not on a through ticket.

Earnings were 66.6% of total personal income; dividends, interest, and rent were 19.0%; and transfer payments were 14.5%. From 1986 to 1996, earnings increased on average 5.7% each year; dividends, interest, and rent increased on average 5.7%; and transfer payments increased on average 5.6%.

Earnings of persons employed in Milwaukee-Waukesha increased from $16.6 billion in 1986 to $29.2 billion in 1996, an average annual growth rate of 5.8%. The largest industries are services, 27.1% of earnings; durable goods manufacturing, 19.2%; and finance, insurance, and real estate, 9.1%.

There has been some structural change in the economic base with decline of the durable goods manufacturing industry that had been the most important industry in 1986. Among the industries that accounted for at least 5% of earnings, the slowest growing was transportation and public utilities (5.4% of earnings in 1996), that increased at an average annual rate of 3.8%. In comparison the fastest growing was finance, insurance, and real estate, that increased at an average annual rate of 8.6%.

The technology sector employs about 79 000 employees. Service sector employment is about 39.5% with a low unemployment rate of 4.5%. Further, six Fortune 500 companies have headquarters in the region.

Milwaukee General Mitchell International Airport handled 2.8 million enplanements in 1997. The main carriers are Midwest Express with 26% (733 790) of enplanements, Northwest with 22% (625 077) and Delta with 7% (202 779) in 1997. It has been estimated that the airport is directly responsible for nearly 5,000 jobs and indirectly for another 1,660 with a further 3 260 jobs being associated with the local purchases made by firms dependent on the airport and another 17,000 from visitor industry jobs through visitors arriving at the airport (Martin Associates, 1997).

10.7.2.5 Indianapolis

Indianapolis enjoyed a per capita personal income of $25 898 in 1996. This personal per capita income ranked it 56th in the US The average annual growth rate of per capita personal income over the past 10 years was 5.5%. In 1996, Indianapolis had a total personal income of $38 million, up from $20 million in 1986. In 1996, earnings were 71.1% of total income (compared with 71.2% in 1986); dividends, interest, and rent were 16.2% (compared with 16.5% in 1986); and transfer payments were 12.7% (compared with 12.3% in 1986). From 1986 to 1996, earnings increased on average 6.6% each year; dividends, interest, and rent increased on average 6.4%; and transfer payments increased on average 7.0%.

The Indianapolis MSA has several educational institutions including Indiana-Purdue University and University of Indianapolis.

Indianapolis International Airport has 183 flights a day. The main air carriers at Indianapolis are United Air Lines and US Airways; Delta, Continental and Southwest also have a significant presence. Of the 7 177 thousand total passenger movements through the airport in 1997, the US Department of Transportation 10% ticket sample survey designates 89% as either originating in or destined for Indianapolis.

In summary, the five urban areas served by the study airports are medium sized, free-standing cities. Their populations have generally grown over the past decade. The performance of the local economies of the five case study cities has fluctuated in recent years in terms of both income and employment (Figure 10.2). In part this is attributable to cycles in the national economy, and local fluctuations largely mirror these, but it also reflects local effects. Since temporal changes in the demand for air travel are closely related to income movements (Boeing Airplane Co., 1997), to assess the importance of these airports to their regional account must be taken of these local differences.[27] Figure 10.3 offers time series data on passenger traffic at the airports.

Structurally, all the urban areas in the study have followed the general national trend in that manufacturing employment has fallen consistently over the past 20 years. It now only constitutes between 12.8% and 18.8% of jobs in the US. The main employment growth in all the cases has been in service sector employment, again reflecting the longer term structural adjustment of the US as it has moved in the 'New Economy' age.

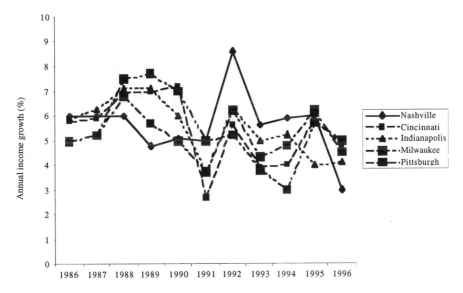

Figure 10.2 Growth in income in case study areas

---

[27] The issue of causality is a vexing one and is considered later in the chapter.

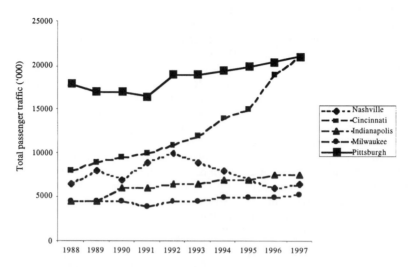

Table 10.3 Passenger traffic at case study airports

Simple comparison of the five airports provides some indication of the higher quality of service that residents of areas adjacent to Cincinnati and Pittsburgh enjoy. Table 10.7, for instance, gives details of the various destinations that are serviced for the five airports. The hubs offer both more direct services and international services than do the non-hub flights.[28]

[28]   Some indication of the general importance of international air services for New Economy employment can be gleaned from an ordinary least-squares regression relating the number of such jobs in 40 US metropolitan regions with varying degrees of international service. The results are:

$$HT = -23257.8 + 0.021POP + 3965.35\text{Ln}ENP + 6122.41\text{Ln}DEST + 0.559MIL - 1235.91TZ + 0.0015TENP \qquad R^2 = 0.82$$

where: *HT* is new economy employment in 1996; *POP* is the population of the surrounding Metropolitan Standard Area in 1996; *ENP* is the logarithm of the number of European on-plane passengers in 1994; *DEST* is the number of European airports served in 1994; *MIL* is military expenditure in 1996; *TZ* is the time zone (East Coast Standard Time = 0); *TENP* is total enplanements in 1994; and Ln represents a variable expressed in natural logarithms

The coefficients by and large take signs that are intuitively sensible. (A number of other variables were tested but added nothing significant to the model fit and were omitted.) In the context of the availability of air transportation, the three key variables all have positive coefficients. The total enplanements variable is small but this may be expected since much of the air transportation affect is taken up by the international dimension of the equation. There is a tendency for larger airports to have more international activities. With regard to international air services, the associated coefficients for both on-plane passengers and the number of destinations served take positive signs. They exert a positive influence on the attractiveness of regions to new economy employers. As important for confirming the robustness of the specification

Table 10.7 Services from the case study airports

Airport	Domestic	International
Pittsburgh	105	8
Cincinnati	102	8
Milwaukee	90	1
Nashville	83	2
Indianapolis	45	6

Inspection of trends in high-technology employment in the five case study locations (Figure 10.4) shows the more rapid and even growth in high-technology jobs in those areas with hub airports. While Milwaukee has seen some growth since the mid-1980s, this has been demonstrably slower than either Pittsburgh or Cincinnati. Indianapolis has also seen growth in its new economy employment numbers but Pittsburgh has been steadily pulling away from it and Cincinnati has gradually, albeit slowly, been catching up. Nashville, which has fluctuated between being a hub and not being a hub has seen a rather erratic growth path.

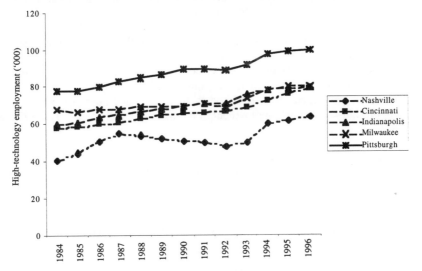

Figure 10.4 Trends in high-technology employment

While the tables are insightful, they cannot allow for variations in the nature of the different cities. The selection of the hub and non-hub cities was designed to

is the fact that variables such as the overall level of air service, population and military employment are positive as would be anticipated.

allow comparisons with similar, medium-sized cities but they are not identical. Further statistical analysis makes additional adjustments for this.

A simple basic model indicates that, in terms of airline traffic, when allowance is made for per capita income differences and levels of high-technology employ-ment, there is more air traffic associated with the hub airport cities than with the non-hubs. Holding these variables constant, Pittsburgh has a significantly higher volume than Cincinnati, with Nashville and Milwaukee, respectively, lagging behind. In detail the model is estimated using ordinary least squares and the preferred specification is (Equation 10.3):

Ln enplanements = 6.99 + 0.97 ln per capita income* + 0.23 ln high-technology
                    jobs + 0.58 Pittsburgh* – 0.58 Indianapolis* – 0.92
                    Milwaukee* - 0.14 Nashville   (10.3)

*denotes statistical significance at 99% confidence level; n = 40, R^2 = 0.96, n = 40. Cincinnati was taken as the base variable. The estimation adjusts for variations in the size of the different cities (heteroscedastcity).

The Nashville variable takes a negative coefficient in the analysis (i.e. there are less enplanements than at Cincinnati, holding other things constant) and while this is not statistically significant, it does require comment. One explanation for this is that the city's airport was formerly an American Airlines mini-hub and, therefore, while not proving commercially viable in this role, nevertheless offers a relatively high quality of service to residents.

One other implicit factor that may account for this pattern of use is the larger number of domestic and international destinations that the hub airports offer when compared to the non-hubs.

As with the macro level of analysis, one can also focus on the creation of high-technology employment in the various urban areas. Again linear regression analysis was performed looking at the factors that have been important in the growth of high-technology employment in the five case study areas. The estimated parameters are:

Ln high-technology employment = – 3.25 + 1.48 ln per capita income * – 0.07
                                  time* + 0.12 hub dummy* – 0.75 Nashville
                                  dummy*   (10.4)

* denotes statistical significance at 99% confidence level; n = 40, R^2 = 0.980. Cincinnati and Milwaukee were taken as the base variable. The estimation adjusts for heteroscedastcity.

The findings for the period to 1997 are that, allowing for factors such as differences in personal income, the particular issue of Nashville and a time path, the existence of a hub airport has exercised a positive and statistically significant effect on the industrial composition of Cincinnati and Pittsburgh. In other words, the effect of a city being a hub, and irrespective of the total volume of airline traffic passing through it, still attract more high-technology employment than a comparable non-hub.

Correlation between variables does not of itself imply causation in any meaningful sense. The econometric literature is full of impressive correlations which are spurious or meaningless. These could include a positive correlation between teachers' salaries and the consumption of alcohol and a superb positive correlation between the death rate in the UK and the proportion of marriages solemnized in the Church of England.

In the case of hubs it could be argued that the economic growth that has been demonstrated at hub airport cities is due not to the services offered by the airlines but rather to the fact that the airlines have moved to these locations simply to exploit strong, natural economic growth. The direction of causation can, however, be tested for. The techniques are not definitive and are somewhat technical.[29]

For Cincinnati, traffic data from 1979 to 1997 are employed. The variable used in the analysis is total passenger traffic by year.[30] The Granger causality test to examine the direction of causality between passenger traffic and indicators of economic health such as per capita income, total income, and employment is used.[31]

Results for the Cincinnati area show that airline passenger traffic has a positive effect on employment in the local metropolitan statistical area. The causal effect of passenger traffic on employment is a reasonable proposition as it signifies increase in demand and earnings that have a multiplier effect in employment. Technically, the test is to see if air traffic does not Granger cause employment; the resultant F-statistic of 6.328, at a probability level of 0.0148, implies that this can be rejected with 95% confidence. Indicating the causality is almost certainly the other way. While increases in passenger traffic may have positive effects on per capita incomes, these are not so evident with the two-year time lags that we used to test for causality. In the short run, employment impacts are more evident than earnings or income effects.

Similar results are found for Pittsburgh. There is again evidence to support the thesis that airline passenger traffic causes employment. Technically, the test is to see if air traffic does not Granger cause employment; the resultant F-statistic of 6.328, at a probability level of 0.0148, implies that this can be rejected with 95% confidence, indicating the causality is almost certainly the other way.

What these econometric calculations show is that increases in air passenger traffic at the hub airports has a positive effect on employment in the surrounding

---

[29]   The Granger (1969) approach to the question of whether x causes y is to see how much of the current y can be explained by past values of y and then to see whether adding lagged values of x can improve the explanation. y is said to be Granger-caused by x if x helps in the prediction of y, or equivalently if the coefficients on the lagged xs are statistically significant. It is important to note that the statement x Granger causes y does not imply that y is the effect or the result of x. Granger causality measures precedence and information content but does not by itself indicate causality in the more common use of the term.

[30]   The data were obtained from the Airports Council International, North America.

[31]   Due to definitional problems, it is not possible to extend the analysis to look exclusively at high-technology employment before 1987.

metropolitan statistical areas. As traffic in hub airports in general is more than at other airports, when controlled for population and other characteristics, it can be inferred that hub airport cities accrue greater economic benefits than non-hub airport cities.

10.8   CONCLUSIONS

Considerable changes have taken place in commercial passenger air transport since the enactment of the 1978 Airline Deregulation Act in the US and the deregulation of airline networks that has occurred elsewhere. The commercial and operational freedoms, as we have seen in earlier chapters, now afforded airlines have resulted in most of the larger carriers developing hub-and-spoke networks.

These radial forms of network have benefited both passengers and airlines. An important issue is the extent to which those living close to hubs, and especially business travelers, pay a premium for that advantage. There are arguments that these people, and especially business users, pay more for air services as a result of their needing to use a hub. The evidence for this, which is not conclusive, is not explored here, rather the concern is with whether these people benefit from their proximity to a hub airport.

Looking at it from a macro, national perspective (i.e. across the set of US Metropolitan Statistical Areas), after initially adjusting for as many other factors as possible, that proximity to an airport hub has important structural advantages for the local economy. The evidence is that it is a stimulus for high-technology jobs to grow in the region.

Exploring a number of case study cities in more detail produces a similar set of findings. This indicates that there are major benefits to be gained by a city in terms of attracting high grade employment and, *ipso facto*, income from being a hub city.

Importantly, it has been shown that the link between jobs and airport services at hub cities flows from the air transport input to the creation of employment and not the other way round. In other words, hubs create employment rather than airlines selecting cities as hubs simply because they are already economically dynamic.

11   AIR FREIGHT TRANSPORT

11.1 INTRODUCTION

It is only a few years ago that freight transportation was relegated to a few pages in most transport books, and even then the emphasis was largely on road, rail and sea modes. The industry was by and large heavily regulated and the sector was generally seen as moribund. New ideas about regulation, the growth of new industries requiring different service attributes and changes in transportation itself, including the introduction of larger aircraft, have revised this situation.

Recent years have seen considerable liberalization of freight transport markets. While the removal of quantity regulation from the UK road haulage sector in 1968 was the first significant action in this movement, the early reforms regarding air transport came in 1977 with regulatory changes in the US.[1] These liberalization measures represented a change in a major world transport market and offered ample demonstration effects indicating positive benefits can accrue from freeing markets of price and quantity controls.

Subsequently the 'deregulation' process has moved from North America, to western Europe, to the transition economies of eastern and central Europe; to the newly industrializing countries (NICS) of Asia and South America and, partly due to the influence of the World Bank, to Third World nations. New Zealand, Canada and Australia have also engaged in large-scale deregulation and privatization that extends beyond their transportation systems.

The aim of this chapter is to focus specifically on the regulation of the air cargo transport industry. It is not all-embracing in its coverage.[2] As with the earlier chapters that dealt mainly with passenger transportation, it looks in particular at economic regulation and gives only limited space to technical regulation and to the detailed consideration of safety and environmental regulation. The global nature of much of the emerging air freight transport sector means that

---

[1]   Deregulation of US trucking came in 1980 with the Motor Carriers Reform Act. Effective liberalization of the rail market came with the Railroad Revitalization and Regulatory Reform Act of 1976 and the Staggers Act of 1980.

[2]   It is also not global in its coverage but focuses mainly on the developments in the US, in Australia and in Europe. This is partly due to space considerations but also, unlike many other areas of deregulation, liberalization of air cargo markets has brought about complex structural changes in addition to price and quantity effects. Many of the changes are comparatively recent and are taking time to manifest themselves as markets adjust.

there is a high level of technical commonality. This is particularly so in the industrialized countries. Aircraft are produced by a limited number of suppliers that have an economic incentive to minimize variations in their products. International agencies, such as the International Civil Aviation Organization (ICAO) of the UN, stipulate technical standards and many operational procedures. While there are many on-going debates concerning technical matters, the main regulatory issues impacting on trade in air cargo services revolve around the institutional environment in which air freight transport is provided.

The chapter initially provides some background information about the air caro sector and its recent developments. It provides some details of why air freight transportation has had a tradition of being a heavily regulated industry, both in terms of international activities and often also with regard to domestic operations. It then moves on to look at the nature of the regulatory reforms that have been taking place, and at the implications of these reforms for the market for air cargo services. Since air cargo transport interacts with air passenger transportation the overlapping nature of regulatory change has been important. Air cargo services, for instance, often use the same airports as passenger services and a large amount of air freight is carried in the belly-hold of commercial passenger planes or in combi-aircraft.[3]

11.2 THE AIR CARGO MARKET

The air cargo market has grown steadily over the post war period. The availability of aircraft after the end of the Second World War that were capable of carrying a significant payload moved air cargo transport away from its role as primarily a postal service supplier. Advances in technology have considerably changed this picture and air transportation is now the preferred mode for many commodities.

The bulk of the world's air cargo (freight and mail) is now carried by combination airlines engaged in scheduled and non-scheduled operations. These carried about

---

[3]   The reforms in other freight transport modes (e.g., trucking and railroads) have, in some circumstances, affect air freight transport. The liberal trucking regulations in the UK, for example, mean that virtually all domestic 'air freight' goes by road. In the US the liberalization of trucking permitted the full development of integrated air cargo operation by Federal Express and others.

Additionally, there have been reforms in sectors that have a demand for air freight services. In particular, these often involve permitting private carriage of packages and mail that had formerly been the monopoly of a state postal system. This has been a stimulus to the growth of express parcel services but has also meant that, as a result of market pressures, there has been the need for traditional postal services to improve their own air freight operations. The UK's Royal Mail's Skynet, for instance, employs ten airlines to operate reroutes centered on Liverpool and East Midlands airports in the UK.

75% of the world's total air cargo in 1996 (in freight tonne kilometers). Approximately 50% of this total was performed using the belly compartments of passenger aircraft, the remaining 25% being carried on freighter aircraft belonging to combination carriers. Air cargo operations conducted by combination carriers are predominantly long-haul, often assisted by feeder services. The balance of the world air cargo – approximately 25% of the total in the late 1990s– was carried by specialized all-cargo airlines and integrated express operators.

More recent developments indicate that the sector's growth will, if anything, accelerate in the future. Whilst, as we have seen in Chapter 4, it is not easy to forecast future trends in air transport, all predictions are that this growth will at the very least continue and probably at a pace faster than envisaged for passenger aviation (e.g., Figure 11.1 provides the projections from the Boeing company to 2015).

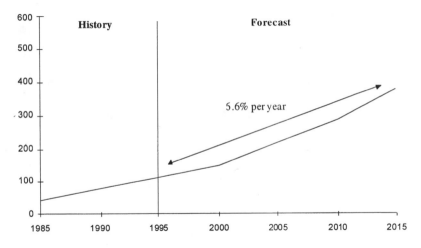

Figure 11.1 Growth in the air cargo market, billions of FTKs, 1985–2015

One reason for this projected growth rate is simply that the demand for freight transportation in general will expand as economies and trade grow. Additionally, the world demand for air cargo services is in the midst of a shift from a 'premium' to a 'mass' transportation market. The air cargo industry is no longer just a premium transportation service, offering highly customized remedies to the deficiencies of the postal system on the one hand, and to the specific transportation needs of perishable, urgent or precious goods on the other hand. It offers a range of services to meet customer's needs.

As recently as in the late 1980s, air freightable goods were perishables of all kinds (e.g., seafood, newspapers and luxury garments), urgent items (medicines, spare parts), or highly valuable goods (gold, jewellery, computers, aerospace products). In contrast, in the late 1990s, the range of air transported products has widened, growth rates in the total market have been determined by economic conditions and by the gradual reduction in trade tariffs.[4]

By weight, the most important air freight commodities are machinery parts, electronics, high tech instruments, cut flowers, live trees/plants, fish, crustaceans, vehicle parts, plastic, consumer durables, apparel, and footwear. Figure 11.2, gives details of the main commodities imported into and exported from the US that are transported by air freight. Overall, as a result of these trends, air transportation of lower-value goods, as well as their share in total air transportation, has reportedly increased since 1993 - the latest year for which formal data is available.

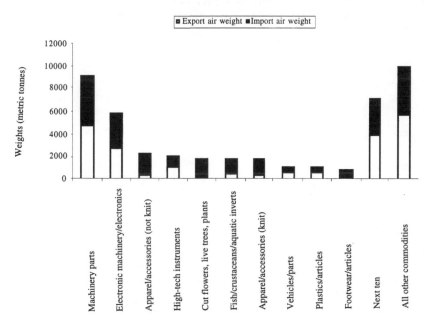

Figure 11.2 US air freight by weight imported into and exported from the US in 1995 (ranked by combined total weight of air exports and imports)

[4]　　Another way of looking at this is in terms of the percentage share of US exports and imports transported by air according to their value group; the table below is for 1993.

Value/weigh groups (US$ per kg):	over $16	$14–16	$12–14	$10–12	$8–10	($0–2)
Air-traded exports (%)	52	10	48	8	5	(0.06)
Air-traded imports (%)	26	10	7	3	2	(0.01)

As pointed out in Chapter 1, air cargo providers are a heterogeneous group offering a variety of logistical services. This is a significant change over two decades ago. A variety of factors, on the demand and the supply sides, have caused this. Of prime importance have been changes in institutional structures and the adoption of new technologies and management techniques. Further, the flows of air cargo are are geographically concentrated with the main flows on the North Atlantic, between Europe and the Far East and in the Pacific Rim. The US dominates the global market but its share of RTKs has declined since the 1970s (Table 11.1).

Table 11.1 Air cargo volumes by market segment, millions RTKs

	1980	(%)	1985	(%)	1990	(%)	1995	(%)
US Domestic								
Scheduled freight	4 780	14.0	4 579	9.8	5 253	7.0	4 576	4.2
Charter freight	425	1.2	1 131	2.4	616	0.8	363	0.3
Mail	1 378.6	4.0	1 768	3.8	2 175	2.9	2 781	2.5
Express carriers	455	1.3	2 383	5.1	6 428	8.5	11 275	2.5
Total domestic	7 039	20.7	9 860	21.1	14 472	19.2	18 997	17.4
US International								
Scheduled freight	3 602	10.6	4 202	9.0	7 966	10.6	11 943	10.9
Charter freight	742	2.2	845	1.8	1 974	2.6	3 120	2.9
Mail	581	1.7	647	1.4	748	0.9	772	0.7
US Total								
Scheduled freight	8 382	24.6	8 781	18.8	13 219	17.5	16 521	15.1
Charter freight	1 167	3.4	1 976	4.2	2 590	3.4	3 483	3.2
Mail	1 959	5.8	2 415	5.2	2 923	3.9	3 513	3.2
Express carriers	455	1.3	2 383	5.1	6 428	8.5	11 275	2.5
Grand US total	11 964	35.1	15 555	33.2	25 160	33.3	34 832	31.9
Europe								
Scheduled freight	8 244	24.2	11 737	25.1	17 465	23.1	23 977	22.0
Scheduled mail	601	1.8	767	1.6	885	1.2	971	0.8
Scheduled total	8 845	26.0	12 504	26.7	18 350	24.3	24 948	22.9
Asia and Pacific								
Scheduled freight	5 789	17.0	10 312	22.0	19 400	25.7	30 216	27.7
Scheduled mail	292	0.9	422	0.9	927	1.2	868	0.8
Scheduled total	6 081	17.9	10 734	22.9	20 327	26.9	31 984	28.5
Total non-US scheduled	19 582	57.5	29 209	62.4	46 741	61.9	67 147	61.5
Total non-US charter	2 516	7.4	2 056	4.4	3 556	4.7	7 174	6.6
Total non-US cargo	22 097	64.9	31 265	66.8	50 287	66.7	74 321	68.1
Total world air cargo	34 061	100.0	46 820	100.0	75 457	100.0	109 153	100.0

Many air carrier markets outside the US are dominated by flag carriers that are protected by government or are state-owned. In Europe, for example, prior to the recent deregulation movement, over 90% of RTKs was performed by the national flag carrier (Table 11.2). In the UK where British Airways was an exception, only about 51% was performed by British Airways. While there has been a trend towards greater market concentration in the US passenger market, large carriers do because of the number of non-scheduled specialist charter cargo operators that serve markets where scheduled operations are constrained.

Table 11.2 Air freight traffic in Europe by market segment, 1993

Carrier	Country	% of country's air freight RTK	% of freight on pax services within Europe		European freight as % of total scheduled freight	
			RTKs	Tonnes	RTKs	Tonnes
Aer Lingus	Ireland	100.0	61.7	53.0	11.9	52.1
Air France	France	97.4	94.6	98.1	1.3	9.2
Alitalia	Italy	99.4	79.4	78.3	3.6	17.8
Austrian Air	Austria	66.9	100.0	100.0	22.8	63.7
British Airways	UK	50.6	100.0	100.0	2.9	17.3
Finnair	Finland	99.7	71,8	70.7	12.7	40.6
Iberia	Spain	98.2	65.2	73.8	8.1	22.7
KLM	Netherlands	100.0	61.9	64.7	2.7	19.4
Lufthansa	Germany	99.9	69.0	72.9	3.1	17.5
Luxair	Luxembourg	90.0	10.0	100.0	100.0	100.0
Olympic	Greece	100.0	100.0	100.0	31.9	36.5
Sabena	Belgium	100.0	100.0	100.0	4.6	24.2
SAS	Scandinavia	95.4	100.0	100.0	11.1	40.4
TAP	Portugal	99.8	99.4	99.4	18.8	40.4

Source: Association of European Airlines (1994).

Table 11.3 Top 10 air freight carriers, 1993

Rank	Carrier	Country	Scheduled freight tonnes carried ('000s)
1	Lufthansa	Germany	737
2	Federal Express	US	557
3	Air France	France	547
4	Korean	South Korea	492
5	KLM	Netherlands	478
6	Singapore	Singapore	467
7	JAL	Japan	432
8	British Airways	UK	429
9	Cathay Pacific	Hong Kong	388
10	Northwest	US	316

Integrated carriers are now a major and growing part of the air freight transport sector. They are not only extensive users of information networks; they also make use of diverse transport networks. Express/courier carriers started with the overnight delivery of paper mail and small parcels. They use dedicated, well performing multimodal transport networks. For higher speed and reliability, they own and often operate their own aircraft, smaller airplanes, trucks, other surface transportation equipment, and automated handling and storage facilities. They have developed this unique capital and know-how basis, which they can use for the express delivery of a wider range of cargo shipments (today they handle shipments of up to 70 kilograms).

Express carriers provide freight forwarding with time-definite delivery properties and continuous shipment trucking by using proprietary intermodal transportation networks. In a number of markets, they are as well off, and arguably better off, when they function at least in part as a forwarder, relying on lower-cost charter and/or interline partners to provide the actual air transport services. They may also recourse to local third party carriers for regulatory reasons.

Express/courier services first developed in the US, and then internationally. There has been substantial growth in the integrated or express carriers market for freight transport. Due to the capital intensity of operations, the scale, network and learning benefits associated with them, as well as the speed of development of the express sector rewarding early participants who pioneered concepts and practices, the market structure of the express segment provokes unusual concentration. The market share of the international leader DHL approaches 40% and the four largest carriers handle 90% of the international traffic (Table 11.4).

Table 11.4 Concentration in the international express sector, daily shipments volume, 1997

Company	Market share (%)	Growth rate 1996/1997 (%)
DHL	39.9	15.4
TNT	12.0	16.7
Federal Express	21.1	17.8
United Parcel Service	14.6	10.0
Airborne Express	1.8	19.5
Other	10.6	20.0

International market developments might follow the earlier rapid growth of express services in the US domestic market. There, express carriers such as FedEx and UPS started their air based services in the early 1970s, and their development was largely favored by the effects of the 1977 Air Cargo Deregulation Act. They have been extremely successful in integrating the activities of the other segments of the industry. In 1996, US express carriers realized 60% of the total air freight traffic (in RTKs) performed in the domestic market.

Europe's internal air freight market has also seen significant growth and development in the express sector, with many of the line haul carriers reducing or discontinuing their intra-European freight operations. Data on Europe's express market are piecemeal, of variable quality and not published or available for all of the EU states. Because this sector has experienced such rapid growth in a relatively short period of time, the lack of data makes it difficult to identify trends and key characteristics of the European sector.

There are important reasons for international markets not fully duplicating the express carriers' predominance in the US market. Neither the regulatory framework nor more energetic competitive responses by strong combination carriers and freight forwarders are likely to encourage a similar domination of the industry by one of its segments. Still, market demands for time-definite, reliable, point-to-point cargo services are pervasive. Air carriers and freight forwarders may in the future be expected to play a larger role in international markets than in the US, by developing assets, capabilities and work organization methods similar to those of international express carriers.

The underlying basis for the pricing of air freight is akin to that found for passenger traffic. The freight rates correspond to a continuum of products with different valuations (notably delivery times) by consignors and consignees, and different operation costs (notably volume and frequency of shipments) by carriers.

Supply-demand balance varies by routes and types of services, and market rates reflect these differences. Because it is closely linked to inventory levels, cargo business turns down early in the business cycle, and total demand is cyclical on individual markets. As with traffic, the N rate level for the same citypair as well as the number and availability of commodity rates can differ significantly according to the direction of the flow of the goods. A similar supply-demand imbalance is observed on particularly busy passenger and tourist routes, where 'excess' belly-hold capacity is permanently available. Cargo rates on these routes are compressed toward marginal costs.

While it is difficult to establish the degree of rate variability due to factors other than cost, one handle is to compare the IATA reference 'N' rate with those actually pertaining in the market.[5] Figure 11.3 plots the results of a distance-based

---

[5]   IATA tariffs are agreed for the purpose of interlining shipments between carriers and apply on all important international routes, except between Canada and US. Each agreement is different according to the areas involved, but all contain the 'N' rate for ordinary shipments of less than 45 kilograms (in some markets, 100 kilograms).

comparison of published 'N' tariffs on various international routes. It shows important deviations of individual tariffs from distance-based industry averages.

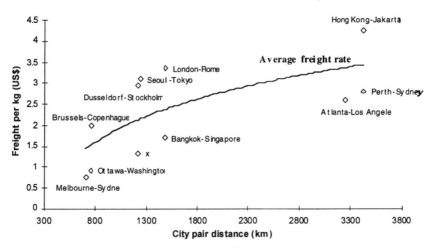

Figure 11.3 Comparison of actual air freight rates with the N rate for 1993

11.3 THE REGULATION OF AIR CARGO

As Chapters 4 and 5 has shown air transportation has had a long history of economic regulation. While much of this has been explicit, some measures of safety and environmental regulation have been used as tools of economic regulation. Much of the recent concern has been with the liberalization of the passenger market, but the regulatory structure has also applied to air cargo activities. This is particularly so in the case of belly-hold operations. There are several types of regulation that are particularly important from an economic perspective. The nature of the regulatory structure is also relevant.

The first air cargo services were mainly for the carriage of mail. Since these services were initially unprofitable, they were given direct subsidies to support them.[6] It was also deemed desirable that networks of stable services should be provided with the result that the subsidies were given to a limited number of carriers that enjoyed route monopolies. This notion of the need to provide a public service tended to influence policy over subsequent years, although in the US Post Office case subsidies were withdrawn in 1953 and the objective switched more to supporting small communities. In many countries postal services remain the

---

[6]   E.g., the Kelly Airmail Act of 1925 in the US.

statutory monopoly of the national PTT and, as such, carry considerable amounts of cargo in the form of packages and parcels. Increasingly this monopoly position is being eroded as courier services are permitted and PTT themselves link with private courier operators.

The development of international air cargo services, as with passenger aviation, has largely been on the basis of the 1944 Chicago Convention's failure to reach agreement on opening the market beyond bilateral agreements. The concern of most nations that a free market in the aftermath of the Second World War would lead to the US domination of trade in both passenger aviation and the embryonic cargo sector ruled out multilateralism. Bilateral agreements emerged that regulated capacity, the carriers allowed on each route and the rates that could be charged. Many of these were, and still are, highly restrictive, embracing revenue pooling and duopoly supply by an airline from each country involved.[7] The bilateral structure of air service agreements has, though, gradually been eroded as the importance of freer trade has become apparent, but a large legacy remains.[8]

Air transport of all types carries a risk of accident and, since there is a strongly held view that this risk cannot be internalized within a market structure, command-and-control regimes are widespread. Each country has its own set of technical regulations, enacted through licensing, but the International Civil Aviation Organization plays an overseeing role in terms of information flows, monitoring and making policy recommendations.

Air transport, as we see in Chapter 13, is also environmentally intrusive and controls over noise emissions, flight paths and fuel emissions result. North American, Asian and European governments have agreed to the phased reduction of 'Chapter 2' aircraft by the end of the decade. The aircraft noise legislation agreed by European ministers of transport related to two areas: non-addition of 'Chapter 2' aircraft to EU aircraft registers after 1992, and a ban on Chapter 2 aircraft and engines after 1997. These are not first best methods of tackling the problems of social externalities but have a general acceptance. The economic issue is primarily to do with circumstances where regulation of this type is used to manipulate the market in favor of particular suppliers.[9].

Air cargo markets are not homogeneous and may suffer from a number of inherent imperfections. The diversity of the sector means that superficially the

---

[7]   There has been a degree of standardization in the form of air service agreements, although this has varied over time, see Doganis (1993).
[8]   Organisation for Economic Cooperation and Development (1997) examines the situation and sets out proposals for liberalizing the system.
[9]   For some all-cargo operators, low utilization rates make newer aircraft uneconomic. New entrants since 1997 have been competing for aircraft equipment purchases/leases as well as trying to compete in offering air services. Higher operating costs in all market sectors place upward pressure on cargo rates, but with consistent adoption of noise and emission standards, competitive disadvantages will not be imposed on particular states and their carriers

problems often highlighted may appear contradictory. The economies of scale, density and scope that can be reaped by large network integrated carriers may, for example, pose perceived threats of monopoly exploitation. This may be seen as requiring interventions on rates and on predatory behavior. In the early days of the air mail service, market instability (an 'empty core'[10]) associated with excessive competition was seen as one reason for subsidies, route allocation and other interventions. A similar situation arose in the US freight market after the SecondWorld War when there were fears that the large number of surplus ex-military aircraft would lead to excess supply (Carron, 1981). This was when the US started regulating freight rates and market entry. In other cases, especially in situations of sparse population, cargo services have been directly subsidized or regimes of licensing involving cross-subsidization have been invoked because economic notions of 'need' have been thought more relevant than effective demand.

Inevitably, with the growth of combi-aircraft and the larger belly capacity of many airliners, the issues of passenger and air cargo regulation have become entwined. Essentially, belly-hold freight cannot be carried if there is no passenger service, hence in many cases the regulation of passenger services has represented a *de facto* regulation of cargo services.[11] The degree to which this has proved a binding constraint has varied between markets but relaxation of passenger airline capacity constraints can release additional belly capacity that creates short-term shocks in the cargo market if traffic had formerly been primarily carried by dedicated freighters. Additionally, as the strategic airline alliance movement has grown, so the scope for large airlines coordinating their freight activities as well as their passenger services has also increased.

The nature of regulation has varied between markets. The largest domestic air cargo transport market.[12] that of the US, was initially regulated in 1947 at the same time as the Civil Aeronautics Board (CAB) was given the power to control fares and entry to the passenger market. The result was that while a number of all-cargo carriers were certified, between 1947 and 1956 there was nearly as much market exit through bankruptcy as there was entry. By 1977, only three all-cargo carriers remained. This did not, however, prevent a rapid growth in the industry in the 1950s (9% per annum) and the 1960s (17% per annum). The regulatory structure, however, could not adjust to changing conditions in the 1970s, notably

[10]   For technical arguments about market stability in transport industries, see Chapter 7.

[11]   As regards terms of US domestic regulation, the controls over rates were designed in such a way that they favored the carriage of freight in belly-holds rather than freighter aircraft (Carron, 1981).

[12]   This excludes postal services.

geographical shifts in demand, higher jet fuel prices and changes in customer service demands.[13]

Unregulated commuter carriers also expanded their cargo services (17% between 1970 and 1978) and offered new competition. Under CAB regulation of air freight, all-cargo operators were unable in the 1970s to generate reasonable profits, with the result that the quantity and quality of service deteriorated. A particular feature of the US system has been that it has involved privately owned and operated air cargo companies.

Other countries have pursued somewhat different policies in line with their more general approach to transport policy. Canada and Australia, for instance, with their smaller populations but large physical areas, have tended to try to stimulate competition through two airline strategies. In the case of the geographically smaller European states, where domestic air cargo transport has traditionally enjoyed a relatively small market share, state-owned monopoly carriers have mainly been responsible for air cargo. Until recently, this philosophy of state provision has also generally extended to international freight operations.

11.4 DEREGULATION OF AIR CARGO NETWORKS[14]

The economic deregulation movement has been global in its coverage and widespread in terms of the sectors affected. It has varied in its intensity and form. As with several other sectors, the analysis of the implications of air cargo deregulation is fraught with problems.

Deregulation, combined with changing demand patterns and regulatory reform of other sectors, has brought about important structural effects that make conventional before and after analysis almost impossible; there is no effective counterfactual. In particular, integrated services have developed considerably and, while deregulation has been a factor, so have new informatics and the growth in demand to transport high-cost/low-volume high-technology products. Deregulation of trucking modes, and to a much lesser extent rail transport, has affected the modal shift for some cross-border feeder services. Changes in ownership and competition policy have affected commercial strategies. Deregulation of passenger air services has affected the supply of belly-hold and combi capacity. The creation of airline alliances, in part to counteract the constraints of existing regulations, has further complicated the picture. More generally, privatization and commercialization have made data collection more difficult, especially in terms of key economic parameters such as actual rates paid and costs.

---

[13]   The sector also enjoyed an implicit subsidy from supplying air-lift capacity to the military. The ending of the Vietnam War reduced this.
[14]   Air cargo transport has been deregulated in many markets; here the experiences of two of the major reforms are examined in detail.

The following looks at some of the important changes that have taken place in a number of the key markets as a result of regulatory change. They are divided between domestic, regional and international experiences.

11.4.1 Major domestic deregulations

The experience in the US, where deregulation was initiated earliest, highlights the significant changes possible under liberalized regulations and there are lessons for the EU in them and developments elsewhere. The US experience receives particular attention because of the key industry trends to emerge there after deregulation in 1977 with the passage of the Domestic All-cargo Deregulation Statute.[15] This initially eliminated control over entry into, and exit from the all-cargo market and reduced the power of the CAB to regulate rates. A year later came complete rate setting freedom. Additionally, carriers were permitted to refuse specific types of freight and were also exempt from the need for approval prior to any consolidation.

Since 1977, domestic and international air cargo markets have greatly expanded in the US (Figure 11.4) giving shippers a wider choice with respect to rates, consequential damages and excess value charges. Scheduled air freight services were commenced to many new communities and, as with passenger services, network reorganization was permitted. Air freight rates had increased prior to 1977 and had increased by an average of 20% by 1980. Rate changes varied according to route and type of commodities. Air freight carriers became liable for the full value of the freight.

Cargo deregulation led to consolidation among the bigger carriers and encouraged the growth of non-certificated carriers like Federal Express.[16] Federal Express, founded in 1971, had become the most profitable US carrier by 1982 and the world's largest air cargo carrier by 1989, when it took over Flying Tiger. Cargo deregulation enabled other courier operators to expand their operations and offer integrated carrier services with door-to-door delivery of freight loads of all sizes. Additionally, since deregulation, air freight forwarders have been permitted to offer line-haul services.[17] All this meant a considerable improvement in service, a point emphasized in 1990 when UPS offered 10.30 a.m. next day delivery in the mainland US and in 1991 when Federal Express set up EXPRESSfreight as its express cargo service.

---

[15] For more details, see Taneja (1979) and Carron (1981).

[16] Several new all-cargo operators entered the market after 1977, and non-certificated carriers, like Federal Express, were awarded certificates and permitted to operate large jet aircraft.

[17] Surface shipments in the US were regulated by the Interstate Commerce Commission (ICC).

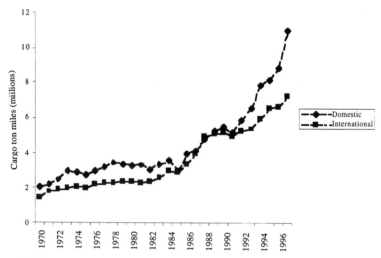

Source: Air Transport Association.

Figure 11.4 US cargo ton miles by scheduled carriers

In 1979, the combination passenger/cargo carriers handled in excess of 75% of the total air freight market. After deregulation, combination and passenger carriers developed interactive hub-and-spoke networks (Reynolds-Feighan, 1994; Reynolds-Feighan and Berechman, 1998). The network structure was driven more by passenger demands than cargo demands.[18] The cargo operations tended to focus on the international gateways operated by the carriers. The combination passenger carriers have gradually been losing their share of the freight market to all-cargo and express operators (their share falling from 83% in 1977 to 44% in 1989).

The all-cargo carriers greatly increased their share of the air freight market between 1977 and 1989 and it has continued to grow steadily to about 60% of the domestic market. Federal Express, even prior to its acquisition of Flying Tiger, had the largest share of the US air freight market. It operates a single hub network system centered on Memphis, Tennessee. The interactive hub-and-spoke system (where multiple regional hubs are interconnected) does not suit the all-cargo air operators. When there are a large number of transfers between aircraft, the reliability of service is reduced as the possibility of damage to the cargo increases.

---

[18]   For example, in 1990, 19.9% of American Airlines' passenger traffic and 17.6% of its freight went through Dallas with another 12.2% of its passengers and 11.5% of freight through Chicago; regarding Continental Airlines, Houston handled 15.9% of the airline's passengers and 12.5% of its freight; Delta Air Lines handled 21.0% of both its passengers and its freight through Atlanta; and 15.5% of USAir's passengers went though Pittsburgh, as did 13.1% of its freight.

Under regulation, it was generally felt that freight carried by air traveled longer distances than was necessary because surface modes could not be used to support the carrier's operation. Integrated carriers now offer multimodal service that takes advantage of the distance/cost/time trade-off that the different modes offer.

US air RTKs declined in the mid-1970s with the all-cargo market share of the US total market (i.e., domestic plus international) being less than 17%. After air cargo deregulation in 1977, the express carrier emerged as a significant new type of operator in the air freight sector. They experienced very rapid increases in their freight volumes throughout the 1980s and 1990s. In 1980 and 1985 for example, the express carriers experienced annual increases of 27.8% and 21.9% in RTKs respectively. By 1993, over half of the RTKs (56%) in the US domestic market was carried by express operators.

The widespread use of discounting and variable rates made possible with modern electronic data interchange and other technologies makes assessing air cargo rates extremely difficult. Added to this the 'product' provided by the industry has changed significantly in the US since deregulation. Figure 11.5 offers some indication of the changes in the relative cost of using air cargo in the US against the other major modes.[19] Since deregulation it has tended to rise more sharply than the other modes. It has also risen faster than the retail price index. In part this reflects the initial short-term adjustments associated with air carriers' full cost cargo after 1978 and the increased demands for the services captured in Figure 11.5. The main effect, however, and one not easily separated, is the higher cost associated with supplying a higher quality of service.

The express carriers have been gradually handling larger shares of standard freight in addition to express freight.[20] These carriers are successfully bidding for market share by offering a diversified range of related services combined with the line-haul requirements (e.g., pick-up and delivery; tracking services; warehousing and stock control; logistics management).[21] The express carriers have become large undertakings and since 1977 there is some evidence of consolidation amongst the all freight carriers. Table 11.5 provides some base data on concentration which offers some guidance on levels of concentration but even this disguises the importance of Federal Express that in 1989[22] was responsible for 41.5% of domestic freight and 18% of international freight and operated from 407 airports

---

[19]   The calculations are based on total revenues accruing to air cargo divided by aggregate ton miles.
[20]   The large express carriers are also increasingly outsourcing to a number of smaller operators who provide marginal capacity (e.g., Atlas Air Inc. does this for Federal Express).
[21]   For example, in early 1993, National Semiconductor Inc. contracted Federal Express to set up and operate its distribution network for its Asian subsidiaries.
[22]   Changes in FAA data after 1989 make longer-term comparisons difficult.

domestically and 108 internationally. This was prior to the merger with Flying Tiger that in 1989 carried 9.2% of US domestic freight and 17.9% of international.

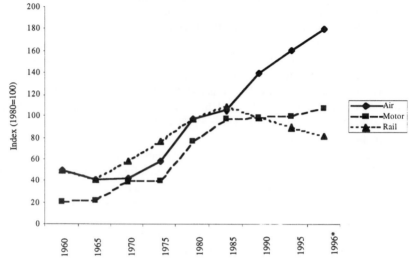

* Provisonal

Figure 11.5 Average US cargo freight revenue per ton-mile

Table 11.5 US all-cargo air operators

| Year | Number of Carriers | Percentage share of the market | | Total |
		Domestic	International	
1977	3	12.7	30.4	16.9
1979	3	21.3	31.7	23.7
1989	11	53.1	60.1	56.0

Regulations governing the operation of other transport modes can have a significant impact on the operators' abilities to diversify. While air transport was deregulated in the 1977 and 1978 Acts, problems remained until recently for the integrated/express carriers who were subject to state regulations in relation to ground operations. These regulations on occasion required that express operators contracted to ship goods by air within a state had to ship the goods by air out of the state before returning to deliver the goods to a location in the original state. Under an amendment to the Federal Aviation Act in 1994, inter-state ground operations of all intermodal all-cargo air carriers were deregulated. The Act extends the definition of carrier types covered by several state regulations, notably Texas.

The Australian air cargo market began to be deregulated in 1977 when the Commonwealth allowed two specialist freight operators to import aircraft and operate air freight services across the bass Strait between the mainland and Tasmania. Prior to this, regulations dating back to the Airline Agreement Act of 1952 had limited the rights to carry freight and mail on the main trunk routes to two carriers. It also controlled the importing of the heavy aircraft required for freight operations. Freight rates were fixed by the Ministry and adjusted periodically mainly *pari passu* with air passenger fares. Discounting was common, and deep discounting not uncommon, meaning the official rates became effective ceilings. It has been estimated that only about 10% of cargo was carried at published rates (Gawan-Taylor, 1984).

Legal reform came in 1981 with an amendment to the existing legislation when reference to air freight was removed from the established regulations. Since about 60% of freight was being carried in passenger planes the effects of reform were largely dependent on the freight capacity of these aircraft. Deregulation of the passenger market bore heavily on the way air cargo developed. This was not fully deregulated until 1990. This could have distorted the development of Australian air cargo over the intervening period as belly hold capacity remained restricted but national economic growth over the period was slow.

The result of the reforms was a degree of market entry although, mainly due to the state of the macroeconomy and the inexperience of new entries, there were a number of bankruptcies. Overall, scheduled air freight rates rose faster in the immediate period following reform than in the years before. Poor data makes assessment of the causes difficult.

There are indications that rates for small packages rose because of high handling costs that could be fully passed on. Also, when comparisons are made with road freight, the main competitor with air cargo, it is found that trucking rates rose faster than scheduled air cargo rates. Allowance is also needed for discounting and for inflation. After adjustments, over the period 1979 to 1981 the change in real yield per ton for one air cargo carrier (TAA) rose 7.3%, but for the period 1981 t0 1983 after deregulation it fell −8.3%. There are also indications that deregulation stimulated capacity growth. Freight tonne kilometers grew by 3.1% per annum in 1971 to 1981 and also by 3.1% from 1981 to 1983 despite an annual decline in GDP of 1% in the second period compared to a rise of 3.1% per annum for 1971–81.[23]

[23]   New Zealand has also deregulated its freight operations. In part because of the geography, the trend has been towards consolidation of carriers and their integration with other freight modes (Bollard and Pickford, 1998).

11.4.2 Macroregional deregulations

By macroregional deregulation we mean market liberalization involving a group of countries. The main example of this has been the development of the common aviation policy within the European Union but there are others. In each case air cargo regulatory reforms are entwined, although not always technically connected, with the creation of a larger, regional trading area. These developments are new and their impacts have yet to fully materialize.

11.4.2.1 North American Free Trade Agreement Area.

The North American Free Trade Agreement (NAFTA)[24] that commenced in 1994 and embraces the US, Canada and Mexico has no explicit air cargo component but has been accompanied by separate liberalizing air transport bilateral agreements. In the case of Canada, the 1995 agreement is not like the Open Skies agreements that the US has developed elsewhere and involves phasing-in of services. The NAFTA has stimulated trade between its members and air cargo transport has grown rapidly (Figure 11.6), and US–Canadian transborder traffic rose a further 25%, to about 700 million revenue tonne-kilometers in 1995. The agreement is too new to assess the role of air cargo because restructuring of trade is still taking place and its short time of operation has covered only a period of general economic expansion.

What does seem to be emerging is that the hub-and-spoke structure of courier operations is increasingly being integrated across national borders. There are, for example, no Canadian scheduled all-cargo services (although belly-hold cargo is carried by the trunk airlines) but Canadian courier carriers participate extensively in transborder activities involving feeding the main US hubs (Table 11.6).

11.4.2.2 The European Union.

Air freight markets in Europe have also undergone significant change. The EU took substantial steps towards liberalizing the internal European air transport market in July 1992 with the adoption of Council Regulations No. L240 relating to several key aspects of the industry's operation including access for community air carriers to intra-community air routes, licensing, and fares. The previous packages represented more modest moves towards liberalization and came in the wake of European Court of Justice rulings applying, for the first time, articles 85 and 86 of the Treaty of Rome (relating to antitrust-type restrictions) to air transport (Button *et al.* 1998).

The Third Package removed the distinction between scheduled and non-scheduled operations in air transport, although the distinctions were already becoming more ill-defined as scheduled carriers had been offering increasing numbers of charter services or were setting up subsidiary charter companies. The

---

[24]   Prior to this was the US–Canadian North American Trade Agreement that was more restrictive on trade.

charter carriers had been offering what amounted to scheduled services on a limited number of north-south intra-European routes for some years. Europe's charter industry accounted for over half of all intra-European passengers and about two-thirds of total intra-European RPKs. These shares had remained relatively constant for the previous ten years (Doganis, 1994)).

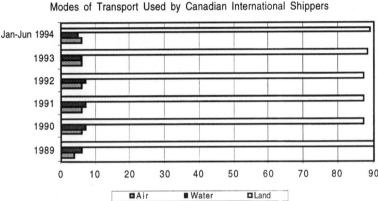

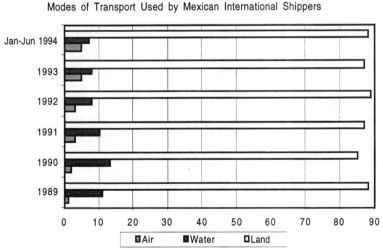

Source: Bureau of Transport Statistics

Figure 11.6 Role of air cargo transport in US/Canadian and US/Mexican trade

Table 11.6 Canadian air cargo carriers providing feed to US hubs, 1996

US courier company	Canadian operator proving feed to US hub
Airborne Express	Knighthawk Air Express
Burlington Express	All Canada Express
DHL	CanAir Cargo
Emery Air Freight Corp.	Bradley Air services
Federal Express	Kelowna Flightcraft Air Charter Ltd.
TNT	Knighthawk Air Express
UPS/TNT	Western Express Airline, Knighthawk Air Express, Perimeter Airlines

Council Regulations No. 2407/92 to 2411/92 cover a wide range of issues in the scheduled and non-scheduled passenger and cargo markets. Council Regulation 2407/92 deals with common licensing arrangements and the rights of community registered carriers to operate aircraft owned anywhere in the Community.

The licensing regulation requires that the principal place of business and registered office be located in the state in which the carrier is registered, that the carrier carries insurance and that air transport is the main concern of the licensee. Licensed carriers are not required to own their own aircraft, but they must have at least one at their disposal. These aircraft must be registered in the state's aircraft register, although it is left to the discretion of the member state to issue a license to the carrier if the aircraft at their disposal are registered elsewhere in the EU.

Council Regulation 2408/92 covers access to intra-community air routes. This includes the abolition of capacity restrictions between member states, and the removal of restrictions concerning fifth-freedom and multiple designation[25] rights along with a gradual phasing-in of cabotage rights.[26] Full cabotage was not required before April 1997.

Council Regulation No. 2409/92 grants freedom for Community carriers to set and rates for services, except in specific limited circumstances. In Council Regulation 2410/92, the Community competition rules are formally extended to the air transport sector while amendments to certain categories of agreements and concerted practices in the air transport sector are made in Council Regulation No. 2411/92.

---

[25] Multiple designation is where multiple carriers are permitted to offer air services on an international route.

[26] Consecutive cabotage is permitted where a carrier uses less than 50% of its seasonal capacity on a service on which the cabotage segment is an extension or preliminary to an inter-state route.

Several of the negative outcomes associated with deregulation in the US are now subject to safeguard provisions in the European liberalization program (i.e., predatory pricing practices and slot allocation issues relating to hub airport dominance.[27] These regulations will impact on the pattern of consumer demand, on carrier profitability and airline industry structure. From a regulatory viewpoint, a number of key difficulties remain in the European market that are expected to slow the development of competition in air freight transport. Several significant barriers to entry and to competition remain in the industry which limit the extent to which a truly competitive market can evolve.

There are capacity constraints at a large number of European airports and new entry, and hence competition, on many routes thus remain difficult.[28] These barriers to entry, and to effective competition, have a significant impact on the extent to which carriers can reorganize and optimize their networks. Reynolds-Feighan (1994) has shown that the European flag carriers in 1990 organized their traffic flows based a single hub network. This system suits passenger and freight operations. The extent to which schedules can be optimally coordinated in time and space is constrained by factors such as air traffic control delays and airport slot availability. One of the most dramatic effects of US deregulation was the move by carriers to concentrate traffic and coordinate its flows through multiple interactive hub-and-spoke network systems. For the air cargo sector, these barriers to competition will constrain its development and its ability to organize carrier networks in an efficient manner.

Within Europe, competition from surface modes has exerted a downward pressure on air freight growth. Additionally, the Boeing 737 aircraft used for many scheduled passenger routes restricts the size of freight that can be carried. This, along with a relatively low overall economic growth rate, explains the below-average long term growth rate for air freight. Air trucking[29] has, however, been

---

[27] E.g. Van de Voorde (1992); Button and Swann (1992); Button *et al.* (1998); Bjarnadottir (1994); Association of European Airlines (1996).

[28] One of the paradoxes of air transport deregulation in Europe is that it has increased the frequency of passenger services, with smaller aircraft being used, causing capacity to be reached more rapidly than anticipated at many airports.

[29] Air trucking, involves the movement of air cargo by road (or rail) under an air waybill. In 1971, international airlines through IATA introduced and adopted IATA Resolution 507b, which clearly defined the circumstances under which trucking could be undertaken; these involved the lack of available space on aircraft, where consignments could not be handled on aircraft operated by an airline due to the size, weight or nature of the consignments (certain commodities may only be shipped in freighter or all-cargo aircraft) or because the carrier refuses carriage on some other grounds, where the carriage by air will result in delayed transit times or in carriage not being accomplished within 12 hours of acceptance and where carriage by air will result in missed connections.

expanding at a rate of 15% per annum since 1975, with an estimated 6 650 frequencies per week in Europe in 1995. The number of routes served within Europe expanded from 38 in 1975 to 386 in 1995.[30] It has become particularly important in some countries. In the UK, British Airways air trucks all domestic freight, while the part of air trucking in the total of 1997 German air cargo volume amounted to some 26% (some 767 000 tonnes of a total of 2.88 million tonnes). Overall, air trucking appears as a new form of multimodal optimization in air freight transportation. The practice of air trucking is predominantly oriented towards moving intracontinental freight traffic to gateway airports (*The Economist*, 1996).

Significant developments and growth in European carrier's air cargo traffic are anticipated in the long-haul markets, which are a large part of the overall European market (Table 11.7). Air express is expected to continue to grow at a much faster rate than 'heavy' cargo or airmail services. The North Atlantic and Europe–Asia markets are expected to record 6.5-7% annual growth rates in RTKs according to Boeing. The forecast for intra-Europe growth is a more modest 2% to 3% per annum over the same period (1993–2012).

The internal air freight market has seen significant growth and development in the express sector, with many of the line haul carriers reducing or discontinuing their intra-European freight operations. Data on Europe's express market are piecemeal, of variable quality and not published or available for all of the EU states. Because this sector has experienced such rapid growth in a relatively short period of time, the lack of data makes it difficult to identify trends and key characteristics of the European sector.

13.4.3 International deregulation.

There have recently been a number of major bilateral, and to a lesser extent, multilateral attempts to liberalize international air transport. The primary focus of most of these initiatives has been on scheduled passenger services. This is because on many routes there has until recently been adequate scheduled, belly-hold and non-scheduled capacity to meet demand, the US–Japan situation being a notable exception to this. Indeed, since most passenger airlines tend to cost belly-hold capacity at short-run marginal cost, it could be argued that freight rates have been artificially low and excess capacity has exceeded the official physical indicators.

Many of the developments in terms of international air cargo services are still evolving but some important structural changes have occurred. Internationally, the

---

[30]   In their report to the European Commission in 1990, Triangle Management Services (1990) suggested that air trucking in Europe, 'initially was a key product of the carriers' effort to provide shippers with a substantial range of services, i.e., a road-based routing where there was no real option. In doing so they have now undermined the basic economics of running a substantial conventional all-cargo operation, particularly Intra-European.'

US has been instrumental, through its Open Skies policy, in the liberalization of a number of important international routes. The Open Sky agreements, although mainly aimed at the passenger market have also removed entry and rate controls in the bilateral agreements to which they apply (see Chapter 4). While the main attention has been on the implications of these developments for passenger services, there is only limited evidence emerging regarding their implications for cargo activities. The alliances that have been permitted have tended to consolidate passenger services (and *ipso facto* belly space capacity) and there is no evidence of any significant increase in air cargo capacity.

Table 11.7 Air freight traffic in Europe by geographical market segment, 1993

Carrier	Country	North American air freight as % of total scheduled air freight		Total long-haul freight as % of total scheduled air freight		Freight only services as % of total scheduled air freight	
		RTKs	Tonnes	RTKs	Tonnes	RTKs	Tonnes
Aer Lingus	Ireland	88.0	42.6	88.0	42.6	50.6	45.0
Air France	France	30.9	29.0	93.9	82.6	52.8	46.0
Alitalia	Italy	49.3	37.9	93.4	58.9	41.4	35.0
Austrian Air	Austria	46.7	18.7	66.9	26.0	0.0	0.0
British Airways	UK	44.7	42.2	90.3	73.6	5.0	2.6
Finnair	Finland	44.0	27.3	86.4	51.8	3.6	11.9
Iberia	Spain	30.0	17.4	80.4	41.3	19.1	24.3
KLM	Netherlands	37.6	37.0	94.2	76.0	18.6	15.3
Lufthansa	Germany	37.6	30.6	90.0	65.7	49.8	43.8
Luxair	Luxembourg	0.0	0.0	0.0	0.0	0.0	0.0
Olympic	Greece	22.8	5.8	56.7	14.1	0.0	0.0
Sabena	Belgium	50.4	40.8	92.9	71.8	0.0	0.0
SAS	Scandinavia	49.9	23.8	84.5	38.3	0.0	0.0
TAP	Portugal	23.7	14.5	73.4	38.8	0.8	1.6

Source: Association of European Airlines (1994).

The liberalization of international markets has provided more scope for the development of air courier services, although the outcome has been mixed. TNT, originally an outshoot of the Australian carrier Ansett, found competition tight when trying to expand into the European market. Equally, Federal Express suffered a $254 million restructuring cost and a $114 million loss when it withdrew from domestic pick-ups/deliveries in Europe during 1992 and linked with the Dutch PPT. In contrast, UPS has adopted a different approach to extending its international activities as deregulation has spread. It has acquired a number of existing national operators; Prost Transport in France (1991), Carry fast in the UK, Star Parcel in Austria and Beemsterboer in the Netherlands (all in 1992). It has also spread from its initial major hub in Germany to secondary hubs in Europe (e.g., East Midlands Airport in the UK and Paris).

Outside of Europe the story has been equally mixed, in part because some large markets are still regulated (notably that between the US and Japan).[31] Federal Express began the development of a $400 million hub in Taipei to serve the gradually liberalizing Asian market. Federal Express has also been active in gaining more rights in the highly restrictive Japanese market both to offer more capacity to the Japanese market itself but also to afford a greater exploitation of beyond activities in Asia.

Japan is important in the Asian portion of any global network of services because of its market size and its location. Technology does not currently enable aircraft to fly non-stop from the US to many major Asia–Pacific destinations beyond Japan. Even as ranges are extended, many of these markets would not justify high frequencies of service. Japan is, therefore, a natural Asian hub for US freight carriers serving the Asian Pacific region. Japan, however, has felt that the 1952 agreement, allowing such things as unlimited US rights for designated carriers beyond Tokyo and Osaka, was signed at a time when it had little political power and is unbalanced. Japan also has claimed that environmental constraints limit the number of additional services that are socially desirable.

The late 1980s, and most of the 1990s, saw efforts to resolve the situation. US carriers, including major freight operators, notably Federal Express with interests in having more capacity through Japan to serve its Subic Bay operations, pressed for more beyond rights capacity and Japan sought to rectify the imbalance in traffic (Prestowitz *et al.*, 1996). The latter frequently delayed necessary clearances for routes and services, leading to regular periods of diplomatic conflict. The opening of Kansai Airport, and the initial denial of clearance for US carriers, led to particular difficulties.

Little significant change occurred until January 1998 when the framework for a new accord was reached. The beyond rights of Federal Express were protected. While the agreement is not Open Skies, it does provide a degree of *de facto* liberalization and provides a more balanced basis for competition. The short-term implications are still unclear. In the longer term, however, if traffic growth matches predictions then a new crisis seems inevitable. The goal posts have effectively been moved out but the rules of the game have not been changed.

What is emerging in virtually all the international markets is the development of large hub-and-spoke air cargo networks. This has clearly been the case with the integrated carriers enjoying considerable economies of scale, scope and density in funneling traffic through a limited number of consolidation and trans-shipment points. Part of this trend in line haul operations, however, has been driven by developments on the passenger side where the large airline alliances simple make

---

[31]   DHL has moved to circumvent many of the problems still posed by market restrictions by selling some 57.7% of its ownership to German and Japanese interests.

it economical to combine passenger and freight activities at their major passenger hubs.[32]

11.5   CONCLUSIONS

There has been a rapid and widespread change in production management that has seen the growth of such things as supply chain management and just-in-time techniques. Many of the products that are transported are now high-value, low-weight items where transport costs are often less important than the speed and reliability of service. As one result, given its comparative advantage in many of the attributes that these types of activity demand, the air cargo industry is one of the fastest growing sectors in transport.

The industry has undergone important regulatory, structural and technical change over the past twenty years. From being essentially a sector providing supplementary services to the postal system and offering specialized freight services, it has now developed into a multifaceted industry. It is dynamic and still undergoing significant structural change. There are now a number of extremely large companies that provide air cargo services. Technology has been instrumental in this, as aircraft lifting power has grown, but it also reflects the needs of the new technology driven and internationalized world productive structures.

Institutional reforms have also been extremely important. The regulatory reforms that have taken place in Europe, the US, Canada, Australasia and elsewhere have stimulated important structural changes to the sector; changes that have not fully worked their way through the system. These changes make it virtually impossible to conduct the normal before and after studies of the implications of market liberalization.

The changes have also occurred at a time of major technical change in the sector and in the nature of the demands placed on its services. Again this mitigates against realistic comparisons of such things as rates and entry levels. The growth in air cargo may be considered indicative of the success of liberalization, but cannot be taken as a strict guide to the benefits of reform; e.g., it might have happened anyway or there might have been a better model to follow. The institutional developments regarding air cargo and complementary sectors have not hindered the growth of the sector or the role that it is playing in enhancing economic growth.

---

[32]   Indeed, concern has been expressed by some of the organizations representing small air cargo airlines that this trend could prove anti-competitive, in the sense that the alliances have sufficient power to act in a predatory manner.

12 INTERACTION WITH OTHER NETWORKS

12.1 INTRODUCTION

Air transportation is closely linked with the provison of other transport and non-transport networks. The objective of this chapter is to look at some of these linkages. These ties are often extremely important for the success of air transport networks but equally often neglected in narrower studies of the sector. The links are also often not transparent and can be complex. In economic terms, there are considerations of complementarity and of substitutablility involved.

Air transport is inevitably part of a multimodal chain. At the most simple level, people and cargoes need to get to and from air terminals, and this requires another mode of transport.[1] But in other cases, non-aviation modes provide important alternatives to air transportation. This can obviously be seen as competition, but in many situations it provides important alternative capacity that leaves air transport infrastructure and inputs free to perform the services for which they offer the greatest comparative advantage. Investments such as the Channel Tunnel, for example, by allowing short distance UK–continental European traffic to switch to car/rail modes release scarce slots at London's airports and some of those on Continental Europe that can be used for other services.[2]

Attention is also given to those non-transport networks that interface, either as a complement or as a substitute, with air transportation. The chapter pays particular attention to information networks that are now important in both the supply of air transportation and influencing their demand for their services. Without developments in information systems, modern air transportation could not exist. CRS systems are an integral part of airline demand management and EDI systems are a cornerstone of modern logistics. Information networks,

---

[1]   Although in the cargo context the most common interactions are between air transport and road and rail networks, there are some instances where shipping is involved. Air-sea transportation is important for shipments between Asia/Pacific and Europe transiting the Gulf (e.g., at Sharjah) and on certain trans-Pacific routes. Generally, air-sea transportation is carried out if the carrier has no traffic rights in the country of origin of the goods, in such a case goods are shipped to destinations where such rights are available to the carriers.

[2]   Additionally, by taking traffic directly from city center to city center, the Channel Tunnel also frees access infrastructure to airports.

however, extend well beyond these two. To get a modern airliner off the ground requires a sophisticated just-in-time process to ensure that all of the myriad of inputs are in place at the correct time. There is also the other aspect of information networks: in some instances they may provide a substitute for travel and reduce some individuals' needs for trip making.

12.2   AIRPORT ACCESS

All air transportation movements ultimately involve accessing and leaving the air terminal. Air movements pose one set of problems but there are also mounting difficulties associated with ground movements. Accessing Europe's major airports is becoming increasing difficult as surface traffic congestion grows. Similar problems exist at many airports in the US and are increasing in less developed economies where surface transport infrastructure is in general often poor. The emerging 'edge city' pattern of urban land use[3] is compounding the problem as local traffic becomes entwined with that using the airport. The problems are often most acute for users traveling from central city sites who have to make radial trips out to air terminals along heavily used cross-cutting commuter routes.

Most movements to and from airports are also by private car and the forecasts are that even with the international trend towards policies involving traffic constraint, car ownership and use will grow. This has the added complication at the airport of multiple loading and unloading areas, parking provision and the movement of passengers to and from parks to terminals.

Land transport movements also pose severe environmental problems, inflicting noise and fumes on those living on access corridors. This is increasingly leading to public pressures to limit the construction of new road access links. The Outward movement of suburbs towards former isolated airport locations adds to this debate.

Mass public transport offers one possible methods of more efficiently moving the forecast number of future air travelers. Some airports already have extensive public transport access. In some cases airlines have also been proactive in attempting to ease the problem for their users by operating public transport services. This has, for instance, been a policy of Lufthansa at Frankfurt, where the airline's 'Airport Express' has provided train services to nearby urban areas.

---

[3]   These are a growing phenomenon in the US and other parts of the world and represent the emergence of self-sufficient concentrations of population and employment close to traditional urban areas but distant from the urban core. This results in more complicated patterns of traffic movement than with the stylized single core urban model.

In many cities there are plans to either introduce new public transport systems to improve access or to upgrade existing ones (Table 12.1). Nevertheless, fixed track transport involves considerable capital investments and in many cases, such as Heathrow, the forecasts suggest that new capacity will merely slow the increase in car traffic growth, not reverse it. The geographical configuration and historic pattern of land use in many European cities also pose serious planning problems that can often only be resolved by using expensive technologies such as tunneling.

Table 12.1 Rail links at selected European airports

Airport	Rail link
Amsterdam	Regional, urban and inter-city rail links in place; potential for high-speed link
Cologne-Bonn	Inter-city link and urban rail links
Copenhagen	Regional and urban rail links planned; potential for high-speed link
Düsseldorf	Inter-city and urban links
Frankfurt	Inter-city and urban links; high-speed rail link planned
Geneva	Inter-city rail link
Hamburg	Metro connection planned; timing depends on funding
London/LHG	Urban rail link
London/LHR	Underground link and Heathrow Express in place
London/Stanstead	Urban rail link
Manchester	Urban rail link
Milan/Malpensa	New high-speed link to city plus links to regional rail system
Munich	Urban rail link
Oslo	New high-speed link to city under construction
Paris/CDG	Regional and high-speed rail links in place
Paris/ORY	Urban rail link
Vienna	City center link to be improved; possible future inter-city connection
Zurich	Inter-city link

Fixed track public transport is particularly attractive if it not only links an air terminal to its parent urban area but also ties it into a region's larger public transport network. Linking high-speed rail and air transport in this way also takes some of the strain of slot congestion at airports by allowing airlines to use more of their capacity for medium- and long-haul services. The openings of the Paris–Lyon TGV and the Channel Tunnel linking the UK to continental Europe are illustrative of this type of effect. Part of the traffic making use of these links has been diverted traffic from the air services.

Outside the EU, the Swiss have already established a precedent by having a mainline rail station located under each major airport and travelers' baggage may be checked in and delivered at any Swiss railway station. The development of the French TGV system and its extensions into the low countries is involving joint rail/air terminals at Charles de Gaulle and Schipol airports.

The idea that the EU airport network should be linked with the wider EU inter-urban transport network formed one element of the Commission's approach to developing the trans-European transport network. The guidelines for developing air transport infrastructure priorities include not only the enhancement of existing airport capacity the development of airport capacity and the enhancement of environmental compatibility but also the development of access to the airport and interconnections with other networks.

12.3 'AIR TRUCKING'

The common objective of freight transportation is to get the right product to the right place at the right time so the costs of holding inventories is minimized.[4] When there are technical difficulties, for example due to weather, it is standard practice to deploy alternative modes to air transport on a short term, emergency basis to circumvent problems. In some markets, however, there is a clear possibility for subsituting an alternative mode for air transport on a more permanent basis when economic conditions put pressure on the costs of air services. In some instances it is the airline that opts to use an alternative mode to meet customer needs. An example of this is air trucking when an airline moves freight by road, with a flight number, rather than by plane. This is an option normally only for relatively short haul movements.

Within Europe and elsewhere, competition from surface modes has exerted a downward pressure on air freight growth. This, along with a relatively low overall economic growth rate, explains the below-average long term growth rate for air freight. As seen in the previous chapter, air trucking has been growing rapidly in Europe and similar things are happening elsewhere. In the US, for example, air trucking frequencies now attain 16 000 a week, and around 1 000 city-pairs are served.

There is an inevitable concern that transportation users could be decieved when cargo is moved by road rather than by air. From an institutional perspective and, in particular, as a measure of consumer protection, efforts have been made to clearly define when air trucking is a legitimate option for an airline to adopt. In

---

[4]   Carrying and holding costs represent 25% to 30% of the value of inventories in US firms in terms of the product, depreciation and interest costs involved.

1971, international airlines through IATA introduced and adopted IATA Resolution 507b, that clearly defined the circumstances under which trucking could be undertaken: [5]

- the lack of available space on aircraft;
- where consignments could not be handled on aircraft operated by an airline due to the size, weight or nature of the consignments (certain commodities may only be shipped in freighter or all-cargo aircraft) or because the carrier refuses carriage on some other grounds;
- where the carriage by air will result in delayed transit times or in carriage not being accomplished within 12 hours of acceptance;
- where carriage by air will result in missed connections.

---

[5]   Air trucking is extensively used in the express operators' service chain which is presented in schematic below.

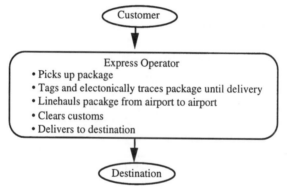

The key advantages of the express operators' service over traditional air freight services are the relatively small lapsed time between pick-up and delivery, and the fact that a single company handles the package or freight from pick-up to delivery. Customers can purchase different services based on speed and delivery requirement. The express operator will typically provide electronic tracking of packages, with customers having access to this tracking facility. Each package/consignment is separately tagged and tracked and will be cleared through customs. Customs services in most European countries now operate electronically, so that consignments receive clearance en route to their destination airport. The customs authority can notify the operator of consignments that will require to be cleared on the ground and this information can be forwarded to the customer via the tracking system. Because each consignment requires separate documentation and custom clearance, charges are levied individually.

Today the practice of air trucking is predominantly oriented towards moving intercontinental freight traffic to gateway airports. This process is described in Figure 12.1.

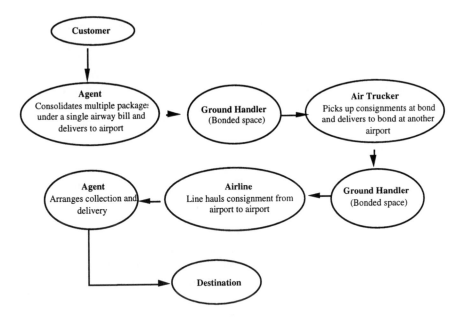

Figure 12.1 Air trucking in the freight logistics chain

12.4 INFORMATION AND FREIGHT SERVICES

Economists are increasingly appreciative of the fact that transportation and information systems are closely interconnected.[6] While there is a growing body of economic analysis looking at the potential substitutability of telecommunications for transport (Button and Maggi, 1995), perhaps the more important link is that of complementarities. In particular, improved information systems can act to improve transport supply. On the passenger transport side, for instance, airlines have developed sophisticated yield management systems to maximize their revenue from any flight based on computer reservation programs (CRSs) that continually

---

[6]   Of course, the importance of information in economics more generally was appreciated much earlier, e.g. in the seminal work of Coase (1937).

adjust fare levels and seat availability as information on sales develops over time.[7] Similarly, electronic data interchange (EDI) has become an integral part of modern logistics.[8] These developments may all be seen as part of the move to intelligent transport systems (ITS).

EDI should not be seen as a single approach to information management but rather reflects a generic attitude to the use of modern computing technology for the control of inventories.[9] It is generally defined as the direct computer-to-computer communication of business documents and information in machine-readable, structured format that permits data to be processed by the receiver without re-keying. Its up take has been driven by a variety of factors (Walton, 1996) linked to the need for shippers and carriers to compete on quality improvements, customer value and cost reductions.

EDI performs a variety of functions not only in terms of contributing to the efficiency of just-in-time production management but also in tracking and in security. It also helps in effective financial management by assisting in the creation of organizational integration and cohesion. In terms of financial returns, analysis by Cooper and Lybrand, for example, found that the firms it surveyed using EDI in the US enjoyed a $1 million year cost saving (cited in Walton and Lewis, 1995). On the demand side, electronic ordering there is evidence of up to 50% sales increases (La Londe and Cooper, 1989). Ultimately the customers of final production should benefit from lower costs and improved services EDI brings

---

[7]   Parallel developments can also be seen in other transport sectors such as shipping (Brooks and Button, 1994).

[8]   The link between economics and transport management is often an uneasy one. Here, however, the view is taken that for economists to fully contribute to debates on freight transport issues and to fully understand how the sector operates it is important to appreciate the factors that influence relevant cost functions and that shape the derived demands for transport services. More generally, there is a growing body of theoretical economics literature that examines the synergies that can develop through the interaction of networks such as transport and communications (Capello and Rietveld, 1998). The empirical literature is lagging some way behind. Equally, economic policies linking transport and the environment increasingly require a more detailed understanding of how network industries operate and interact (Button, 1997a).

[9]   Using a broad definition, Walton and Lewis (1995) estimated that about 68% of EDI users were in the US, with only 10% in the UK and another 11% in the rest of Europe. A common information technology infrastructure for cargo transactions is being developed by airlines. The function of such a cargo community system differs from that of passenger computer reservation systems. It is not designated to differentiate carriers' services from competitors', but aims at providing a common technical infrastructure to all participants. In parallel, express carriers develop proprietary information technology systems, which are at the core of their product differentiation and competitive strategies.

to logistics (Felkner, 1992)

While this section is concerned with the interaction of EDI use and air cargo transport,[10] it also focuses on the broader economic issue of the extent to which it is important for economists to have a more complete understanding of what goes on within firms.[11] It takes a case study to explore in detail the ways in which EDI is now becoming an integral part of logistic chains involving air freight transport. Later sections of the chapter set the case study in its broader context, in terms of developments in logistics and of the market for air freight services.

New technologies in transport generally take time to permeate the sector. This is because of the legacy effects inherent in the existing capital stock and managerial structures. ITS, of which EDI is a sub-component, can embrace major hardware changes that are difficult to introduce but here the emphasis is on the more immediate implications of essentially introducing electronic management devices into the production process. In general, ITS of this type can influence both the demand side and the cost side of an operators activities.

On the demand side the main benefits come from structurally changing the nature of the transport service that can be offered. This may take the form of faster, more frequent and more reliable services that reduce the time element in consumers' generalized cost functions in the conventional way. Inventory holdings can be reduced as a consequence of EDI application. More important for many companies engaged in just-in-time production is the reliability of transport services and, when there are delivery or collection problems, speedy relaying of information so that contingency plans can be put in place.

On the supply-side, ITS can assist in the reduction of input requirements for a particular level of output or the more effective use of a given input level. This reduces the costs of providing transport services. These changes manifest themselves by permitting the supplier to reap more fully economies of scale, density and scope through the ability of management to manipulate factor inputs more efficiently and, in the longer term, in larger volumes. While these implications can affect both the capital (K) and labor (L) inputs into the provision of transportation services, in the short term they are more likely to impact on the variable factors. In terms of simple cost function analysis, this means an asymmetric shift of the cost function, of the form seen in Figure 12.2 to C*.

---

[10] The empirical literature on the use of EDI is relatively small and much of that relating EDI to logistics is in relation to trucking rather than air freight; e.g., Walton and Lewis (1995) and Crum *et al.* (1996). It also tends to focus on aggregate uptake rates.

[11] In this sense it moves away from the more common methodology of economics with its basis abstract modeling and back to a more institutional approach to economic issues.

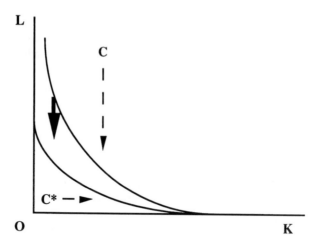

Figure 12.2 Shift in the cost function

More specifically, the ways in which information systems are used in logistics can vary considerably, but analysis of a particular case can help pinpoint some of the details of the current situation as well as highlighting some of the challenges that exist in incorporating information systems into economic models. The interest here is in the use made by an air cargo forwarder of EDI. Much of the specific information in this chapter is, therefore, the result of extensive interviews with a mid-sized privately owned air freight forwarder located in the Washington area of the USA.[12]

The forwarder has a contract agreement with an umbrella air-freight forwarding organization, establishing an institutional network throughout the US and Canada, along with formal and informal agreements with forwarders and customs brokers outside the US and Canada (Figure 12.3).[13] The forwarder uses an informal network of cartage companies, airlines and integrators for cargo transportation. In this context, the forwarder must maintain a communications network, capable of tracking and facilitating the movement of freight throughout the system.

The communications network not only has a role in its own right but also acts to integrate the formal and informal networks within the forwarder's systems architecture. The technology level of communications used within these formal and informal networks is often out of the control of the forwarder but has a direct effect on the forwarder's productivity, and on its ability to fulfill the demands of

[12]   Some indication of the nature of the overall regional economy in which the forwarder operates is to be found in Stough (1997).
[13]   The figure also offers some indication of the features of the various components of the forwarder's systems architecture.

shippers. Because air freight forwarders are susceptible to inroads made into their business by large integrators, their ability to remain competitive in the transportation and logistics arena often hinges on their capacity to keep pace with information technology advances and to utilize these advances in value-added services to their customers.

The fast-paced, global expansion of the package express companies, now often referred to as integrators, has been closely linked with information technology advances, including EDI, advanced cargo tracking and handling techniques, hub facilities for overnight package sorting, and computerized truck routing systems. Additionally, FedEx and UPS now have technologies that route freight through the most cost-effective mode of transportation (Page, 1996b).

The global explosion of the express and logistics industries has developed in a synergetic relationship with industry's demands for inventory reductions and just-in-time deliveries (Brown, 1997). Nationally, logistics and transportation now account for at least 25% of the cost of finished goods and have increased supply chain productivity.

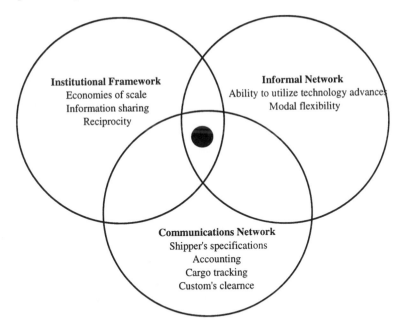

Figure 12.3 Airfreight forwarders' systems architecture

One manufacturing firm based in Indianapolis saw a 57% increase in productivity and a reduction of inventory of 65% with the implementation of a logistical information system. It is estimated that, at any given time, 10% of the volume of the US's inventory is in motion, a number dependent on information logistics. None of this would be possible without the information technology developed, in large part, because of pressures from the transportation industry (Graham, 1995).[14]

As an example of the extended networks used by the integrators, UPS communications technologies include UPSnet, a system composed of a dedicated satellite, 500 000 miles of communications lines, and links to 1 300 distribution sites world wide. The system currently tracks about 821 000 packages per day. The cost of technology improvements at UPS between 1986 and 1991 was $1.5 billion, and expected benefits include increased operating efficiencies. DHLNET, a TCP/IP communications network used by DHL, also provides routing, delivery times, and cargo tracking and customs clearances, and increases system efficiencies.

By 1989, the large express firms such as FedEx, Airborne, UPS, and DHL were using their own trucks for on-demand pick-ups, making investments in cargo aircraft, operated under single vendor control, developing systems dependent upon large scale small package deliveries, but also increasingly responsive to customer demands for value-added services such as logistics management and just-in-time deliveries. The capital investment cost of entrance into the now global package express market has become so great, that no new companies are likely to emerge within the current market (Ligon, 1992).[15]

Air cargo tonnage has continued to increase globally, and at a faster rate than airline passenger services. The integrators, continually looking to increase their market share, have branched out from overnight document and small package delivery to acceptance of heavier cargo, making inroads into the scheduled airlines cargo market. With integrators now controlling about 75% of the domestic air cargo market, airlines and forwarders alike are looking to new and improved technologies to increase productivity and gain back some of the cargo market that has been lost.

The smaller forwarders have had tried to remain competitive without the ability to invest heavily in capital assets or to implement the sophisticated communications systems used by the integrators and large freight forwarding companies. These smaller companies have been looking for competitive solutions,

---

[14]   Brown (1997) offers a number of other US examples of the impact, such as the 10% cost saving Whirlpool has enjoyed in bringing its materials into its plants within improved logistics information systems provided by Ryder Integrated Logistics in 1994.

[15]   Specialist firms such as USCO have also grown up to link into companies' computer systems to analyze the way that products flow through a customer's business and then provide advice on how the customer can set up its own computerized system and modify such things as warehouse locations.

including greater use of technologies, alliances, and *ad hoc* working agreements (Page, 1996a).

One result has been the emergence of networked air-freight companies; formal umbrella organizations that handle accounting for the cartage and airline bills, and customer invoicing, while allowing the forwarders to maintain independent operations. In this case study, the umbrella organization offers its forwarders reduced air cargo fees, because the group as a whole purchases a greater volume of cargo space, and because of cash flow benefits, a continual problem for many forwarders due to airline demands for fast invoice payment.

The networks offer the advantages of economies of scale, density and scope, a forum for information sharing among otherwise independent forwarders, and a system of reciprocal care of the cargo shipped. These are joined by the combined purchasing power of the network and availability of other service benefits such as group health insurance and legal advice. The system also provides an electronic accounting system, with e-mail transfer of receivables and airline and cartage payables, which are then processed by the corporate office. An internet system is capable of handling electronic internet bidding for the individual forwarders within the system, when appropriate for large scale or renewable cargo contracts.

A freight forwarder may own its truck operations. In this institutional network, some of the forwarders have opted to run local cartage operations, but this is not obligatory and the Washington office does not own or operate trucks, making it dependent upon external cartage operations. This forwarder, then, does not usually have direct contact with the cargo that is being handled; it is dependent upon the cartage companies, airlines and, in some cases integrators, for cargo transportation and tracking and, in tandem with this, is dependent on the other companies' information sharing technologies or communications systems. But it also has the flexibility to choose the mode or intermodal transportation, whether the choice is based on transport timing, cost, or both.

Because the productivity level of the forwarder depends upon its ability to synthesize information quickly within the informal operations of the network, it has developed into a hybrid, a communications and transportation consulting firm, selecting and coordinating the modes of transportation according to the time-definite demands of the shipper, the distance the cargo is to be transported, the weight and dimensions of the shipment, the shippers' pricing limitations and, when necessary, the carriers' cargo tracking capabilities.

Cargo tracking is critical to an air freight forwarder's operations. Often, the forwarder is given a window of time by a customer in which to make a pick-up, then must meet cargo drop deadlines for the airlines, be informed of the cargo boarding the intended flight, know when cargo is ready for pick-up at the airlines, meet delivery deadlines and then provide the shipper with an immediate proof of delivery. Tracking the freight as it passes through the intermodal system is essential in order to compensate for problems as they arise, and in order to complete the transaction with the shipper. Ideally, the communication network should provide the forwarder with real-time information. Figure 12.4 provides an indication of the complexities of such a system.[16]

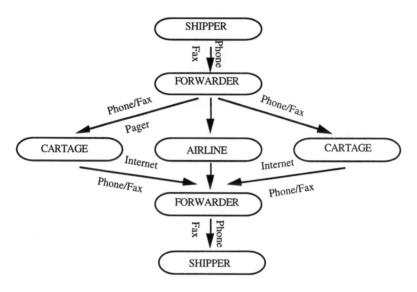

Figure 12.4 Communications network

In the case of the Washington forwarder, the local cartage company of choice is HBI. HBI traditionally used either two-way radios or pagers to contact drivers while en route. The system failed when numerous busy signals were received,

[16]   As an example, a shipment moved by air within the informal transport network, with cartage and airline selections made upon receipt of the shipper's orders, requires the following:
- shipper contacts forwarder (by telephone or fax) with job specifications;
- forwarder contacts cartage firm (by telephone and fax or in cases of night or weekend pick-ups, pages drivers who respond by telephone) with job specifications including airline drop;
- forwarder reserves airline cargo space (by telephone);
- forwarder receives confirmation of drop from the driver (by telephone or internet);
- forwarder receives boarding confirmation from airline (by telephone or internet);
- forwarder alerts driver of cargo pick-up time at airline and job specifications (by fax and/or telephone);
- forwarder receives proof of delivery (POD) from driver (by telephone, fax or internet);
- forwarder contacts shipper with POD (by telephone, fax or internet).

reception was poor, the driver not in the truck, etc. The system did not allow for computerized dispatching of drivers. HBI changed to a computerized dispatching and tracking system in December 1997, with software custom designed by Datatrac. Vehicles were equipped with on-board mini-computers, allowing instant messaging of cargo data, such as PODs, along with e-mail capabilities between the driver and the dispatcher. The mainframe computer processes driver positions, along with new orders as they are received, increasing the productivity of the driver and dispatching operations. The computer also relays pick-up and drop times, and PODs, within a 45 second time frame to the forwarder, via fax or the internet.

While HBI is the main cartage firm used by the Washington office, it is not the only one. In October 1996, the forwarder handled 396 shipments at a total weight of 275 671 pounds for domestic transport. It used the services of 82 cartage firms, contracted four exclusive line haul trucks and used twelve airlines, four integrators, and six overnight expediters.

Modal choice often means expedited freight travels on the ground, with the transport solutions taking priority over mode (Bell, 1996). Few cartage companies used by the forwarder have computerized systems and, if they do, they would not necessarily be compatible with the system used by HBI. Each additional system has the possibility of requiring separate software for computer tracking by the forwarder, possibly negating the convenience of computerized cargo tracking on the office system.[17]

The airlines have become increasingly sensitive to the relative loss in air cargo to the integrators. Cargo comprises only 10% of airline revenues (20% on some international lines), but it is often cargo that tips the balance between a profitable or non-profitable flight (Hill, 1996). Between 1980 and 1995, freight revenue ton-miles by airlines that are primarily passenger carriers grew by 88% in the domestic US market and 173% in the international market, but the revenue ton-miles produced by the all-cargo air carriers grew even faster. The seven major all-cargo carriers flew 9.3 billion revenue ton-miles in 1995, up 405% from 1980 (US Department of Transportation, Bureau of Transportation Statistics, 1997).

Although forecasting in this field is notoriously difficult,[18] the volume of air

---

[17] The problem of standardization is unlikely to be solved in the short term given that there are numerous mobile communication systems operating in competition with each other within the US. The technology, using either cellular, satellite or wide-band radio communications, is becoming increasingly affordable (Cooke, 1996) and, whereas these systems have been employed by large courier and trucking fleets in the past, the market is moving within reach of the small to mid-sized cartage companies.

[18] There are many possible reasons for this, not least are the problems of attaining data (Button, 1999). The impacts of the changing regulatory regime under

freight is expected to increase at an annual rate of 7% over the next 20 years, with a 92% revenue increase expected in the ten years between 1994 and 2004 (Boeing Commercial Airplane Group, 1996). In 1995, the US revenue for air freight totaled $61.3 billion. With this business at stake, the industry has been turning toward computerized cargo tracking systems in an effort to stop the flow of business to the integrators and to satisfy forwarders' demands. Predictability and information are seen as being more important than the actual shipment. Information access is not only the ability to increase quality of service but also a means of increasing the productivity levels along the links in the transport chain.

The large airlines now have computerized cargo tracking systems but most have not reached the sophisticated levels of the integrators. There are a number of reasons for this. The forwarder will book a shipment on a specific flight with the airlines. When the freight is dropped, it is entered into the airline's computers. It is loaded on a pallet and brought to the tarmac for boarding. However, due to unknown cargo demands made by either the quantity of passenger baggage, US mail, or other cargo with priority boarding, the cargo may not be loaded into the airplane. Because the boarding manifest is hand entered into the computer after the plane has departed (the freight is not scanned as it goes on), the forwarder is not aware the cargo is not on board until up to an hour after the flight leaves the airport. This causes a problem with the cartage company attempting to make the pick-up at the destination airport and with meeting shipper's time-sensitive deadlines.

An additional set of problems occurs. The freight left on the tarmac is not necessarily entered into the airline's computers as booked for the next flight out, even though it is physically next in line for boarding. The booking agents, not aware of this freight, will show space available on the next flight, and continue to book cargo on an airplane that has already been committed. Hence, even though the process is computerized, the airlines are unable to provide the correct, real-time information, whether over telephone or the internet, that the forwarders require for efficient operations.

The airlines are aware of these problems and are moving toward a standardized cargo tracking system, one able to provide the forwarders with real-time information.[19] The forwarders will have the ability to relay these messages to their customers; large forwarders such as AEI have already begun to do this. With global shipping and interline agreements, airline cargo alliances are moving toward standardized products and automated systems. Forwarders will receive the added

---

which most air freight is carried add to the forecasting problems (Reynolds-Feighan and Durkin, 1997).

[19]   Singapore Airlines, for example, have been doing this for a number of years.

benefit of being able to sell global systems to their shippers.[20]

Bar coding of air freight cargo is now being done by at least one major European cargo carrier. The cargo facilities have gained significant improvements of freight management. The bar codes on containers, palletized freight, and the air bills accompanying each piece of freight are scanned with portable units. Not only does it provide real-time information on cargo position, but the system automatically prepares manifests and tracks temperature-sensitive cargo (Newton, 1994).

The small to mid-sized air freight forwarder has traditionally depended on the telephone to conduct business. The entry of the facsimile machine made significant changes to the efficiency of the forwarders' operations. Before facsimiles, forwarders would have to maintain staff to send and receive messages during the business hours of differing time zones. With the ability to fax alerts to cartage companies retrieving freight from a distant shipper or airport and, conversely, to receive fax alerts from other forwarders, staff hours could be reduced. Facsimiles are used extensively to coordinate customs clearance of cargo with overseas brokers, before the freight arrives at the airport. This is important because simple technologies, such as fax machines and pagers, have given important positive efficiency gains to small freight forwarding operations.

The integrators, however, have applied new pressures on forwarders. Not only have forwarders lost business to the integrators, but customers are beginning to expect technologies, such as internet access to freight tracking, from some of the smaller forwarders. And some members of the cargo community question whether shippers are demanding too much in tracking capabilities, draining airline profits without adding any real value to the services provided. Conversely, some shippers use the forwarders because of the personal service provided - the subjective quality of telephone contact with someone personally familiar with the freight shipped and its transportation status.

Many freight forwarders must depend upon cartage companies and airlines to invest in the more sophisticated technologies. This is not only because of freight handling procedures themselves but also because forwarders have tended to work on small margins, with a narrow asset base (Malkin, 1992). Once they are in place, the cost of use of EDI systems to the forwarder is minimal − a computer with a modem and an internet connection. However, the cost of delay in the adoption of new technologies caused by waiting for others to implement new services may be

[20] Cargo Multinational EDI Association (Cargo MEDIA), established through the International Air Transport Association (IATA), has been working on a standardized messaging system using EDI for booking, cargo tracking and billing purposes. Additionally, a bar code labeling program is being prepared in order to ensure international consistency and to facilitate real-time tracking.

great, with loss of business due to lack of real-time freight tracking capabilities and loss of marketability of the forwarders' services.

System benefits to the new tracking technologies come in a number of different forms and can prove to be significant for many actors in the overall freight movement element of the logistics process (Figure 12.5). They can cut costs and enhance the overall quality of service offered. The advantages are not gained without cost in terms of investment and training but these are falling over time and systems are becoming increasingly user-friendly.

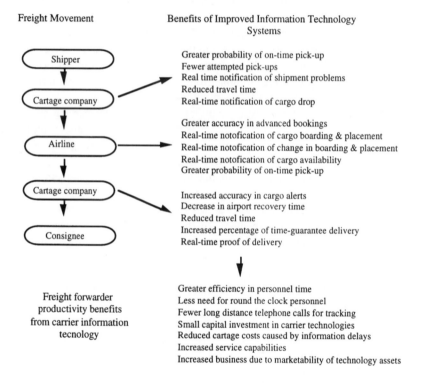

Figure 12.5 Forwarder benefits

There would, therefore, seem to be important potential improvements to performance for each segment of the intermodal transport of cargo if improved tracking technologies were deployed. Major benefits of more widespread use of EDI would seem to include a virtual elimination of errors, reduction in paperwork, better use of resources including personnel, reductions in travel time for cartage vehicles and the ability to handle greater quantities of freight.

The development of the supply-side of transport economics has broadly mirrored developments in the discipline more generally. The economic theory of production revolves around a 'Black Box' in which various factors are combined by a profit maximizing entity with the intention of producing a minimum cost output. From a policy perspective, this tradition is epitomized by the 'structure, conduct, performance' framework that looks at how an undertaking behaves but only in terms of external factors such as the number of sellers, barriers to market entry and prevailing demand conditions.

Economists, such as Leibenstein (1966), have questioned the extent to which allocative efficiency is attained and others, such as Baumol (1959), have argued that motivations often have little to do with traditional ideas of profit maximization. The growth in managerial economics and management studies has helped to shed more light on production processes and how they change over time. The freight transport element of this is the development of a more thorough understanding of logistics. It inevitably complicates economic modeling but it can add to the appreciation of how transport markets function and provides a more complete basis upon which cost functions may be specified.

The introduction of EDI, or indeed any consideration of information systems, into transport economics poses problems as well as offering new insights.[21] Traditional economic assumptions of homogeneity may well not apply. As the case study illustrates many actors can be involved in the decision-making process when information systems become more diverse and many of the channels of information may be informal in nature. It is much less clear who the consumer of transport services is when intermediaries interact with final consumers.

Forwarders are an important intermediary in the sector but their demands on services are somewhat different to many direct customers. In many cases they also have more direct access to information channels. There are a variety of economic benefits to the freight forwarder when cartage companies and airlines implement computerized information systems, especially cargo tracking technologies.[22] With little investment in capital assets, the forwarder would be able to enjoy the investments of the other firms. Small to mid-sized forwarders, like other similarly sized companies, can become free-riders for EDI standards and systems to be established (Saccomano, 1996). The cost of waiting, however, may be significant, as the integrators further erode the cargo market and shippers' demands for real-time technologies increase.

Barriers to the establishment of tracking technologies available to the forwarder are not insignificant. Many cartage firms, like the forwarders they

[21]   This is equally true on the passenger side, where traditional demand modeling assumes full real-time information about costs of alternative routes, modes, etc. In fact, new on-board information systems may make this a more realistic assumption now than in the past.

[22]   A Ryder Dedicated Logistics manager, for instance, states that ability of drivers to cope with the value-added services is a major concern.

service, are too small to afford the investment in tracking technologies. To some small companies, the telephone, facsimile, and pager systems work well enough, and the need for additional technologies cannot be justified. Additionally, there may be problems in finding and hiring drivers who are able to adjust to the increasingly sophisticated tracking software and hardware.[23] Airlines, however, are moving quickly to establish standards and information systems, and to make the information available quickly to the forwarders. The concern of the forwarder is that the information be accurate and current, and the new systems promise to be both.

A barrier to the forwarders' implementation of services based on established tracking systems is the lack of time and expertise. Typically, a small firm owner is involved in day-to-day operations and has difficulty in allocating the time to investigate new avenues of technologies, such as internet access to airline cargo tracking. In this respect, the networked systems have given forwarders the opportunity to share information on industry developments and take advantage of technologies as they are available.

In his assessment of the future of economics, Hahn (1991) argued that 'Not only will our successors have to be far less concerned with the general (leave alone the 'generic') than we have been, they will have to bring to the particular problems they will study particular histories and methods capable of dealing with the complexity of the particular.' Recent work in transport economics has benefited considerably from advances in pure theory (particularly regarding regulation and demand), in econometrics (e.g., flexible production functions and stochastic frontier analysis) and has made some efforts to draw upon the advances in programming (e.g., data envelopment analysis). It has made fewer advances in understanding the inner workings of transport services suppliers and how they are responding to new information systems.[24] The new technologies are, however, changing the ways in which freight transport is being supplied and, as the case study illustrates, the inner workings of even a small concern are far from simple.

12.5 CONCLUSIONS

Transport networks are seldom independent entities. They often overlap geographically, can involve a number of modes and are inter-linked with a variety

---

[23]   There are also many social benefits from improving freight transport (van de Riet and Twaalfhoven, 1998).

[24]   Much of the work that has been done has been with regard to passengers' transport; e.g., on the instruction of information systems and the substitutability of electronic communications for trip making (telecommuting, video conferencing, etc.).

of non-transport networks. In the case of air transport, all of these features are present. The various modes of transport offered, including air transportation can combine to provide an integrated service to users, or they can act as substitutes and compete for the customer's demands. Airlines cannot function without modern information systems that allow then to manage their assets effectively and match the services that they may offer to the demands of potential customers.

These links are growing rather than contracting as technology moves forward and as the demands on air transport services rise over time. Technology, for example in the guise of CRS systems, has already led to remarkable changes in the ways in which customers interact with airlines via travel agents and now the advent of e-commerce has began to reshape this relationship. Whilst in the past airlines have tended to think of themselves as providing medium and long haul transport, with other modes dealing mainly with short-distance movements, congested infrastructure and the demand for different service attributes by users is leading to them thinking more in terms of integrated transport and to reassessing their comparative advantages in some types of market.

13 SAFETY AND ENVIRONMENTAL ISSUES

13.1 INTRODUCTION

The number of major aircraft accidents in 1996, combined with concerns expressed by the aircraft manufacturer Boeing, that, while in statistical terms civil aviation may be slowly getting safer or, at worst, no more dangerous, the sheer growth of aircraft movements in future years will result in a rise in the absolute number of accidents, has brought forth a response from the aviation sector (*The Economist*, 1997). In the US, for instance, there has been the White House Commission on Aviation Safety and Security.

This has also happened at a time when the air transport market is experiencing considerable change. As with many other sectors, air transport service suppliers are responding to commercial pressures for increased internationalization to reap benefits on both the cost and demand sides. The growth of international airline alliances is the most transparent manifestation of this although there has been an even more rapid growth in point specific alliances (see Chapter 2). Alliances are seen by carriers as a means of exploiting economies of scale, density and scope in the provision of services and as a means to exploit economies of market presence in terms of patronage.

The growth in number and the nature of modern alliances have raised a series of policy issues concerned mainly with antitrust issues. The concern of this chapter is to look at another aspect of the globalization of the airline industry and of the growth of various forms of airline alliances and that is the potential effect of these developments on airline safety. In particular, it looks at the way market forces change and can influence the commercial incentive for airline operators to offer safe services. Public policy regarding safety has been reacting to changing conditions in aviation markets, but such reaction should be in the context of the new commercial environment in which airlines provide their services.

The chapter initially outlines some of the broad trends in globalization that are influencing and being influenced by developments in commercial aviation. It then turns to look at exactly what is taking place regarding airline alliances, and particularly those of a strategic nature. An important point here is that conceptually the details of any airline alliance may have specific safety implications. A model of how airline safety is incorporated in both corporate and public policy is then developed and subsequently the implications of strategic alliances are set within this context. The discussion is entirely concerned with aviation markets in what might be termed the industrial world. Strategic airline alliances do exist in many parts of the world but here we content ourselves with considering those involving partnerships between carriers based in the major, economically developed countries. The arguments may be somewhat different for other parts of the world.

13.2 GLOBALIZATION, AVIATION AND STRATEGIC ALLIANCES

Globalization and internationalization are two of the major industrial trends of the late twentieth century (Thurow, 1996). Part of these trends are reflected in the significant growth of trade that has taken place in the 1990s, with real export growth in the industrialized countries that make up the Organisation for Economic Cooperation and Development (OECD) running at over 7% per annum. Put another way, from 1964 to 1992, first world production was up by 9%, but exports were up by 12%, and cross-border lending was up 23%. Equally, there has been a significant rise in foreign ownership of assets that are now estimated to total about $1.7 trillion.

Whether these trends are passing fads or represent genuine long-term adjustments to the way that production and trade are conducted it is perhaps premature to judge. There are for, example, arguments in the economic literature that the advances in communications and information systems that are occurring represent a major shift in production akin to those seen in the Industrial Revolution. The preliminary indications are that, whatever the rhetoric, they are more than transient trends.

As we have seen, this has also been taking place at a time when the institutional structure in which air transport services are provided has seen significant developments. The US's deregulation of its domestic markets combined with its subsequent commitment to an Open Skies approach to international aviation, have been instrumental in changing, through both demonstration effects and direct knock-on effects, the ways in which many other air transport markets are now regulated (Button, 1990; Button and Swann, 1989a). The intra-European market has moved towards a situation akin to that found within the US (see Chapter 5). The EU has since 1988 through a succession of 'packages' has moved to a position that by the middle of 1997 left air transport within the Union largely free from economic regulation (Button, 1996a; Button and Swann, 1992). Intra-European market liberalization has also been accompanied by liberalization of many bilateral agreements involving European states and the US.

Outside of Europe and North America, the majority of national markets in South America have been liberalized with extensive privatization programs of different types. The markets in Australia and New Zealand have also been deregulated. Additionally, the establishment of the World Trade Organization has also brought into play, albeit in an extremely small role, a new and geographically wider policy making institution to supplement the roles already played by bodies such as the International Civil Aviation Organization (ICAO) and the International Air Transport Association (IATA). Aviation issues are also on the agenda of new regional groupings such as the Asian-Pacific Economic Council. There is continued pressure, therefore, for this international liberalization process to continue (Organisation for Economic Cooperation and Development, 1997).

This combination of market trends and institutional reforms, together with rising incomes and increased leisure time, have contributed to the steady growth in demand that have taken place in aviation markets. Additionally, technology advances have meant that aircraft efficiency has risen and air traffic control systems, despite their continued inadequacies, can handle greater volumes of traffic. This has exerted positive effects on the cost side of the international air transport equation.

As a result of these trends, air passenger traffic has grown considerably worldwide. Further, all the indications are that as a sector it will continue to expand into the foreseeable future albeit at differential rates in various geographical submarkets.

In line with many other sectors, aviation has experienced significant moves towards globalization and internationalization in terms of its market structure. Indeed, it is the stated objective of the major UK carrier, British Airways that it intends to become a 'global carrier'. In pursuit of wider market coverage, and in an effort to enhance their own internal efficiency, airlines have followed a number of courses. The recent development of various forms of airline alliances is perhaps currently the most controversial of these (Button, 1997).

The exact definition of what constitutes an airline alliance, as is clear from earlier chapters, is a vague one especially given that the institutional arrangements linking airline activities is continually changing. The notion of airline alliances is, however, one that has recently come under public scrutiny in the wake of several much publicized efforts by a number of major international airlines to link their operations. The nature of the ties differs between groupings and so has the success of airline partners in gaining both official ratification and in the subsequent way partners have been able to operate and manage their alliances.

Historically, international alliances in aviation can be traced back as far as 1945, when the IATA was established primarily to coordinate international air fares. The bilateral structure of agreements that emerged following the inability of the 1994 Chicago Convention to initiate free international aviation markets regulated fares, routings, schedules, designated carriers and often embraced revenue pooling. The primary aim of the immediate post-war structure was to protect non-US carriers at a time when, as a result of the Second World War, the US had built up a dominant fleet of aircraft that could be transferred to commercial uses. Subsequently, the regime was often used to protect economically inefficient state-owned carriers from the rigors of market competition.

The late 1980s and the 1990s saw the growth of new forms of international alliances that have embraced somewhat different characteristics and that serve different purposes. They have been less institutionalized, in that they have generally been formed by privately owned commercial airlines outside any governmental or intergovernmental agency initiative. The main growth has also been in international alliances. The first of these, between American Airlines and Qantas, was signed in 1985 and the number has grown rapidly since.

Alliances, however, are in a continual state of flux. According to the *Airline Business* survey, for instance, the Spanish carrier Iberia reduced its alliances from 27 in 1995 to 13 by May 1996. Over the same period Austrian Airlines canceled six agreements and added four new ones, Swissair added six agreements and dropped three, while United Air Lines canceled six but added two. These changes generally are part of a tidying-up process as carriers formulate more coherent network strategies.

The exact number of airline alliances that now exists is unclear, not only because of the dynamic nature of the arrangements that make it almost impossible to keep abreast of changes, but also because the term alliance is a generic one with no precise definition. It can, in a strict legal sense, mean some degree of equity ownership of one carrier by another but it is more often interpreted in looser terms to embrace such things as code-sharing agreements, interchangeable frequent flyer programs and coordinated scheduling of services. Equally, airlines are often involved in a large number of different alliances, sometimes embracing a single partner but which may involve several others carriers. A more recent feature is that increasingly several major carriers are linking their activities in so-called 'galaxies'.

An annual survey by *Airline Business* attempts to track alliances involving the major carriers and to report changes in the main features of the alliances (see Chapter 2). The growth in strategic airline alliances is immediately obvious as is both the relatively small quantitative importance of alliances involving an equity stake and the slow growth in their numbers.[1]

The North Atlantic market embraces a number of major strategic alliances that involve the airlines code sharing and cooperating in other ways across a large number of routes so as to strategically link their networks. This type of strategic alliance dates back to the formation of the Global Excellence alliance formed by Swissair, Singapore International Airlines and Delta in 1989.

Other alliances, such as that between Continental and Alitalia and United and British Midland, are regional in their orientation, involving code sharing between specific regions. The vast majority of alliances, point-specific alliances, are, however, relatively minor, targeted affairs that usually generate few controversies. Blocked-space agreements are often a feature of point-specific alliances with airlines purchasing and reselling blocks of seats on each other's flights.

Point specific alliances, in their various guises, may in some cases lead to fears of the prospect of monopoly domination of an individual route. The multifaceted, strategic alliances in which the large international carriers are increasing becoming engaged are now seen as potentially posing challenges of a somewhat greater magnitude.

In detail, alliance arrangements may take a number of different forms (Button, 1997b).

---

[1] The data presented is not, however, definitive and one finds, for instance, *The Economist* in 1995 producing slightly different figures and claiming that there were then 401 alliances, double the number it estimated four years earlier. The overwhelming conclusion, though, is that the number of alliances is large and increasing.

Full mergers of domestic airlines were a feature of the US domestic market following deregulation under the 1978 Airline Deregulation Act as the initial period of instability moved into one of consolidation and rationalization.[2] Mergers of this type are the most extreme form of alliance and have been a traditional way in which carriers can coordinate their operations and other activities. They are claimed to enjoy the advantage that complete control of a carrier is in the hands of a single board and that resources can, therefore, be allocated more effectively.

In practice, though, mergers are not always successful. As a generalization, mergers linking overlapping networks in any transport industry tend to offer fewer economies than those that combine interfacing networks (either in geographical terms or with respect to the types of service offered). In some instances problems also arise because those involved have miscalculated the costs of transition. In particular, airlines have individual management styles and have particular forms of labor contracts that are ofetn very difficult to marry across carriers.

Mergers generally involve the need to obtain institutional approval from various authorities. Traditionally, in virtually all cases cross-border mergers are not possible because of regulations limiting the degree of permitted foreign ownership in an airline. a notable exception to this being the joint ownership of SAS. Cross-border mergers also pose problems in terms of the implications for international air transport agreements since the nationality of a carrier can become blurred in these circumstances.

Even within countries mergers are often controlled by national governments, although the degree of control can vary. In the US, for instance, the Department of Transportation took a very passive stance on mergers following deregulation of the domestic market. Individually, European countries have taken a variety of positions as has the EU in recent years. In many cases mergers, such as those between British Airways and British Caledonia and Air France and UTA, have only gained approval by the airlines relinquishing routes or slots.

The strongest form of airline alliance short of direct mergers or take-overs involves either unidirectional (as with the USAir/British Airways and Northwest/ KLM alliances) or cross-equity holdings. While mergers still take place, more recently there has been a tendency for the level of equity holdings to fall short of a full merger. This is particularly so when airlines from two countries are involved and national laws limit the extent of foreign ownership. What the evidence does not show, however, is the degree of control that equity holdings can afford an airline; and, in particular, voting rights are often less than the relative amount of capital involvement.[3]

---

[2]   For example, of the 34 new jet scheduled carriers to enter the US market between 1978 and 1992, only two remain operating, with the vast majority of the others being merged with incumbents.

[3]   The relative importance of airline alliances involving equity stakes tends to be declining, with *Airline Business* recording about 10% of agreements in May 1999 involving equity investments, compared with 16% 1996, 18% in 1995 and 21% in 1994. This, nevertheless, does not mean that there has not been a large increase in

Potential travelers have traditionally suffered from a dearth of information regarding the air transport options open to them. The problem was compounded from the late 1970s as fare deregulation and the widespread adoption of yield management techniques by airlines introduced a massive array of continually changing fare options. The use of computer reservation systems (CRSs) provides the interface between the carriers and the potential travelers. Airlines combine to make use of the information channels provided by CRS systems to stimulate their joint traffic flows. This involves code sharing. Code sharing is now often seen as the main feature of any airline alliance and the number of code shares has grown considerably in recent years.[4]

Hub-and-spoke operations, and in particular the 'banking' of flights, that are a concomitant of effective hub-and-spoke operations, can be more efficient if carriers coordinate their flight schedules. Hub-and-spoke operations, by allowing traffic to be consolidated and trans-shipped between flights can enhance load factors and allow airlines to reap any economic benefits of economies of scope and scale that exist. By agreeing to coordinate schedules, two allied airlines increase the potential amount of traffic that can on-lines across their combined networks.

Franchising has been almost a tradition in sectors such as fast food and clothing. Its appeal in aviation is that it allows a major carrier to spread its brand name and generate revenues on thin routes without the necessary commitment to major capital investments. It is now a form of alliance that is growing in popularity in international markets and especially in Europe, where British Airways has been particularly successful in developing franchising activities. Some other carriers have been less enthusiastic about franchising arrangements and have been slower to adopt them.

13.3 THE AVIATION SAFETY EQUATION

The incentive for any airline to provide safe services is the potential for lost business that it would suffer if its accident rate or, more strictly, its perceived accident rate, exceeded the net benefits that passengers enjoy from making use of its services. Safety is one of the attributes of an airline's characteristics that

their absolute importance and other surveys indicate that from 1992 ownership stakes of above 20% have predominated.

[4] Technically, a code share is a marketing arrangement between two carriers that allows them to sell seats on each other's flights under their own designator code. In the case of connecting flights of two or more code-sharing carriers, the whole flight is displayed as a single carrier service on a CRS. From the customers' perspective, what it does is to give the impression of an on-line service or, at the least, to offer some features of an on-line service such as single check-in, common frequent flyer program and coordinated flight schedule. Code shares can be across a wide range of services, as with the major strategic alliances, but more often just involve a single service or a small network of services. A stronger form of code sharing involves blocked space arrangements. In this case one carrier buys space on another airline's aircraft that it then sells in its own right and using its own designator code.

potential customers, and subsequently investors, look at in making decisions.[5] This inherent market pressure is boosted by regulations and codes of conduct imposed on the industry by government. Government involvement is usually justified because of imperfections in the market that make it impossible for potential passengers to understand fully the risks confronting them or, even if information is adequate, they have insufficient market power to ensure levels of safety are optimized.

One simple way of looking at air transport safety from an analytical point of view is to think in terms of the incentives that influence the actions of those providing air transport services. Essentially, the incentive function takes the general form (equation 13.1):

$$S = f(E, G, I) + \varepsilon \qquad\qquad (13.1)$$

where: S reflects the safety standard level adopted by an airline; E reflects the private economic incentive to be safe (reputation, insurance premiums, lost business, share price and the interest of flight personnel); G represent the government safety codes and policies (e.g. regarding aircraft safety features, maintenance standards and crews' working hours and conditions); andI represents infrastructure considerations (airport design and air traffic control).

There is an additional random element in the function, ε, indicating the risk of something else, such as a missile or bomb, causing the accident.[6]

With respect to safety levels pursued by a carrier, there is no reason to assume that it is socially desirable for an airline to be 100% safe. There are opportunity costs associated with devoting resources to safety and it is clear from individuals' decisions on such things as the speed they drive at or the choices they make regarding car travel over air travel that factors such as time savings or cost saving often override safety considerations. Indeed, many argue that aviation is excessively safe and with better information about relative safety records, society would put fewer resources into aviation safety (Kahn, 1988).

Regarding the items on the right hand side of the equation, while these may be expressed as independent factors they will almost certainly exhibit some degree of correlation. The nature of infrastructure provision, for instance, is inevitably linked to the safety regulatory regime adopted by the authorities. Equally, the internal economic incentives influencing an airline's pursuit of safety cannot be separated from the institutional regime within which the carrier operates. Nevertheless, the three-way division is helpful in tying together the implications of globalization and strategic alliances with aviation safety considerations.

---

[5]   Safety is a very general term for which there is no strict definition. This is because accidents can take a variety of forms and be of differing intensity. Also the actuarial probability of an accident may differ from an individual's perception of the chance of being in an accident (Moses and Savage, 1990). No attempt at a strict definition of safety is offered here but rather the subject is treated in general terms.
[6]   The issue of terrorism and the growth of strategic airline alliances is outside the domain of our discussions.

13.4 STRATEGIC AIRLINE ALLIANCES AND THE SAFETY EQUATION

If we consider equation 13.1, there are a number of ways in which changes in the institutional structure of the airline industry, including the creation of strategic alliances, can have a bearing. These are in terms of the internal structure of the airlines' operations and in the ways in which the authorities may respond to them.

What we do not have at present is a very large body of rigorous empirical evidence linking strategic airline alliances to safety questions. Alliances are too new for detailed statistical analysis of the type required; short term fluctuations in airline accidents rates involving a very small number of incidents does not make for easy econometric work. The concept of an alliance is also a rather broad one. What one must generally rely, therefore, on in looking at the safety implications of alliances is parallel experiences of aviation developments that have also influenced the structure of the sector and on anecdotal evidence gleaned from the experiences of alliances to date.

13.4.1 Aggregate air travel demand

The creation of strategic alliances is seen to generate, when controlled within an appropriate economic regulatory regime, significant consumer benefits (e.g., US General Accounting Office, 1995; UK Civil Aviation Authority, 1994). In particular, the various economies enjoyed by carriers combined with service enhancements and lower fares for users have led to more travel by air, the latter being a reflection of enhanced consumer surplus. This, however, only occurs provided carriers do not excessively exploit any monopoly powers associated with the market strength that alliances could potentially generate.

More air travel beyond the increase that would occur without the growth of alliances would of itself lead to more aviation accidents according to the arguments presented by Boeing in 1996. The added economic efficiency that alliances bring about and the accompanying additional traffic will inevitably increase the potential aggregate number of aviation incidents. Public policy (G in equation 13.1) is inevitably going to respond to this. In the US, for example, the Federal Aviation Authority (FAA) has already begun releasing more information on safety in an effort to keep the public better informed, although the complexity of aviation safety issues suggests that such information will in practice not really offer any great insights.[7]

Equally, in terms of I in equation 13.1, the provision and use made of aviation infrastructure may be changed. At present many airports and air traffic systems are

---

[7] Moses and Savage (1990) make the argument that, after any institutional change, the safety authorities may adjust their preferred level of safety - essentially recognizing that the economic benefits associated with the new regime are worth trading for possibly lower safety criteria. This does not, however, mean that no safety reforms are needed to meet this new safety standard; put simply, all the parameters have shifted and adjustments may be needed to safety regulations etc. to allow for this even at a new safety level.

working at, or above their design capacity and are also, in many cases, using out-dated technologies. There will be enhanced pressures both from a purely air transport perspective and from a safety standpoint to ensure that existing infrastructure is used better and new infrastructure provided where justified.

There is, though, another way of looking at this aspect of the safety issue. What is missing from many calculations on the implications of increased demand for air travel is the opportunity cost element. If individuals were not traveling by air they would be engaged in some other activity that of itself has a safety aspect attached to it. In this sense, it is not altogether clear that more air travel will result in more deaths and injuries in aggregate.

Little empirical work has been conducted into this aspect of airline safety. What evidence there is mainly relates to experiences with domestic airline liberalization in the US after the enactment of the 1978 Airline Deregulation Act (Rose, 1989; Morrison and Winston, 1988; Oster and Zorn, 1989). The limited amount of analysis undertaken here indicates that on many routes where US airlines could compete with car travel then the diversion effect from car to plane as the result of improved services offered by airlines reduced the number of road deaths. The calculations are made difficult, however, because of the inherent problems in defining counterfactuals, but Bylow and Savage (1991) estimate that some 275 highway fatalities were avoided by the modal switches to air travel.

Not only are the US estimates very tentative for technical reasons, but extrapolation to the effect of strategic airline alliances poses particular difficulties. While the alliances do involve situations where new structures of fares, services and routes can induce modal transfers, many of the really important alliances focus on long distance travel, often over oceans, where commercial aviation is the only viable transport option.[8]

What the alliances do seem to do within the narrow confines of transportation is to induce travelers away from carriers outside alliances. This, for instance, is seen very clearly in the analysis that has been completed on the strategic alliances affecting the North Atlantic market where the KLM/Northwest and British Airways/USAir alliances demonstrably took traffic from competitors (Gellman Research Associates, 1994; US General Accounting Office, 1995). From the safety perspective, the issue then becomes one predominantly of discovering whether the alliance carriers are safer than their non-alliance counterparts. This issue is addressed separately later.

13.4.2 Consumer information
Airline alliances affect the type of information that travelers enjoy regarding the actual carrier they fly with. As can be seen from Figure 13.1, that provides a simple schema of the links involved for Swissair in the Global Quality alliance in 1994, alliance structures even in the early 1990s can be very complex. It is not

---

[8]   There still remains the broader issue of what induced travelers would have done with their time even if they would not have been traveling by an alternative mode of transport. All human activities have risks of accidents associated with them and many of those exceed those risks to do with flying.

difficult to see, in this case, why, for instance, someone booking a multi-segment flight with Swissair could be puzzled at being carried on a Delta aircraft. Blocked space agreements are potentially even more confusing.

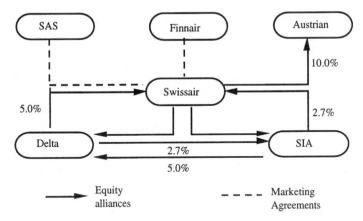

Figure 13.1 Swissair and the Global Quality alliance, 1994

In terms of safety, consumer information raises two important questions; these concern the identity of the carrier actually taking the passenger and the type of aircraft used for the flight.[9]

Although the variations are very small, airlines do have differing historic safety records. This is not only in terms of the number of accidents they have experienced but also relates to the degree to which they have been held negligent for accidents. Airlines also offer different frequencies, qualities of service and fares. In a perfect world, potential passengers should be able to make their choices and trade off the various attributes of carriers when selecting the airline they wish to fly. In the case of alliances, it is often difficult to know exactly what are the various portfolios that are available because the actual carrier providing the flight is not immediately transparent.

There have been public policy efforts to ensure that alliance code-sharing arrangements are not used to misinform or disadvantage passengers. This involves not just direct issues revolving around individuals having information on the exact airline they will travel on but extends to such things as responsibility for missed connections, direction to connecting flights and ensuring appropriate information systems are available at airports. To prevent screen padding on CRS systems, the European Union now limits code-shared flights to being displayed twice. The United States has no such limit on displays in this way. What the US rules do require is that passengers are informed by US airlines of the actual carrier with

---

[9] There is also the supplementary issue of who is responsible for an accident involving passengers from several airlines on an alliance flight and how compensation is to be extracted. This is not dealt with here.

which they travel. The European Civil Aviation Conference (ECAC) has a similar code for disclosure but is not legally binding on member states.

It is not just airlines that have differing safety records, aircraft also do.[10] There are arguments that that potential travelers' perception of the safety of different aircraft types can affect their decisions and that information on plane types should be transparent. Airline alliances could hide or make it more difficult for passenger to have information regarding aircraft type.

The most documented case of the commercial impact of an aircraft crash on its producer relates to the McDonnell Douglas DC-10 after two major crashes (one in 1979 and the other in 1989). Here there was evidence of significant falls in the producer's share prices immediately after the 1979 incident that could only be accounted for in terms of lower anticipated sales (Chalk, 1986). Karels (1989) extended this analysis to look at the share prices of airlines such as American that flew DC-10s and found that their share prices were also adversely affected after the accident.[11] In contrast to this the 1989 DC-10 crash seemed to have no long-term adverse effects on the McDonnell Douglas share prices. There is also no evidence that the share prices of Boeing or Lockheed have fallen significantly after an accident, suggesting the impact of the 1979 DC-10 crash was atypical (Chalk, 1986).

13.4.3 Alliances versus non-alliance carriers
One very vocal concern expressed at the time of the liberalization of the US domestic air transport market in 1978 was that free markets would force some carriers to cut corners with regard to safe operations to keep their fares competitive. The argument was resurrected after a series of accidents in the mid-1980s and the fining of a number of carriers for violating maintenance and safety regulations (Nance, 1986). In fact, the evidence seem to be that in this case market changes seem to have had little effect on the overall level and trend of accidents in the US market (Morrison and Winston, 1988).

What the experience has shown, though, is that there do seem to be variations in the inputs airlines put into safety. The US National Transportation Safety Board, for example, expressed concern about budget constraints restricting maintenance, although this may well have reflected the actual safety regulations in place for such operations (US Congress, Committee on Government Operations, 1977). Following deregulation in the US domestic market, a number of studies produced evidence of reduced expenditure on potentially safety-related activities, such as maintenance and training, in some segments of the market (Lederer and

---

[10]   In general, jet aircraft have a better safety record than turboprop aircraft, but there are also difference within these two broad categories. For example, Boeing 747 (100, 200, 330 series) aircraft have about 1.6 crashes per million departures; Airbus A300-600 aircraft have about 1.4 per million departures while Boeing 737 (300, 400, 500 series) aircraft have about 0.5 per million departures.

[11]   Focusing on patronage rather than financial performance, however, Barnett and LoFaso (1983) found that the crash had no impact on the market shares of routes where DC-10s were flown.

Enders, 1989). Even if this did not produce more incidents immediately, there is an argument that in the longer term a legacy effect would result in accidents. Assessing the validity of this argument is not easy. Technical advances, especially in jet engines, have reduced maintenance needs and isolating this shift in the maintenance cost function from the impact of institutional changes is difficult.

There is also another set of findings of importance, namely linkages between the actual financial position of an airline and an airline's accident record. Rose (1989; 1990) finds, in analysis of US domestic carriers, that there was a one year lagged positive effect on accident rates of higher operating profits, although the effect is negligible amongst the largest carriers.

Where does this lead with regard to the growth in strategic alliances? From the evidence obtained on North Atlantic routes, alliances tend to attract passengers from non-alliance carriers. One consideration relates to the financial pressures on alliance carriers; are the market pressures to cut corners on such things as maintenance and to employ cheaper, less experienced crew greater for alliance carriers? In general, the evidence is that alliance carriers, especially when there are mergers or equity holdings involved, have a larger resource base and are, therefore, less prone to liquidity difficulties. Indeed, in the case of many alliances (e.g., British Airways/USAir, KLM/Northwest and American/Canadian) significant financial injections were made by one partner into the other to bolster a flagging financial position. This suggest, *a priori*, that many alliance airlines are in stronger financial positions than they would be operating in isolation. This in itself, though, may not mean overall improved safety even if it were true that a strong financial performance correlates with less accidents. This is because the non-alliance carriers on these routes would be the subject of greater financial pressures.

Comparisons between alliance carriers and non-alliance carriers also bring two other different elements into consideration.

First, blocked space alliance arrangements, whereby a carrier buys capacity on another plane, and coordinated scheduling by code-sharing partners can lead to the use of larger aircraft on the routes involved. The evidence that is available is that larger aircraft tend to be safer than smaller ones (Oster and Zorn, 1989).

Second, and to complicate the situation, where alliances do in some way rationalize the use of the partners' capacity this can free up the market to allow new entry. This may come about for purely commercial reasons or it may be driven by institutional factors. For instance, in several mergers involving European carriers' slots were relinquished by the partners to meet anti-trust requirements. Similar arrangements seem important in the efforts of British Airways and American to form a strategic code-sharing alliance. This raises questions as to whether the new entrants are safer than incumbents.[12] The

---

[12]   One of the problems with the work that has been completed in this area is that many new entrants into scheduled aviation are not new to airline operations *per se*. In many cases they are charter carriers that have extended their operations (Levine, 1989). This may not have been a problem in the past; after all, where the newcomers originate is not relevant to the safety equation which is merely concerned with the implications

evidence, which again is mainly from US experiences, is that there is little difference in the safety record of established carriers and incumbents measured in terms of accidents (Oster and Zorn, 1989; Rose, 1989).[13]

The airline switch effects of strategic alliance on safety are, therefore, far from clear. It does not seem, however, that there are strong forces likely to lead to reduced safety as a result of the way traffic may switch between airlines once an alliance is formed in a particular market. Indeed, there could be made a case that, if anything, the changes would, on balance, have a positive effect on safety.

13.4.4 Managerial incentives

There are also a number of other ways in which the E component in equation 13.1 may change as a result of alliances being created. Does the establishment of an airline alliance, for example, influence the management incentive of the partner carriers to change their approach to safety? The available evidence is not altogether conclusive as to the implications for airlines of accidents. Much depends on the circumstances involved and on how the airline manages the crisis.

One argument is that accidents will discourage people from using the carrier concerned even after the immediate impact has passed (Borenstein and Zimmerman, 1988). While this may or may not be true, measurement of this effect is made difficult by the natural response of any carrier who is adversely affected in this way to lower fares so as to keep its market share (Rose, 1990; 1992).

An alternative way of looking at the topic is the impact of accidents directly on the financial status of an airline. Simply eye-balling the share prices of ValuJet and TWA showed a significant declines in their respective share prices (both actual and against a moving average) following crashes involving their aircraft in May 1996 and July 1996, respectively.[14] The contrast is particularly clear when compared to American Airlines.[15] American did, though, experience a major crash during this data period, the loss of a Boeing 757 in Columbia during December 1995, but this does not seem to have adversely affected the smoothed share value index. The difference would seem to lie in the location of the crash, the American incident being outside the US, and in the perception of who was at fault.

This rather uneven pattern of stock market implications is in conformity with more rigorous studies that have been completed looking at the financial implications for an airline of crashes. In this context there has been work on a number of themes, much of it concerned with US experiences.[16]

---

of a change in supply on accidents, but in many markets there are now more genuinely new airlines and their potential safety characteristics are now important.

[13]   Incidents involving new entrants, other things being equal, however, tend to result in more fatalities, possibly due to the lesser experience of pilots.

[14]   The ValuJet case is complicated by the temporary closure of the airline by the FAA for violation of safety and maintenance codes just after one of the airline's DC9s crashed in Florida.

[15]   This lack of any apparent immediate link between airline safety records and profits is also consistent with the findings of Golbe (1986).

[16]   Outside the US, the *Edwards Report* in the UK concluded in 1969 that independent operators were less safe than regularly licensed carriers for the period 1955

An accident seldom costs an airline in terms of immediate payments because all carriers tend to be extensively, and frequently excessively, insured. What it may do, however, is to affect an airline's image and to impact on future insurance premiums it must pay. Mitchell and Maloney (1989), for instance, looked at insurance rate adjustments after crashes and 'brand name effects' and found that share price falls can be attributed both to the projected future costs of higher insurance and to a brand name effect associated with at-fault attribution. In contrast to this, Chance and Ferris (1987) find an immediate dip in share price of an airline involved in an incident, although it is extremely short-lived, but no impact on the industry in general. Golbe (1986) in his study of the early years of US domestic deregulation concluded, 'There does not seem to be a statistically significant relationship between safety and profits.' Borenstein and Zimmerman (1988), in contrast found that airlines suffered an equity loss of about 1.0% as a result of an accident. The picture is not, therefore, very clear on this topic.

Where does the establishment of alliances fit into this picture? Much depends upon the nature of an alliance. If the structure is extremely loose then there would seem to be little reason or pressure for the management of any carrier to change its behavior patterns with regard to safety. Where there is, however, a closer relationship, especially involving equity holdings, there may be grounds for expecting airlines to closely monitor each other's safety performance, especially if each fears that any diminution in reputation of one airline would adversely affect the other. Empirical evidence on this is simply not currently available; the strategic airline alliances are simply too new and their structures too variable to allow any sort of detailed testing.

13.4.5 Lobbying power

As well as looking at the implications of alliances for the internal effects they may have on airlines' attitudes towards safety, and managements' reactions to this, we must also bear in mind that airlines often exercise considerable political power. In general, large suppliers exercise more political power than do smaller ones and so one would expect alliances to have more political sway than individual airlines. Looked at in another way, airline alliances effectively change supply conditions and therefore, this could potentially have implications for the G component of equation 13.1.

One possible way of looking at this more systematically is to treat those involved in supporting any aviation policy as a coalition (Keeler, 1984). Following this approach, strategic alliances serve the interest of a number of different parties. In terms of an airline alliance acting to alter government policy on aviation safety, one must look, in the context of coalitions, at the factors motivating those in the 'ruling coalition'. There would seem to be little reason for the users of aviation to try to reduce safety standards unless they were initially felt to be excessive. From a competitive perspective, there would seem to be little reason for member airlines of an alliance to compromise on standards since,

to 1966 and that smaller carriers and charter operators were more susceptible to accidents.

generally, they are the larger carriers that have solid safety records giving them a comparative advantage over non-alliance rivals. The exception to this is when an alliance has a monopoly position and it is to the combined advantage of the partners' to reduce overall safety standards and to save on their costs. There are few incentives for the bureaucracy responsible for safety to compromise on existing standards since this would reduce their power and influence. Equally, airline producers would seem to be little affected in their attitude to safety and in their lobbying positions by the formation of a strategic alliance.

What one can concluded from these few observations is that there is unlikely to be any significant changes in the attitudes of those concerned with alliances to manipulate public policy in a way that would be detrimental to current safety conditions.

13.5 AIR TRANSPORT AND THE ENVIRONMENT

The state of the natural environment is a continuing public concern in most countries. The impact of transport on the environment in general has received particular attention in recent years (Button, 1993b). Transport has been the subject of major pieces of legislation at local, national and international levels as policy makers and those supplying transport services have acted to respond to this public concern.

The underlying difficulty is that, because of a number of intrinsic features that are associated with transport, it is seen to lead to particular environmental difficulties. These features include the following:[17]

- It is a major sector in its own right,
- It is a growth sector,
- It is highly visible,
- Transport is demanded where people are,
- It is a mobile source of pollution (in the widest sense),
- It generates a diverse range of environmentally intrusive effects,
- It is a major contributor to many forms of environmental damage.

In comparison with many other transport modes, however, air transport has been left largely outside many of the recent mainstream environmental debates. Where there has been concern it has mainly been in relation to issues of local importance (most notably aircraft noise around airports and fears concerning safety for those under flight paths).

The situation is, however, now changing. Air transport is clearly growing in importance as a mode of transport. Existing markets are expanding and new networks are emerging. Air transport is becoming more visible than in the past,

---

[17]   These features have led to one commentator describing transport as 'Industry on Wheels' although 'Industry on Wings' might be more appropriate in our context.

especially as urban sprawl leads to encroachment on airports.[18] The forecasts provided by Boeing and others also indicate that this growth is likely to continue into the foreseeable future. This growth is also taking place within a much less regulated market than in the past (Organisation for Economic Cooperation and Development, 1997). The trend is towards the privatization of airlines and air transport infrastructure and towards more commercially driven markets. This has raised public concern about how the wider social interests are to be represented in decision making.

Aviation needs significant amounts of surface infrastructure to function effectively but many airports are now congested and there are also land access problems at some. Adding new airports or expanding existing ones imposes a variety of environmental costs on those living nearby, but these may be costs that have to be borne if growth in air transport is to take place. There is amounting conflict between those living near airports and those who use them as a result (Button, 1998b). The perception of trends in environmental problems is often compounded because, although many of the adverse effects of air transportation and especially noise round airports have been reduced for individual flights and the noise envelopes for many airports are now consequently smaller, people's expectations have risen, in part because of rising living standards.

Additionally, many of the concerns about the environmental degradation that is associated with surface modes of transport have been addressed (albeit with varying degrees of success) and one can perceive a feeling that there is now the need to move on and to look at other forms of transport.

The following sections initially outline the main environmental implications of modern air travel. In particular, they seek to set this in the more general context of environmental concerns. We then move on to offer a brief consideration of how one can look at the underlying reasons why air transport does create these difficulties, paying particular attention to the way economists tend to look at these types of problem rather than being driven by pure engineering considerations. We consider ways in which the scale of the problem may be evaluated to enable more balanced judgments to be made.

Finally, we pay attention to the policy tools that may be deployed to confront the worst of the difficulties. In tackling this last task, the aim is rather to look at the options that are available than to be prescriptive. This is for no other reasons than that the choices are often difficult and, in many respects, we still have limited knowledge concerning key parameters that underlie the adoption of a viable policy package. There is also the wider issue that air transport interacts with other transport modes and there is a need to review policy options in a broader context.

13.5.1 The issues

This economic success of air transport has been accompanied by increasing concerns about the longer term and its wider implications for society. While

---

[18]   For example, the Air Transport Association recognized the increasing role that environmental concerns will play in air transport policy making in a statement in 1996.

environmental matters have not been at the forefront of air transport policy concerns in the past they are now attracting increasing attention. Also, while most people concur that environmental preservation is important, what constitutes an environmental concern is not always agreed upon. At the macro level, notions of sustainability and sustainable development have gained a widespread general acceptance following the publication of the Brundtland Report in 1987 (World Commission on Environment and Development, 1987).

While the notion that current generations should leave as a legacy a natural resource base for future generations comparable with the one it inherited itself has an intuitive appeal, operationalizing this at a global level has proved problematic. At the level of individual sectors such as transport it is even more difficult and becomes even more so at the level of the individual industry.[19] There are simply too many possible trade-offs that could potentially lead to a sustainable path.

13.5.2 The scale

More traditional approaches to looking at environmental protection focus upon micro concerns, on particular issues and on individual environmental problems. These approaches, while less holistic in their basis, do provide a framework of analysis that is more consistent with normal policy making. Thus, while not intellectually ideal they offer tractable tools of immediate use in such areas as project appraisal, regulation and pricing.

In this context, aviation can be seen to have environmental effects at various levels.[20] Some of these are local and concern such things as noise, land-take and soil contamination at airports and emissions of pollutants into the air by aircraft while at airports or during the landing and take-off cycle. Among these emissions are those of VOC due to fueling of aircraft and fuel handling in general, and CO emissions of aircraft due to incomplete combustion while being in the idle and taxi mode. For these pollutants the shares emitted at altitudes lower than 1.5 kilometers are dominant (from 50% to 80%).

On a larger spatial scale the emissions stemming from climbing, approaching and cruising take the form of CO_2, NO_X, SO_2, CO, CH, and VOC. On a global scale emissions are important that take place in the stratosphere (i.e. the layer above 12 kilometers where the ozone layer is located). Since many aircraft cruise at about 10 to 12 kilometers, a non-negligible part of the aircraft effluent is emitted in the stratosphere.

In terms of what is actually taking place regarding empirical and applied research, this traditional approach has mainly manifested itself in studies concerned with noise and pollution at airports and with certain aspects of safety.[21] A recent

---

[19]   See papers in Banister and Button (1993).

[20]   Space precludes a detailed outline of the implications of these types of emissions for health, etc. For details, see papers in McMichael and Fletcher (1997).

[21]   Safety is often not considered an environmental issue and this is sensible for many aspects of the topic. However, there is the issue of whether people living close to airports have their quality of life reduced through the fear of a plane crashing on them.

small-scale survey by Morrissette (1996) looking at the activities of consultancy firms specializing in environmental work in relation to airports, for example, found that issues concerning wetland damage was of most importance followed by air quality, noise and storm water pollution work.

A considerable amount of work, by academic and government economists, has been done on the social costs of noise nuisance. A variety of techniques have been developed in order to place a monetary valuation on such nuisances so that they may be traded off against the more narrowly defined economic benefits of air transport. Generally, this has involved efforts to express noise nuisance in terms of the financial implications of living near a major noise source, such as an airport, on house prices; for example, see Table 13.1 for a summary of some of these values (Johnson and Button, 1997).[22]

Table 13.1 Estimates of the implications of noise nuisance effects on property values (percentage change per decibel increase)

Study	Year	% of House Price	Country	Data
Abelson	1979	0.45	Australia	Disaggregate
Collins and Evans	1994	0.45	UK	Disaggregate
DeVany	1976	0.80	US	Aggregate
Dygert	1973	0.60	US	Aggregate
Emerson	1969	0.57	US	Disaggregate
Gautrin	1875	0.35	UK	Disaggregate
Levesque	1994	1.30	Canada	Disaggregate
Maser	1977	0.62	US	Aggregate
McMillan	1978	0.50	Canada	Disaggregate
McMillan	1980	0.87	Canada	Disaggregate
Mieszkowski	1978	0.40	Canada	Disaggregate
Nelson	1979	1.10	US	Aggregate
O'Byrne *et al.*	1985	0.52	US	Aggregate
O'Bryne *et al.*	1985	0.57	US	Aggregate
Paik	1972	0.65	US	Disaggregate
Pennington *et al.*	1990	0.60	UK	Disaggregate
Price	1974	0.83	US	Aggregate
Uyeno *et al.*	1993	1.13	Canada	Disaggregate

More recently, researchers have concerned themselves with trying to gain more direct valuations through sophisticated questioning of those affected.[23] These

In the broad definition favored here, this aspect of safety is seen as an environmental concern as much as something such as noise nuisance.

[22]   Full citations to the surveyed studies are contained in the article.

[23]   Technically, these two approaches are referred to by economists as the revealed preference and the stated preference methodologies.

studies indicate that noise nuisance costs may have been underestimated in earlier work. Feitelson *et al.*'s(1996) work implies the valuation per decibel to be up to 4.1% of property values.

In terms of atmospheric pollution, air transport also imposes adverse effects. However, the evidence on this, and in particular the particular implications of individual pollutants is still not always solid. It does contribute No_x to the atmosphere and is, thus, contributing to acid rain, but the evidence indicates this contribution is very small. At altitudes between one and twelve kilometers, aircraft emissions would seem to impact on the creation of global warning gases and at higher altitudes (where there is supersonic flight) to ozone depletion.

As a mode of passenger transport, air transport is slightly less fuel efficient than the car but offers significant benefits in terms of time savings over longer distances (See column 2 of Table 13.2, although care must be exercised in the way this type of data is handled). In aggregate, air transport is responsible for about 5% of the world oil consumption and 12% of that consumed by the transport sector. The International Civil Aviation Organization estimates that civil aviation consumed about 138 million tonnes of aviation fuel in 1990 and that this will rise, given existing policies but allowing for improved technology, to about 220 million tonnes by 2020.

Table 13.2 Relative fuel consumption of air transport

	Energy per pkm (MJ/pkm)	Average Speed (km/hour)	Energy use per Travel Hour (MJ/hour)
Aviation	2.2	500	1 100
High-speed rail	0.7	150	106
Intercity train	0.7	80	56
Car	1.5	50	75

While one can always question these types of calculation, translating this into damaging emissions, the Air Transport Action Group in Geneva finds that air transport only contributes about 2–3% of CO_2 emissions that are, in turn, responsible for about 1% of any global warming effect. Even more tentative are the estimates of the monetary costs of air pollution. A US study by Hansson and Markham estimated this to be about 1.08 cents per passenger ton kilometer, Kagerson's work in Scandinavia puts it at 0.70 cents, while German analysis by INFRAS/IWW offers a range between 0.18 and 1.09 cents.

There have also been efforts to place a larger set of values on the social costs of air transport and, in particular, to set these costs in the context of alternative modes. These studies rely on a combination of syntheses of previous work with new findings. The results of one recent study by Levinson *et al.* (1998) generated the estimates found in Table 13.3. The difficulties with such work are numerous and the findings should be treated with some care.

Table 13.3 Comparison of long-run average social costs of passenger transport

Cost Category	Air System ($/pkt)	Highways ($/pkt)
Noise	0.0043	0.00045
Air Pollution		
CO	0.0000018	0.000033
VOC	0.0001530	0.0026
NO_x	0.0001700	0.00067
SO_2	–	0.00021
PM10	–	0.000057
Carbon	0.0005800	0.00017
Accidents	0.0005	0.0200
Congestion	0.0017	0.0069

Measuring many other environmental effects, let alone attempting to place a monetary value on them, is even more difficult than with items such as noise and air pollution. Airports, for example, despite often innovative design are not normally seen as visible delights. There are problems of drainage at and near airports as work courses are diverted and fuel seepage from storage tanks can take place.

13.6 ENVIRONMENTAL VALUATION DIFFERENCES

Benefit-cost analysis, in one way or another, now forms the backbone for much of the analysis that underlies public policy making regarding air transport. For example, US federal requirements are that major regulatory programs must 'not be undertaken unless the potential benefits...outweigh the potential costs' (National Archives and Records Administration, 1985). The benefit-cost approach is not, however, without critics, and questioning ranges from such details as the legitimacy of attempting to place monetary values on all items in the benefit-cost account to the intellectual validity of using partial equilibrium analysis in public policy making (e.g., Hoehn and Randall, 1989).

The focus here is on the more detailed level of assessing the viability of a particular approach to benefit-cost analysis and in particular the increasing use made of benefit transfers when conducting such analysis. Benefit transfers involve deploying valuations based on primary data gathering in a specific study to estimate changes in consumer's surplus with regard to another policy[24]. The implicit assumption doing this is that parameters derived in one location, at one time and for one type of policy making decision, can legitimately be employed in other decision making exercises. This implies that either there is some common parameter applicable to all studies or at least one can explain variations between studies so that parameters taken from one exercise can adequately be modified to be used in a second exercise. If neither of these conditions holds, original independent analyses may be required for each case study.

The issue is one of degree. No modeling exercise produces a completely accurate picture, and benefit transfers are no exception. The practical point is whether benefit transfers provide sufficiently acceptable accuracy for the task at hand. Acceptance criteria are likely to differ quite considerably across a range of applications (Smith, 1992).[25] The focus here is on one particular type of transfer relating to the use of aircraft noise nuisance valuations, although the findings may have wider implications.

This study is concerned with examining which benefit transfers may be legitimate in the context of applying aircraft noise nuisance valuations derived at one airport location to decision making at other sites. Airports are considered environmentally intrusive, but as air transport is growing rapidly, there are pressures for both the expansion of air transport infrastructure and a more extensive use of existing facilities. Benefit-cost procedures now normally form an integral part of assessing any major developments of large airports and are increasingly being used in appraisals of smaller, local facilities. High levels of aircraft noise are usually the main concerns expressed by objectors to expanding airports infrastructure or when there are efforts to push more traffic through existing terminals.

There is a well developed methodology for placing monetary values on aviation-related noise nuisance, but the approach to date has generally been to rely on individual case studies for each assessment. For reasons of economy and to speed up decision-making benefit, transfer may be seen to offer a tractable method of improving current practices. This study initially elaborates on both the benefit transfer concept and the airport noise nuisance issue prior to conducting an analysis of variations in noise nuisance values that have been found in a range of individual cases, the underlying hypothesis being that, if there are wide and difficult to explain variations in the values found, then it is difficult to legitimize the use of benefit transfers in this context.

---

[24]   Benefits here may be viewed as either cost or benefit items in a benefit-cost calculation, with a cost simply being a negative benefit. Much of the early analysis using the technique was in the water resources field and involved transferring monetary values of such things as recreational benefits from one study site to another policy site. The term often takes a wider meaning and many of the controversies surrounding its use apply to the general transfer of economic parameters.

[25]   Brookshire (1992) offers some guidance as to the degree of accuracy required in estimated benefits and costs according to the use they are put to. These consideration may influence the extent to which benefit transfers may be deemed acceptable.

13.6.1 Benefit transfers

The underlying idea of benefit transfers is that one can take findings or parameters from one case study and adopt them to assist in policy making elsewhere.[26] Conceptually, this is not a particularly new idea, and economists have a long tradition of applying parameters such as demand elasticities in consumer analysis or input-output coefficients in macroeconomic policy assessments in work other than that from which they were initially derived. Even in public appraisal procedures where non-market factors are of importance, benefit transfer has a long pedigree; in the United Kingdom's Department of Transport's computerized COBA framework of road investment appraisal, standardized values and parameters synthesized from previous studies are often included in the benefit-cost calculus. This has included values for reduced risks of accidents, for travel time savings and for changes in vehicle operating costs. In the US, unit-day values were used as early as 1962 to evaluate recreational resources.

In practice, benefit transfer applications can be divided into three broad types: estimates based upon expert opinion; estimates based upon observed, revealed behavior; and estimates based upon stated preference elicitation mechanisms (Brookshire and Neill, 1992). The distinctions, however, are somewhat blurred. Expert opinion, for example, is seldom formed in a vacuum but normally relies on judgments arrived at after assessing either revealed or stated preferences studies. The bases of these assessments are subjective and usually opaque.

The recent interest in benefit transfer is mainly associated with more fully incorporating environmental externalities into the benefit-cost framework.[27] The issue is whether one can legitimately transfer non-market valuations of these externalities, particularly those valuations deploying stated preference (contingent) valuation techniques that have become a major focus of the literature (O'Doherty, 1995). This may be seen as a belated switch in emphasis from methodological concerns about intellectual legitimacy of alternative non-market evaluation techniques to questions of application and policy relevance of empirical findings.

While there have been important developments in evaluation methods in terms of revealed and stated preference methodologies, external environmental costs and benefits are often given only sparse and partial coverage in many benefit-cost analyses. Increasing public concern about environmental implications of various

---

[26]   Brookshire and Neill (1992) define benefit transfers as 'an application of a data set that was developed for one particular use to a quite distinct alternative application.' Boyle and Bergstrom (1992) talk of 'the transfer of existing estimates of non-market values to a new study which is different from the study for which the values were originally estimated...[T]his is simply the application of secondary data to a new policy issue.' This is the broad form of definition adopted in other studies, e.g., Opaluch and Mazzota (1992). The journal, *Water Resources Research,* carried a special edition on benefit transfers in volume 28, number 3, 1992.

[27]   Some of the issues were highlighted in the UK in the context of road investment appraisal (UK Department of Transport, 1992). Demand for valuation studies in the US rose at the federal level with the enactment of Executive Order 12291 that caused the Environmental Protection Agency to use benefit-cost analysis to assess policy (Freeman, 1984).

policy options is leading to a broader approach to benefit-cost analysis being sought. This is also taking place at a time when many intergovernmental (ranging from the European Union to World Bank), national and local agencies are being committed to the adoption of comprehensive appraisals of policy options and project proposals.

From a pragmatic perspective, benefit transfer has a number of attractions. In terms of financial expediency, taking parameters from one study or a synthesis of a set of previous studies and employing them more widely is much less costly than conducting separate evaluations for each individual decision made. Linked to this is a growing body of studies providing estimates of case specific parameters, and it appears sensible to see if they can usefully be mined for additional and useful insights (Bergh *et al.*, 1997). Benefit transfer can also help streamline decision making. Deploying previously derived monetary valuations estimates of environmental externalities can significantly speed up what is often considered a lengthy process of information collection, collation, and analysis.

From a methodological viewpoint, benefit transfer may be seen to introduce a degree of consistency into decision making through the use of common parameters across studies. This may be particularly relevant when the degree of accuracy in parameters does not have to be very high, as in the initial screening of projects. Luken *et al.* (1992), for example, discuss benefit transfers in terms of establishing limits within which parameters may lie. It is also relevant when a large number of relatively standard but linked policy issues are being addressed.

Additional to public policy making, legal requirements to provide forms of compensation to those adversely affected by environmental degradation and legal processes often seek out evidence from earlier cases as precedents.

Benefit transfers have their limitations. A central issue is the decision regarding which values can legitimately be transferred as calculated and which require additional analysis. In the latter case, benefit transfers may remain legitimate if appropriate adjustments can be made to allow for specificity in individual case studies.[28] One criterion for deciding on the potential transferability of results is to examine the variability between previous case studies and to explore the extent to which that can be explained and allowed in subsequent transfers.

13.6.2 Airport noise studies

The growth in air transport has taken place with comparatively limited expansion in the physical capacity of airport infrastructure. Initial excess capacity and better utilization of existing space have been the main facilitators of growth. The ability of segments of airport infrastructure to handle the forecast growth in traffic is now in doubt. Capacity has already been reached at ten of the largest 46 airports in Europe and is being approached at another sixteen. As a consequence, there are

---

[28]   McConnell (1992) essentially argues that, at present, benefit transfer is rather more an art than a science and, '[T]here is no simple, acceptable way mechanically to transfer a model.'

pressures for additional capacity to be built (Comité des Sages for Air Transport, 1994). Similar problems exist in several parts of North America.

Investments in new airports and expansions, together with the updating of existing ones are financially costly. Airports also impose a variety of serious adverse environmental effects on those living nearby. Despite much-improved technology residents and businesses experience considerable aircraft noise. For these reasons, airport investments are generally the subject of benefit-cost analysis. Putting a monetary value on the aircraft noise nuisances stemming from airport development as part of benefit-cost calculations has a long pedigree dating back at least to the seminal work of the Commission on the Third London Airport (1971). The vast majority of evaluations have been case specific, and the methodology generally deploys some form of revealed preference, hedonic price approach. These studies sought to place indirectly a non-market monetary value on the noise nuisance by examining the impact on property values in residential areas adjacent to an airport.[29] Traditionally, they have looked at marginal changes in real estate values associated with additional units of airport-related noise nuisance.

Recently, there have been a number of innovations in the evaluation methods employed, and several stated preference models deploying contingent valuation techniques have sought to elicit directly from individuals their willingness to pay for aircraft noise abatement (e.g., Feitelson *et al.*, 1996). This broad dichotomy of approaches poses some problems for benefit transfers. Revealed preference and stated preference frameworks are based upon differing sets of underlying assumptions. The appropriate use of one or the other requires that the entire benefit-cost framework into which they are fitted conform to their underlying theoretical basis. This is not a problem in itself, but it does mean there are inherent limitations to its general application.

More problematic is the considerable diversity of values generated both within and between the two groups of evaluation methodologies. With the hedonic pricing method, conventional surveys have produced a range of estimates of the impact of airport noise on local property values. Nelson (1980), for example, looked at thirteen studies and produced a property value discount range of 0.4% to 1.1% for each additional decibel of aircraft noise nuisance. These values compare to the 2.4% to 4.1% per decibel for house prices in Feitelson *et al.* (1996) stated preference work.

13.6.3 Meta-analysis

Meta-analysis was initially developed in the physical sciences and involves the statistical synthesis of existing case studies to extract additional information concerning, for example, representative parameters or factors (moderator variables) that result in study specific results. Glass (1976) provides a widely accepted formal definition as 'the statistical analysis of a large collection of analysis results from

---

[29]   These calculations have taken the general form:

$$\ln H = \beta_0 + \beta_1 NEF + \Sigma \beta_i \ln X + u$$

where β_1 is the noise coefficient, NEF is a measure of noise nuisance, β_i are non-noise coefficients, X are corresponding property characteristics and u is an error term.

individual studies for the purpose of integrating the findings. It connotes a rigorous alternative to the casual, narrative discussions of research studies which typify our attempts to make sense of the rapidly expanding research literature.'

Most of the statistical synthesis work concerned with environmental evaluation has employed some form of meta-regression procedure. In particular, it has been concerned with moderator variables that account for differences in the values of environmental externalities found in various case studies. Meta-regression analysis takes the general form (Stanley and Jarrell, 1989):

$$b_j = \beta + \Sigma \alpha_k Z_{jk} + u_j \quad (j = 1,2,...L) \ (k = 1,2,...M) \tag{13.2}$$

where b_j is the reported estimate of the relationship of interest in the jth study from a total of L studies; β is the summary value of b, Z_{jk} are variables that reflect the relevant characteristics of an empirical study that could explain variations amongst studies; α_k are the coefficients of the M different study characteristics that are controlled for and u_j is the error term

Transport-induced noise nuisance values can be explored in this framework. The general functional form that seems appropriate when seeking meta-analysis moderator variables in this context can be summarized along the lines of equation 13.3. The right-hand side of the equation effectively extends the argument of Hunter *et al.*, (1982) that much of the observed variance in correlations across studies can be accounted for by three statistical artifacts: unreliable data due to small sample size, inter-study differences in the reliability with which dependent and independent variables are measured, and inter study differences in restrictions of range.

$$Y = f(P, X, R, T, L) + \text{Error} \tag{13.3}$$

where:
* Y represents an outcome of interested. This may be a single measure, such as dbA in the case of noise, or it may reflect a variety of differing effects, such as level, duration and pitch;
* P can be treated as the specific cause of the problem (such as air traffic levels and proximity to source);
* X represents features of those affected by the nuisance (such as individuals' age and income);
* R, since the analysis is not based upon primary data but rather the combination of other studies, represents the characteristics of the research methods used in each study (such as econometric or survey) and the data used (e.g. time series or cross-sectional);
* T indicates the period covered by each study to allow for any underlying dynamic effects (such as systematic changes in social preferences); and
* L is the location of the study (which could be spatial, such as urban and rural, or may relate to the country forming the basis for each data set).

Justification for the above type of framework is necessary. First, much of the work using meta-analysis in the physical sciences tends to focus on P and X in equation 13.3. This is mainly because of the ability of those working in these fields to compare strict experiments where methodologies are identical and results tend to be reported in a more standardized way. The importance of so-called 'artifact effects', that are normally embraced in R in the social sciences, would seem to be much greater where the need for quasi-experimentation has often resulted in a considerable range of diverse model specifications, information-gathering procedures and econometric estimation methods being adopted. This obviously poses practical problems when attempting to express various studies' approaches consistent with the inherently numerical variables that are the basis of most scientific meta-analysis.

The question of estimation methodology may also be particularly important in many sub-areas of economics now expanding. Such is the case with several aspects of the environmental economics because different procedures can embrace differing components of cost (Pearce and Markandya, 1989). In part, this is due to the elements that make up the external cost of many environmental considerations. Boulding and Lundstedt (1988), for example, argue that individuals' values influence behavior in at least three ways: observed choice (i.e., revealed preference), people's conversations (i.e., stated preference), and adaptations as part of the learning process. Smith (1989) suggests that all three provide insights into measuring the economic value placed on environmental amenities, although there is no reason to expect the values to be the same. A simpler breakdown argues that individuals' preference for environmental protection consists of three components:

$$\text{Total Economic Value} = \text{User Value} + \text{Option Value} + \text{Existence Value} \quad (13.4)$$

User value is that which may be observed from behavior, option value is the result of individuals desiring to keep an environmental asset in case they wish to use it in the future, and existence value is the importance individuals attach to the very existence of an asset, even if they never have personal contact with it. These categories can be further refined, but the point is that estimation techniques that rely only on revealed preference tend to understate option and existence values. Stated preference techniques can embrace them more fully, thus yielding a higher valuation.[30] Similar types of issues can emerge in other areas of economics.

The same sort of argument apply to T and L, especially when time series and cross-sectional work is combined in the meta-analysis or there is considerable geographical variation in the sources of the data used. The importance of when and where the studies were conducted stems from the underlying economic preference model. At one level, preferences are context-specific, and differing contexts may result in varied valuations. One of these elements is information. Before the 1960s, lead additive was added to fuel and was felt to have negligible

---

[30]   This may be seen as a further form of potential upward bias in benefit-cost ratios that are the subject of Hoehn and Randall's (1989) critique of benefit-cost methods.

environmental effects. But medical work brought this into question and, thus, preferences were changed. We are now moving back in the other direction and concerns are being expressed about the health implications of the additives being used in place of lead. Equally, local conditions can be important because they can influence the choice set. A wealthy country or region could provide a richer choice set than a poorer one and preferences may be affected. Added to this are the constraints imposed by political and technical environments that are often space specific.

Applying meta-analysis to environmental evaluations has been done before, generally in the context of revealed preference valuations of externalities.[31] Smith (1989) considered the empirical work of 35 hedonic price studies and found consistency in the results that emerged once allowance was made for local conditions and assumptions. Smith and Huang (1995) examined some 167 hedonic models of the marginal willingness to pay for reducing particulate matter in the air, although their meta-analysis forced them to rely on only 86. The results show that market conditions and the procedures used to implement the hedonic models were important in explaining variations in the values individual studies produced.

Smith and Kaoru (1990) examined some 200 studies of recreational demand employing travel cost evaluation methods. They used meta-regression analysis to examine the results of 77 of these studies. One of the main conclusions that can be drawn from this body of analysis is that variations across studies can often be explained in terms of the specific nature of the recreational resources and the underlying assumptions made in the estimation models employed.

While variations exist in the parameters examined, the evidence from this body of environmental literature is that they can, in part, be explained in a way that potentially allows for adjustments if they are adopted in benefit transfers.[32]

In terms of putting monetary values on airport noise nuisance, empirical findings of eighteen economic studies deploying hedonic price techniques are examined using a simple meta-regression analysis.[33] Looking at results produced through the application of a single revealed preference evaluation methodology is likely to produce conservative estimates of any limitations in adopting benefit

---

[31]   A more comprehensive account of this literature is to be found in Bergh *et a.l* (1997).

[32]   Findings from other related areas are less strong. Waters' (1996) meta-analytical work on travel time savings values and Button and Kerr's (1996) on the effectiveness of urban traffic restraint policies do not offer any statistical confidence that benefit transfers can readily be recommended in these fields. Similar conclusions can be drawn from the meta-analysis of the output elasticities of infrastructure investment (Button and Rietveld, 1997).

[33]   Selecting a set of case studies for a meta-analysis is fraught with problems. In this instance, a standard computerized search was conducted. Studies were then selected in part according to the information made available within them. Studies were not included if information on the main variables in the regression was missing. Since the aim is not to actually find a representative parameter or to seek out appropriate moderator variables, the possible lack of a full set of case studies would tend to bias the results in favor of benefit transfers.

transfers since the technique has been more uniformly applied than contingent valuation methods. If there is little consistency across hedonic price studies then there is likely to be even less across contingent valuation estimates.

Results of these studies, all based on hedonic price index methods and offering a common measure of noise value (the change in property value associated with a change in noise level) provide a range of estimated airport noise nuisance values (see again Table 13.1). The set of estimated values has a standard deviation of 1.28. The studies differ in terms of when they were conducted, location of the airport considered and the level of aggregation at which the hedonic estimation was completed. To assess the importance of these case-specific features there is a need to transfer the entire demand function. The meta-regression embraces such effects in the form of dichotomous variables (Boyle and Bergstrom, 1992).

Table 13.4 shows the parameters from the meta-regression exercise with indicators of their statistical significance.[34] The results provide little by way of overall explanation for the variability in results or of any important influence that may be relevant. The low overall degree of explanation for variations in the noise nuisance values provided by the meta-regression, even allowing for the essentially cross-sectional nature of the analysis, offers little objective support for adopting any of the reported values, or an average of them, for benefit transfer purposes.

Table 13.4 Meta-regression parameters

Variable	Coefficient	Standard Error	2-tail significance
Constant	0.3761	1.3552	0.7854
US	−0.1563	0.9779	0.8753
Year	0.0562	0.0479	0.2604
Disaggregated data	−0.0351	0.9303	0.9704
R^2: 0.1340	Standard error of regression: 1.3085		Log likelihood: −28.1201

This does not mean benefit transfers are invalid; any one of the values found in the case study may be appropriate for transfer in specific situations. The problem is rather one of selection. The mean value of case study parameters would certainly not seen appropriate. Any selection of a noise nuisance value from these previous studies would inevitably be subjective. Although the importance of expert opinion should not automatically be discounted (Button, 1998a), this must inevitably raise questions about the widespread usefulness of benefit transfers if they amount to little more than legitimizing established judgments.

---

[34]   A previous meta-analysis that looked at a range of transport noise nuisance evaluation studies covering a variety of transport modes, including a limited number of airport studies, could only explain 40% of the variation in the values reported (Button and Nijkamp, 1997).

The argument about judgments in benefit transfers can actually be extended into the evaluation process itself. While all benefit-cost exercises require making a large number of assumptions, the real issue is making these as transparent as possible. Therefore, if it does ultimately come down to the analyst selecting a particular case study's parameter to transfer, justification for the selection should be transparent.

Benefit transfers are increasingly seen as cost-effective and expeditious in incorporating environmental effects into benefit-cost studies. In some areas, there is evidence that one can adopt, with due care and caution, parameters derived in similar contexts for some aspects of benefit cost analysis. A major issue, however, is the generality with which this can be done across various types of parameters, especially when dealing with non-market valuations of external benefits and costs.

Examination of a range of values obtained for noise nuisances associated with airports indicates that there is little justification for applying benefit transfer procedures at this time. The relatively wide range of airport noise nuisance values previously obtained and the difficulty of explaining it also raises further questions involving the overall legitimacy of the techniques that have been employed. The range of parameters cannot be explained by factors such as the country concerned or the data based employed and this raises concern about the overall usefulness of the hedonic method or, at the very least, the way it is applied.

13.7 THE ECONOMIC ISSUES

13.7.1 The theory

Economists have long had an interest in the environment, although the focus of their thinking has changed over time as new issues have evolved and new policy debates have taken the stage. The economic perspective is that at the margin any additional activity should generate benefits at least as great as the costs that are imposed. In standard accounting terms this would just mean weighing up the financial pros and cons of options. The welfare economic view that underlies public policy making takes a much broader perspective and embraces a full range of social costs. There is a trade-off between the different effects of any action that is multidimensional in its nature and this should be allowed for. What it does not mean, however, is that all environmental degradation is intrinsically undesirable; if the benefits to society exceed the costs then they are justified.

At the most basic level, economists view the underlying problem of excessive environmental degradation in terms of there being a market failure. In the very strictest terms this stems from the lack of adequate 'property right' allocations. In other words, there is no clear ownership of environmental attributes and, as a consequence, there is excessive consumption of them. They are called 'commons' in the environmental economics literature.

The environmental attributes are, therefore, external to the market process and to ensure their appropriate and efficient use they need to be brought within the market. As obvious as this may seem, it was not really until the work of the

Nobel Prize winner Ronald Coase in the 1960s that this became generally accepted. If every environmental attribute were owned then there would be a market for them and, of course, there may be good reasons why property rights are not allocated. It may be difficult to define exactly what they are and to police a market system. There may be wider social reasons why it is felt the market process may prove inefficient (e.g., due to monopoly elements) or to be socially undesirable for income distribution reasons. Nevertheless, a lack of property right allocation is the underlying cause of excessive environmental degradation.

Ideally, techniques such as cost-benefit analysis, therefore, include the environmental costs of activities as well as those immediately evident from the market. This is not, however, always straightforward to put into practice. There are, for instance, problems of valuation, it may not be possible for practical or political reasons to pursue some policy approaches and there are normally knock-on effects elsewhere in the system that are difficult to foresee.

One simple way of looking at the more pragmatic economic approach to environmental matters favored by practitioners rather than pure theoreticians, be it to do with air transport or some other activity, is to think in terms of a chain effect. Figure 13.2 provides a simple outline of what is meant by this. If the market does not work then government has a responsibility for trying to rectify the situation.[35] If it cannot create an appropriate market to internalize the underlying issue because property rights cannot viably be allocated then it can act at a second level to attain a level of environmental intrusion nearer the optimum. It has the ability to impose various forms of regulation, adjust prices, provide subsidies and influence complementary activities (e.g., in the case of airlines, investments in infrastructure such as airports). These are all measures that can directly or indirectly be aimed at the environmental problem.

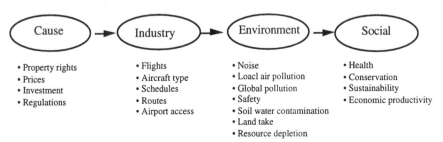

Figure 13.2 The stages of the environmental chain

The long-standing standard microeconomic position is that 'Pigouvian taxes' can be imposed on those generating the adverse environmental externality to bring it more nearly to the socially desirable level. Those causing the environmental

---

[35]   In some cases government interventions may actually make the situation worse or lead to excessive environmental damage when none would have occurred without it, see Button (1992).

damage are charged by the authorities for so doing. This is not, however, strictly a market measure but rather a method for attaining a particular environmental standard - it is rather a fiscal instrument. Whether such taxes, or indeed subsidies in some cases, are preferable to other measures such as regulations on emissions has long been debated.

Linked to this is the appropriate way to treat investment in air transportation infrastructure. If standard financial techniques are used (e.g., the pay-back criteria or the internal rate of return) then without environmental considerations being included excessive capacity will be provided in the system. The standard public policy way around this is to adopt some form of cost-benefit analysis (CBA) that takes both a suitable wide view of all the effects of investment and combines this with a long view to reflect the durability of most infrastructure. Conducting a full CBA is not easy and inevitably a degree of subjectivity is involved in the evaluations, nevertheless much pioneering work in this area has been done in the context of airport developments.[36]

In any case, the underlying economic issue is one of externalities. These externalities, however, manifest themselves in the way air transportation is provided (the second link in Figure 13.2). If the full costs of air transport are not made transparent to suppliers of air transport services then they will make decisions that are environmentally detrimental.

If the social costs of noise imposed on people around airports are not taken into account then there will be excessive aircraft movements and their timing will not allowing for possible differing temporal sensitivities of local people to noise. Inadequate allowance for the atmospheric pollution effects of air travel will influence the fleet composition of carriers and their route choices. On the ground, traffic to and from airports causes a particular set of environmental problems and if this is not reflected in the prices that are paid for surface transport use, then airport planning will fall short of environmental requirements.

These distortions to the air transport market then have effects for the environment (the third link). In general, the existence of negative environmental activities in transport leads to an excess in the total supply of transport services; there is no exception to this in air transport. It also leads to sub-optimal modal splits with excessive traffic being carried by modes that exhibit the highest relative external costs. The overall outcome of these, and other industrial distortions, is the atmospheric poolution, noise, land-use take and other environmental costs that cause social concern.

The final link in the chain is the impact of environmental degradation on society. After all, it is generally the social well-being of this and future generations that is the concern of people. An excessively degraded environment has immediate health implications (e.g., high levels of noise causes stress) and can reduce traditional economic output (again, noise can affect sleep and this is reflected in lower levels of labor productivity). In many cases there is the simple

[36]   In particular the work on the UK Commission on the potential siting of a new airpirt for London (Third London Airport, 1971)

loss of welfare in knowing that the environment has been damaged and irreplaceable resources have been lost.

In the longer term there is the much wider question concerning sustainability and whether it is possible for the global ecosystem to provide the resources necessary for future generations if current levels of utilization continue. This can be extended to the consideration of whether current political, social and institutional structures can be sustained as the resource base is reduced.

13.7.2 Policy options

It is often taken for granted that there are few private sector reasons for taking account of environmental costs in decisionmaking other than that government policy requires this or that government action will follow if private sector management does not act itself. This is not always the situation, however, in practice. Airline managers may well have incentives to take at least some account of the effect of their actions on the environment when making commercial decisions.

When there is the need for official action, policy makers have a variety of instruments that may be used. In broad terms, policy interventions can be made at any of the four stages of the chain set out in Figure 13.2. The government also has a wide portfolio of potential policy instruments at its disposal that can be applied at the various stages. Table 13.5 offers a taxonomy of some of the possible measures that are available to policy makers, the dividing lines being drawn according to whether they act directly on the environmental source or are of a less direct nature.

Table 13.5 Taxonomy of policy instruments

	Market-based Incentives		Command and Control Regulations	
	Direct	Indirect	Direct	Indirect
Plane	• Emission fees • Tax allowances	• Tradable permits • Feebates	• Emissions standards	• Inspection and maintenance • Compulsory scrappage
Fuel	• Fuel taxation	• Fuel composition	• Fuel economy standards	• Flying speeds
Traffic	• Slot pricing • Airport access pricing		• Routing • Timing • Aircraft type • Airport design • Noise insulation	• Flight limitations

Ideally, but also probably unrealistically, from an economic perspective property right allocations could be made more comprehensive, but, failing that, other remedial measures relating to pricing or directly regulating the use of environmental resources could be initiated. In fact, there are effective ways of making use of some of the features inherent in property rights. The use of tradable permits, whereby actors are allocated rights to make use of a predetermined quantity of environmental resources has proved effective in related areas such as the reduction of lead in gasoline.

Government interventions can come through a variety of other direct channels (Button, 1994). Since full property right allocation is difficult, many economists favor the use of pollution charges of various kinds as mechanisms for reducing the environmental intrusion of air transport. They are seen, because of their flexibility and because they equalize the marginal costs of abatement, as being the best way of attaining an administratively established level of pollution.

Besides the need to have a fairly good idea of how sensitive users are to various levels of charge, there is the political difficulty that, without some form of pay-back, these charges extract revenue from the sector in a way that fully allocated property rights would not. They essentially take resources from airlines and give them to government. A property right structure involves trade between airlines and those adversely affected, with the automatic outcome that there are measures of compensation for those who are still adversely affected and penalties for those who continue to inflict damage on the environment. Further, it yields an optimal level of abatement rather than simply resulting in some level that has been deemed appropriate (albeit often with expert advice) by the authorities.

At the second stage seen in Figure 13.2, the way the industry operates and its scale could be controlled, again to reduce the environmental intrusion of air transport if this is felt excessive. In practice this is often the chosen approach of policy makers. Instruments of direct regulation abound. Examples include airport curfews, designated flight paths around airports, safety regulations, airport planning requirements, and regulations over destinations served (e.g., the perimeter rules in the US discussed in Chapter 10). Fuel taxation may also be seen as important in this context as can airport charging regimes.

The problem with acting at this stage in the chain is that air transport policy itself has more than an environmental dimension to it. Acting indirectly on the environmental problems by influencing market conditions can affect – and potentially adversely affect – the competitive environment in which air services are provided. While this may be done in a purely incidental way, there is always the underlying danger that actions purporting to be environmentally desirable in their orientation can be driven by secondary considerations to favor a particular carrier or airport.

At the third stage there is direct remedial action on environmental damage. In terms of noise, reductions in environmental intrusion are often achieved by insulating certain aspects of the environment (e.g., the construction of noise barriers) or by fitting aircraft with mufflers. The global warming problems associated with CO_2 emission can be mitigated by remedial measures such as the creation of 'carbon sinks'. Essentially, the air transport sector would be left to its own devices, but measures would be taken to adapt the environment to it.

The main objections to this type of strategy are mainly to do with distribution considerations. The problem is that the costs of insulating the environment are not directly borne by the air transport industry. There are also questions of effectiveness. Most of these types of measure only partially reduce the adverse effects and may themselves have secondary out-comes that are undesirable (e.g., most noise barriers are not aesthetically pleasing).

Finally, society could 'treat' itself when afflicted by the adverse environmental effects of air transport. This may be in the form of compensation or it may be more direct, for example better medical care for those affected by noise-induced stress or for the effects of VOC on chest ailments. While theoretically this is a possible option, it is generally treated very much as a last resort. The full social costs of many forms of environmental pollution for individuals is not known and many treatments for those that are understood are far from satisfactory.

13.8 CONCLUSIONS

Air transport is a major growth sector in the global economy. It not only brings with it improved communication for those in business but has opened up a whole range of leisure possibilities. At the same time it is bringing with it increased concern about the implications that this rise in air transport activity may have on the environment.

The sector has, to date, been reactive in a number of ways to meet these concerns, some of the reactions the result of market pressures and others the outcome of policy initiatives by governments. Compared to surface modes of transport, however, the environmental debate has been relatively subdued regarding aviation. This may continue to be the case, but even if this is so there is still a social need to ensure that air transport does not cause excessive environmental damage.

Policy makers have a variety of policy instruments that can be used to help ensure that air transport conforms to the long-term needs of sustainable development, but there are problems. Information on the monetary equivalent costs of many forms of environmental damage is still scant and this makes comparisons of policy instruments difficult. There is still relatively little information concerning the effectiveness of many of the policy instruments. A problem here is not only that individual instruments are often still largely untried but also in practice policies have a multidimensional nature involving a number of tools applied simultaneously with consequential interactive effects. Further, most policy instruments have impacts other than those purely on the environment and the magnitude and nature of these are generally not fully know in advance.

REFERENCES

Abe, M.A. (1979) Skytrain: competitive pricing, quality of service and deregulation of the airline industry, *International Journal of Transport Economics*, 6: 41-47.

Abelson, P. (1979) Property prices and the value of amenities, *Journal of Environmental Economics and Management*, 6: 11-28.

Aiger, D.J. and Chu, S. (1968) On estimating the industry production function, *American Economic Review*, 53: 826-929.

Aigner, D.J., Lovell, C.A.K. and Schmidt, P. (1977) Formulation and estimation of stochastic frontier production function models, *Journal of Econometrics*, 6: 21-37.

Air Transport Association of America (1995) *The Airline Handbook*, ATAA, Washington.

Airbus Industrie (1993) *Air Cargo Market Trends*, Airbus Industrie, Blagnac.

Aivazian, V.A. and Callen, J.L (1981) The Coase Theorem and the empty core, *Journal of Law and Economics*, 24: 175-81

Alexander, D.R. and Hall, J.W. (1991) ACN-PCN concepts for airport pavement management, in *Aircraft/Pavement Interaction: An Integrated System*, Proceedings of the Conference, American Society of Civil Engineers, New York.

Altshuler, A. and Teal, R. (1979) The political economy of airline deregulation, in Altshuler, A. (ed.) *Current Issues in Transportation Policy*, Lexington Books, Lexington.

Alperovich, G. and Machnes, Y. (1994) The role of wealth in the demand for international air travel, *Journal of Transport Economics and Policy*, 28: 163-173.

Archer, S.H. (1983) Regulatory lag, *Economia Aziendale*, 11: 176-84.

Aschauer, D.A. (1990) Why is infrastructure important?, in Munnell, P (ed.) *Is There a Shortfall in Public Capital Investment?*, Conference Series, 34, Federal Reserve Bank of Boston, Boston.

Ashford, N. and Wright, P.H. (1992) *Airport Engineering*, 3rd Edition, John Wiley, New York.

Association of European Airlines (1995) *EU External Relations*, AEA, Brussels.

Association of European Airlines (1999) *Towards a Transatlantic Common Aviation Area: AEA Policy Statement*, AEA, Brussels.

Association of European Airlines (various years)*Yearbook*, AEA, Brussels.

Australian Bureau of Industry Economics (1994) *Aviation: International Performance Indicators,* Research Report 59, BIE Canberra.

Bailey, E.E. (1980) Deregulation and regulatory reform of U.S. air-transportation policy, in Mitchell, B.M. and Kleindorfer, P.R. (eds) *Regulated Industries and Public Enterprise,* Lexington Books, Lexington.

Bailey, E.E. (1981) Contestability and the design of regulatory and antitrust policy, *American Economic Review: Papers and Proceedings,* 71: 178-183.

Bailey, E.E. (1985) Airline deregulation in the United States: the benefits provided and the lessons learned, *International Journal of Transport Economics,* 12: 119-44.

Bailey, E.E. (1986) Deregulation: causes and consequences. *Science,* 234: 1211-16.

Bailey, E.E. and Baumol, W.J. (1984) Deregulation and the theory of contestable markets, *Yale Journal of Regulation,* 2: 111-37.

Bailey, E.E. and Panzar, J.C. (1981) The contestability of airline markets during the transition to deregulation, *Law and Contemporary Problems,* 44:125-45.

Bailey, E.E. and Williams, J.R. (1988) Sources of economic rent in the deregulated airline industry, *Journal of Law and Economics,* 31: 173-202.

Bailey, E.E., Graham, D.R. and Kaplan, D.P. (1985) *Deregulating the Airlines,* MIT Press, Cambridge.

Baker, S.H. and Pratt, J.B.(1989) Experience as a barrier to contestability in airline markets, *Review of Economics and Statistics,* 81: 352-6.

Baldwin, J. (1975) *The Regulatory Agency and the Public Corporation,* Ballinger, Cambridge.

Balfour, J. (1994) The changing role of regulation in European air transport liberalisation, *Journal of Air Transport Management,* 1: 27-36.

Balinski, M.L. and Sand, F.M. (1985) Auctioning landing rights at congested airports, in Peyton, H. (ed.) *Cost allocation: Methods, Principles, Applications* Elsevier Science Publishers, Oxford.

Banister, D. and Button, K.J. (eds) (1993) *Transport, the Environment and Sustainable Development,* E and FN Spon, London.

Barnett, A. and LoFaso, A.J. (1983) After the crash: the passenger response to the DC-10 disaster, *Management Science,* 35: 1-21.

Barone, S.S., Javidan, M., Reschenthaler, G.B. and Kraft, D.J.H. (1986) Deregulation in the Canadian airline industry: is there room for a large regional carrier?, *Logistics and Transportation Review,* 22: 421-48.

Barrett, S.A. (1987) *Flying High: Airline Prices and European Regulation,* Avebury, Aldershot.

Barrett, S.A. (1990) Deregulating European aviation – a case study, *Transportation,* 16: 311-27.

Bass, T.C. (1985) Passenger transport: regulation of international transport, *Proceedings of the 10th International Symposium on Theory and Practice in Transport Economics* European Conference of ministers of Transport, Berlin.

Bauer, P.W. (1990) Decomposing TFP growth in the presence of cost inefficiency, nonconstant returns to scale and technological progress, *Journal of Productivity Analysis*, 1: 287-99.

Baumol, W.J. (1959) *Business Behavior, Value and Growth*, Macmillan, London.

Baumol, W.J. (1982) Contestable markets: an uprising in the theory of industrial structure, *American Economic Review*, 72: 1-15.

Baumol, W.J. and Willig, R.D. (1986) Contestability: developments since the book, *Oxford Economic Papers*, 38: 9-36.

Baumol, W.J., Panzar, J.C. and Willig, R.D. (1982) *Contestable Markets and the Theory of Industrial Structure*, Harcourt Brace Jovanovich, New York.

Baumol, W.J., Panzar, J.C. and Willig, R.D. (1983) Contestable markets: an uprising in the theory of industrial structure: reply, *American Economic Review*, 73: 491-6.

Bell, J. (1996) Expanding a small world, *Distribution*, 95 (July): 56.

Bennett, R.D. and Craun, J.M. (1993) *The Airline Deregulation Evolution Continues: the Southwest Effect*, USDOT, Washington.

Bergh, J. van den, Button, K.J., Nijkamp, P. and Pepping, G.C. (1997)*Meta-analysis in Environmental Economics,* Kluwer, Amsterdam.

Berechnman, J. and de Wit, J. (1996) An analysis of the effects of European aviation deregulation on an airline's network structure and choice of a primary west European hub airport, *Journal of Transport Economics and Policy*, 30: 251-75.

Berry, T. (1990) Estimating a model of entry in the airline industry, Yale Working Paper.

Bhagwati, J.N. (1982) Directly unproductive, profit-seeking (DUP) activities, *Journal of Political Economy,* 90: 988-1002.

Bittlingmayer, G. (1982) Decreasing average cost and competition, *Journal of Law and Economics*, 25: 201-29.

Bittlingmayer, G. (1985) Did antitrust policy cause the great merger wave?, *Journal of Law and Economics*, 28: 77-118.

Bjarnadottir, V. (1994) Air transport, in European Free Trade Association, *European Economic Integration: Effects of '1992' on the Services Sectors of the EFTA Countries*, Occasional Paper no. 49, EFTA, Economic Affairs Department.

Blumestock, J.W. and Thochick, E.A. (1986) Deregulation and airline labor relations, *Logistics and Transportation Review*, 22: 389-403.

Boeing Commercial Airplane Group (various years a) *Current Market Outlook, 1996,* Boeing, Seattle.

Boeing Commercial Airplane Group (various years b) *World Air Cargo Forecast*, Boeing, Seattle.

Bollard, A. and Pickford, M. (1998) Deregulation and competition policy in the transport sector in New Zealand, *Journal of Transport Economics and Policy*, 32: 267-76.

Borenstein, S. (1992a) The evolution of US airline competition, *Journal of Economic Perspectives*, April: 45-73.

Borenstein, S. (1992b) Prospects for competitive air travel in Europe, in Adams, W.J. (ed.) *Singular Europe: Economics and Polity of the European Community after 1992*, University of Michigan Press, Ann Arbor.

Borenstein, S. and Zimmerman, M.B. (1988) Market incentives for safe commercial airline operation, *American Economic Review*, 78: 913-35.

Borins, S. (1981) Meiszkowski and Saper's estimate of the effects of airport noise on property values: a comment, *Journal of Urban Economics*, 9: 125-8.

Boulding, K.E. and Lundstedt, S.B. (1988) Value concepts and justifications, in Peterson, G.L., Driver, B.L. and Gregory, R. (eds.) *Amenity Resource Valuation: Integrating Economics with Other Disciplines*, Venture Publishing: State College.

Boyle, K.J. and Bergstrom, J.C. (1992) Benefit transfer studies: myths, pragmatism and idealism, *Water Resources Research*, 28: 657-63.

Brander, J.R.G., Cook, B.A. and Rowcroft, J.E. (1989) Entry, exclusion and expulsion in a single hub airport system, *Transportation Research Record* 1214: 27-36.

Brenner, M.A., Leet, J.O. and Schott, E. (1985) *Airline Deregulation*, ENO Foundation for Transportation, Westport.

Breyer, S. (1982) *Regulation and its Reform*, Harvard University Press, Cambridge.

Breyer, S. and Stein, L. (1981) Airline deregulation: the anatomy of reform instead of regulation, in Poole R. (eds) *Alternatives to Federal Regulatory Agencies*, Lexington Books, Lexington.

Brooks, M. and Button, K.J. (1994) Yield management: a phenomenon of the 1980s and 1990s?, *International Journal of Transport Economics*, 21:177-96.

Brooks, M. and Button, K.J. (1995) Separating track from operations: a look at international experiences, *International Journal of Transport Economics*, 22: 235-60.

Brookshire, D.S. (1992) Issues regarding benefits transfer, paper to the Association of Environmental and Resource Economists Workshop, Snowbird.

Brookshire, D.S. and Neill, H.R. (1992) Benefit transfers: conceptual and empirical issues, *Water Resources Research*, 28: 651-5.

Brown, E. (1997) Costs too high? Bring in the logistics experts, *Fortune*, 10 November: 200C-200T.

Brown, S. and Watkins, W. (1968), The demand for air travel: a regression study of time-series and cross-sectional data in the US domestic market, *Highway Research Record,* 213: 21-34.

Brueckner, J.J. and Spiller, P.T. (1994) Economics of traffic density in the deregulated airline industry, *Journal of Law and Economics*, 37: 379-415.

Bureau of Transport and Communications Economics (1996) Techniques for managing runway congestion, Working Paper 27, BTCE, Commonwealth of Australia, Canberra.

Button, K.J. (1987a) High-technology companies: an examination of their transport needs, *Progress in Planning*, 29: 79-146.

Button, K.J. (1987b) The effects of regulatory reform on the U.S. inter-city bus market, *Transport Reviews*, 7: 145-66.

Button, K.J. (ed.) (1990) *Airline Deregulation: An International Perspective,* David Fulton, London.

Button, K.J. (1992) *Market and Government Failures in Environmental Policy: The Case of Transport*, OECD, Paris.

Button, K.J. (1993a) *Transport Economics*, 2nd Edition, Edward Elgar, Cheltenham.

Button, K.J. (1993b) *Transport, the Environment and Economic Policy,* Edward Elgar, Cheltenham.

Button, K.J. (1994) Overview of internalising the social costs of transport, in *Internalising the Social Costs of Transport*, ECMT/OECD, Paris.

Button, K.J. (1995) Transport in the twenty-first century, in European Conference of Ministers of Transport, *New Problems, New Solutions*, ECMT, Paris.

Button, K.J. (1996a) Aviation deregulation in European Union: do actors learn in the regulation game?, *Contemporary Economic Policy*, 14: 70-80.

Button, K.J. (1996b) Liberalising European aviation: is there an empty core problem, *Journal of Transport Economics and Policy*, 30: 275-91.

Button, K.J. (1997a) Regulatory reform, networks and economic efficiency, in Capineri, C. and Rietveld. P. (eds) *Networks in Transport and Communications: A Policy Approach*, Ashgate, Aldershot.

Button, K.J. (1997b) *Why Don't All Aviation Marriages Work?,* The Institute of Public Policy, George Mason University, Fairfax.

Button, K.J. (1997c) Lessons from European transport experience, *Annals of the American Academy of Political and Social Science* 553: 157-67

Button, K.J. (1998a) The three faces of synthesis: bringing together quantitative findings in the field of transport and environmental policy, *Environment and Planning C*, 16: 516-28.

Button, K.J. (1998b) Environmental factors in airport competition, in the *Les Aéroports de Demain*, Laboratoire d'Economie des Transports, Lyon.

Button. K.J. (1998c) *Opening U.S. Skies to Global Airline Competition*, CATO Institute, Washington.

Button, K.J. (1999a) The usefulness of current international air transport statistics, *Journal of Transportation and Statistics*, 2: 71-92.

Button, K.J. (1999b) Airline safety and the increase in inter-airline operating agreements, in Meersman, H., Van de Voorde, E. and Winklemans, W. (eds.) *World Transport Research Volume 1. Transport Modes and Systems*, Pergamon, Oxford..

Button, K.J. and Gillingwater, D. (1986) *Future Transport Policy,* Croom Helm, London.

Button, K.J. and Johnson, K. (1998) Incremental versus trend-break change in airline regulation, *Transportation Journal*, 37: 25-34.

Button, K.J. and Keeler, T. (1993) The regulation of transport markets, *Economic Journal*, 103: 1017-28.

Button, K.J. and Kerr, J. (1996) Effectiveness of traffic restraint policies: a simple meta-regression analysis, *International Journal of Transport Economics*, 23: 214-25.

Button, K.J. and Maggi, R. (1995) Videoconferencing and its implications for transport: an Anglo-Swiss perspective, *Transport Reviews*, 15:59–75.

Button, K.J. and Nijkamp, P. (1997) Environmental policy assessment and the usefulness of meta-analysis, *Socio-economic Planning Sciences*, 31:231-40.

Button, K.J. and Nijkamp, P. (1998) Economic stability in network industries, *Transportation Research E*, 34: 13-24.

Button, K.J. and Owens, C. (1999) Transport and information systems: a case study of EDI development by the air cargo industry, *International Journal of Transport Economics*, 26: 3-21

Button, K.J. and Rietveld, P. (1998) Infrastructure policy and pan-European regional development, in Kohno, H., Nijkamp, P. and Poot, J. (eds) *Regional Cohesion and Competition in the Process of Globalisation*, Springer-Verlag, Berlin.

Button, K.J. and Swann, D. (eds.) (1989a) *The Age of Regulatory Reform*, Oxford University Press, Oxford.

Button, K.J. and Swann, D. (1989b) European Community airlines – deregulation and its problems, *Journal of Common Market Studies*, 27: 259-82.

Button, K.J. and Swann, D. (1992) Transatlantic lessons in aviation deregulation: EEC and US experiences, *Antitrust Bulletin*, 37: 207-55.

Button, K.J., Arena, P. and Stough, R. (1999) Relaxing the Perimeter and high density rules: implications for Washington Dulles International Airport, *Journal of Air Transport Management*, 5: 97-104.

Button, K.J., Haynes, K. and Stough, R. (1998) *Flying into the Future: Air Transport Policy in the European Union*, Edward Elgar, Cheltenham.

Button, K.J., Lall, S., Stough, R. and Trice, M. (1999) High-technology employment and hub airports, *Journal of Air Transport Management*, 5: 53-9.

Bylow, L.F. and Savage, I. (1991) The effect of airline deregulation on automobile fatalities, *Accident Analysis and Prevention*, 23: 443-52.

Byrnes, J.L.S. (1985) *Diversification Strategies for Regulated and Deregulated Industries: Lessons from the Airlines*, Heath Lexington, Toronto.

Canadian Department of External Affairs (1975) Non-scheduled air service agreements between the Government of Canada and the Government of the United States of America, Canada Treaty Series, No. 16, Department of External Affairs, Ottawa.

Canadian House of Commons Standing Committee on Transport (1982) *Domestic Air Carrier Policy*, Ninth Report of the House of Commons Standing Committee on Transport, HMSO, London.

Canadian Parliament (1982) *Minutes of Proceedings and Evidence of the Standing Committee on Transport Respecting the Document Entitled "Proposed Domestic Air Carrier Policy (Unit Toll Services)"*, August 1981, Parliamentary Session 32, 1st Session, Ottawa.

Canadian Transport Commission (1984) *Interim Report of the Air Transport Committee of the Canadian Transport Commission on Domestic Charters and Airfare Issues*, Ottawa.

Canadian Transport Commission, Air Transport Committee. Department of External Affairs (1966) Air agreement between Canada and the United States of America, Canada Treaty Series, No.2, Department of External Affairs, Ottawa.

Capineri, C. and Rietveld, P. (eds), *Networks in Transport and Communications: A Policy Approach,* Ashgate. Aldershot

Capello, R. and Rietveld, P. (1998) The concept of network synergies in economic theory: policy implications, in Button, K.J., Nijkamp, P. and Priemus, H. (eds) *Transport Networks in Europe: Concepts, Analysis and Policies*, Edward Elgar, Cheltenham.

Carlton, D.W., Landes, W.M. and Posner, R.A. (1980) Benefits and costs of airline mergers: a case study, *Bell Journal of Economics*, 11: 65-83.

Carron, A.S. (1981) *Transition to a Free Market: Deregulation of the Air Cargo Industry*, Brookings Institution, Washington.

Castles, C. (1997) Development of airport slot allocation in the European Community, paper presented at the Privatization and Reregulation in Transport seminar, Oxford.

Caves, D.W., Christensen, L.R. and Tretheway, M.W. (1981) US trunk airlines, 1972-1977: a multilateral comparison of total factor productivity, in Cowing, T.G. and Stevenson, R.E. (eds.) *Productivity Measurement in Regulated Industries*, Academic Press, New York.

Caves, D.W., Christensen, L.R. and Tretheway, M.W. (1983) Productivity performance of U.S. trunk and local service airlines in the era of deregulation. *Economic Inquiry*, 21: 312-34.

Caves, D.W., Christensen, L.R., Tretheway, M.W. and Windle, R.J. (1987) An assessment of the efficiency effects of U.S. airline deregulation via an international comparison, in Bailey, E.E. (ed.) *Public Regulation: New Perspectives on Institutions and Policies,* MIT Press, Cambridge.

Caves, R.E. (1962) *Air Transportation and its Regulators: An Industry Study,* Harvard University Press, Cambridge.

Center for Economic Education, University of Cincinnati (1997) *The Economic Impact of the Cincinnati/ Northern Kentucky International Airport: the Next 20 Years,* Center for Economic Education, University of Cincinnati.

Centre for Delay Analysis (1997) *Delays to Air Transport in Europe Annual Report 1997,* EUROCONTROL/ECAC, Brussels.

Chalk, A. (1986) Market forces and aircraft safety: the case of the DC-10, *Economic Inquiry,* 24: 43-60.

Chalk, A. (1987) Market forces and commercial aicraft safety, *Journal of Industrial Economics,* 36: 61-81.

Chance, D.M. and Ferris, S.P. (1987) The effect of aviation disasters on the air transport industry: a financial market perspective, *Journal of Transport Economics and Policy,* 21: 151-65.

Charnes, A., Cooper, W.W. and Rhodes, E. (1977) Measuring the efficiency of decision-making units, *European Journal of Operations Research,* 2: 429-44.

Coase, R.H. (1937) The nature of the firm, *Economica* (NS) 4: 386-405.

Coase, R.H. (1960) The problem of social cost, *Journal of Law and Economics,* 3: 1–44.

Coase, R.H. (1981) The Coase Theorem and the empty core: a comment, *Journal of Law and Economics,* 24: 183-187

Coley/Forrest Inc. (n.d) *Ready for Takeoff: The Business Impact of Three Recent Airport Developments in the US,* Colorado National Banks.

Collins, A. and Evans, A. (1994) Aircraft noise and residential property values: an artificial neural network approach, *Journal of Transport Economics and Policy,* 28: 175-97.

Comité des Sages for Air Transport (1994) *Expanding Horizons,* European Commission, Brussels.

Commission of the European Communities (1981) *Scheduled Passenger Air Fares in the EEC,* COM(81) 398 Final, Brussels.

Commission of the European Communities, (1995) *Consultation paper on Airport Charges, Commission of The European Communities,* Directorate General VII, CEC, Brussels.

Commission of the European Communities (1996) *Impact of the Third Package of Air Transport Liberalization Measures,* COM(96) 415 Final, Brussels.

Commission on the Third London Airport (1971) *Report,* HMSO, London.

Cooke, J.A. (1996) Mobile communications: getting a fix on your freight, *Traffic Management,* 35: 66.

Creager, S.E. (1983) Airline deregulation and airport regulation. *Yale Law Journal*, 93, 319-339.

Crum, M.R., Premkumar, G. and Ramamurthy, K. (1996) An assessment of motor carrier adoption, use, and satisfaction with EDI, *Transportation Journal*, 36: 44-57.

DeVany, A.S. (1974) The revealed value of time in air travel, *Review of Economics and Statistics*, 56: 77-82.

DeVany, A.S. (1975) The effect of price and entry regulation on airline output, capacity and efficiency, *Bell Journal of Economics*, 6: 327-45.

DeVany, A.S. (1976) An economic model of airport noise pollution in an urban environment, in Lin, S. (ed) *Theory and Measurement of Economic Externalities*, Academic Press, New York.

Distexhe, V. and Perelman, S. (1994) Technical efficiency and productivity growth in and era of deregulation: the case of airlines, *Swiss Journal of Economics and Statistics*, 130: 669-89.

Dodgson, J., Katsoulacous,Y. and Pryke, R. (1991) *Predatory Behaviour in Aviation*, EC Official Publications, Luxembourg.

Doganis, R. (1991) *Flying Off Course: The Economics of International Airlines*, 2nd Edition, Harper Collins, London.

Doganis, R. (1992) *The Airport Business*, Routledge, London.

Doganis, R. (1993) The bilateral regime for air transport: current position and future prospects, in Organisation for Economic Cooperation and Development, *International Air Transport: The Challenges Ahead*, OECD, Paris.

Doganis, R. (1994) The impact of liberalization on European airline strategies and operations, *Journal of Air Transport Management*, 1: 15-26.

Doganis, R. (1995) The Airline Business, Routeledge, London.

Doganis, R. and Dennis, N.P.S. (1989) Lessons in hubbing, *Airline Business*, March: 42-45.

Douglas, G.W. and Miller, J.C. (1974) *Economic Regulation of Domestic Air Transport: Theory and Policy*, Brookings Institution, Washington.

Dresner, M. and Tretheway, M.W. (1987) Policy choices for Canada in international air transport, Working Paper No. 1220, Faculty of Commerce and Business Administration, University of British Columbia.

Dresner, M. and Tretheway, M.W. (1992) Modeling and testing the effect of market structure on price: the case of international air transport, *Journal of Transport Economics and Policy*, 25: 171-83.

Dresner, M., Hadrovic, C. and Tretheway, M.W. (1988) The Canadian–U.S. air transport bilateral: will it be freed?, paper presented to the Canadian Transportation Research Forum, Ottawa, 1988 and reproduced in a shorter form in *Air Transport Management*, March/April, 9-12.

Dygert, P. (1973) Estimation of the Cost of Aircraft Noise to Residential Activities, PhD dissertation, University of Michigan.

Eads, G.C. (1972) *The Local Service Airline Experiment,* Studies in the Deregulation of Economic Activities, Brookings Institution, Washington.

Eckel, C., Eckel, D. and Singal, V. (1997) Privatization and efficiency: industry effects of the sale of British Airways, *Journal of Financial Economics,*43: 275-98.

Economides, N. (1996) "The economics of networks", *International Journal of Industrial Organisation,* 14: 673-699.

Edgeworth, F.Y. (1881) *Mathematical Physics: An Essay on the Application of Mathematics to the Moral Sciences,* London, Kegan Paul.

Ellison, A.P. (1984) Regulatory reform in transport: a Canadian perspective, *Transportation Journal,* 23: 4-19.

Emerson, F. (1969) The Determinants of Residential Value with Special Reference to the Effects of Aircraft Nuisance and Other Environmental Features, PhD Dissertation, University of Minnesota.

Emerson, F. (1972) Valuation of residential amenities: an econometric approach, *Appraisal Journal,* 40: 268-78.

Encanoua, D. (1991) Liberalizing European airlines: cost and factor productivity evidence, *International Journal of Industrial Organization,* 9: 109-24.

European Air Shippers Council (1995) *Airfreight 2000 and Beyond: A Shippers' 'White Paper' on Airfreight* , EASC, Brussels.

European Civil Aviation Conference (1981) *Report of the Task Force on Competition in Intra-European Air Services,* ECAC.

Eurostat (1997) *EU Transport Statistics in Figures,* 2nd Edition, Eurostat, Brussels.

Fawcett, S.E. and Fawcett, S.A. (1988) Congestion at capacity–constrained airports: A question of economics and realism, *Transportation Journal,* Summer: 42-54.

Feitelson, E.I., Hurd, R.E. and Mudge, R.R. (1996) The impact of airport noise on willingness to pay for residences, *Transportation Research D: Transport and Environment D,* 1: 1-14.

Felkner, J. (1992) Transportation customers benefit from EDI, *EDI World* (December): 22-4.

Fisher, F.M. (1987) Pan American to United: the 'Pacific Division Transfer Case', *Rand Journal of Economics,* 18: 492-508.

Fisher, J.B. (1989) Managing demand to reduce airport congestion and delays, *Transportation Research Record,* 1218: 1-10.

Freeman, A.M. (1984) On the tactics of benefit estimation under Executive Order 12291, in Smith, V.K. (ed.) *Environmental Policy under Reagan's Executive Order: the Role of Benefit Cost Analysis,* University of North Carolina Press, Chapel Hill.

Fujii, E., Im, E. and Mak, J. (1992) The economics of direct flights, *Journal of Transport Economics and Policy*, 26: 185-95.

Galbraith, K.J. (1967) *The New Industrial State*, Houghton Mifflin, Boston.

Gautrin, J. (1973) The Economics of Aircraft Noise: An Essay with British Data, PhD thesis, University of London.

Gautrin, J. (1975) An evaluation of the impact of aircraft noise on property values with a simple model on urban land rent, *Land Economics*, 51: 80-86.

Gawan-Taylor, M. (1984) *The Australian Domestic Air Freight Market: Consequences of Partial Deregulation*, Australian National University, Centre for Economic Policy Research, Discussion Paper 87.

GECAS (1994) *Air Cargo: An Industry Study*, GECAS, Shannon.

Gellman Research Associates (1994) *A Study of International Airline Code Sharing, Office of Aviation and International Economics*, Office of the Secretary of US Department of Transportation, Washington.

Gillen, D.W. and Lall, A. (1997) Developing measures of airport productivity and performance: and application of data envelopment analysis, *Transportation Research E*, 33: 261-73.

Gillen, D.W., Oum, T.H. and Tretheway, M.W. (1985) *Canadian Airline Deregulation and Privatization: Assessing Effects and Prospects*, Centre for Transportation Studies, University of British Columbia.

Gillen, D.W., Oum, T.H. and Tretheway, M.W. (1986) *Airline and Performance Implications for Public and Industrial Policies*, Centre for Transportation Studies, University of British Columbia.

Gillen, D.W., Oum, T.H. and Tretheway, M.W. (1988a) Survival under free skies, *Air Transport Management*, 1: 10-13.

Gillen, D.W., Oun, T.H. and Tretheway, M.W. (1988b) Entry barriers and anti competitive behaviour in a deregulated airline market: the case of Canada, *International Journal of Transport Economics*, 15: 29-41.

Gillen, D.W., Ourn, T.H. and Tretheway, M.W. (1990) Airline cost structures and policy implications, *Journal of Transport Economics and Policy*, 24: 9-34.

Gillen, D.W., Stanbury, W.T. and Tretheway, M.W. (1988) Duopoly in Canada's airline industry: consequences and policy issues, *Canadian Public Policy*, 16: 16-31.

Glass, G.V. (1976) Primary, secondary, and meta-analysis of research, *Educational Researcher*, 5: 3-8.

Golbe, D.L. (1986) Safety and profits in the airline industry, *Journal of Industrial Economics*, 34: 305-18.

Gomez-Ibanez, J.A., and Morgan, I.P. (1984) Deregulating international markets: the examples of aviation and shipping. *Yale Journal of Regulation*, 2: 107-44.

Good, D.H., Röller, L-H. and Sickles, R.C. (1993) US airline deregulation: implications for European transport, *Economic Journal*, 103: 1028-41.

Good, D.H., Röller, L-H. and Sickles, R.C. (1995) Airline efficiency differences between Europe and the US: implications for the pace of EC integration and domestic regulation, *European Journal of Operations Research*, 80: 508-18.

Gordon, K. (1981) Deregulation rights and the compensation of losers, in K.D. Boyer and W.G. Shepherd (eds) *Economic Regulation: Essays in Honor of James R. Nelson,* Michigan State University Press, East Lancing.

Graham, B. (1995) *Geography and Air Transport*, John Wiley & Sons, Chichester.

Granger, C. (1969) Investigating causal relations by econometric models and cross-spectral methods, *Econometrica*, 37: 424-38.

Gronau, R. (1970), *The Value of Time in Passenger Transportation: The Demand for Air Travel,* Columbia University Press, New York.

Greene, W.H. (1980). On the estimation of a flexible frontier production model, *Journal of Econometrics*, 13: 101-15.

Grether, D.M., Isaac, R.M. and Plott, C.R. (1979) *Alternative Methods of Allocating Airport Slots: Performance and Evaluation,* Polinomics Research Laboratories, Inc., Pasadena.

Haanapel, P.P.C. (1980) Bilateral air transport agreements between Canada and the United States, *Annals of Air and Space Law*, 5: 133-153.

Hahn, F. (1991) The next hundred years, *Economic Journal*, 101: 47-50,

Hamzawi. S.G. (1992) Lack of airport capacity: exploration of alternative solutions, *Transportation Research A*, 26: 47-58.

Hanlon, P. (1994) Discriminatory fares; identifying predatory behaviour, *Journal of Air Transport Management*, 1: 89-110.

Hanlon, P. (1996) *Global Airlines: Competition in a Transnational Industry*, Butterworth-Heinemann, Oxford.

Hansen, M. and Kanafani, A. (1990) Airline hubbing and airline economics *Transportation Research A*, 24: 217-30.

Harberger, A.C. (1954) Monopoly and resource allocation, *American Economic Review Proceedings,* 44: 77-87.

Hardaway, R.M. (1991) *Airport Regulation, Law and Public Policy: The Management and Growth of Infrastructure*, Quorum Books, New York.

Harris, R.G. and Sullivan, L.A. (1986) Horizontal mergers policy: promoting competition and American competitiveness. *Anti-Trust Bulletin,* 31: 871-933.

Heaver, T.D. (1987) Transport regulation and privatization in Canada, paper presented to the Canada–U.K. Colloquium on Privatization and Deregulation in Britain and Canada, Gleneagles.

Hill, H. (1996) European shippers demand greater voice, changes in the air cargo shipping world, *Traffic World*, 245: 25-7.

Hoehn, J.P. and Randall, A. (1989) Too many proposals pass the benefit cost test, *American Review of Economics*, 79: 544-51.

Hooper, P.G. and Hensher, D.A. (1997) Measuring total factor productivity of airports - an index number approach, *Transportation Research E - Logistics and Transportation Review*, 33: 249-260.

Humphreys, B.K. (1991) Are FFP anticompetitive?, *Avamark Economist*, July/August: 12-15.

Humphreys, B.K. (1994) *New Developments in CRSs*, ITA Documents and Reports 32, Paris.

Hunter, J.E., Schmidt, F.L. and Jackson, G. (1982) *Advanced Meta-analysis: Quantitative Methods for Cumulating Research Findings across Studies*, Sage, Beverly Hills.

International Air Transport Association (1986) *Deregulation Watch: Third Report*, IATA, Geneva.

International Air Transport Association (1986) *Air Transport in a Changing World: Facing the Challenges of Tomorrow*, IATA, Geneva.

International Civil Aviation Organization (1994) *The World of Civil Aviation*, ICAO, Montreal.

International Foundation of Airline Passengers Associations (1988) *European Airline Mergers: Implications for Passenger and Policy Options*, IFAPA, Geneva.

Ippolito, R.A. (1981) Estimating airline demand with quality of service variables, *Journal of Transport Economics and Policy*, 15:7-15.

James, G. (1988) Overview: pre- and post-deregulation U.S. airline system, presentation to the Transport Research Board Annual Meeting, Washington.

Johnson, K. and Button, K.J. (1997) Benefit transfers: are they a satisfactory input to benefit cost analysis? An airport noise nuisance case study, *Transportation Research D*, 2: 223-31.

Jordan, W.A. (1970) *Airline Regulation in America: Effects and Imperfections*, Johns Hopkins Press, Baltimore.

Jordan, W.A. (1986a) Results of US airline deregulation: evidence from the regulated Canadian airlines, *Logistics and Transportation Review*, 22: 297-337.

Jordan, W.A. (1986b) Economic deregulation and airline safety, in Canadian Transportation Research Forum, *Proceedings of the 21st Annual Meeting of the Canadian Transportation Research Forum*, CTRF, Vancouver

Jordan, W.A. (1987) *Comparative Analysis of Airline Performance in Canada and the United States*, report for Transport Canada Submitted to the Standing Committee on Transport, House of Commons, Ottawa.

Jordan, W.A. (1988) Problems stemming from airline mergers and acquisitions, *Transportation Journal*, 27: 9-30.

Juan, E.J. (1995) *Airport Infrastructure: The Emerging Role of the Private Sector*, CFS Discussion Paper Number 115, World Bank, Washington.

Jung, J.M. and Fujii, E.T. (1976), The price elasticity of demand for air travel – some new evidence, *Journal of Transport Economics and Policy,* 10: 257–62.

Kanafani, A. and Ghorbial, A.A. (1985) Airline hubbing: some implications for airport economics, *Transportation Research A,* 19: 15–27.

Kahn, A.E (1988a) Airline deregulation-a mixed bag, but a clear success nevertheless, *Transportation Law Journal,* 16: 229-51.

Kahn. A.E. (1988b) Deregulatory schizophrenia, *California Law Review,* 75: 1059-68.

Kahn, A.E. (1988c) Surprises of airline deregulation, *American Economic Review: Papers and Proceedings,* 78: 316-22.

Kahn, A.E. (1988d) *The Economics of Regulation, Principles and Institutions,* MIT Press, Cambridge.

Karels, G.V. (1989) Market forces and aircraft safety: an extension, *Economic Inquiry,* 27: 345-54.

Katz, R. (1995) The great GATS, *Airline Business,* September: 81-2.

Keamey, C. and Favotto, I. (1993) *Peak Period Pricing in Australian Aviation: The Experience at Sydney's Kingsford Smith Airport,* Research Paper, University of Western Sydney, Sydney.

Keeler, T.E. (1972) Airline regulation and market performance, *Bell Journal of Economics,* 3: 399-424.

Keeler, T.E. (1978) Domestic trunk airline regulation: an economic evaluation. *Studies on Federal Regulation,* US Senate Committee on Government Affairs, Washington.

Keeler, T.E. (1984) Theories of regulation and the deregulation movement, *Public Choice,* 3: 399-424.

Keeler, T.E. (1990) Airline deregulation and market performance: the economic basis for regulatory reform and lessons from the U.S. experience, in Banister. D. and Button, K.J. (eds) *Transport in a Free Market Economy,* Macmillan, London.

Keyes, L. (1951) *Federal Control of Entry into Air Transportation,* Harvard University Press, Cambridge.

Kyle, R. and Phillips, L.T. (19850 Airline deregulation: did economists promise too much or too little? *Logistics and Transportation Review,* 21: 3-25.

La Londe, B.J. and Copper, M.C. (1989) Electronic interchange and other third-party services, in *Partnerships in Providing Customer Service: A Third Party Perspective,* Council of Logistics Management, Oak Brook.

Labich, K. (1986) Why bigger is better in the airline wars, *Fortune,* 113(7): 40-42.

Labich, K. (1988) The show down at Eastern Air Lines, *Fortune,* 117(8): 53-5.

Lederer, J.F. and Enders, J.H. (1989) Aviation safety: the global conditions and prospects, in Moses, L. and Savage, I (eds), *Transportation Safety in an Age of Deregulation,* Oxford University Press, Oxford.

Leibenstein, H. (1966) Allocative efficiency, X-efficiency and the measurement of welfare losses, *American Economic Review*, 56: 392-415.

Levesque, T. (1994) Modeling the effects of airport noise on residential housing markets: a case study of Winnipeg International Airport, *Journal of Transport Economics and Policy*, 28: 199-210.

Levine, M.E. (1965) Is regulation necessary? California air transportation and national regulatory policy, *Yale Law Journal*, 74: 1416-47.

Levine, M.E. (1975) Regulatory airmail transportation, *Journal of Law and Economics*, 18: 317-59.

Levine, M.E. (1981) Revisionism revised: airline deregulation and the public interest, *Law and Contemporary Problems*, 44: 179-95.

Levine, M.E. (1987) Airline competition in deregulated markets: theory, firm strategy, and public policy, *Yale Journal of Regulation*, 4: 393-494.

Levine, M.E. (1989) Discussants observation on the evidence of linkages between economic deregulation and safety, in Moses, L. and Savage, I. (eds), *Transportation Safety in an Age of Deregulation*, Oxford University Press, Oxford.

Levine, M.E. (1993) Scope and limits of multilateral approaches to international air transport, in Organisation for Economic Cooperation and Development, *International Air Transport: The Challenges Ahead*, OECD, Paris.

Levine, M.E. (1995) The airlines of the future, paper to the 8th High Level Symposium, Montreal.

Levinson, D.M., Gillen, D. and Kanafani, A. (1998) The social costs of intercity transport: a review and comparison of air and highway, *Transport Reviews*, 18: 215-40

Lieb, R.C. and Molloy, J.F. (n.d.) The major airlines: labor relations in transition, Northeastern University.

Ligon, G. C. (1992) Development of the US air express industry: 1970–1990, *Transportation Quarterly*, 46: 279-94.

Loomis, J.B. (1992) The evolution of a more rigorous approach to benefit transfer: benefit function transfer, *Water Resources Research*, 28: 701-5.

Luken, R.A., Johnson, F.R. and Kibier, V. (1992) Benefits and costs of pulp and paper effluence controls under the Clean Water Act, *Water Resources Research*, 28: 667-74.

MacAvoy, P.W. and Snow, J.W. (eds) (1977) *Regulation of Passenger Fares and Competition Among the Airlines,* American Enterprise Institute, Washington.

Mackie, J. (1988) U.S. regulation policy, in Button, K.J. and Swann, D. (eds) *The Age of Regulatory Reform*, Oxford University Press, Oxford.

Maillebiau, E. and Hansen, M. (1995) Demand and consumer welfare impacts of international airline liberalization, *Journal of Transport Economics and Policy*, 29: 115–36.

Malkin, R. (1992) A pragmatic view of air freight, *Distribution*, 91 (May): 60-64.

Mandel, B.N. (1999) *Airport Choice and Competition: A Strategic Approach*, Mkmetric GmbH, Karlsruhe.

Martin Associates (1997a) *The Local and Regional Economic Impact of Washington National and Dulles International Airport*, Washington

Martin Associates (1997b) *The Local and Regional Economic Impacts of General Mitchell International and Lawrence J. Timmerman Airports*, County of Milwaukee.

Martin O'Connell Associates (1989) *The Local and Regional Economic Impact of Washington National and Dulles International Airports*, Washington.

McConnell, K.E. (1992) Model building and judgment: implications for benefit transfers with travel cost models, *Water Resources Research*, 28: 695-700.

McCraw, T.K. (1984) *Prophets of Regulation: Charles Francis Adams, Louis Brandeis, James M. Landis and Alfred E. Kahn,* Harvard University Press, Cambridge.

McDonald, F. E. (1987) Contestable markets – a new ideal model. *Economics,* 23, 183-86.

McGowan, F. (1994) *The EEA Air Transport Industry and a Single European Air Transport Market*, Occasional Paper No. 47, European Free Trade Association, Economic Affairs Department, Geneva.

McGowan, F. and Seabright, P. (1989) Deregulating European airlines, *Economic Policy*, October: 283-344.

McGowan, F. and Trengrove, C. (1986) *European Aviation: A Common Market?* Institute for Fiscal Studies, London.

McKenzie, R.B. and Shughart, W.F. (1988) Deregulation's impact on air safety: separating fact from fiction, *Regulation,* 11: 42-51.

McMichael A.J. and Fletcher, A.C. (eds) (1997) *Health at the Crossroads – Transport Policy and Urban Health*, John Wiley and Sons, London.

McMullen, B. S. (1986) Employee protection after airline deregulation. *Transportation Journal*, 25: 20-4.

Mencik von Zebinsky, A.A. (1996) *European Union External Competence and External Relations in Air Transport*, Kluwer, The Hague.

Meyer, J. R., and Oster, C.V. (1981) *Airline Deregulation: The Early Experience,* Auburn House, Boston

Meyer, J.R. and Oster, C.V. (1984a) *Deregulation and the New Airline Entrepreneurs*, MIT Press, Cambridge..

Meyer, J.R. and Oster, C.V. (eds) (1984b) *Airline Deregulation: The Early Experiences*, Auburn House, Boston.

Meyer, J.R., and Oster, C. V. (1987) *Deregulation and the Future of Intercity Passenger Travel*, MIT Press, Cambridge.

Mieszkowski, P. and Saper, A. (1978) An estimate of the effects of airport noise on property values, *Journal of Urban Economics*, 5: 425-40.

Miller, J.C. (1975) Statement before U.S. Senate Committee on the Judiciary, *Oversight of Civil Aeronautics Board Practices and Procedures,* Washington, 94th Congress, 1st Session, February–March.

Mills, G. (1990) Pricing of congested runways: the case of Sydney Airport, *Papers of the Australian Transport Research Forum,* 15: 291–310.

Mitchell, M.L. and Maloney, M.T. (1989) Crisis in the cockpit? The role of market forces in promoting air travel safety, *Journal of Law and Economics,* 32: 329-55.

Moore, T.G. (1986) Airline deregulation: its effects on passengers, capital, and labor. *Journal of Law and Economics,* 29, 1-28.

Morgan, I. P. (1987) International consequences, in Meyer, J.R. and Oster, C.V. (eds) *Deregulation and the Future of Intercity Passenger Travel,* MIT Press, Cambridge.

Morrison, S.A. (1983) Estimation of long-run prices and investment levels for airport runways, *Research in Transportation Economics,* 1 : 103–30.

Morrison, S.A. (1987) The equity and efficiency of runway pricing, *Journal of Public Economics,* 34: 45-60.

Morrison, S.A. (1989) U.S. domestic aviation, in Button, K.J. and Swann, D. (eds) *The Age of Regulatory Reform,* Oxford University Press, Oxford.

Morrison, S.A. (1997) Airline Deregulation and Fares at Dominated Hubs and Slot-controlled Airports, Statement before the Committee on the Judiciary, US House of Representatives, Washington.

Morrison, S.A. and Winston, C. (1986) *The Economic Effects of Airline Deregulation,* Brookings Institution, Washington.

Morrison, S.A. and Winston, C. (1987) Empirical implications and tests of the contestability hypothesis, *Journal of Law and Economics,* 30: 53-66.

Morrison, S.A. and Winston, C. (1988) Air safety, deregulation, and public policy. *Brookings Review,* Winter: 10-15.

Morrison, S.A. and Winston, C. (1995) *The Evolution of the Airline Industry,* Brookings Institution, Washington.

Morrissette, S.E. (1996) A survey of environmental issues in the civilian aviation industry, *Journal of Air Transportation Worldwide,* 1: 22-35.

Moses, L.N. and Savage, I. (1990) Aviation deregulation and safety, *Journal of Transport Economics and Policy,* 24: 171-88.

Mutti, J. and Mural, Y. (1977), Airline travel on the North Atlantic, *Journal of Transport Economics and Policy,* 11: 45-53.

Nance, J.J. (1986) *Blind Trust,* William Morrow, New York.

National Archives and Records Administration (1985) *Presidential Proclamations and Executive Orders,* USGPO: Washington.

Nelson, J. (1979) Airport noise, location rent, and the market for residential amenities, *Journal of Environmental Economics and Management,* 6: 320-31.

Nelson, J. (1980) Airports and property values: a survey of recent evidence, *Journal of Transport Economics and Policy*, 14: 37-52.

Newton, J. (1994) Improved bar codes for freight tracking, in *World Freight Technology*, Sterling Publications, London.

Nythi, M., Hooper, P. and Hensher, D. (1993) Compass Airline: 1 December 1990 to 20 December 1991 – what went wrong?, *Transport Reviews*, 13: 112-49 and 13: 185-206.

O'Byrne, P., Nelson, J. and Seneca, J. (1985) Housing values, census estimates, disequilibrium, and the environmental cost of airport noise: a case study of Atlanta, *Journal of Environmental Economics and Management*, 12: 169-78

O'Doherty, R.K. (1995) A review of benefit transfer: why and how, *British Review of Economic Issues*, 17: 1-15.

Olsen, C.V. and Traplain, J.M. (1981) Who has benefited from regulation of the airline industry?, *Journal of Law and Economics*, 24: 75-93.

Opaluch, J.J. and Mazzota, M. (1992) Fundamental issues in benefit transfer and national resource damage assessment, paper to the Association of Environmental and Resource Economists Workshop, Snowbird.

Organisation for Economic Cooperation and Development (1988) *Deregulation and Airline Competition*, OECD, Paris.

Organisation for Economic Cooperation and Development (1997) *The Future of International Air Transport Policy: Responding to Global Change*, OECD, Paris.

Oster, C.V. and Pickrell, D.H. (1988) Code sharing, joint fares, and competition in the regional airline industry, *Transportation Research A*, 22: 405-17.

Oster, C.V. and Strong, J. (1988) Competitive strategies of commuters, in Meyer, J.R. and Oster, C.V. (eds) *Airline Deregulation: Rebirth of the Entrepreneur*, MIT Press, Cambridge.

Oster, C.V. and Zorn, C.K. (1983) Airline deregulation, commuter safety, and regional air transportation, *Growth and Change*, 14: 3-11.

Oster, C.V. and Zorn, C.K. (1989) Airline deregulation: is it still safe to fly?, in Moses, L. and Savage, I. (eds), *Transportation Safety in an Age of Deregulation*, Oxford University Press, Oxford.

Ostrowski, P.L. and O'Brien, T.V. (1991) Predicting Consumer Loyalty for Airline Passengers, Department of Marketing, Northern Illinois University.

Oum, T.H. and Park, J-H. (1997) Airline alliances: current status, policy issues and future directions, *Journal of Air Transport Management*,3: 133–44.

Oum, T.H. and Tretheway, M.W. (1984) Reforming Canadian airline regulation, *Logistics and Transportation Review*, 20: 261-84.

Oum, T.H. and Tretheway, M.W. (1990) Airline hub-and-spoke system, *Transportation Research Forum Proceedings*, 30: 380-93.

Oum, T.H. and Yu, C. (1995) A productivity comparison of the world's major airlines, *Journal of Air Transport Management*, 2: 181-95.

Oum, T.H., Stanbury, W.T. and Tretheway, M.W. (1991) Airline deregulation in Canada and its economic effects, *Transportation Journal*, 30: 4-22.

Oum, T.H., Zhang, A. and Zhang, H. (1996) A note on the optimal pricing in a hub-and-spoke system, *Transportation Research B*, 30: 11–8.

Page, P. (1996a) Consolidation, competition cross borders, change shape of air cargo wordlwide, *Traffic World*, 245: 32-3.

Page, P. (1996b) New competition, shipper options drive Emery Worldwide's air freight revamp, *Traffic World*, 245: 44-5.

Paik, I. (1972) Measurement of Environmental Externality in Particular Reference to Noise, PhD thesis, Georgetown University.

Panzar, J.C. (1980) Regulation, deregulation, and economic efficiency: the case of the CAB, *American Economic Review: Papers and Proceedings*, 70: 311-15.

Panzar, J.C. (1983) Regulatory theory and the U.S. airline experience. *Zeitschrift ftir die gestamte Staatswissenschaft*, 139: 490-505.

Panzar, J.C., and Willig, R.D. (1977) Free entry and the sustainability of natural monopoly, *Bell Journal of Economics*, 8: 1-22.

Pearce, D.W. and Markandya, A. (1989) *Environmental Policy Benefits: Monetary Valuation*, OECD, Paris.

Pelksman, J. (1986) Deregulation of European air transport, in Jong, H.W. and Shepherd, W.G. (eds) *Mainstreams in Industrial Organisation*, Martinuss Nijhoff, Dordrecht.

Peltzman, S. (1976) Toward a more general theory of regulation. *Journal of Law and Economics*, 19: 211-40.

Pels, E. (2000) Airport Economics and Policy: Efficiency, Competition, and Interaction with Airlines, PhD dissertation, Free University of Amsterdam.

Pennington, G., Topham, N. and Ward, R. (1990) Aircraft noise and residential property values adjacent to Manchester International Airport, *Journal of Transport Economics and Policy*, 24: 49-59.

Pirrong, S.C. (1992) An application of core theory to the analysis of ocean shipping markets, *Journal of Law and Economics*, 35: 89–131.

Posner, R.A. (1975) The social costs of monopoly and regulation, *Journal of Political Economy*, 83: 807-27.

Prestowitz, C.V., Hilty, D., Chimerine, L. and Sweeney, L. (1996) Turbulence over the Pacific, Economic Strategy Institute, Washington.

Price, T. (1974) The Social Cost of Airport Noise as Measured by Rental Changes: The Case of Logan Airport, PhD dissertation, Boston University.

Prodromidis, K.P. and Frangos, T. (1995) Public or private enterprises in the airline industry, *International Journal of Transport Economics*, 22: 85-95.

Proussaloglu, K. and Koppelman, F. (1995) Air carrier demand: an analysis of market share determinants, *Transportation*, 22: 371-88.

Quandt, R.E. and Baumol, W.J. (1983) The demand for abstract transport modes: theory and measurement, *Journal of Regional Science*, 6: 13-26.

Rastatter, E.H. and Stein, R. (1988) The US experience with deregulation, presentation to the Transportation Research Board Annual Meeting, Washington.

Reed, A. (1992) Grandfather is well and living in Europe, *Air Transport World,* May: 65-7.

Reynolds-Feighan, A.J. (1994) The EU and US air freight markets: network organisation in a deregulated environment, *Transport Reviews,* 14: 193-217.

Reynolds-Feighan, A.J. and Berechman, J. (1998) Network impacts of changes in the European aviation industry, in Button, K.J., Nijkamp, P. and Priemus, H. (eds) *Transport Networks in Europe: Concepts, Analysis and Policies,* Edward Elgar, Cheltenham.

Reynolds-Feighan, A.J. and Button, K.J. (1999) An assessment of the capacity and congestion levels at European airports, *Journal of Air Transport Management,* 5: 113-34.

Reynolds-Feighan, A.J. and Durkin, J. (1997) *The Impact of Air Transport on Ireland's Export Performance,* Institute of International Trade of Ireland, Dublin.

Reynolds-Feighan, A.J. and Feighan, K.J. (1997) Airport services and airport charging systems: a critical review of the EU Common Framework, *Transportation Research E,* 33: 311-20.

Rietveld, P. (1997) Drie mainpoortsystemen voor Nederland, *Economische Statistische Berichten,* Hague

Rose, N.L. (1989) Financial influences on airline safety, in L. Moses and I. Savage (eds), *Transportation Safety in an Age of Deregulation,* Oxford University Press, Oxford.

Rose, N.L. (1990) Profitability and product quality: economic determinants of airline safety performance, *Journal of Political Economy,* 98: 944-64.

Rose, N.L. (1992) Fear of flying? Economic analysis of airline safety, *Journal of Economic Perspectives,* 6: 75-94.

Royal Commission on Transportation (1961) *Report,* Ottawa: Queens Printer, Ottawa.

Ruppenthal, K.M. (1987) U.S. airline deregulation-winners and losers. *Logistics and Transportation Review,* 23: 65-82.

Saccomano, A. (1996) Baltimore aims for logistics-friendly climate, *Traffic World,* 245: 39.

Sandler, R. D. (1988) Market share instability in commercial airline markets and the impact of deregulation. *Journal of Industrial Economics,* 36: 327-35.

Sawers, D. (1987) *Competition in the Air – What Europe Can Learn from the USA,* Institute of Economic Affairs Research Monograph 41, London.

Scarf, H.E. (1962) An analysis of markets with a large number of participants, in *Recent Advances in Game Theory,* Princeton University Press, Princeton.

Scarf, H.E. and Debreu, G. (1963) A limit theorem on the core of an economy, *International Economic Review*, 4: 235-46.

Schwartz, M. (1986) The nature and scope of contestability theory, *Oxford Economic Papers*, 38: 37-57.

Schipper, Y. (1999) Market Structure and Environmental Costs in Aviation: A Welfare Analysis of European Air Transport Reform, PhD dissertation, Free University of Amsterdam

Sharkey, W.W. (1977) Efficient production when demand is uncertain, *Journal of Public Economics*, 8: 369-84.

Simat, Helliesen and Eichner Inc. (1986) *Economic Impact of Dulles International Airport: An Up-date*, Washington.

Simmons, J. (1994) Benefits of different transport modes, in ECMT Economic Research Centre, Round Table 1993, ECMT, Paris.

Sjostrom, W. (1989) Collusion in ocean shipping: a test of monopoly and empty core models, *Journal of Political Economy*, 97: 1160-79.

Sjostrom, W. (1993) Antitrust immunity for shipping conferences: an empty core approach, *Antitrust Bulletin*, 38: 419-23.

Small, K.A., Winston, C. and Evans, C.A. (1989) *Road Work: A New Highway Pricing and Investment Policy*, Brookings Institution, Washington.

Smith, T.K. (1995) Why air travel doesn't work, *Fortune*, April 3: 26-36

Smith, V.K. (1989) Can we measure the economic value of environmental amenities?, *Southern Economic Journal*, 56: 865-78.

Smith, V.K. (1992) On separating defensible benefit transfers from 'smoke and mirrors', *Water Resources Research*, 28: 685-94.

Smith, V.K. and Huang, J-C. (1995) Can markets value air quality? A meta-analysis of hedonic property value models, *Journal of Political Economy*, 103: 209-27.

Smith, V.K. and Kaoru, Y. (1990) Signals or noise – explaining the variation in recreation benefit estimates, *American Journal of Agricultural Economics*, 72: 419-33.

Spalding, T.L. (1979) Civil aviation policy in Canada and its effects on international and domestic charter services, in Reschenthaler, G.B. and Roberts, B. (eds) *Perspectives on Canadian Airline Regulation*, Institute for Research on Public Policy, Montreal.

Spence, A. M. (1983) Contestable markets and the theory of industrial structure: a review article, *Journal of Economic Literature*, 21: 981-90.

Spraggins, H.B. (1989) The impact of airline size upon efficiency and profitability, *Journal of Transportation Management*, 23: 73-104.

Stanbury, W.T. (1987) Direct regulation and its reform: a Canadian perspective, *Brigham Young University Law Review*: 467-539.

Stanbury, W.T. and Reschenthaler, G.B. (1977) Oligopoly and conscious parallelism: theory, policy and the Canadian cases, *Osgoode Hall Law Journal*, 15: 617-700.

Stanbury, W.T. and Tretheway, M.W. (1986) Airline deregulation: a bibliography, *Logistics and Transportation Review*, 22: 449-89.

Stanbury, W.T. and Tretheway, M.W, (1987) *Analysis of the changes in airline regulation proposed in Bill C-18*, Minutes of Proceedings and Evidence of the Standing Committee on Transport, Issue 17.

Stanley, T.D. and Jarrell, S.B. (1989) Meta-regression analysis: a quantitative method of literature surveys, *Journal of Economic Surveys*, 2: 161-70.

Starkie, D., and Starrs, M. (1984) Contestability and sustainability in regional airline markets, *Economic Record*, 60: 274-83.

Stasinopoulos, D. (1992) The second aviation package of the European community, *Journal of Transport Economics and Policy*, 26: 83-7.

Stasinopoulos, D. (1993) The third phase of liberalisation in community aviation and the need for supplementary measures, *Journal of Transport Economics and Policy*, 27: 323-28.

Statistics Canada (1989a) *Aircraft Movement Statistics: Annual Report 1987,* Aviation Statistics Centre, Ottawa.

Statistics Canada (1989b) Aviation Statistics Centre – Service Bulletin, 2(8).

Stevens, H. (1997) *Liberalisation of Air Transport in Europe*, The European Institute, London School of Economics, London.

Stevenson, R. (1980) Likelihood functions for generalized stochastic frontier estimation, *Journal of Econometrics*, 13: 57–66.

Stigler, G. (1971) The theory of economic regulation, *Bell Journal of Economics*, 2: 3-21.

Stough, R. (1997) (ed.) Proceedings of The Fifth Annual Conference on the Future of the Northern Virginia Economy, Center for Regional Analysis, Institute of Public Policy, George Mason University, Fairfax.

Stough, R., Riggle, J. and Kulkarni, R. (1996) Technology in Virginia's Regions, prepared for the Virginia Center for Innovative Technology, Institute of Public Policy, Fairfax.

Swann, D. (1988) *The Retreat of the State – Deregulation and Privatisation in the UK and USA*, Wheatsheaf, Hassocks.

Swoveland, C. (1980) Airport Peaking and Congestion: A Policy Discussion Paper, Quantalytics, prepared for Airport Services and Security Branch, Canadian Air Transport Administration, Vancouver.

Taneja, N. (1979) *The U.S. Air Freight Industry*, Lexington Books, Lexington.

Telser, L.G. (1978) *Economic Theory and the Core*, University of Chicago Press, Chicago.

Telser, L.G. (1987) *A Theory of Efficient Cooperation and Competition*, Cambridge University Press, Cambridge.

Telser, L.G. (1990) Theory of corporations: an application of the theory of the core, *Journal of Accounting, Auditing and Finance*, 5: 159-201.

Telser, L.G. (1991) Industry total cost functions and the status of the core, *Journal of Industrial Economics*, 39: 225-40

Telser, L.G. (1994) The usefulness of core theory in economics, *Journal of Economic Perspectives*, 8: 151-64.

Telser, L.G. (1996) Competition and the core, *Journal of Political Economy*, 104: 85-107.

The Economist (1996) Air freight: rigged, 17th August.

The Economist (1997) Fasten your safety belt, 11 January, 55-7.

Thurow, L. (1996) *The Future of Capitalism: How Today's Economic Forces will Shape Tomorrow's Future*, William Morrow, New York.

Toms, M.R. (1994) Charging for airports: the new BAA approach, *Journal of Air Transport Management*, 1: 77-82.

Transport Canada (1985) *Freedom to Move: A Movement for Transportation Reform*, Transport Canada, Ottawa.

Transport Canada (1988) *Aviation Industry Review: Second Quarter 1988*, Air Statistics and Forecasting Branch, Economic Analysis Directorate, Policy and Co ordination Group, Transport Canada, Ottawa.

Transportation Research Board (1999) *Entry and Competition in the US Airline Industry: Issues and Opportunities*, National Science Foundation, Washington.

Treitel, D. and Smick, E. (1996) All change, *Airline Business*, 12: 34-6.

Triangle Management Services (1990) *Airline Freight under Air Waybill, by Road, in the EEC*, Report to the Commission of the European Communities (DG-VII: Air Transport Division).

Tucci, G. (1985) Regulation and 'contestability' in formulating an air transport policy for the European Community, *Rivista di Politica Economica,* 19: 3-23.

Tullock, G. (1967) The welfare costs of tariffs, monopolies and theft, *Western Economic Journal*, 5: 224-32.

UK Civil Aviation Authority (1988) *Statement of Policies on Air Transport Licensing – June 1988*, CAP539, CAA, London.

UK Civil Aviation Authority (1993) *Airline Competition in the Single European Market*, CAP623, CAA, London.

UK Civil Aviation Authority (1994) *Airline Competition on European Long Haul Routes,* CAA, London.

UK Civil Aviation Authority (1995) *Slot Allocation: A Proposal for Europe's Airports*, CAP644, CAA, London.

UK Civil Aviation Authority (1998) *The Single European Aviation Market: The First Five Years,* CAA: London.

UK Department of Transport (1992) *Assessing the Environmental Impact of Road Schemes, Report of the Standing Committee on trunk Road Assessment*, HMSO, London.

UK House of Commons Standing Committee on Transport (1982) *Ninth Report Domestic Air Carrier Policy, Ninth Report*, HMSO, London

US Civil Aeronautics Board (1975) *Report of the CAB Special Staff on Regulatory Reform*, Civil Aeronautics Board, Washington.

US Congress, Committee on Government Operations (1977) *Airline Deregulation and Aviation Safety*, Hearings, 95th Congress, 1st Session (8-9 September) Washington.

US Congress Senate, Committee on the Judiciary (1975) *Oversight of Civil Aeronautics Board Practices and Procedures*, US Government Printing Office, Washington.

US Department of Transportation (1988) *Study of Airline Computer Reservation Systems*, DOT-P-37-88-2, Office of the Secretary of Transportation, Washington.

US Department of Transportation (1990) *Airline Marketing Practices: Travel Agencies, Frequent-flier Programs and Computer Reservation Systems*, Secretary's Task Force on Competition in the US Domestic Airline Industry, Washington.

US Department of Transportation (1996a) *Airport Activity Statistics of the Certificated Route Air Carriers*, USDOT, Washington.

US Department of Transportation, Bureau of Transportation Statistics (1996b) *Transportation Statistics Annual Report 1996*, USDOT, Washington.

US Department of Transportation, Bureau of Transportation Statistics (1996c) *Transportation Statistics Annual Report 1996*, USDOT, Washington.

US Department of Transportation, Bureau of Transportation Statistics (1997) *Transportation Statistics Annual Report 1997*, US Government Printing Office, Washington

US Federal Aviation Administration (1991) *A Case Study of Potential New Connecting Hub Airports*, Washington, USDOT.

US General Accounting Office (1986) *Airline Competition: Impact of Computerized Reservation Systems*, General Accounting Office, Washington.

US General Accounting Office (1990) *Airline Competition: Higher Fares and Reduced Competition at Concentrated Airports*, GAO/RCED-90-102, Washington.

US General Accounting Office (1995a) International Aviation: Airline Alliances Produce Benefits but Effect on Competition is Uncertain, GAO/RCED-95-99, Washington.

US General Accounting Office (1995b) DOT Needs Better Data for Monitoring and Decision-making, GAO/T-RCED-95-240, USGAO, Washington.

US General Accounting Office (1998) Airline Competition: Barriers to Entry Continue in Some Domestic Markets, statement of John H. Anderson to the Subcommittee on Transportation, Committee on Appropriations, US Senate, GAO/T-RCED-98-112, Washington.

US National Commission to Ensure a Strong Competitive Airline Industry (1993) *Change, Challenge and Competition*, US Government Printing Office, Washington,.

Uyeno, D., Hamilton, S. and Biggs, A. (1993) Density of residential land use and the impact of airport noise, *Journal of Transport Economics and Policy*, 27: 3-18.

Van Boening, M. and Wilcox, N. (1992) Avoidable cost: ride a double-auction roller coaster, paper to the Economic Science Association, Tucson.

van de Riet, O. and Twaalfhoven, P. (1998) Models and tools to design strategies for freight transport: an example for the Netherlands, in Button, K.J., Nijkamp, P. and Priemus, H. (eds) *Transport Networks in Europe: Concepts, Analysis and Policies*, Edward Elgar, Cheltenham

Van De Voorde, E.E. (1992) European air transport after 1992: deregulation or re-regulation? *Antitrust Bulletin*, 37: 507-28.

Varian, H.R. (1999) Market structure in the network age, presented to the *Understanding the Digital Economy Conference*, Washington.

Vasigh, B. and Hamzaee, R.G. (1998) A comparative analysis of economic performance of US commercial airports, *Journal of Air Transport Management*, 4: 209-16.

Vickrey, W. (1971) Responsive pricing of public utility services, *Bell Journal of Economics*, 2: 337-46.

Vincent, D. and Stasinopoulos, D. (1990) The aviation policy of the European community, *Journal of Transport Economics and Policy*, 24: 95-100.

Viner, J. (1931) Cost curves and supply curves, *Zeitschrift für Nationalokonomie*, 3: 23-46.

Walton, L.W. (1996) The ABC's of EDI: the role of activity-based costing (ABC) in determining EDI feasibility in logistics organizations, *Transportation Journal*, 36: 43-50.

Walton, L.W. and Lewis, A.L. (1995) Shipper, carrier and consultant perspectives of EDI: strategies for successful implementation in the motor carrier industry, *Transportation Journal*, 35: 28-37.

Waters, W.G. (1996) Values of travel time savings in road transport project evaluation, in Hensher, D., King, J. and Oum, T. (eds) *World Transport Research: Volume 2, Transport Policy*, Pergamon, Oxford.

Wheatcroft, S. and Lipman, G. (1986) *Air Transport in a Competitive Market*, Economist Intelligence Unit, London.

White, L.J. (1979) Economies of scale and the question of natural monopoly in the airline industry, *Journal of Air Law and Commerce*, 44: 545-73.

Windle. R.J. (1991) The world's airlines: a cost and productivity comparison, *Journal of Transport Economics and Policy*, 25:31-49.

Williams, G. (1993) *The Airline Industry and the Impact of Deregulation*, Ashgate, Aldershot.

World Commission on Environment and Development (1987) *Our Common Future*, Oxford University Press, Oxford.

INDEX

Abe, MA 29
Abelson, P 327
accidents *see* safety
Acts; Aeronautics Act 1922 (Canada) 116; Airline Agreement Act 1952 (Australia) 281; Airline Deregulation Act 1978 (US) 92,93–109*passim*,120,155,231, 264, 318; Canadian Air Transport Board Act 1919 (Canada) 117; Civil Aeronautics Act (US) 1938 85,117; Competition Act 1986 (Canada) 125; Federal Aviation Act (1958) 86; Interstate Commerce Act (1887) 85–6; Kelly Mail Act 1925 (US) 273; Motor Carriers Act 1938 (US) 85; Motor Carriers Reform Act 1980 (US) 265; National Transportation Act 1967 (Canada) 118; National Transportation Act 1987 (Canada) 124; Railroad Revitalization and regulatory Reform Act 1976 (US) 265; Staggers Act 1980 (US) 265; Trans Canadian Airlines Act 1937 (Canada) 117; Transport Act 1938 (Canada) 117
Aiger, DJ 25
air fares *see* prices
air service agreements 158–60,162; Bermuda Agreements 63, 64; bilateral 56,131,133–5,145, 149–50,155,157,158–9,164,166, 274,312; multilateral 160
air traffic control 74,99,148,162,166, 209,211
Air Transport Association of America 100,325
air trucking 285–6,293–9
Airbus Industries 3

Airline Business 67,313,314
airports 65,163,339; access 291–3; capacity 71,128,145,148,166, 196 –7,199,208–26,332; congestion 49–50,71,109,110, 191,203–5 *passim*,212–14,227; economic development 231–64; ground handling 203–4,207; hub-and-spoke 13,59–8,101,102–103, 110,126,150,151,171,231–64, 278,282,287,315; investment 71; ownership 120, 133,200,206; pricing 109–10,142,166–7, 190–230 *passim*,341; productivity 28; Ramsey Pricing of 194,227; scheduling committees 50
Airports Council International 213, 215,216,217,218
alliances 3,32,39,67,76,145,288–9,310, 312–5,316,317–24; strategic 56, 310,313,322; *see also* code-sharing
Altshuler, A 86
Archer, SH 116
Armington Index 254
Aschauer, DA 169,239
Ashford, N 210
Asian-Pacific Economic Council 2, 84, 311
Association of European Airlines 3, 4,74,134,160,168,205,211,212, 270,285,287
atmospheric pollution *see* environmental costs
Australian Bureau of Industry Economics 28
Avmark Aviation Economist 5,67

Bailey, EE 92,93,97,98,103,108,127

Baker, SH 24
Baldwin, J 119
Balfour, J 205
Balinski, ML 196
Banister, D 326
banking of flights 54,71
bankruptcy 177–8
Barnett, A 320
Barone, SS 119
Barrett, SA 66,133,139
Bauer, PW 28
Baumol, WJ 78,87,92,113,173,307
Becker, G 12
Bell, J 303
benefit transfers 329–34
Bennett, RD 25
Berechman, J 77,278
Bergh, J van den 332
Bergstrom, JC 331,337
Berry, T 25
Bertrand, J 175–6
Bhagwati, JN 25
Bittlingmayer, G 174
Bjarnadottir, V 295
Blumestock, JW 106
Boeing Commercial Airplane Group
    3,9,70,317
Bollard, A 281
Borenstein, S 84,322,323
Boulding, KE 335
Boyle, KJ 331,337
Brander, JRG 196
Brenner, MA 113
Breyer, S 90,91
Brooks, M 170,183,296
Brookshire, DS 330,331
Brown, E 8,299,300
Brown, S 1,8
Brueckner, JJ 24,233
Bureau of Transport and
    Communications Economics 186
business travel 17,18,236–9,253–4,
    276
Button, KJ 2,6,40,65,71,72,73,77,
    80,81,85,94,114,134,163,170,
    174,181,183,204,296,235,240,

254,282,285,295,296,303,311,
    312,313,324,325,326,327,338
Bylow, LF 318

cabotage 63,142,284
Canadian Parliament 119
Capello, R 170,296
Carlton, DW 101
Carron, AS 275,277
Castles, C 71
Caves, DW 21,22,23,28,116
Caves, RE 88,89
Center for Delay Analysis 213
Chalk, A 320
Chance, DM 323
Charnes, A 25
charter services 117,118,121,122–3,
    131,139,142,144,158,283
Chicago Convention 63,131,134,
    149,161,167,274,311
Chicago school of economics 62,85
Chu, S 25
coalition theory 90
Coase, RH 177,191,198,295,339
code-sharing 21,35,75,315,319
Coley/Forrest Inc 253
Collins, A 327
collusion 175–6
Comité de Sages for Air Transport
    154,205,333
Commission on the Third London
    Airport 71,333,340
competition 76,86,92,103,109,114,
    122,125,128,135,137,140,145–
    6,172,205; excessive 40, policy
    61,76,86,136,155,165,188,203,
    276; with surface modes 120
computer reservation systems 5,6,
    31,71,76,110–113,129,131,140,
    157,165,290,295,309,315,319;
    regulation of 20,129
congestion costs 49–50,92,93,101,
    113
consumer satisfaction 109,121
contestability 92,93,101,113,176
Copper, MC 296

core theory 40, 172–89
cost-benefit analysis 71,80,778
costs; covering 119,286; functions
  21–8,77–8,175–84 *passim*;
  generalized 278–9; replacement
  78; *see also externalities*
courier services 271–2,287,296
Crandall, RL 31
Crum, MR 297

data envelopment analysis 28
DeVany, AS 18,88,327
De Wit, J 77
Debreu, G 172
demand 16–21; derived 8,21,31,34;
  forecasting 68–70; peaks 171,
  195–8,201
Distexhe, V 28,152
Dodgson, J 43
Doganis, R 53,78,114,166,192,205,
  274,283
Douglas, GW 88
Douglas, P 89
Dresner, M 75,119,123
Durkin, J 10

Eads, GC 87
Economides, N 37,310
Eckel, C 133
Eckel, D 133
economies of density 21,22,23,70,
  104,110,126,233,301,310;
  experience 21,24,52,70; market
  presence 52,152,234; network size
  21,22,51,70; scale 5,22, 23,104,
  193,194,233,301,310; scope 21,
  23,70,104,110,193,194,233,301,
  310; standardization 5,24
Edgeworth, FY 172
elasticities of demand; income 18;
  price 17–19,46,120,174,179–8
electronic data interchange 296–7,
  299,305–7
Emerson, F 122
Encanoua, D 28
Enders, JH 321

environmental costs 15,49,65,72–3,
  80–81,163,209–10,228,310–43
  passim; *see also* externalities
EUROCONTROL 136,139,210,211,
  229
European Civil Aviation Conference
  211–3
European Union 10,24,43,59,64,77,
  79,81,83–4,131–147 *passim*,
  148,150–2,156,159,160,161,
  164,165,169,170,187,188,198,
  204,205–30,282–6,293,311,314;
  Commission 136–40 *passim*,
  143,144,145,160,204; Single
  European Market 2,170,205,282
Evans, CA 327
express carriers 267, 269; *see also*
  courier services
externalities 15,40,42,340; network
  47,50

Favotto, I 196
Fawcett, SA 196
Fawcett, SE 196
Feighan, KJ 227
Feitelson, EI 73,328,333
Felkner, J 297
Ferris, SP 232
Fisher, FM 102
Fisher, JB 196
flag carriers 23,57,137,168,269
Fletcher, AC 326
franchising 315
Frangos, T 133
free rider problem 310
freedom of the skies 63,135,142,144
Freeman, AM 331
freight forwarders 6,8,297–9,301–2,
  305,306,308
frequent flyer programs 16,18–20,21,
  110–11,127,236,239
Fujii, ET 58

Galbraith, KJ 125
Gautrin, J 327
Gawan-Taylor, M 281

Gellman Research Associates 318
General Agreement on Trade in
    Services 68,157,158
Ghorbial, AA 239
Gillen, DW 28,120,123,124,127,161
Gillngwater, D 85
Glass, GV 333
globalization 1
Golbe, DL 98,322
Gomez-Ibanez, JA 114
Good, DH 28,134
Gordon, K 45
Graham, B 300
Granger, C 263
Greene, WH 27
Grether, DM 110
Gronau, R 18

Haanapel, PPC 122
Hahn, F 308
Hamzawi, SG 196
Hanlon, P 42,59
Hansen, M 77
Harberger, AC 25
Hardaway, RM 205
Heaver, TD 124
Hensher, D 79,200
high density rule 240–52 *passim*
high speed rail 292
Hill, H 303
Hoehn, JP 329,335
Hooper, P 79,200
Huang, J-C 336
Humphreys, BK 5
hubs *see* airports
Hunter, JE 334

industrial location 232–265 *passim*
information and communications
    technology 169
intelligent transportation systems
    296–7
International Air Transport
    Association 64,66,71,73,81,83,
    114,149,153,188,201,272–3,
    274,285,294,311,312,

International Civil Aviation
    Organization 64,73,78,81,83,
    134,152,153,161,163,168,200,
    201,210,227,266,311,328
investment 38,40,45; *see also* airports
Ippolito, RA 19

James, G 102,115
Johnson, K 307,327
Jordan, WA 88,104,117,119,127,130
Juan, EJ 205,208
just-in-time production 7,291,296,
    297,299,300

Kahn AE 91,93,105,107,124,194,
    206,316
Kanafani, A 239
Kaoru, Y 336
Karels, GV 320
Katz, R 2,157
Keamey, C 196
Keeler, TE 88,90,181,235,323
Kerr, J 336
Keyes, L 88
Keynes, JM 237
Koppelman, F 19
Kraft, DJH 31
Kyle, R 113

La Londe, BJ 296
Labich, K 93
Lall, A 28
Lederer, JF 320
Leibenstein, H 25
leisure travel 17,111,131,236
Levesque, T 327
Levine, ME 87,88,91,103,110,113,
    151,321
Levinson, DM 80,328
Lewis, AL 296,297
licensing 61,124,137
Lieb, RC 105,106
Ligon, GC 7,300
Lipman, G 114
LoFaso, AJ 320
low cost carriers 19,29,96–7,227

Luken, RA 332
Lundstedt, SB 335

MacAvoy, PW 88
Maggi, R 295
mail services 86–7,205,266,273,275
Maillebiau, E 77
Malkin, R 6,305
Maloney, MT 323
Mandel, BN 144
Markandya, A 335
market stability 90,98,116,132,
    169–89; *see also* core theory
Martin Associates 242
Martin O'Connell Associates 242
Mazzota, M 331
McConnell, KE 332
McCraw, T K 91
McGowan, F 114,134
McKenzie, R B 80,99,100
McMichael AJ 326
McMullen, BS 106
mergers 54–5,101–3,117,126–8,131,
    155,314,321
meta analysis 81,333–8
Metcalfle's Law 55
Meyer, JR 95,96,97,111
Mieszkowski, P 327
Miller, JC 88,98
Mills, G 196
Mitchell, ML 323
Molloy, J F 105,106
monopoly 25,36–7,40,52,86,87,92,
    103,118,127,132,144,151,168,
    176,206,238,274
Moore, T G 103,113
Morgan, IP 114
Morrison, SA 19,76,84,99,100,103,
    113,167,196,238,239,318,320
Morrissette, SE 327
Moses, LN 316,317
Mural, Y 18
Mutti, J 18

Nance, JJ 320
need 40

Neill, HR 331
Nelson, J 327,333
neo-classical economic 21,91,191
networks; definition 11–12,13,46;
    regulation of 170–2; *see also*
    economies
Nijkamp, P 174,337
noise nuisance 40,73,274,329,332–
    3,340,343; *see also* externalities
North American Free Trade Agreement
    160,282
Nythi, M 25

O'Brien, TV 236
O'Byrne, P 327
O'Doherty, RK 331
Olsen, CV 90
Opaluch, JJ 331
Open Skies Policy 2,64,75,114,123,
    134,160,232,287,288,311
Organisation for Economic
    Cooperation and Development
    1,2,9,60,159,169,274,311,312,
    325
Oster, CV 95,96,97,99,111,318,321,
    322
Ostrowski, PL 236
Oum, TH 17,28,31,32,76,84,120,
    124,179,238
Owens, C 6
ownership, foreign 142,150–1,161;
    private 120,133,162,164,276,
    312,325; state 60,120,135; *see
    also* airports

Page, P 299,301
Paik, I 327
Panzar, JC 87,90,92
Pareto optimality 172,178,192
Park, J-H 76
Pearce, DW 336
Pelksman, J 134
Pels, E 204
Peltzman, S 85
Pennington, G 327
Perelman, S 28,152

perimeter rule 240–52 *passim*,342
Phillips, LT 113
Pickford, M 281
Pirrong, SC 174,183,184
Posner, RA 25
Pratt, JB 24
predatory behavior 42–3,67
Prestowitz, CV 288
Price, T 327
prices airline 28–30,96–9,100,101,
    118,120,124,143–4,145,149,
    273,279–81; discrimination and
    discounts 30,31,97,100,120,121,
    140–1,233–6; fuel 121; limit 127;
    regulation 86,118,122,135,137,
    138–9,149–50; *see also* yield
    management
Prodromidis, KP 133
profits 3,5,86,107,127,153–4,175,
    192,200,276
property rights 167,338
postal services *see* mail services
public goods 40
public interest theory 38

Quandt, R. 78

Randall, A 329,335
regulatory capture 89
Reschenthaler, GB 119
Revenue pooling 132,135,137
Reynolds-Feighan, AJ 10,204,227,
    278,285
Rietveld, P 170,237,296,336
Rose, NL 318,320
route structures 15–47 *passim*, 50– 58
    passim,129
Royal Commission on Transportation
    118
Ruppenthal, KM 113

Saccomano, A 307
safety 40,65,72,79–80,87,99–100,
    132,142,310–42 *passim*
Sand, FM 196
Sandler, R D 98

Savage, I 316,317,318
Sawers, D 114–15
Scarf, HE 172
schedules 95–6,127
Schipper, Y 143
Schwartz, M 92
Seabright, P 134
Shughart, WF 80,99,100
Simat, Helliesen and Eichner Inc 242,
    254
Sjostrom, W 173,174,182,183
Small, KA 195
Smick, E 234
Smith, TK 168,173
Smith, VK 330,335,336
Spalding, TL 121
Spence, A M 92
Spiller, PT 24,233
Spraggins, HB 22
Stanbury, WT 116,119
Starkie, D 115
Starrs, M 115
Stasinopoulos, D 134
Stein, L 91
Stein, R 101,109
Stevens, H 134
Stigler, G 85
Stough, R 254,298
subsidies; cross 119–20,124,
    200,339; direct 43–4,58,60,86,
    87,138,151,162,163–4,183,200,
    208
Swann, D 134
Swoveland, C 196

Taneja, N 277
taxation 60,70,130,339,341
telecommunications 14,302; *see also*
    electronic data interchange
Telser, LG 173,174,177,187,188
terrorism 316
The Economist 67,286,310,312
Thurow, L 1,310
traffic forecasts 3,9,10,62,69–71,75,
    76–7
Transport Canada 123,127

Transportation Research Board 43,
  84,94
travel agents 111–12
Traplain, J M 90
Treitel, D 2,34
Trengrove, C 114
Tretheway, MW 75,116,119,120,124
Tullock, G 25
Twaalfhoven, P 308

UK Civil Aviation Authority 66,133,
  142,143,144,166,196,317
UK Department of Transport 67,331
UK House of Commons Standing
  Committee on Transport 121
US Civil Aeronautics Board 85–93
  passim, 131,232,275–7
US Congress Senate, Committee on
  the Judiciary 91
US Congress, Committee on
  Government Operations 320
US Department of Transportation 8,
  19,42,93,102,109,112,155,205,
  232,303
US Federal Aviation Administration
  72,78,86,87,98,110,191,213,
  233,239,254,279,317,322
US General Accounting Office 19,
  20,75,112,233,235,317,318
US Interstate Commerce Commission
  277
US National Commission to Ensure a
  Strong Competitive Airline
  Industry 236
Uyeno, D 327

Van Boening, M 182
van de Riet, O 308
Van De Voorde, EE 285
Varian, H. 55
Vickrey, W 195
Vincent, D 134
Viner, J 172,178,179

Walton, LW 296,
Waters, WG 336
Watkins, W 18
Wheatcroft, S 114
White, LJ 22
Wilcox, N 182
Williams, G 59
Williams, JR 91,108,127
Willig, RD 92
Windle, RJ 75,77,113
Winston, C 19,76,84,99,100,103,
  113,239,318,320
workable competition 139
World Bank 208,265,332
World Commission on Environment
  and Development 326
World Trade Organization 2,60,68,83

X-efficiency 25,28,37,66,70,90

yield management 31–9,78
Yu, C 28,179

Zelner, A 21
Zimmerman, MB 322,323
Zorn, CK 99,318,321,322